Please dear reader, excuse my literary limitations. I have written this straight from the heart, and with little formal education past the age of thirteen. When I decided to write my story it came forth in a torrent of words and emotion that surprised even myself. I fear my lack of training exposes me to the public rather like a woman who has accidentally tucked the back of her dress into her knickers then walked out her front door on the way to the shops. So indulge me, smile with me, and be gentle. This story is what it is, and it's told honestly.

This book is a record and also an explanation. I admit it contains probably more detailed information regarding my family, and medical procedures than is strictly necessary for the casual reader. But please either bear with me, or if you must, skip over those pages. They are intended, in the first instance for my children and wider relatives to understand the truth of my story that was often screened from them; and in the latter for my fellow trans travellers who seek the scalpel to achieve their harmony with life. I hopefully will reveal surgery can and often works, despite what other may say. You can be fixed.

For Danni

Acknowledgements

I would like to thank two people who helped me with proofreading and edits, Richard Grey, and in particular my dear friend Jean Thirtle. Thank you for your time and patience.

Disclaimer

This story is the truth. Some identifying details have been changed to protect the privacy of individuals. I have tried to recreate events, locales and conversations from my memories of them. In order to maintain their anonymity in some instances I have changed the names of some individuals and places, I may have changed some identifying characteristics and details such as physical properties, occupations and places of residence.

Prologue

March 2005

Norwich, England

The day had arrived. Finally, I was about to lose my virginity 'as a woman' whatever that meant. It had been a long road to get here. Would it be everything a woman dreams of? Would he be gentle, would he be able to notice the difference, would he be grateful? Actually the last question was an easy one. He had no need to feel grateful, he was only getting what he'd paid for – sex with me.

The other questions did worry me, though. I certainly hoped he'd be gentle. My neovagina, courtesy of Dr Suporn, my Thai sex reassignment surgeon, was only a year old and had never been penetrated by a man. My client didn't know I hadn't been born with a vagina. Would he be able to tell? Would it function as it should? Would I enjoy it? So many questions, but I had to know.

This was the test, and the fulfilment of an agreement I had made with Alice, my lesbian partner of over fourteen years. The deal was that he would fuck me first, and then her. I can't pretend it was anything about making love. The important thing was simply that I would be fucked, and it wasn't just my idea – this was our pact. But in order to protect our relationship, Alice and I had also agreed there could be no romantic motive for the man who would take my virginity. It was to be a business transaction, pure and simple. I wanted to experience sexual intercourse with a man, to answer all of my questions. Alice would then do likewise with the same man, in the same situation, and for the same price. That would keep everything equal. Neither of us could ever accuse the other of screwing around with a man, because we both had done exactly the same thing. He was also my final punter – we had always said we would stop when it was no longer financially necessary, which it wasn't since all my surgery and travel costs had already been covered.

His name was Clive, the unwitting but very willing accomplice to our plan. We had specifically chosen him because we both felt comfortable with him. He was a thirty-year old British Army soldier, an Afghan war veteran home on leave, attractive, single and looking for a bit of fun. He was a really nice guy, unlike some of my previous punters. I liked him.

Clive had originally contacted me through my website. I'd been involved with escorting, or if I'm honest, prostitution, for several years to help fund my sex change surgery. At this stage of my sex work career I worked as a dominatrix escort, always wearing a leather corset, chain link bra, thigh-length boots and a cobalt blue wig. I consistently wore the same clothes to make me easily identifiable in the grid of online photographs where I was advertised. Alice helped out as my 'maid' and we shared the money.

The great thing about working as a dominatrix is that you don't have to endure penetrative sex with men. It essentially just involves spanks and wanks. You tied up the punter, then teased and tormented him until he was begging for sexual release. Then, when the time was right, you gave either oral sex or a hand job. A lot of the time they were well ahead of you, so neither would be required. Clive was one of those few punters who always asked for more. He had visited me several times previously and always gone away happy, but he was desperate for full sex, and had offered the sizeable fee of three hundred pounds (and the same to Alice a few nights later). Ordinarily I would have refused point blank. If nothing else, by providing full sex the mystery was gone and with it the punter's fantasy. But now, after a suitable period since my surgery, I felt it was time to try out my new body and Clive seemed like the perfect candidate to help me. The money he was paying was actually irrelevant, other than the fact that it complied with my pact with Alice.

It was time. Clive and I were alone in the subdued light of the bedroom, while Alice was in the next room. Leonard Cohen played softly on the stereo. Rather than have him lie on the bed I insisted it would be best if he sat on the office chair I usually used for my submissive ('sub') punters. I stood over him as he sat naked on the stool. This allowed me stand above and in front of him, and to dominate him with the advantage of height (old habits die hard). My plan was that I would lower myself on to him and thus stay in control of the situation in case things went wrong. Remember, this was my first time…

Chapter 1 'I Just Don't Know What To Do With Myself'

Scotland 1960's

My earliest memory seems implausible. It was a bright dry day. The sky was blue but it wasn't hot. I know this because I was tucked up with blankets as I lay on my back. I could see only a rectangle of azure above me, framed by the sides of my coach built pram. My mum was pushing the pram and we were waiting to board a train. When the train arrived at the platform a man I didn't recognise, probably a passing stranger, helped my mother to lift me and the pram into the train carriage.

I said that the memory seems implausible because I would only have been pushed around in a pram like this up until the age of about two. I've heard that we generally don't have any memory of our lives before the age of three, but I remember that day, my mother, the sky, and the unfamiliar man as if it were yesterday. My life journey had begun and this was the first time I was conscious of that fact.

My family was fairly typical for the industrial area of West Scotland where I grew up. We lived in a town just outside Glasgow called Alexandria, but known more commonly to the locals as The Vale (short for Vale of Leven, named after the river that flowed from Loch Lomond through our valley to the Clyde). We were working class in the days when that meant you actually had work to go to. Both my parents always had jobs.

My father, Joseph, left school with no qualifications at the age of fourteen and immediately went to work for the Co-Operative Society. Jobs for school leavers were plentiful in those days shortly after World War II, so Dad's lack of qualifications was no bar to his obtaining employment. His own father, Danny, had died when Dad was only twelve, and so he became the man of the house at an early age.

I never discovered the precise circumstances of my grandfather Danny's death. It was apparently cancer that killed him when he was only in his late thirties. He worked in the local 'Silk Factory' at Balloch, which was part of the large chemical fabric dying industry that had sprung up in the Vale area, made possible by the supply of fast-flowing fresh water from Loch Lomond.

My dad did have an older brother, Robert, but he was considered 'a bit daft' and also suffered from epilepsy. Robert must certainly have been different in some way, for his younger brother to supersede him in the family pecking order. It has more recently been speculated by family members that he might have been gay, as he was also referred to as being 'saft' (soft) at a time when men were expected to be tough. Robert never married and his life is something of a mystery. It occurred to me only a few years ago that, if Robert had indeed been gay, it would have been a source of major embarrassment to the family, and that might partly explain my dad's extreme homophobia. Sadly, Uncle Robert's circumstances will remain largely unknown since, like his father before him, he also died in his late thirties, in the same year that I was born, 1964. His official cause of death was thrombosis, but I know very little about his life. The family always seemed very reluctant to talk about him as I was growing up.

For Dad, the fact that his father and brother had both died before the age of forty left a morbid and doom-laden impression on him. He always said he never expected to reach old age. As he eventually did grow older, this melancholy must have changed to a feeling of grim satisfaction, as he often mentioned when drunk that he had outlived all the men in his family.

It must have been a very difficult time for the family when my grandfather Danny, the breadwinner in the family, died, forcing my dad at such a young age to become the head of the family. But Dad was always very quiet on the subject and rarely mentioned his own father to me. One thing I do know about Danny was that he was a Roman Catholic of Irish origin, and probably from a gypsy/traveller family. His religion caused a great deal of anxiety to my grandmother Agnes' family, the Wilson's, at the time when he was courting her.

My grandmother's father was Jock Wilson, a staunch protestant and the local Orange Lodge Grand Master. It must have caused quite a stir for old Jock

Wilson to have a Catholic-born son-in-law in those times when religious bigotry was rife and deeply ingrained. However, it would appear that Danny was not a particularly committed Catholic, because he and Agnes did marry and the children were all brought up as Church of Scotland protestants. Old Jock must have been relieved.

So, due to his own father's early demise, my dad was the one who had to take responsibility for the family, which included a younger sister Nan and his older brother Robert, as well as his mother Agnes. They lived in Naperson Terrace, Jamestown, Alexandria on the banks of the River Leven. Despite the exotic-sounding address, it was in fact a sandstone tenement building that was typical of what we now think of as private landlord slum accommodation.

Dad always described his job throughout his working life as a driver. Starting off as a 'van boy' in the local Co-op as a teenager, he travelled all over the local area selling milk, bread and vegetables to people who lived in the countryside that surrounded the town. After working for the Co-op for a few years, they decided to train him up for his own delivery route. The Co-op paid for his driving lessons and after a couple of attempts at passing his driving test he finally succeeded. The Co-op subsequently presented him with his own delivery route. However, they also presented him, much to his dismay, not with a van of his own, but a horse and cart! This was a humorous anecdote often retold within the family over the years. But Dad persevered with the horse anyway, and within a year or two was eventually rewarded by being given his very own van and route.

It was around this time, while he was a Co-op van boy, that he met my mother, Helen Holloway. Aged sixteen, she was three years younger than him and still at school when they first got together. Mum's family home was directly across the River Leven from my dad's home, in a slightly better area of the Vale, a council estate called Levenvale. Fortunately there was a bridge across the river between their homes, known locally as the Stuckie Bridge.

And so the courtship commenced.

Mum's family was slightly better off financially than Dad's, not least because her father Tommy Holloway was alive and earning a living right up until his retirement from the same Silk Factory that my other grandfather had worked in. Both my grandfathers must have known each other and may even have worked together at some point. One family story that seems to confirm their mutual acquaintance concerns the time when my parents were preparing for their wedding and were filling in the required legal forms, together with my grandfather Tommy. One question asked of my father on the form was, what was his own (deceased) father's job title? Grandad Holloway sarcastically joked, "Just put fucking 'Harp Player'". That comment gives you an idea of Tommy's sarcastic character.

Unlike my paternal grandfather, I do have some memory of Tommy because he was alive for the first few years of my childhood. I remember he used to take me up to the pubs in Balloch when I was around three years old. At that time children were not allowed into public houses (neither were women, for that matter), but Tommy would take me in and sit me on the bar of the Glenroy pub with a glass of lemonade as he held court with his pals. Even today the smell of whisky and beer transports me back to that time. I loved being the centre of attention. The barmaids would always make a fuss and give me a kiss, and occasionally some of the men would give me a penny or a 'threepenny bit', so I usually went home with some money in my pocket.

On one memorable occasion someone gave me a silver half crown, quite a lot of money in those days. After the pub closed, we walked back home along the River Leven towpath. I decided to copy some older kids as they skimmed stones across the water. I took the half crown from my pocket and, as my grandad watched in horror before he could do anything to stop me, threw it into the river. Old Tommy wasn't so much angry with me as amused. But money was never to be wasted, let alone literally thrown away. So off came his boots and socks, he rolled up his trousers, and with the aid of his walking stick he waded drunkenly into the fast-flowing river and retrieved the coin. Old Tommy hadn't got to where he was without knowing the value of money.

Another family story, also told with some amusement, concerned Tommy's six-month visit to Barlinnie Prison during the 1930s depression for stealing chickens from a local farmer. There was no shame attached to this story – he had a family to feed, after all – the only unfortunate part was that he'd been caught.

I heard many tales about Tommy over the years from my mum and aunts. His marriage to my grandmother Chrissie was fractious, to say the least. Domestic violence was not unusual, and certainly not all directed one way. Tommy would come home drunk and fighting, and Chrissie would give as good as she got. One time she threw an axe at him, narrowly missing his head as it thudded into the kitchen door next to where he was standing. But they still managed to get on well enough to produce seven children, of which my mum was the youngest. They managed to reach their golden wedding anniversary just before he died at the age of sixty-seven. So they must have met and married as teenagers.

Sadly, my abiding and lasting memory of Tommy is one of shock, horror and fear. In the final year of his life he suffered a stroke which left him badly paralysed, unable to walk or speak much at all. He was reduced to spending his days sitting on a chair in the living room in front of the flickering black and white TV. Everything from dressing, eating, washing and going to the toilet had to be done for him by my grandmother or one of my aunts. Tommy did not accept his situation gracefully, and instead became a seething angry presence in the home, frustrated and bitter at what he'd become.

Tommy was looked after, all his basic needs met. But after his stroke he was shown very little respect from the women of the house who now held the power over him. I spent most of my days at my grandparents' house during this time because I was too young for school and my parents were both out working. But even at that young age I detected a sense of revenge and payback towards Tommy, who had always been something of a tyrant towards his wife and his daughters when they were growing up. The only concession of control allowed to him at this time was the uninterrupted watching of his TV. It was always his choice of channel and volume level, and woe betide anyone who got between him and the black and white TV screen.

One day, I accidentally made the mistake of walking in front of the TV as Tommy watched the news, and I blocked his view for a few seconds. I was only around four years old and of course had no idea about what I was doing. But Tommy erupted, made a frightening bellowing sound and grabbed his wooden walking stick with his good hand. He began smacking me with it as I howled in pain and fear. The commotion soon brought my grandmother Chrissie and my Aunt Mary rushing into the room from the kitchen and all hell was let loose. Mary grabbed the walking stick from Tommy's hand and began to beat him violently with it on his head, arms and legs. Meanwhile Chrissie punched and kicked him at the same time. Poor Tommy never stood a chance as both women screamed and swore at him for daring to strike me. The beating he got was systematic and prolonged, with dire warnings and death threats shouted in his face. At one point he was knocked out of his chair, and still the beating continued. I learned very early on that women were not necessarily the gentler sex, at least not in our family. That was one of my earliest memories of domestic violence. It wasn't the last I would see, and it certainly wasn't the worst.

It wasn't long after that incident that Tommy died and he was finally released from his torment. Amusingly, his legacy lives on even today, through the repetition of one his favourite expressions. "I've had nothing to eat for three days," he would lament to my grandmother. This was actually a dig at my granny's cooking skills, which to be fair were modest at best, and which he claimed made the majority of his meals inedible most days. But the phrase lived on as it was passed on to my parents who would jokingly say it any time they were hungry, as do I to this day, and as do my own children (his great-grandchildren), who have no idea who Tommy was.

* * * * * * *

I don't remember how old I was when it first dawned on me that despite being born a boy, I would rather have been a girl. It was certainly before I started school. I remember one time when my older sister Carolyn received a pretty dressing gown for a birthday present. It was aqua-blue, soft and fluffy, and I fell in love with it straight away. I wanted to try it on, but I was shooed away by my grandmother who told me it was a dressing gown for girls and not for me. It was probably the first time I can remember being told I was different from my sister. I couldn't really comprehend it, but I just accepted it as something that was confusing to me at the time, but which I hoped I would understand later when I asked my sister about it. The dressing gown hung in the bedroom that Carolyn and I shared, so occasionally I would go in to touch it and rub the soft fleece fabric on my cheek. I didn't dare try it on, though. That would only come years later…

I also began to notice that Carolyn often received different gifts from me. One Easter my other grandmother Agnes brought round a small basket of beautiful chocolate Easter eggs. They were all wrapped in pretty coloured foil with ribbons tied round them. Carolyn and I gasped when we saw it. But, as I reached towards this gorgeous gift, my grandmother stopped me.

"They're for your sister," she said. "Don't touch!"

I held back and walked away with tears burning down my cheeks while Carolyn grabbed the basket and she and my grandmother cooed over how pretty it looked. I hid my face, not wanting everyone to see me crying. Then my mum, who must have noticed how upset I was, asked Agnes what had she brought for me? Agnes was dismissive. "I just got this for Carolyn," she replied. "I didn't get him anything." Not surprisingly, this caused a row with Mum, who shouted at Agnes that she shouldn't have got something for one without getting something for the other. By this time I was in full flow and wailing.

"Look what you've done!" Mum shouted at Agnes as she pointed to me snivelling on the sofa.

"Oh fucking all right," Agnes conceded at last. Grabbing me, she dragged me crying across the estate to the little corner shop. Once inside she said, "Right, pick a bar of chocolate from the shelf." I was eyeing up the boxed chocolate eggs and those pretty ones wrapped in cellophane that sat in cups; but no, I'd been told I could only get a bar of chocolate. So, reluctantly, I chose a bar of Galaxy, which Agnes then paid for. Clearly annoyed, she dragged me back home, shouting, "Are you happy now? Good, so fucking shut up and stop fucking crying then." Ah, happy days...

So, the difference between girls and boys was gradually introduced and reinforced in me by many little situations like this. Don't get me wrong, I wasn't deprived of anything compared to Carolyn; it was just that we were given different things.

On another occasion I was given a football, but there was no attempt to stop Carolyn from playing with it. In fact she was a much better footballer than I was at that age. What struck me, though, was that it seemed that she had the freedom to play with anything, including 'boys' toys', without attracting any derogatory comments. "She's just a bit of a tomboy," was the accepted thinking, no big deal. But I wasn't allowed to play with her things without being criticised. The only exception to this rule was when I was on my own at my grandmother Chrissie's house, where I spent a lot of my pre-school years.

Just prior to reaching school age, I remember one Christmas being given an Action Man toy. Carolyn had been given dolls before and I'd played with them and been told off because they were hers and therefore 'girls' toys'. To my eyes this Action Man was just another doll, but one that for some unexplained reason I was allowed to enjoy playing with all by myself. It was confusing, to say the least.

Anyway, I wasn't too keen on the uniform Action Man was wearing. It looked very drab and boring to me, so I decided his wardrobe needed some improvements. My grandmother Chrissie had previously taught me to sew. I had watched her doing this as she mended clothes or took up hems, and became fascinated. I wanted to try it and she was more than happy to teach me. Soon I had learned how to thread a needle, use single or double thread, tie a knot and to finish off a piece so it wouldn't unravel. She also taught me how to knit and it was something I really enjoyed. It seemed like a magic trick to take a long piece of woollen yarn and turn it into a different shape, and then, by adding a different coloured yarn it would change again to make a pattern. I loved it.

Before long I'd started designing small sweaters for my Action Man and cutting old pieces of fabric material into a pattern to make tiny shirts. I'm sure my parents must have seen this and thought it slightly unusual for a boy, but no one said anything to me, so I carried on quite happily whenever I was at Chrissie's house.

By the time I was five years old and starting school I was already quite accomplished at designing, sewing and knitting. I remember proudly showing off my handiwork to my primary school teachers and receiving their encouragement. It must have been a novelty for them to see a boy so happy doing 'girls' things', but in those early years they never tried to deter or discourage me. As far as I was concerned, this was just something creative to which no gender need be attached. And whenever it came to anything artistic or crafty I was right in there, showing off what I could do, whether it was making Christmas decorations or woollen pom-poms.

Was this a sign of things to come? Was it just part of my nature, or did the encouragement I received from Granny Chrissie and those early years teachers influence me towards a more feminine outlook?

* * * * * * *

How I became transsexual is not a question I have a good answer to. Did it come down to genetics or conditioning, nature or nurture? I certainly grew up surrounded by women, but that wasn't unusual in those days when the men usually worked and the women looked after the home.

Was it medical? I learned about DES Syndrome back in the 1990s and wondered if perhaps that applied to me. DES was a synthetic form of oestrogen that doctors prescribed from the 1930s until the 1980s in order to help some pregnant women who had experienced numerous miscarriages or premature deliveries. My mum was certainly a pill-popper all her life, and always kept a stash of tranquillisers, diet pills, and god knows what else. She had no qualms about drinking alcohol or taking pills when she was pregnant. But I discovered that prenatal DES exposure may be linked to increased rates of homosexuality, transgender and transsexual conditions. Could that have been the reason?

The truth is I don't know why I was born transsexual. I've read all the theories and tried to apply them to my own situation, but there simply isn't one single factor that I can point to. Frankly, looking back now after fifty years' experience, I can now say that I don't really care what the reason was. There's nothing I can do about it now, or could have done back then. I just accept it. I certainly cannot pinpoint anything in my pre-school relationships with women that may have made me this way. Most of the women I grew up with were very strong characters, even more so than the men. But I do have very clear memories of my confused and annoyed reactions as a child, as I tried to process and understand the gender stereotypes towards children that prevented me from playing with the things I wanted to play with.

* * * * * * *

As Christmas 1969 arrived, I remember Carolyn and I receiving our comic annuals. She would be given Mandy and Bunty, while I would get Hotspur or something equally boyish. My annuals were all about soldiers or footballers. The war wasn't that far behind us and was a topic often spoken about, not surprisingly since many people then still had vivid first-hand recollections. I did read my books, but I also read Carolyn's, and they were so much better. I loved the stories about girls who were sent off to boarding schools and would play hockey, deal with bullies and have midnight feasts in the dorm. All that seemed fascinating to me and I wanted to be part of it, much more so than the stories in the boys' books where enemy soldiers were all killed and the British Army triumphantly won the day.

Later on, when I was a bit older and gender divisions were becoming more striking, I was forced to read my sister's comics in secret to avoid derision. When I was following Enid Blyton's Malory Towers series (my favourite), I had to wait for Carolyn to read them first, discard the book, and then I would find and take her copy, hide it, then read it quietly and in secret.

As the 1970s began, a whole new area of interest would open up for me: fashion, music and particularly Glam Rock. I may have been too young to appreciate the swinging sixties but I was right on time for this decade of long hair and platform shoes.

Chapter 2 'You Wear It Well'

1970's

The early 1970s were a good time to be alive. Looking back, that was probably the easiest time for someone like me to be growing up. I was able quite easily to express myself without attracting too much adverse attention. Also, the NHS had recently started a new service specifically designed for people like me. Charing Cross hospital in London had a Gender Identity Clinic for a new type of patient, transsexual people. Of course I knew nothing of that at the time, but the GIC would be established and providing hormone treatment and sex change surgery by the time I was old enough to access treatment. In that regard I was very fortunate indeed.

By now we had moved house, to a council estate in the Vale called Rosshead. These days people would think it was a rough and deprived area, but if you didn't know any different, then you don't think that way; it was just home. We had a two bedroom council house with a garden in a small tight-knit square of houses at one end of the estate. All the neighbours were friends, and people would pop into our house most days, as we would go to theirs. Carolyn and I called all the adults 'Auntie' or 'Uncle', and it would be some years before I realised they were not actually related to me in any way. Everyone just looked out for each other, from the babies to the pensioners.

We kids all played together in the street. There was a crowd of us about twenty strong. We were never lonely or bored since there was always something going on outside like street football or Chinese skipping, and some of the older kids ran card schools. Looking back, it was idyllic. No one had much money, but what we did have was a community. We were always building bikes from spare parts, or 'bogies', a kind of four-wheeled go kart made from old pram wheels and wooden planks. There was also a wood nearby where we would go and build tree houses or rafts to use in the lade (canal). There was virtually no supervision from the adults. We left home to go out to play and came back when it was dark. No one's parents worried about us. The kids looked after themselves with the older ones taking some unspoken responsibility. Even today I can still reel off the names of all the families in our square and their house numbers.

The only time I was ever taken to school by my parents was when my mum took me, aged five, for my first day at Levenvale Primary School. She brought me to the gates, handed me over to a teacher and walked away. That was it. From then on I was expected to get to and from school every day on my own. Fortunately, it wasn't difficult. It was impossible to get lost as I just followed the group of other kids who also made the mile and a half walk from school to Rosshead. I couldn't walk with Carolyn because she was three years older than me and her friends didn't want a little kid hanging around with them. Instead I walked with Irene who was my age and in my class, while both of our older sisters also walked together. I'm still friends with Irene today, and she didn't seem a bit surprised when, having lost touch with her for over twenty years in our late teens, I contacted her in the late 1990's, to let her know I'd changed sex.

One day one of the younger kids drowned in the canal. Walter was only three or four years old and had wandered down there with his friend Craig. As I said, this wasn't unusual for children at that time. But on that particular day, Walter fell into the canal, the same canal I and my friends had fallen into many times. For some reason he couldn't get himself out and there was no one older to help. The current dragged him under and carried him away to the whisky distillery that was fed by the canal. Little Craig ran back to the square and raised the alarm. All the adults ran down there to try and get to Walter, but it was too late. Walter's dad, also called Walter, dived in and swam along the canal under the fence into the industrial area and found his small body, floating but lifeless. 'Uncle' Walter carried his son's body back to the square surrounded by all the neighbours, the women crying and the men swearing.

That was the first time I faced my own immortality. I'd never experienced the death of a child in our community before, and it was a terrible time for everyone in Rosshead. However, even this tragedy caused no additional restrictions on the kids. We were occasionally warned to take care when we went near the canal. "Remember wee Walter," we'd be told as we went out to play in the same place where he'd drowned. And for many years after that, whenever the adults got together in one of the houses for a drink at night, Uncle Walter and Auntie Isabel would get maudlin drunk and the story of wee Walter would be retold over and over.

House drinking parties were very popular in our square. Often I'd come in at night and find several neighbours, Uncle Jim and Aunty Jessie, or whoever, getting drunk and loud. Records would be playing and the singing would be going strong. As kids we all knew this was a good time to hang around as we might get some money from the adults who would sometimes empty their pockets of loose change and tell us "go and get yourself an ice cream from Gallonie's van". Or we might be told to go to the van to buy them twenty fags or a bottle of lemonade, "and keep the change." Everybody smoked back then, or so it seemed, and kids could easily buy cigarettes for the adults without any question, if we were asked to get them.

One night when I was around seven years old, I remember Mum telling me to go and buy ten Embassy tips from the van and to keep the change. Somehow I got it mixed up and I asked the ice cream van man, Carmen, for five cigarettes. He happily took the money and got the fags from an open packet, wrapped them in paper and gave them to me, together with the change. I was very pleased to see there was more change than the usual penny or two, so I bought myself a bag of bonbon sweets. But when I handed the five cigarettes to Mum she went crazy, screaming and shouting that I'd stolen her money and bought sweets with it. She chased me around the kitchen until I managed to escape through the back door. Later on I sneaked back in, but by then she and Dad had had a few drinks and my 'thieving' was forgotten.

I knew Carmen Gallonie (a.k.a. the 'ice cream van man') for most of my life in the Vale. His was one of quite a few Scots/Italian families in the area, and they owned an ice cream parlour as well as the van. When I was at secondary school Carmen would bring his van down to the school at lunchtime and the kids could buy sweets, ice cream, and even a 'single fag' for five pence, from him. Different times…

Occasionally, the house drinking parties in the square became quite violent. It wasn't so surprising, really, since all the adults seemed to drink every night, so any slights or quarrels would inevitably be magnified by the booze. A fight would usually start between a husband and wife, and then others would pile in on either side. As kids, though, we were quite used to it, so we weren't fazed. We had all been brought up to see this as normal behaviour.

The licencing laws at that time meant that the pubs closed at nine o'clock, so most drinking was done at home. Often we'd see men coming home from the pub, staggering along as they made their way home with a fish supper and a 'carry oot', usually bottles and cans they had bought at the pub off licence. These men were fair game for us kids if they fell over drunk. We'd crowd around them and ask for money, which in their inebriated state might be forthcoming. Sometimes one or two of us might be daring enough to dip into their pockets if they were pissed enough. Any money we got was then shared between us at the sweetshop.

It wasn't unusual to see an 'aunt' or 'uncle' the next morning, in the cold light of day, with a black eye after the previous night's shenanigans. It might sound violent and dangerous, but this was at least at a time before drugs were prevalent. Alcohol was the norm and there was virtually no heroin or even cannabis around. They would come later.

* * * * * * *

It was just after we'd moved into the house at Rosshead that Dad got a new job. He had applied to the oil company Shell to be a tanker driver, and had got a place on their training scheme. Shell paid for Dad to go through his HGV training, and once he got his driving licence he was given a decent job delivering oil all round the west of Scotland. He celebrated that night in the pub and came home completely drunk and singing, with a dog in tow. Somehow he had managed to be given a puppy that night in the pub. So now we had a new addition to the family, a little black terrier of unknown and dubious parentage. When asked what breed the dog was, my dad would always reply, "He's a cross between a mossy dike and a packet of Woodbine," whatever that meant. Anyway, he was a beautiful little black dog and I loved him. As far as I was concerned he was mine. The next day we had to pick a name for him and it was agreed that he would be called 'Shell', to commemorate the day Dad got his new job.

Shell was just like any other dog on the Rosshead estate in those days. We would open the door in the morning and let him out into the street, and then he would fend for himself until he decided it was time to come home for some food. Everyone else did the same thing with their dogs. As kids we used the estate dogs' territories as geographical markers. The square was Shell's area and everyone knew him. Over on Baxter's Lane was where Roy, a large Old English Sheepdog, patrolled. There were no dog wardens in those days, so dogs and cats just came and went as they felt like it.

Shell was a tough little dog. We always said he had nine lives after all the near-death scrapes he managed to get himself into. On one occasion, it was a warm sunny afternoon and the family was relaxing together in the garden. Carolyn and I were sunbathing while our parents were drinking, when Shell suddenly appeared. Nothing unusual in that, but he ran in past us using only his front legs as he dragged his back legs, bloodied and splayed out flat, behind him. We all did a double take, and looked at each other for confirmation as to what we'd just witnessed. Then we all ran into the kitchen, only to find Shell eating his dinner from his bowl as usual, seemingly unconcerned with his clearly broken back legs. No whining or concern from Shell, though. He simply ate his food, then climbed into his basket and fell asleep, as if nothing had happened. It turned out, we learned later, that he'd been run over by a car but had somehow managed to save himself. Several people had witnessed it and ran after the driver, but he had sped off without stopping.

Dad took Shell to the vet the next day and he was fixed up with heavy bandages and splints. Within a few months he had healed and was back running around as normal with just a hint of a limp. I imagine that even if we hadn't taken him to the vet he would have just carried on anyway as a two-legged dog without any complaint. That was Shell, a tough little Rosshead dog.

* * * * * * *

In the early seventies my thoughts of being a girl were still all in the realm of fantasy. I thought about it often but never took it any further than dreaming. I thought that all boys probably had similar feelings. I mean, why wouldn't they? It was something that was always at the back of my mind, but I was happy enough with my situation. I had many female friends and I was always included in their games and social activities.

At home Carolyn and I shared a bedroom, and we put up posters on the walls. At one stage Donny Osmond and David Cassidy were our favourites, and every night we would kiss them goodnight before turning off the light and going to sleep. Later on my crush would be David Essex and his cheeky sparkling eyes.

The pop charts were really important to us. Finding out who was at number one and what new songs had been released was a major weekly event for us. We only had a radio on which to listen to the songs, but we also bought weekly magazines that were full of information and stories about our favourite pop stars. These magazines were a little more sophisticated by now, since we were that bit older. I loved reading Jackie and Diana. As well as having all the posters, they also included picture board stories that were mostly about girls meeting either horses or boys. And then there was the Cathy & Claire problem page, where I began to discover what being a girl was all about. Or at least what stuff was important to girls. I identified entirely with these problems and accepted them as completely relevant to me too. I read the fashion and make-up tips religiously, despite the obvious fact that I couldn't put them into practice.

Until one day I did.

I was probably about seven or eight years old when I first began to cross-dress in secret. It was easy enough in our shared bedroom with Carolyn's clothes when she was out. I would try on her skirts, tops and shoes, then pose in front of the dressing table mirror. I tried on her school uniform and thought about how lovely it would be to wear her clothes to school rather than the drab boys' uniform I had to wear. But I knew enough to understand what I was doing would be seen as wrong and shameful. I knew I could never share this with anyone else. It literally became my guilty secret and in a way it was comforting because I had a safe place to daydream that was enough to satisfy me, for now at least. I knew in my heart I would never be able to walk down the local town dressed like this. It was as unlikely as ever bumping into David Essex on my way to the shops. But in the meantime, at least I could dream.

Dad, meanwhile, was trying his damnedest to bring me up as a son he could be proud of. Sometimes he'd take me to watch Rangers play football. One Saturday afternoon I fell asleep whilst leaning against a stanchion inside the stadium with a crowd of fifty thousand fans screaming and cheering all around me. My dad and his friends were highly amused by this.

To tell the truth I wasn't really that interested in sport, at least not at that age. Sometimes I did kick a ball around in the garden, and while I quite enjoyed it, Carolyn was always bigger and more skilful than me at that age. I could sense Dad's disappointment that I wasn't better, and that I was too frightened to head the ball.

Some days, if Dad had a long distance delivery to make in his oil tanker he would bring me along. In those pre-seatbelt days I would sit on the giant gearbox cover as he drove to Rothesay or Greenock. We'd stop at a friendly pub where Dad knew he could sneak me in and get himself a drink. While I enjoyed these trips, I also had a clear realisation that this was not the life I wanted for myself.

Dad also took the opportunity to begin my 'street' education. He would explain how he managed to steal from the customers he was delivering to by giving them a short load of oil. He had his own special measuring dipstick that he would use to demonstrate to the customer how much oil he had pumped off the tanker. But Dad's stick was not regulation size, which meant that he was able to skim off a little from each delivery. Then, on the way home, he would sell the stolen oil to a regular trusted customer for a cash bung.

Although we weren't wealthy, we were never short of money in our council estate house. In fact no one seemed to be in our area. We were among the first families to enjoy the package holidays to Spain that were just becoming popular in the late seventies. Everyone seemed to have some kind of fiddle going on, and no one was out of work. It all seemed perfectly normal to me to steal and thieve from anywhere you could if you got the chance, so long as it wasn't from your own community. I was taught that this behaviour was the working man's privilege. And so, while still a boy, this was my initiation into that way of thinking.

Even at home my dad fiddled the electricity meter and, when I was old enough, showed me how to do it. The meter was located under the stairs in an awkward cupboard. One day, when I could only have been eight years old, Dad crawled in there with me and showed me how to remove the lead seal that was attached to the casing, then unscrew the cover that revealed two rows of screws. One of those screws was brass coloured and this was the one to unscrew carefully until the metal disc inside stopped turning and the meter stopped recording the electricity that was being consumed. Dad also explained to me how dangerous this procedure was. If you touched the wrong screw with the screwdriver, then you could easily receive an electric shock that might kill you. Then, after the meter was stopped, the cover was replaced and the lead seal left hanging, ready to be crimped on quickly if a meter reader turned up.

On more than a few occasions I had to dive under the stairs on my own, tighten the screw and reset the meter, then replace the seal and crimp it back on with pliers. All this while Mum or Dad kept the meter reader talking at the door, as sweat streamed down my face for fear of getting electrocuted.

That little space under the stairs soon became my own secret domain. Once Dad had trained me, he became quite lazy since he never had go in there to do the fiddle himself. And since it was such a small and awkward place to get into, I began to use it as a place to store my secret stash of female clothing that I had begun to acquire from Carolyn's cast off's. Then, whenever I found myself home alone, I would be able to take out these clothes and get dressed as a girl.

Meanwhile, Dad involved me in his thieving exploits at every possible opportunity. It was like I was on some kind of training course or apprenticeship. Another of his tricks would be to drive up to local parks or public spaces. He'd park the car next to some flower beds or a nice ornamental tree he wanted for our garden. Then he'd take a spade out of the boot of the car, dig up the plants or whatever it was he wanted, and then put them carefully in the car boot on spread-out newspaper.

The overall lesson was that you can get away with almost anything if you're bold as brass and confident, even right in front of anyone who passed by. If anyone did stop to question us, he would then demonstrate his real talent, which was the ability to talk his way out of any situation. Always friendly, always plausible, but most of all, always very confident.

It was an important lesson for me.

Chapter 3 'Show Me The Way'

I left primary school in 1976. I had turned 12 years old and this was the beginning of my first transition. I entered puberty that year and it was a transformation that I found far more heart-breaking and painful than the sex change I was to go through years later.

That summer I had been invited by a school friend, Billy, to go for a week's holiday by the seaside. We were to stay at a bed and breakfast hotel in Ayr on the west coast of Scotland. Also coming along were Billy's mum and two elder sisters. The idea was that Billy wouldn't feel left out when his mum and sisters teamed up for the week, because he would have me to do 'boys' things with. Not surprisingly, things didn't go entirely to plan.

As it turned out, I got on famously with the sisters and enjoyed hanging out with them much more than with poor Billy. More often than not I spent the week sunbathing on the beach with the girls, playing bingo in the arcades, or back in the hotel at night listening to music on the radio and playing board games with them. Meanwhile Billy usually resorted to wandering around the park on his own with a football, wishing he had someone to play with.

I was enthralled by these girls. Especially the older one, Linda was seventeen, and with her high heels and make-up I desperately wanted to be just like her and so I followed her around like a puppy, watching how she applied eyeliner, shadow and mascara, which not only transformed her face but also seemed to infuse her with sophistication and confidence. I would fantasise that maybe one evening she would suggest to me that we would get dressed up in her clothes and go out together. It was just daydreaming, though; it would never really happen and I was saddened by that thought.

One day, Billy asked me to go down with him to the Green, which was a grass area just behind the beach. As usual he had brought his football and we kicked it around between us. Billy was happy enough but I desperately missed the laughs and fun I'd been having with the girls. But even though I was bored to tears I knew I had to make the effort to be Billy's pal.

I remember that day clearly. It was particularly hot and sunny (it did happen sometimes, even in Ayr), and soon we were thirsty after our kick around. I suggested we go get an ice cream from the kiosk at the edge of the Green.

That was when I met Jan.

* * * * *

Jan MacDonald was my first real girlfriend. I mean 'real' in the sense that we were more than just friends, as had been the case with all the other girls I'd known at primary school. In school I'd 'gone out' with almost all the girls in my class at one time or another. These were mostly just childish pairings that lasted for a few weeks at a time, and which usually involved awkward kisses and cuddles. I usually just ended up having another pal by the end of it. But with Jan I felt something different. For one thing she was two years older than me and much more experienced. When she served me and Billy with ice cream that day, I couldn't help noticing that she was very focused on me, smiling and laughing, and all but fluttering her eyelashes. I had never experienced that level of attention towards me before, and I was besotted with her immediately. Something was awakened within me. This was special, and I knew I needed to spend much more time with her.

Jan was beautiful, with long auburn hair, laughing eyes and a feminine figure with wide hips, full breasts and a narrow waist. I'd never really noticed anything like her before in my previous childish encounters with girls. In fact she was practically a woman!

I'm pretty sure it was her idea that I come back to collect her when her shift ended, so we could go for a walk together along the esplanade. And so, I duly met her later that evening when she finished work, much to the annoyance of Billy and his family. I was excited when I left the hotel and raced down to the beach kiosk where she was waiting for me. We walked along the seafront, Jan showing me around her home town and telling me about herself, her school and friends, and where she lived. She told me she was fourteen, which was two years older than me. And so I did what any self-respecting boy would have done in the same situation: I lied, and told her we were the same age.

The time just disappeared that night and before I knew it, it was dark. I knew I should have gone back to the hotel because no doubt Billy's family were worried about me. I was just a child, they had taken me on holiday with them and they were responsible for me. But I simply couldn't drag myself away from Jan. We ended up sitting together in a bus shelter that night, not far from the pier. I can still remember listening to the music that came from the variety show that was playing there, as we cuddled each other to stay warm and shared a bag of chips. I remember hearing the Carpenters song 'I'm on top of the world' drifting from the music hall.

I finally left Jan that night after seeing her off at the bus stop with a long and real lingering kiss, the first one I'd ever experienced. There was no doubt about it – I was in love! On cloud nine, I made my way back to the hotel where I was met with frosty looks from Billy and his sisters. His mum gave me a stern lecture about staying out after dark and leaving Billy on his own. I didn't care; they could never understand what I had experienced that evening. It had been amazing, and that night nothing else mattered.

For the first time in my life I actually believed completely that I was normal after all. All it had taken was to meet a girl and fall in love – that's what made you a man. Or at least in my case, a normal boy and not some freak who dreamed about being a girl. I just needed to meet the right girl and from now on everything would be okay. I went to bed that night happier than I could ever remember.

For the rest of the holiday I spent every moment I could with Jan. During the day I would persuade Billy to come down to the Green where we would kick a football around. But every minute I was looking across to the ice cream kiosk where Jan worked, knowing she would be watching me. As soon as she was free to leave I would meet her and we'd spend the evening hanging around the pier, holding hands and basking in the joy of being together. Meanwhile Billy would slope off back to the hotel on his own. Much later, and after I'd finally left Jan at her bus stop, I'd go back to the hotel to face the same stony faces from Billy's family. It was clear I'd abused their hospitality in inviting me on the holiday and paying for my board. I was supposed to be Billy's companion; sadly, I was oblivious. I didn't care – I was in love.

All too soon it was time to go home. The week's holiday was over and we were to drive back to the Vale in the morning. I had a tearful last night with Jan, and we promised we would write to each other. This was of course in the days before email, and even a phone call was considered an expensive extravagance. I knew I would keep our promise and desperately hoped that she would too. In the morning we departed, and all too soon I was back home in the Vale, lovesick. Only fifty miles separated us, but to me it seemed like I had left Jan behind on the other side of the world.

* * * * *

The summer of 1976 was exceptional for its weather. Even today people still talk about it. The heatwave that year engulfed Scotland and the rest of the UK. Rivers dried up and reservoirs became pans of cracked, baked mud. As the lazy days dragged on, I hung around with my friends from primary school and Rosshead, playing tennis in the street or swimming up the bay at Balloch on Loch Lomond. We had come to the end of something, seven years together in the same class going through school. Soon we would all be at the much larger comprehensive school, split up into different classes and being compelled to make new friends. It was also a scary time because we had all been told by older siblings how tough the Vale Academy was. Soon we'd be mixing with kids from all around the area in a school of almost 2000 pupils, some from the roughest and most deprived areas in Scotland.

School wasn't the only thing that changed in 1976. Our bodies were changing too. Mine definitely was, and I wasn't too sure I liked it. I lost most of my puppy fat that year and stretched several inches in height. Previously I'd been quite short and chubby compared to my peers, but now I towered over many of them. I liked the added height, but my shoulders were still narrow and my bottom hadn't lost any fat. This was commented on, much to the disgust of my dad, when we went to Glasgow to buy my new school uniform. The middle-aged shop assistant became exasperated trying to find a pair of black school trousers for me. Every pair she brought to the changing room didn't fit, and finally she said to my mum, "he's got a girl's bum".

* * * * *

That summer was also the first time I can remember being specifically picked out for bullying because of my body shape. Previously I'd gone unnoticed by the bullies, small and lost in the crowd, and no one really bothered with me. But now I'd gotten taller and very slender, with a smooth complexion and a big bush of thick dark hair. It was a form of tall poppy syndrome I suppose. Suddenly some of the older kids decided I needed to be cut down. I was an easy target, having no elder brothers to protect me. I was friends with more girls than boys and not in any of the gangs. My interests were art and sport, and I read a lot. I was easy meat, and I never stood a chance.

One day during that hot summer I was walking back home with a couple of my friends. Minding our own business, I saw two older tough nut boys approaching us. They had been at our primary school but were two years older. Everyone knew each other at that school so they knew who I was. They came up to me, and as if to double check, asked my name. I confirmed who I was, smiling and trying to be friendly, laughing about the fact that I'd got taller.

Next, before I could react, I was punched full on the face by one of them. His name was Rab McGlinn, and he and his companion Andy Cook laughed as they walked off. My two friends were looking stared at the ground, as if embarrassed both by what had happened, as well as and their inaction failure to intervene. I didn't blame them at all; these were two of the toughest and most notorious bullies in town and everyone was scared of them. Physically, I wasn't badly hurt; I had a black eye later on that night and a sore jaw. But the embarrassment was far more upsetting than the physical pain.

We trailed off home trying to ignore what had happened. After all, the Vale was a tough place, the kind of place where people were often attacked with random acts of violence on a regular basis, usually in or around the pubs. At least I hadn't been attacked with a knife, or worse. Looking back, I think the older kids were probably high on glue. Glue sniffing was a very popular pastime back then for a lot of kids.

By the time I arrived home my face had become swollen and my eye was bruised, puffy and half closed. My dad naturally noticed and demanded to know what had happened. I broke down and startled snivelling, the hurt and the shock of the unprovoked assault finally kicking in. My dad was livid when I told him the story, incredulous that I hadn't retaliated. I was ashamed and knew I'd let him down. After eventually calming down, he promised he would deal with it himself. But when I told him who my attacker was, I saw a concerned expression crossing his face. As I said, everyone knew everyone else in our area, and my dad must have known what a tough lot this family was. But, to give him his due, my dad stood up for me that night. I suppose he felt he had to, after he'd given me the lecture about standing up for myself and fighting back.

And so, after a few drinks for courage, he grabbed me and drove round to the McGlinn's house and banged on the door while I sat outside in the car. Rab's dad came to the door, as he stood there in the doorway, it appeared to me that he was at least a foot taller than my dad and twice as wide. He stretched his arms up to lean on the top of the inside of the door frame and looked menacingly at my dad. I was pretty sure that Rab's dad was resting his hands on some kind of weapon secured out of sight above the frame. It could have been a club, knife or even a gun.

My dad carried on, he explained what had happened to me, and that his son (who, he emphasised, was two years older than me) had inflicted the injury. There was no anger from my dad; he was never a big fighter himself, but he was a trained trade union negotiator, and so those were the skills he used. He appealed to what he hoped was Rab's dad's reasonable side, and the fact that an unprovoked attack on a weaker and younger opponent was just not on in the rules of the streets we lived in. Amazingly it seemed to work, and Rab's dad was soon agreeing with my dad. He said it wasn't the first time this had happened, that he knew Rab could be violent and a bully, and that he'd sort him out when he came home. My dad climbed back into the car and I had never been so relieved in my life. That giant could have snapped him in half.

Unfortunately, that incident was just the prelude of things to come. I would continue to be a target for bullies over the next couple of years. My dad had stepped in on that occasion, but he had also made it clear I needed to toughen up and fight my own battles in future.

* * * * *

Jan, meanwhile, had written to me and I was so happy that we could perhaps continue our romance, even long distance, but it was so precious to me. We exchanged letters every week and occasionally, when I had some cash, I would call her. We used public phone boxes because her family didn't have a phone installed, and we had only just got one ourselves. Ours was a 'party line', which meant we shared the line with at least one other neighbour. It's difficult to imagine now, but often when you picked up the receiver to make a call, you would find yourself butting into the middle of someone else's call. There was very little privacy. But somehow, Jan and I maintained contact through the rest of the summer, and before long, the holiday had ended and it was time for me to start secondary school. I was still madly in love with Jan and wanted to see her again.

Throughout this period I still shared a bedroom with my elder sister Carolyn. We did our best to create some private space for ourselves by putting a dividing curtain down the middle of the room, but it was far from ideal. We were both growing up, and at fifteen she was now a young woman. Meanwhile, I was going through puberty and hated the changes that were happening to me. I would still lie in bed at night and pray that I would wake up as female. I often dreamt that I had somehow magically transformed, and these dreams were very beautiful. I would be taken around the neighbourhood by my parents and introduced to all our friends and relations. My mum would say something like, "This is my new daughter. We discovered a mistake has been made, so from now on please call her Sally," or Angela, or whatever was the current favourite name I had for my secret alter ego at that time. All the people we met were genuinely happy for me, kissed me and wished me love. I would regularly wake up bathed in this glow of love and acceptance, until reality would inevitably bite and I'd be back in the real world. Getting up, dressing for school in my awful boy's uniform, while my sister laid out her girl's clothes that I envied so much.

I had been dressing up in my sister's and mother's clothes for as long as I could remember. But opportunities to do so didn't come along too often, and they were always done in secret. Being three years younger than my sister, I had always managed to fit into her clothes and shoes easily, but now, as puberty rampaged through my body, her clothes were now becoming tight as my body developed muscle mass. But that was the least of my problems.

One day I noticed I had hair on my top lip. Soon, to my absolute horror, hair was sprouting everywhere – all over my legs, arms, and even on my chest. That Christmas I was given a shaving kit as one of my presents, and I reluctantly came to accept that physically there was no escape for me. Testosterone was slowly but steadily poisoning my body, and it was wrecking everything. My voice began to break, too. I went through that awful phase when my voice would crack dramatically and drop halfway through a sentence. People would laugh and joke with me about this, oblivious that for me this was like being consumed by a monster. My mind was in turmoil; I knew exactly what was happening and that it was perfectly normal, but inside I was drowning in despair, with no one to talk to or to throw me a lifeline.

* * * * *

I started secondary school, I was put in a registration class at my new comprehensive, and everyone was a stranger. There was no one at all from my old school and I really missed my friends. We would sometimes meet up at break time and lunch, but inevitably the ties between us all soon unravelled as we all made new friends. I felt that my whole world was gradually being dismantled. Everyone I knew, all my old girlfriends and pals were growing up and growing away from me. Even when we did get together, the girls I'd known for years began to treat me differently. I was no longer part of the crowd. I wasn't able to gossip and laugh with them like I used to. Of course, they were going through their puberty phases too, beginning to have periods, grow breasts and have serious boyfriends. These were all things I was excluded from, and so now we had much less in common than ever before. One of the most hurtful things that could be said to me back then was when some of my old girl pals would whisper things to each other, then when I excitedly asked what the story was, one of them would reply, "Oh, it's just girly talk." It felt like a dagger in my heart.

Perhaps, back then, I should have opened up and told the girls how I was feeling. But I was scared I'd be laughed at and have even less access to my old friends. As my own body changed, I felt a chasm was opening up between us and I was beginning to lose confidence in myself. At that time transsexuality was a word I'd never heard of; no one had. Even being gay was such an unlikely concept that it was unheard of except in jokes, and even then we didn't really understand what homosexuality was. My parents had never spoken to me about heterosexuality, much less about any other variations of love. I felt I was completely alone with the biggest, worst secret imaginable.

I was also absolutely certain that I was the only person in the history of the world who had felt like this.

I decided I must see Jan. We had been in regular contact since the previous summer through letters and the occasional phone call, and I missed her so much. She had made me feel accepted, she had loved me and made me feel like I could be a man for her. All I needed to make me normal was the right woman, I told myself.

One morning the opportunity unexpectedly arrived. I got up and slowly dressed for school. As usual my sister

Carolyn was already up and dressed long before me, and she had already left for school by the time I came downstairs. My mum had also left for work so I sat alone in the living room eating my toast, when I looked up and saw an envelope on the mantelpiece above the fire. Written on the envelope was 'coal money.' I looked inside and there was about £7 in cash, which was quite a lot of money in those days. My dad was upstairs in bed sleeping, having come off a night shift. I knew he wouldn't be up for hours.

My plan crystallised in my mind immediately. I would borrow the coal money and take a bus into the centre of Glasgow, where could change and take another bus direct to Ayr. With the money left over from the bus fares, I could feed myself for a few days until I found a job, and then maybe I could live with Jan. It all seemed so easy in my mind. Jan would of course be delighted to see me and we'd work out all the details later. But just as long as we were together, everything would be fine.

I sneaked back upstairs and packed a bag with some clothes, a few books, and my little alarm clock. Back downstairs, I quietly made up a couple of sandwiches to keep me going until I reached Ayr. I was quiet as a mouse, terrified that I'd wake up my dad who would come down and foil my plan before I'd even left the house. Soon, however, I was out the door, bag in hand and the coal money in my pocket. I was terrified all the way along the street to the bus stop, expecting at any moment to see my dad appear, demanding to know where the money was and why I wasn't at school. Once on the bus I breathed a sigh of relief and began to calm down. I'd done it! I couldn't believe I'd had the nerve.

The journey to Ayr went as planned and I arrived sometime in the afternoon. I'd had no chance to warn Jan I was coming. I could only ever phone her if it was prearranged for her to be at the phone box at the time and date set in one of our letters. But it didn't really matter – I had her address and so I'd find her house soon enough.

Once I'd arrived in Ayr, my first priority was to find somewhere to sleep that night. I found a derelict office building that I could enter from a broken back door. It was cold and completely empty, devoid of any furniture, and with mostly smashed windows. It did have a stone floor and a roof though, so I decided it would do for the first night of my new life. I'd find something better later. And if I couldn't live with Jan, at her house, then perhaps we could both stay here for a while, I decided. I laid out my bag and clothes on the floor, and put my alarm clock on a cardboard box next to my makeshift bed.

As I wandered through the streets of Ayr, I noticed how different it all looked now, compared to what I remembered from the summer. We were now in the depths of winter and all the tourist attractions were closed up. The weather was cold and wet and I was feeling a bit homesick already. I'd also begun to have the realisation that turning up unexpectedly to see Jan might not be the fantastic idea that it had seemed earlier that day. However, I pressed on and, after asking around, eventually found her house. I'd never been to her home during the time we'd spent together in the summer. She lived on a rough council estate, much like my own home. By this time, I was quite fearful of the reception I'd get when I saw Jan. But I'd come this far, so I took a few deep breaths, gathered up my courage and knocked on the door. A teenage boy answered, about sixteen. I could see by the resemblance he was probably Jan's brother. He looked at me aggressively and demanded what I wanted. I said I was looking for Jan, was she home? No, she's at school, he replied as started to shut the door. When is she coming back, I quickly asked? He looked at me and grinned. She'll be getting off at that bus stop at about a quarter past four, pointing to a bus shelter across the road from where we stood. Then he slammed the door.

It had never occurred to me that Jan had a brother. Why didn't I know that? In fact, I realised that I knew nothing much at all about her family setup. I'd never asked, and Jan had never said anything about them. I didn't even know what school she went to; she'd certainly never mentioned a school in her letters. But of course why didn't I understand that a fifteen year old girl would be at school? I felt like such an idiot. What had driven me to steal money and travel halfway across Scotland to visit Jan, without any warning? And what made me think that she would be happy to see me in those circumstances? Was I going to tell her that I came to see her because she was the only person who could make a man of me? It all seemed so ridiculous now, as I slumped in the bus shelter.

Jan's bus duly arrived and she got off. I stood up and smiled at her. At first she seemed not to notice me. She was wearing her school uniform, no make-up, and shouting and screaming with her school friends as they messed around teasing each other, pushing and shoving as kids do. Then she stopped and did a double take, looked directly at me, and smiled. "What the fuck are you doing here?" she screamed. We hugged and I began babbling about how I needed to see her, how much I missed her. At least she seemed pleased to see me, so I felt a whole lot better.

I explained to Jan that I missed her so much and had decided to come and live in Ayr so we could be together. To give her credit, she didn't make a fuss about my crazy revelation. She just told me to wait here while she went and changed out of her school clothes. I waited at the bus stop, and about twenty minutes later Jan reappeared. She had changed and put on her make-up. She now looked much more like the Jan I remembered. We hugged again and kissed, and after more hugging we starting walking into town.

Jan looked amazing. I was almost lost for words at her presence beside me again. We couldn't stop touching and holding each other. But I could also see in her eyes that she was concerned as to why I was there.

"Have you got somewhere to stay tonight?" she asked. "How long are you here for? What about school, have you got a holiday?" In the face of such obvious and reasonable questions, my original plan of living in Ayr with Jan, dreamt up that morning as I had stared at the coal money envelope on the mantelpiece, seemed a bit presumptuous to say the least.

I asked Jan to come with me and see my temporary accommodation, the derelict office block. It was dusk when we arrived and I took her round the back, through some bushes and trees to the broken rear door. It didn't look like much when I left it that afternoon. But now, in the gloomy twilight and biting cold, it seemed much worse. My little alarm clock sitting on a cardboard box looked particularly pathetic.

"You can't stay here," Jan said." And you definitely can't stay at our house, we have no room and my dad will go mad if he finds out about you and me." She said this in a kind way, not trying to put me down, just explaining the realities of life to a lovesick kid, which is what I was. Jan still didn't know I was still only twelve, so the situation was even worse than she imagined. I knew she was right.

By this time I was also beginning to think about the carnage I'd left behind. "What have you told your parents?" was her next question, as if reading my mind. "They don't know where I am," I replied." I nicked some money that was meant for the coal man and on impulse came here. I had to see you. I love you."

Over the years I've met and loved many people, encountered through my impetuous actions. It's not something I would recommend, impulsiveness is part of my nature and these things are never pre-planned. I often, especially when I was younger, just made a crazy decision and followed through with it, hoping luck would see me through. Jan was one of those wonderful level-headed people. She didn't judge or ridicule me; she just gave me the wise council that I needed, and she took control of the situation.

"Okay, the first thing you have to do is call your parents, they'll be worried sick about you. Then somehow you need to get back to Glasgow tonight before the buses stop running. I'll stay with you until we get this sorted, but we have to do it now because you cannot stay in this slum, you'll freeze to death." I knew she was right.

I would have to make that call, and I would no doubt get a beating for stealing the money and putting my parents through such worry. But, with Jan by my side to give me courage, I'd face the music.

I called home and Dad answered. He seemed quite calm. I told him I was okay and that I'd stolen the money to come and see Jan because I missed her so much. It was my plan, not hers. I was sorry. "Right,"Dad replied," get the bus back to Glasgow and I'll meet you at Buchanan Street bus station. Call me when your bus gets in." So far, so good.

We had about an hour to kill until my bus was due to leave for Glasgow, so we spent that time with each other, cuddling up and sharing a bag of chips. It seemed we had spent most of our time together in bus shelters, Jan and me. When it was time to get on the bus we kissed and said goodbye. I was frightened to say too much about our future in case she dumped me. After all, following this ridiculous stunt, who could blame her? So I just climbed on the bus and waved through the glass as the bus pulled out. "I'll write soon" she mouthed, as we lost sight of each other in the dark wet night.

Jan's promise to write buoyed me up on the long journey back to Glasgow. Whatever punishment I would inevitably receive after this day of madness, I was confident that I could survive, so long as Jan still loved me and wanted to continue our relationship.

At around midnight the bus pulled into the bus station in Buchanan Street, Glasgow. I got off and was casting my eyes around looking for a phone box when I heard a familiar voice. "Ally, over here." It was my uncle Jake. Before I could express my surprise at him being there, he just told me to get into the car. I complied, still fearful of what was coming. We drove back to the Vale in virtual silence. Jake didn't try to engage me in much conversation, he just told me everything was going to be okay. "Don't worry, your dad is at work on the night shift. He'll speak with you in the morning."

I arrived back home half an hour later and my mum was still up, waiting for me. Here it comes, I thought, bracing myself for the onslaught. But no, she just told me to get to bed, and I gratefully slid past her and rushed upstairs. My sister was still awake when I got into bed, she was the other side of the curtain and whispered "Where the hell have you been?" "Ayr", I replied. That was it. Then I turned over and fell asleep.

The remarkable thing about this entire episode was that it was never mentioned, ever again, after that night. My parents never asked who I was with, what had happened, why I'd left, or even where the money was. The next day we just carried on as if it had never happened. This was a pattern that I would see develop over the subsequent years with my parents. Any emotional or embarrassing incident would simply be ignored, as they didn't have the necessary emotional tools to deal with it, or talk about it, and another glass of rum usually helped with that process of forgetting anyway.

* * * * *

As that dreary winter continued, I trudged to school every day with a loathing I'd never experienced before. In primary school I'd always enjoyed school and looked forward to it every day. Now, I hated every minute, I hated being a boy, I hated wearing boy's clothes, and I hated the loss of my girl friends. I started smoking, which was very common in those days. You could buy cigarettes at any age and they were very cheap. I'd hang out behind the bike shelters during every school break. smoking with a lot of the other kids, some of whom had come from different schools.

Fortunately, slowly but surely, I began to make some new friends.

One boy I was particularly fascinated with. His name was Glen and he really stood out from the crowd. He was the most popular kid in our year and I got to know him during our smoking breaks. He had bright blond spiked hair and wore the most amazing clothes: black leathers, Doc Marten boots dyed fluorescent green, and a heavy chain padlocked round his neck. The punk era had arrived! It turned out he was a fan of punk music, something I'd never heard of, but was definitely interested in finding out more. It seemed to me that, if you can dress any way you want and be as outrageous as you like, then maybe I should be a punk too.

It was Glen and his older brother Alan who first introduced me to punk music. They invited me back to their house one day to listen to a record by the Ramones. I loved it! They had other records by the Damned and the Buzzcocks, and these blew me away when they were put on the turntable. The energy and the noise was just so refreshing. I'd felt suffocated for years, but this new music was like an invitation to just explode with joy.

When they put on the Sex Pistols album Never Mind The Bollocks I just erupted; we all did. Soon we were all jumping around Glen's front room with wild abandon, screaming the lyrics of Pretty Vacant along with Johnny Rotten. We jumped and bounced and pogoed and slammed into each other as we literally bounced off the walls. I loved this feeling. It felt like I'd been a coiled spring and now I exploded with raw power and emotion. As so often happens with adolescent discovery of music, I'd finally found my tribe with Glen and Alan and punk music. Over the next year, this was something I'd throw myself into completely, meanwhile trying to put to the back of my mind the transsexual feelings that had been growing stronger as puberty progressed.

The fantastic thing about punk when it started was that nothing mattered. There were no fashion rules – you could wear what you liked. You could form a band – it didn't matter if you couldn't play or if your singing was rubbish. It was gloriously equal at the beginning; everyone was welcome, and no one was excluded if they wanted to be part of it.

It's no exaggeration to say that punk kept me just about sane throughout my puberty. For me it was all-consuming. Glen, Alan and I became firm friends and soon we were joined by Lynn and Lesley, two girls who loved the music too. I bought all the records I could afford and we went to the Glasgow Apollo whenever a punk band was playing. I saw all the early punk bands there: Eddy and the Hot Rods, Generation X, Sham 69, The Clash, and what turned out to be my favourite band, the Stranglers. Sadly I never did get to see the Sex Pistols live, but I followed their story in every article in the music papers and bought all their music and memorabilia.

Punk also opened up the clear possibility and viability of different lifestyles to me. It was quite clear, for example that Pete Shelly, founder of the Buzzcocks, was apparently gay or bisexual, but it didn't matter; no-one cared. Sid Vicious was a heroin addict and that was cool too. Everyone was welcome in the punk tent. The first completely naked woman I ever saw was as a thirteen year old kid at a Stranglers concert in 1977 at the Apollo where they had two strippers dancing along to the song Nice and Sleazy. I watched their movements with intensity, seeing how they moved their bodies and emphasised their sex appeal. It was for me fascination coupled with regret and sadness. As I looked around at the rest of the audience watching the girls, it struck me how powerful the female form was, and also how far away I was from achieving that female shape and power.

* * * * *

Jan and I had surprisingly kept in touch. We still wrote to each other regularly. Amazingly she hadn't dumped me after my surprise visit to see her. Then one day she wrote to tell me she wanted to come to the Vale to visit me. I was so excited, wanting this meeting to be perfect, especially after the last disastrous time I'd saw her. I worked out a day when I knew there would be no one at home. I was supposed to be at school but I'd begun regularly bunking off most days and the way the system was then, no one from the Department of Education seemed to notice my absences. If I was ever questioned, I'd write my own notes, supposedly from my mum, saying I'd been at the dentist, doctor, or whatever. I always got away with it.

I'd basically given up on education anyway. As soon as everyone else in the house left for work or school, I'd throw off my hated boy's clothes and go upstairs to my secret stash of girl's clothes and get dressed again. Then I'd spend the day either drawing and listening to music, or occasionally going out to the local parks or taking a train into Glasgow. I had to be very careful, though, because anyone of school age could easily be stopped by the police in those days, to ask why they weren't in school.

Looking back now, I'm sure some of our neighbours must have seen me leaving the house some days dressed as a girl. It was a very tight neighbourhood, and everyone knew everyone, and their business. But I was never challenged and so somehow managed to get away with it. I never wore any make-up but my hair was long and could be put in a female style. I had also got my ears pierced, much to the bemusement of my family and friends. It just wasn't done in those days for a boy to get even a single ear pierced, let alone two. But I didn't care; I just walked brazenly into the salon one day and asked for both to be done. Even the woman who did it tried to dissuade me, but I was adamant. I had also begun plucking my eyebrows, which hadn't gone unnoticed. My excuse was that I had a monobrow that I hated so I was just tidying it up a bit. It's amazing what you can get away with, if you just do it.

Jan arrived one morning for her visit and our long-awaited reunion. I met her off the bus. We walked hand-in-hand through the town back to my house. We had no money to go anywhere, so it was to be a day in together for us, maybe listen to some music cassettes and I could cook her some lunch. I didn't really care what we did – I was just so happy to see her. When we got back to my house we snuggled up in front of the coal fire and I drew the curtains. We smoked cigarettes and drank coke, just catching up with each other's lives. She would be leaving school in the summer and was already looking for a job. Meanwhile, I still hadn't told her my true age.

Eventually, after we had both warmed up in front of the fire, we went and sat together on the sofa. As usual, we had our arms around each other, kissing and cuddling, and soon we were both lying on the sofa. She had taken off her cardigan and just wore a strappy top and a pair of jeans. The next thing I knew, she was taking off her top and wore only a white bra underneath. She looked at me in a way I'd never seen before, then suggested I might want to help her get her jeans off.

How naive I was! I still didn't understand what was happening. I genuinely thought she must be too warm with the coal fire and everything, and just wanted to cool down a bit. We had never actually gone any further than kissing and cuddling before, usually in a cold bus shelter, so I was totally unprepared for what happened next. She was pulling my shirt off and at the same time I was taking down her jeans. Then she stretched out just wearing just bra and pants and pulled me down beside her. I was shocked at her directness and aggression. She grabbed my hand and put it under her breast inside the cup of her bra. I didn't know what to do so I started squeezing gently and kissing her. This went on for about five minutes. I was impassive and just hoped she was enjoying this. Next she took my hand and put it down to her pants and then inside on top of her vagina. I had no idea what she expected of me, so I just repeated doing what I'd done with her breast, gently squeezing and rubbing. Again, this went on for some time, while she squirmed and pushed herself on to my hand. I was taken aback. I'd never seen this side of Jan before; she had always been so soft and gentle.

You have to remember I'd received absolutely no sex education, either from my school or parents, so I couldn't even pretend to know what was happening. I felt no sexual stirring on my own behalf. I'd never even masturbated and didn't understand what an erection was. But probably more to the point, it didn't automatically come naturally to me as to what I should do. Looking back, I had no sexual desire for Jan. I just loved her and wanted to hold and kiss her.

The truth was I wanted to be just like her.

After several minutes, Jan started bucking her hips and groaning. I felt my hand get warm and wet next to her vagina. Even then I didn't understand. I just presumed she had wet herself or something. But Jan didn't seem embarrassed in the least, so I just withdrew my hand and hugged her close while she shuddered in my arms. After a while she was lying with eyes half-closed and breathing quietly. I got up to wash my hands and get cigarettes for us.

I sat on the floor while she lay on the sofa as we both smoked. She seemed a bit annoyed, and was asking for reassurance if I really loved her. I was surprised, and assured her I did, that I adored her. I meant it; I had missed her so much.

We both got dressed again and spent the rest of the day listening to music, but Jan still seemed a bit distant. I thought I'd upset her somehow. Was it the house, or my lack of money? I honestly had no idea.

This was my first sexual experience and, although not a complete disaster, I would remember that day forever. I was so inexperienced and naive about what was expected of a man. Most noticeably, though, I was completely incapable of figuring it out naturally.

* * * * *

As 1977 rolled in, I began to really fill out physically. I continued to develop muscle mass and strength to add to my height, which wasn't all that tall now, compared to my peers. I was 5' 10" and my family genes gave me my dad's body hair pattern. I was capable of growing a beard and had hair on my chest. But I still stood out, and I was still a target for the bullies.

One day at school, and for no reason at all, I was challenged to fight by an older kid Jim, whom I barely knew. He lived on my council estate and was a couple of years older than me, but a little shorter. He told me he'd be waiting for me when school finished that day. I felt sick all afternoon but could see no way to avoid a confrontation. At least Glen and Alan said they would be there to make sure it was fair, one-on-one, and make sure the rest of his gang didn't jump in. I left school at four o'clock and went out the front gates. Jim was there waiting for me, strutting around with his pals geeing him on. The whole school seemed to know about this fight, and a huge crowd had expectantly gathered around us on the street. I was feeling really sick now, my stomach churning and a sense of fear causing a weakness going through my body. I literally felt I needed to lie down. But there was no escape with the hundreds of kids gathered round us in a tight circle.

We had to do battle; there was no avoiding it.

Jim rushed straight towards me, arms swinging wild punches. Acting on instinct and fuelled by fear, I reached out with both hands and grabbed his hair and pulled down. I was pumped up by adrenalin but still surprised to see how easy this was. I was so much quicker than him. Now I had a firm hold of this swirling, spitting bundle of rage and I just swung him round, like I was holding a rag doll. I swung him to one side then the other, he was struggling to keep his feet but I felt I had total control. I felt I could stand like this for hours. He was never going to get out of my grip, or get close to hitting me. But he wouldn't give up, he kept struggling and trying to get to me. I realised I had to do something else if this was ever going to end. So without any prior plan, I started to kick him in the face while still holding his hair. I must have kicked him really hard about six or seven times. I felt my Doc Marten boots thudding into his nose, throat and eyes. After the first couple of kicks he was struggling less and become limp, but in my panic I kept going. The crowd were screaming for me to knock him out, kill him, shouting my name over and over.

It was at this point I felt strong hands on my shoulder and I was lifted up and back rapidly. I was still hanging on to Jim's hair and wondering what was happening when a policeman came into my view in front of me and wrestled Jim out of my grasp. The hands on my shoulder were soon identified as another policeman. It turned out that a patrol car had been passing the school when the cops saw the huge crowd of kids blocking the road, and had stopped to see what was going on. Quickly recognising it was a fight, they had charged in to break it up.

Jim and I were put into the back of the police car and they drove us away quickly as the mob of baying kids screamed and banged on the side of the vehicle. It was only a mile or so to the police station and we drove through the back gates into the garage area. Once there the policemen dragged us both out of the car. But, instead of arresting us or calling our parents, one of the cops just stood Jim and me facing each other in the middle of the garage. He said" Okay, there are lots of tools lying around on the floor or hanging on the wall. I want you to grab anything you want and finish the fight here. Don't worry, we won't step in until one of you has won. Get to it!"

They were obviously quite street smart, these cops. It's hard to imagine anything like that happening these days. But Jim and I just looked at each other, and I knew there was no fight left in him. I hadn't wanted to fight in the first place, so we both turned to the cop and he understood that the lesson had been learned. He told us to shake hands, then took us inside the station and helped to clean us both up. Jim's face was covered in blood and bruises, but I was virtually unscathed. Ten minutes later we were released out the front door of the police station and told to get home.

Jim and I started walking slowly back to Rosshead where we both lived. There was no animosity between us. We'd had a shared experience to talk about. On the way we were joined by a couple of boys from Jim's gang who had caught up with us. What had happened? How had we managed to get out of the police station? I half expected to be attacked, now that there were three of them, but that didn't happen. We all walked back to the estate together, if not as friends, then at least no longer as enemies. Importantly, I had managed to gain some respect from them. They were really shocked that I could fight like that.

To be honest, no one was more surprised than I was.

I had turned a corner. After that day, I was much less likely to get picked on at school. I still had a few encounters but on the whole people left me alone. It was nice not to be bullied, but I was also quite frightened about my own actions. Where had that brute strength come from?

* * * * *

As well as my punk music, I decided to get much more involved in sport and athletics. Anything to take my mind off my transsexual thoughts and desires. I was always average at sport until I got to secondary school and then puberty gave me a strong lithe body that was perfectly suited to running in particular.

One day this was noted by my P.E. teacher Dougie Morrison. The class was to play rugby that day, a game I had no real understanding of. None of the boys wanted to play rugby. Working class kids were only interested in football. But Dougie had been a very good rugby player in his day and so he made us play his game. Most of the boys were just messing around. We didn't know the rules or tactics and Dougie was struggling to get us interested.

He threw the ball to me and said "Right, you and your team need to get that ball over the line 50 meters away, behind the posts. Our team will try to stop you. Let's go!"

I picked up the ball and ran as fast as I could through Dougie's team. I easily outpaced everyone trying to catch me and avoided their tackles. I got to the posts and just stood there holding the ball. "Okay, I've done that, what next?" I asked. Dougie just stood there staring at me, open-mouthed. He gathered the teams together again into each half, ready to start again. He explained that I should also use my team mates and pass the ball between us as a team, because it was very unlikely I'd be able to get the ball over the line on my own again. We restarted, then someone threw the ball to me and off I went. I immediately darted up the line as fast as I could. I looked around for someone on my team to pass to, but they were all way back behind me. I just put my head down and carried on by myself, ending up once more under the posts with the ball. This carried on all through the P.E. session. Occasionally someone got close to me and tackled, then I went down like a felled tree. I couldn't handle the tackling, but as long as I found room to run, no one could catch me.

After the session finished Dougie came up to me and asked if I was entering the school sports that year. I hadn't even thought about it. The fact was, a year before I was short and tubby, and I had never stood out in sports before. It's true that my elder sister was an accomplished athlete. She had been the girls' sports day champion three years running at our school. My mum had also been a runner when she was young, with some old medals to show from her school days; and my dad had been a very good amateur footballer and gymnast. I'd assumed the athletic gene had passed me by. But Dougie insisted I enter, telling me I had a great chance and that I should definitely take part.

I talked to Carolyn about it at home that night. What did she think I should do? Carolyn encouraged me: "Yes, go for it," she urged. I think even she was surprised that her formerly chubby kid brother had suddenly transformed into an athlete right under everyone's noses and without anyone noticing.

The upshot was that I did enter. Dougie even took me for training and time trial sessions after school, just to see how fast I was. He was amazed at the times I clocked for the sprints in particular. At thirteen years old I was regularly doing sub-twelve seconds for the 100 metres. Running on grass, with no spikes or training. Dougie was impressed, and he contacted my dad to tell him I should concentrate on athletics and that I needed proper running spikes.

That year I won the sports day championship easily. I won every event I entered except the 1500 metres. I was given the school boys' silver cup to keep for a year and my name was engraved on it. My sister won the girls' trophy. I went on to win it for the following two years too, so my name appears engraved three times on the cup, as does Carolyn's on the girls' cup.

Dougie even decided to take me along with a team to the Scottish Schools National Championships in 1977, held in Glasgow. I won the 100 and 200 metres that year. It was the first time our deprived and frankly disaster zone of a school had ever had a national champion in anything. I was even a hero for a while.

One thing in particular about that day sticks in my mind more than anything else. After I had stripped off ready for my first race, I decided I needed to go to the loo. So I returned to the changing rooms. Our school was sharing changing facilities with a couple of other much posher schools, and when I entered the room to get to the toilets I encountered a boy from my school, Shug, who was our long distance runner. He was casually rifling through the pockets and bags of the posh school kids, stealing cash, jewellery and watches. He looked up as I entered and smiled when he saw it was me.

"I'll split it with you later," he said. I nodded, quickly used the loo, then left. This was seen as absolutely acceptable. That was just the kind of school we went to.

For the rest of my time at secondary school I concentrated on athletics and art, the only things I showed any interest in and aptitude for. I rarely turned up for any other classes and no one seemed to miss me. The bullying had almost ended, too. There had been a couple of other occasions where I'd been physically attacked but had managed to hold my own. I also had some backup, now; everyone knew I was friends with Glen and Alan, and that afforded me some protection.

* * * * *

I had began drinking around the age of thirteen. This wasn't that unusual back then in the Vale. Lots of kids were drinking by that age and even before. My parents drank themselves into oblivion every night. It often ended up in a fight between them and I'd see my mum getting beaten up by my dad, or sometimes the other way round. My dad in particular could be quite violent within the home. Occasionally he would attack Carolyn or me for some perceived insult he'd imagined we'd given him. If he was in a nasty mood, we'd all tiptoe around him and tried to escape his attentions. I lost count of the number of dinners he threw against the wall. We had to decorate quite often. Sometimes it didn't matter what you did, it was just your turn to get it.

Carolyn came home from school one day when she was around fifteen. She went into the kitchen for a bowl of cereal. My dad was slumped in a drunken stupor, half-on, half-off his armchair. I was trying to watch TV. Next, Carolyn came into the living room.

"I think the milk is off," she announced with her nose wrinkled up at the stench from the half-full bottle. For some reason this innocent statement set my dad off. He lurched off his chair and threw himself across the room at my sister, grabbed her by her long hair and pulled her down to the floor. Then he took the milk bottle from her and poured its smelly contents all over her head. He was ranting and raving, saying there's nothing wrong with the milk, calling her a fucking bitch and dragging her by her hair around the room. I jumped up to try and get between them, Carolyn screaming and crying by now, terrified at this sudden unprovoked attack. When my dad saw me, he turned his attention away from her and grabbed me by the throat and pushed me up against a wall. I could smell the stale rum on his breath as he pushed his face into mine.

"D'ya think yer man enough to fight me yet?" He screamed. I too was sobbing by now, slumped against the wall, terrified. I was growing bigger and stronger, but I was still too scared of him to hit back. But racing through my mind was the thought, One day, one day soon, I'll fucking get you. He released me without a blow this time, and Carolyn quickly grabbed me and we ran upstairs to our bedroom. Dad was shouting and cursing at us from the bottom of the stairs, telling us to get to bed and not to come down again or we'd "get it". Carolyn and I got into our bedroom, dragged furniture in front of the door as a blockade, and sat down on our beds. I rubbed my bruised throat while she tried to brush out the sour milk from her hair. We hoped that if we sat quietly for long enough, Dad would fall into a drunken slumber and leave us alone. Mum was at work and wouldn't be home for several hours. Not that she would have been much help to us, but when she came home, at least she might become the focus of his rage, instead of us.

This kind of incident was typical of how we lived through my teens. You never knew from one night to the next what you'd be coming home to. Would it be happy drunks or nasty drunks? You never knew, but it was always drunks. You might imagine that episodes such as these would have put me off alcohol for life. But it doesn't work that way when you're trapped in a family dependent on alcohol. One of the reasons I started drinking myself was to cope with the fear. It also gave me some courage, and eventually my own drinking was encouraged by my parents, since it gave them another drinking buddy. Carolyn, on the other hand, took the opposite stance and wouldn't drink at all. It disgusted her to see my parents inebriated, argumentative and violent.

Being three years older than me, she knew she it wouldn't be long before she could leave home and escape the situation. I, however, would have no choice but to remain in the abusive situation on my own after she left. Frankly, I felt it was easier drinking with them, rather than being the sober object of their drunken violence.

As I grew older and taller as a teenager, my dad began challenging me more and more. He would call me out for a fight in the garden, call me a sissy and tell me he knew I didn't have the balls to be a real man like him and fight. I was too scared to stand up to him and I had nowhere else to go, so I would accept this with a tearful burning rage inside of me. It didn't help that the backdrop to all this was my increasing desire to be female. I spent most of my free time dressed in girls' clothes, and it became my release from the violence and fear. But I was also ashamed because it proved him right: I was weak, feminine and scared. If he knew how I spent my time alone, he would have killed me and felt justified in doing it. There was no attempt at understanding LGBT in our house. It was just a joke; they were all poofs, people to laugh at and ridicule.

Looking back, I'm amazed that my parents never caught me dressed as female during my teenage years. It did almost happen once. One day I bunked off school as I often did. Carolyn had left home by then, mum was at work until 8pm and my dad wasn't due home until 3pm. As usual I threw off my boys' clothes and went upstairs to dress in my secret stash of girls' clothes. I planned on going up to Loch Lomond, just to do touristy things for the day. I put on my bra (padded with socks) and pants, black tights, a knee-length tan skirt, with a tie-bottom cheesecloth top. I was sitting in front of my dressing table mirror trying to decide how to do my hair when suddenly I heard the front door open and my dad come in. He knew I was at home because the front door wasn't locked and he shouted up to me, asking why I wasn't at school. Moments later I heard his feet thudding up the stairs. I was in a blind panic. I had no time to get changed and I knew my bedroom door would burst open in just a few seconds. I threw myself into my bed and covered myself up with the blankets, just before he entered the room. He came over to me and I pretended to be asleep. Then he shook me and asked why I was in bed. I feigned sleepiness, pretending to be half awake and told him I'd been sent home from school because I had the flu. He mumbled something about him having the day off because of heavy fog, then he left the room, apparently satisfied with my answer, and no doubt desperate to get back downstairs to his precious rum bottle.

I lay in bed, terrified. That was too close for comfort. After he left, I undressed whilst still under the covers, fearful he would come back. When I had everything off I crept out of bed silently, and hid my girls' clothes back in their usual place before returning to bed. I was so scared that I remained in bed all day, just to make my flu story seem plausible.

* * * * *

Carolyn did catch me out, once. Well, kind of. Before she had left home, while we still shared a bedroom, I had gone upstairs one evening while she was out with her friends. She had just bought some new clothes and I knew she had bought a new bra. I wanted to try it on for size, just to see how it looked on me. I stripped down to just my jeans, took the new bra out of her top drawer and carefully put it on, making sure not to mark it or stretch the material. There I was, filling the cups with rolled up tights, when I heard the door behind me open. I turned, terrified, to face my sister as she breezed into the bedroom. For an awful moment we both just stared at each other, saying nothing. Then, her reaction surprised me. She never asked why I was wearing a bra. All she was concerned about was the fact I was wearing her bra.

"Take that off, it's brand new!" she said. It might as well have been a pen or magazine she'd caught me with. She didn't seem at all bothered that I was wearing a bra, just that it didn't belong to me. I took it off and handed it to her. She put it back in the drawer and stormed out, telling me to leave her things alone.

* * * * *

Given my family background, you can perhaps understand my reticence when in later years I was advised by the NHS Gender Identity Clinic at Charing Cross in London to tell my immediate family and friends by way of a nice informative letter that I was undergoing surgery to change sex. More fool me; I took their advice and did it anyway. Unfortunately this advice was clearly based on some middle class perception of how these matters were best handled within polite society, as determined by the professional medical people who'd thought up the plan. I doubt that many of them were the products of West Scotland's working class council estates. Needless to say, my letter to family and friends didn't go down at all well. But we'll come back to that later.

* * * * *

My sporting prowess began to get me really noticed from about the age of fourteen, and suddenly I became more popular than I'd ever been before. Hanging out with Glen and the punks had helped too, and I was no longer the victim of bullying. In fact, a lot of the bullies now wanted to be friends with me! I admit it all went to my head, and my desire for acceptance influenced my choices of friendship. I began hanging out with a gang from my own rough council estate who had previously been the very same people I would fear and avoid. The wrong crowd.

There's a buzz you get from being in a gang, there's no denying it. You feel safe as part of the crowd and then, with rampant testosterone coursing through the strong body of an adolescent male, mixed with some alcohol, and you can feel invincible. It was a potent combination, and one I would later discover I couldn't handle.

We would gather each night for drinking sessions, usually cheap Eldorado or Vordo extra-strong fortified wine which was more like a sherry, cans of Tennent's lager, and bottles of Old English cider. Sometimes if money was harder to come by it would be tins of glue, which would be poured into a bin bag and then passed around the group in a circle. When it was your turn you put your whole face into the neck of the sack, covering your mouth and nose, and deeply inhaled the fumes. The sensation is like having you brain explode over and over. I was never a much of a glue sniffer but I did partake when it was all we had to share. My favourite was Vordo wine, which we could buy almost anywhere.

There was another reason why my popularity soared. I looked older than most of my friends, so I was often the one who was given the money by everyone else to go into the local off licence or pub to buy the booze. This became a nice little earner for me as I would often encounter other kids hanging around outside the shops who begged me to go in and buy alcohol for them too. I would charge the kids who were not my friends 50p a time to buy for them, and so I usually ended up making enough money to pay for all my own drinks, with a little extra left over in my pocket as profit.

Once we had got our booze for the evening we would gather round in some abandoned flats on the council estate. During the summer we'd go into the woods and drink, sometimes with added glue sniffing, or even a bit of hash, as cannabis was just becoming widely available. Our aim was simple: to get as drunk or high as possible. Fights would often break out among our group, and I was as guilty of this as anyone else.

We were like a pack of wolves. Trainspotting meets Lord of the Flies. There was a clear pecking order among the ten to fifteen regulars in our gang, and I started at the bottom. But pretty soon I was challenging others for a step up in the hierarchy. I knew I was fit and strong, and most importantly, I was fast. With the addition of alcohol, I soon found I had the courage to use my natural physical attributes. I fought almost everyone in our gang at least once over the next few years. Sometimes it would just be a quick punch-up, other times it could be a prolonged vicious fight with whatever was close to hand – bottles, knives, clubs or bricks. It really was that basic. It didn't matter if you lost one of these fights, so long as you didn't turn away from a challenge. Better to take a beating than back down and be forever ostracised from the gang.

We didn't just fight among ourselves, of course. Once we'd got tanked up on booze, drugs and glue in the woods, we would head into the area of town where the pubs were, where we'd often meet up and fight with other gangs, or even strangers. Several of the local pubs turned a blind eye to underage drinkers, so naturally and we would go to those, usually hanging out in their pool room.

Another way to raise your status in the group was by challenging members from other gangs that lived in other parts of town. Conflict was never far away, since everyone in all the gangs went to the same handful of pubs in the evenings, and would frequently cross paths. This was where I came into my own as a fighter. After working my way up the ranks of my own gang I had nothing to prove to them, and I knew they would back me up if I got into a fight with someone from a different council estate. It also made me a marked face if I travelled into gang territories outside my own area. I had acquired something of a reputation and so was a target for anyone if they caught me or my friends outnumbered outside our own territory. This happened to me a few times.

One night I found myself with, unusually for me by this time, my old friends Glen and Alan, the punks. We were walking over a bridge in town and two older members of a well-known gang came across us. They started by messing around and slapping Glen and Alan, asking for money. But there was clear menace in their actions and I knew what was coming. I stepped in.

"Do you want to have a go?" I shouted, issuing the standard gang challenge. I knew Glen and Alan weren't the fighters that I was, but there were three of us against two, so to my mind we had to go for the attack first. But, to my shock and horror, my friends turned and ran. They lived only a short distance away and they ran for home, leaving me standing on my own. I felt I had no choice, so I ploughed into both of them, arms flaying and boots flying, but it was soon apparent I was not going to get the better of them on my own. I was taking a real beating, but in times like those I never felt any pain, just the surge of adrenalin. I knew there was a taxi office a little further up the street, so I headed straight for that, hoping I might find a friend in there to even things up, or if not, at least some other people who would break up the fight I was clearly going to lose.

I crashed through the front door of the office but to my dismay saw that the seating area was empty. I was still on my own and the fight carried on with the chairs and tables flying. I knew I was beaten and my strength was draining. I just hoped they weren't tooled up with knives because if they were, I was likely going to be stabbed to death or at the very least, badly scarred. Suddenly, I heard a woman's screeching voice above the grunting and swearing. I saw Mary P, who lived behind my house in the flats. She was the radio operator for the taxi firm and was now charging from the office door with her telephone headset still on. She launched herself kicking and punching into the two guys who were beating me up and screaming that she'd called the police.

Whether it was the threat of the police or Mary's fury that stopped them I'll never know, but they soon fled, running out the door, shouting curses about how I was going to get chibbed (stabbed) the next time they saw me.

Once the panic was over I pulled myself up and sat on a chair with Mary. She went for a wet cloth to clean me up and to see if I'd received any stab wounds. Luckily I had not. I asked if she had really called the police. Of course she hadn't. People on our estate never called the police. I thanked Mary and eventually limped my way home.

I learned a few things that night: first, that Glen and Alan weren't like me and my gang friends. I had become a member of a different tribe from them now. Second, I now knew that I had been marked out by other gangs as a prize scalp to be had for anyone who wanted to enhance their own reputation. They hadn't even tried to chase Glen and Alan; it was me they had wanted all along, and I knew they would be boasting about the kicking they had given me. My third realisation that night was Mary's courage. What an amazon she had been! With no thought for her own safety, she had weighed into two guys who were twice her size to protect me, just because we had the shared background of growing up and living on the same council estate. Local gangs enjoyed a fierce loyalty towards them on the council estates. That's the way it was. Probably still is. Even if you were not in a gang, you never knew when you might need them to help you one night.

* * * * *

There were many more fights during this period of my life as I tried to rationalise some kind of reason for living, or even existing. I lived a double life, desperately trying to avoid the thoughts in my head and my desire to live and be female. My life with the gangs, the fights and the violence was not what I wanted, but I was good at it. It was an area of my life where I had found friendship and acceptance and a way of blocking out my inner feelings. At least, it did so long as I was drunk enough, so naturally I drank enough every night to make sure I was.

I became increasingly detached. I could quite easily be one of two different people, and one helped to cancel out the other. Deep down I knew I could never have the female life I fantasised about. I had been born male and the evidence was plain to see every time I looked in a mirror or whenever someone spoke to me. That was when I first experienced suicidal thoughts.

I never really considered hanging myself or jumping off a bridge; it was never so straightforward for me. Instead I placed myself in increasingly risky and dangerous situations. I now believe that subconsciously I was hoping that I may somehow die accidentally. I still had some religious faith in those days. After all, I had prayed and begged God to help me, to turn me into a girl or to let me die and be reborn female. I felt a mistake had been made in my creation, and who else could fix that, except my creator?

This internal death wish helped me to build a reputation as a fearless gang fighter. I began to think, what have I got to lose? And when you believe that you don't have much of a life to lose, you can become a very dangerous person.

I remember going up one night to the Loch Lomond Rock festival, I think in 1979. As usual, my friends and I had got tanked up with cheap wine and cider in the woods before heading up to the pubs in Balloch. Thousands of people had come from all over Britain to attend this weekend rock concert. As far as we were concerned, however, they were in our gang territory and so we needed to make ourselves known to them.

It wasn't just our gang; all the local gangs from the Vale, Renton, and Dumbarton area were there. Predictably, after the pubs shut and we were all turfed out onto the streets, the fights began. There were gangs from all around Glasgow and the west of Scotland, and a huge pitched battle took place on the street outside the Glenroy pub in Balloch. Our gang charged into the middle of the melee, throwing punches, kicking and slashing knives. To be considered the enemy, you simply had to be someone we didn't know locally. It was that simple, and I was right in the middle of it all.

This fight went on for ages. Hundreds of youths, Hell's Angels, and all the punk rock fans that had come from all over Britain to see the bands that weekend were involved. Fuelled by alcohol and my death wish, I charged a group of around fifteen guys on my own. After about half an hour, most of my gang had either got beaten up or were lying drunk somewhere. The fight continued with just me and Davy B at my side. At one point I had some guy in a headlock, but no matter how hard or how many times I punched him, he wouldn't go down. I shouted to Davy to hit him with the bottle he had in his hand. My opponent knew what was coming so he struggled for dear life as I tried to wrestle him into position for Davy to get a clean hit. Unfortunately, Davy was by this time far too drunk and dazed from his own battles, and he actually smashed me over the head instead. I went down, knocked unconscious but still hanging onto the guy I was fighting. When I came round a few moments later, I was still holding his legs while he rained down blows on my head. Davy, meanwhile, was lying asleep on the pavement. I'd had enough. I let go of the guy and got to my feet. I was very unsteady and covered in blood. It was at this point the police turned up. A patrol car stopped directly opposite me. I staggered over to them and asked if they could get me to hospital as I suspected I had split my skull from the bottle blow to the head. The cop just looked beyond me to the fights that were still raging behind me in the street. "Don't worry," he said,"We'll be back soon, but there's an urgent call somewhere else." They drove off, and I collapsed next to Davy.

The next thing I remember is the police coming back about fifteen minutes later. By this time the fighting had all but ceased. Those who were able to had made off, and those who couldn't lay all around in the road. There were bodies everywhere. The police scooped up everyone from the street and pushed us into the backs of vans and took us back to the police station where we were all left in cells to sober up. In the morning everyone was charged with a breach of the peace. Guilty attacker or innocent victim, it didn't matter.

At the Sheriff court in Dumbarton the next day I pleaded guilty, along with the guy whose legs I'd been hanging on to. It turned out he was from Paisley. We had a laugh together outside the court and went our own separate ways as friends.

In the morning, after the hearing, I did challenge the policeman, the one I'd asked to take me to hospital when I'd been bottled. Why hadn't he picked me up then, when I was so clearly badly injured? If he had, I wouldn't have ended up getting charged. He said, quite candidly, it was too dangerous. There were still a lot of fights going on and they didn't want to get involved. So the cops had just driven up the road a few hundred metres and waited for the fighting to die down. And then, when all that was left were bodies lying in the street, they came back and arrested everyone. I had to admire his honesty.

I don't relate these stories to glorify the behaviour, just to demonstrate what a common feature of my life it was at that time. In my world, my reputation grew immeasurably because of that fracas. I had led the charge despite being vastly outnumbered, I'd kept fighting even after being knocked out, and I'd got arrested and fined. Three ticks! People remembered that night and often related the story for years afterwards to me. I'd proved myself a man. Oh, the irony!

Looking back now, I know I was very lucky to escape that period without getting killed or seriously injured. Even more, I was fortunate not to have killed someone else. Three of our gang members ended up getting convicted of murder during that period, and another close friend achieved the same result, though he wasn't himself a gang fighter.

I did have a very lucky escape one evening, along with one of my intended victims. I'd been drinking with several of our gang in a bar, when we decided to leave and go to another pub. The pub we approached was just by the railway station in the Vale, and two young men were leaving the station platform just as we noticed them. They were members of a Dumbarton gang. Why they had turned up here on their own was as crazy as it was a mystery. Everyone knew the rules. You don't enter another gang's territory unless you're there to fight. There were four of us against the two of them.

As soon as they saw us they realised their error and ran back towards the station as we charged towards them. It was a cold winter's evening that night and the roads were icy. There were very few people around. As I chased one of the guys, he slipped on the ice and fell over. He was on his hands and knees circling round like a spinning top as I approached at full speed. He stopped spinning and his face was presented to me at the perfect height for a full-blooded kick to the head from my steel-toe-capped Dr Martens boots. As the distance between us narrowed I readied myself for the blow I was about to deliver. His face was a mask of pure terror because he knew what was coming but could do nothing to prevent it. Just as I swung my boot to his head, however, I too slipped on the ice. I missed him completely and slid past him, landing on my back. By the time I got up, he had jumped the railway fence and was nowhere to be seen.

I have been haunted throughout my life by many what ifs and maybes since that night. I'll never forget his handsome youthful face looking up at me in terror. I could easily have killed a beautiful young man and sent myself to prison for life in that moment if I'd connected. And for what?

Most of the gang murders and other deaths from that period were pointless, usually fuelled by testosterone and alcohol, and completely senseless. I hated myself and hated men, but I feared being labelled a poof even more. I was too much of a coward to face up to myself and too cowardly to kill myself.

It wasn't just fighting that killed people. One day I was walking through town at lunchtime with a school friend, Kenny. We were pals in the same class, but he wasn't into gangs or fighting. It must have been a rare occasion because I had actually been to school that morning, and now we were going to buy lunch at the City Bakery cafe.

As we walked along the main street I saw this guy heading towards us. He was wide-eyed and his nose was running. He was a couple of years older than me and wearing old ragged clothes and had a menacing air. I recognised him immediately; he was H from my council estate and one of the gang. As he staggered up to me and Kenny, people were swerving out of the way of his staggered gait. His eyes lit up in recognition.

"Do me a favour, big man," he smiled. "I need some glue from the cobblers but they won't sell it to me." I could understand from the state he was in why he'd been refused. He was obviously completely off his head from glue sniffing and booze, with the tell-tale ring of red and yellow spots round his mouth as further proof of his habit. He pushed some coins into my hands, approximately 75p, and told me to get me a tube of Bostick, and you two can keep the change. Kenny and I looked at each other; the change would be enough to buy a couple of single cigarettes, so we quickly agreed.

The short story is we went into the cobblers for H and bought the glue. We laughed as we handed it to him outside and went off with the change. A few days later I found out that H died that night after we'd given him the tube. He had gotten so wrecked on glue that he choked on his own vomit and suffocated in the woods. Neither Kenny nor I mentioned that day ever again. But one thing was becoming increasingly clear to me: I had to get out of the Vale.

* * * * *

Not long after the train station incident I began systematically to turn against my fellow gang members. I realised I hated them; I was disgusted to be part of what we were, a directionless bunch of juvenile idiots, and I was one of the worst. I'd spent years proving to them, but mostly to myself, that I was a man. They might have believed it, but I didn't. And I couldn't run away from myself any more.

It was at this time, when I was at my lowest ebb, that something absolutely remarkable happened one rainy winter's day. I had been at school, or at least pretending I'd been at school, and came home at the appropriate time to back up that fiction. Both my parents were home, which was unusual. I remember I had toothache and was feeling pretty miserable. We were watching TV when we all heard a knock at the front door. My mum was cooking in the kitchen and my dad slouched half-pissed in the armchair, so he motioned for me to answer it. I got up reluctantly and went to the hallway and opened the door. What I saw before me was as unlikely as seeing a couple of Martians in our dreary council estate. It was two twenty-ish year old, blond-haired, blue-eyed, suntanned and absolutely stunning women. My first thought was they were lost. Apparently not.

"Is this the McIntyre residence?" asked one hopefully in an American accent and a full on American smile.

"Er, yeah," I stammered in reply. I must have looked pretty stupid as I stared at them. They were so incongruently out of place standing there that I was lost for words. Eventually I asked who they were looking for and they mentioned Helen, my mum, who she said was her cousin.

"My name is Bethany, and this is Cathy. We're from California and travelling around Europe this year. I'm related to Helen, and my mother is Dorothy." I had no real understanding of all the family connections, but I did know we had family in America whom I'd never met. It turned out Bethany's grandmother and my own grandmother were sisters. So, Bethany and I were second cousins! Cathy was not a relation, she was just Beth's friend. I welcomed them inside and by this time my mum had come through and cottoned on to who they were. And then we gave them a taste of traditional Scottish hospitality: we boiled the kettle and a brought out a bottle of whisky.

The girls stayed all evening and we managed to catch up with who was who, and what had happened to my grandmother's sister Dorothy, who had left Scotland some time in the 1920s. We had no idea of who was left among the many sisters and brothers from my mum's family who had all emigrated to America at that time. It turned out Beth and Cathy were staying in Scotland for a few weeks, trying to track down ancestors and living relations.

Straight away I was fascinated by Beth. She was several years older than me and so beautiful, confident and friendly in the way Americans tend to be. The day had suddenly become so much brighter with this interesting and intelligent woman appearing from nowhere, and here she was sitting in our council house front room like an exotic flower planted in a wasteland. I was smitten; I couldn't take my eyes off her. Even stranger, she seemed to be looking at me in the same way.

That night I walked Beth and Cathy back to their hotel in town to make sure they didn't get lost. We'd had quite a celebration back at my house and lots of drinks, so it was very late when we reached their hotel, and the front door was locked. Rather than bang the door and cause a fuss, I went round the back and found a ladder. The girls went up to their first floor room and climbed in through the window with much tipsy hilarity and shushing.

The next day Beth and Cathy checked out of the hotel and moved into my grandmother's spare bedroom. She was also family, of course, so they were welcome to stay there. Fortunately for me, my grandmother's house was just around the corner from our own house on the same estate. Beth and I became inseparable for the next few weeks of her stay. I showed her around town and took her to the local pubs. I made sure to avoid the gang members and steered her away from any possible contact with them. I didn't want her to know what kind of person I was, and to be honest, after meeting Beth, I thought maybe I could be something else? She was so inspirational to me, and I realised by being with her that there was another world out there. One that wasn't all booze, drugs, fights and the grey poverty of living in the Vale. She told me all about her life back in California. She was at university and had a part-time job with a travel agency that allowed her to get free, or very cheap, worldwide flights.

Right from the start she insisted I must visit California and stay with her. I could get a job and eventually even become a citizen. This was all relayed to me with the confidence of someone who was on a much higher social standing. She said I could do it, and so it would happen – why not? I even began to believe it myself.

One night I took her to a football match and she was surprised at the dereliction of the area around Celtic Park in Glasgow. I'd never really noticed it before she mentioned it, but now I was also looking at things through a different lens. She was right – the area had become a triumph of urban decay.

Over the next couple of weeks we had a lot of fun together, just hanging out. It just seemed right, as if we'd known each other for years. We were like best friends, but aside from hugs and occasional kisses, nothing remotely romantic was on my mind. And then one day, at the grand old age of 15 years it finally happened.

It was a Saturday morning. We had been out together at a pub the night before, and as usual I'd left her at my gran's house, saying good night and making my way home. Beth turned up at my house early next morning to call for me, and I was still in bed. My mum told her I was still asleep and Beth simply walked past her and said I'll go and wake him up. She entered my bedroom and started pulling the covers off, laughing and telling me to get up. Then before I knew it she was lying on top of me. I was a virgin, I had never had sex before, though I'd sometimes bragged to my friends that I had. I really had no idea what was going on. Beth was very experienced, her fingers were already expertly stroking and pulling gently at my penis as she grinned at me with her blond hair falling over my face and her confident knowing eyes smiling at me.

I was in a state of panic; for one thing, what she was doing to me seemed to be working and I was getting an erection, an experience I usually hated. But at the same time I wanted to please her and be what she wanted me to be. At the back of my mind was also the fear of my mum walking into the room. But carefree and confident, Beth didn't seem to worry about any of that. She started pulling off her jeans and pants and then she was on top of me, guiding my penis into her. She sat up with her back arched and began moving up and down rhythmically as if in a world of her own. I was both terrified of the door opening and amazed that, apparently, I was capable of having sex, and this seemed to be what having sex was. I tried to relax and leave what was happening to Beth. She was happy to take the lead and I just went with the flow. Before too much longer we both climaxed. Just at that moment my mum called up the stairs, something about bringing up a cup of tea. I was petrified; I couldn't let my mum catch us doing this! But Beth, who must have seen the look in my eyes, just put her finger to her lips and said, It's okay, and smiled. She carried on until she was fully satisfied, then gently stepped off and pulled on her jeans. She was laughing at her own pleasure and my panic. What a woman, she was absolutely fearless! Then she ran downstairs and sat drinking a cup of tea with my mum as if nothing had happened.

So, that was how I lost my virginity, and how I learned that, even though I detested having a penis, it did at least seem to be in working order.

Beth was an amazing woman. I was left madly in love with her. Not so much for the sex, but more for the outrageous big-hearted, strong and beautiful woman she was. She was a force of nature and I adored her. Even more than that, I wanted to be just like her.

* * * * *

Things between my dad and me also came to a head one night during Beth's visit. We had all been out at a local drinking club one evening: my parents, my sister Carolyn, Beth and me. We all walked back together to the council estate at the end of the evening, and as we arrived at my gran's house I walked Beth to the door while the others waited for me on the street. I told my parents to carry on, I would catch up later, I wanted to talk a bit longer with Beth at the door. But my dad insisted I should come right then. I ignored him, telling them all to go on. But my dad insisted that I leave Beth there, and he stayed there, waiting for me at the end of the path.

What happened next was a turning point in our relationship. My dad whistled at me and told me to come. Just like he would command a dog. He did it deliberately to try and put me down in front of Beth. By this time it was clear to everyone how much we loved each other's company, and he knew I was in awe of her. I suppose he thought that by belittling me in front of her, he'd show us both who was boss. Shamefaced, I reluctantly mumbled good night to Beth and left her, just as my dad began whistling again for me to come.

I was embarrassed and angry as we walked back to our house, and the further we walked, the madder I became. By the time we got home I was livid with him for treating me like that in front of Beth. All the built-up resentment of years past had come to surface, all the times he had hit my mum, my sister or me. How he used to terrorise the whole family so that we crept around him, terrified to say the wrong word that would set him off. All the dinners flung against the walls, the drunken rants, the times when he grabbed me by the throat and challenged me to fight.

"Don't ever do that to me again, humiliate me by whistling at me like a dog."

"What are you going to do about it?" he replied, laughing. It was a challenge too far. This time I flew at him. I'd been fighting in the gangs for years by now and I knew what I was capable of, but the fear of this man was still so strong that I attacked him more in panic than by design. I grabbed his hair, pulled him down and kicked him several times in the face. He fell over on his side and looked up at me in shock. His nose was bleeding and his brow was cut. His mouth was opening and closing with no sound coming out. He was completely bemused by my actions and hadn't seen it coming at all.

Mum and Carolyn soon chimed in, shouting at my dad that he deserved that. It was like a dam bursting, and all the pent-up emotions and resentments poured out as they screamed and shouted at him lying there. He looked frightened, and suddenly I felt sick. I'd never seen him like this before, he was beaten and knew it. I actually felt sorry for him. He was still my dad after all. I blurted out something like "And don't you ever raise your hand to my mother or sister ever again or you'll have me to deal with!"as if it was some BBC kitchen sink drama. Then I ran out the door and walked the streets for hours in fear and sorrow at what I'd done.

Things were never going to be the same between me and my dad after that night. He never forgave me for using violence against him, and I don't think I ever really forgave myself. But one good thing did come out of that night: he never raised his hand to any one of us ever again.

* * * * *

Eventually it was time for Beth and Cathy to go back home. The time we had spent together had been fantastic. Beth had opened my eyes to life's possibilities and had given me some hope for my future. We promised we would keep in touch by writing every week. These promises are often made but we meant it and both stuck to it. I would buy a blue airmail letter every week and send it off to California with my thoughts and dreams, and by return I'd receive her letter with its distinctive US Mail stamp. We kept this up for about two years, also with occasional long distance phone calls. She desperately wanted me to go to California and have a better life. The thought of one day going there to be with her kept me sane during the next couple of years. I promised myself I would go.

Chapter 4 'London Calling'

I left for London in the autumn of 1980. Aged sixteen, it was a new start for me and I travelled south on a coach with my favourite aunt Mamie who had come up to Scotland to collect me. The plan was for me to live with her and Uncle George in Barkingside, East London. There I would get a job, save up some money and then in a few months go to California to live with Beth and Cathy.

The previous year had been a crazy time. I had really struggled with my identity and had got into countless fights. On any given night I'd be out, full of booze, aggressively angry and picking a fight with anyone I came across who looked sideways at me. Then the next day I'd be walking quietly in the countryside, dressed in clothes I'd borrowed from my sister. My life was an absurd contradiction, yet I could see no way to resolve it. No one else knew about my female side, and the pressure to keep it hidden was driving me crazy. By uprooting my life and moving to London, I desperately hoped that my inner gender turmoil would be forgotten by the change of location and the new people I would be living with. Perhaps I just needed to grow up a bit and have new experiences, I told myself. Not for the first time I cursed my body, then I cursed my brain that seemed so diametrically opposed to it. I watched friends and strangers with envy. How wonderful it must be to know who you are and to be accepted by yourself, and by everyone else, as that gender. It seemed so effortless and natural for everyone else.

* * * * * * *

As the youngest, I'd always been Aunt Mamie's favourite of all the nieces and nephews in the family. She was my mother's older sister, and since she and George had sadly never had any children of their own, they were always very generous to me.

When we arrived at their house they showed me to my room. It was their front bedroom facing on to Barkingside High Street and was full of all the usual stuff that spare rooms contain: George's fishing rods, boxes of papers and files, and so on. I opened the wardrobe to hang my clothes and discovered rails of Mamie's spare clothes: dresses, skirts and coats, all lined up. In one set of drawers there was more of her clothing: underwear, bras, pants, underskirts, and tights. Most of the clothes were brand new still in the packaging or had labels attached. Mamie was clearly a hoarder.

As soon as I saw her clothes I knew it wouldn't be long before I started trying stuff on – I simply wouldn't be able to resist. I felt guilty but also optimistic and upbeat. My head was racing. Maybe this was a sign, my opportunity to finally come out to the family? Perhaps I would be able to speak with Mamie about the way I felt. We had always been so close so I was confident she would understand. George, on the other hand, would be more of a problem. He was a real old-school cockney East ender and a former British Army paratrooper. He had always been good to me, but there was no doubt he was a man's man. I decided I would wait a while, get settled in and play it by ear. One thing was certain, though: changing my location did not bring about any change in my inner feelings. I still desperately wanted to live and be accepted as female.

* * * * * * *

I found a job within a week of being in London. It was very easy in those days. I borrowed Aunt Mamie's bicycle, rode down to Ilford and started by looking around the cards at the unemployment office. There were lots of office jobs but I had no secretarial skills such as typing or shorthand. The only paid work I had ever done was painting with my Uncle Jake. There was a local building firm called C J Smith who were was looking for a 'young lad' at an address just two minutes along the street from the dole office, so I thought I'd give them a try. Perhaps they needed a painter and decorator? I could play the part of a young lad, after all that's what I looked like, and I really needed the money if I was going to save enough to get to for America.

The address was a building site on Connaught Lane, Ilford. I walked in and asked for the foreman. I was told that Paddy was somewhere within the half-finished office building, and I finally found him. Paddy was in his fifties, Irish with grey hair and a weather-beaten face. He was mixing cement with a shovel as I introduced myself and told him the unemployment office had sent me. He looked me up and down, clearly not convinced. I was tall and slender, but stronger than I looked.

"Can you handle a broom?"

"Yes I can, and I can paint too." Paddy looked wearily at me.

"We don't need painters," he said, but they did need a 'gofer', which was basically a general dogsbody who was sent out to go for this, go for that, make the tea and sweep up and tidy the Portakabin where the workers had their lunch breaks.

"Yeah, I can do that," I said, and that was it, I was hired. Paddy told me to report for work the following Monday at 8:00am sharp.

In the beginning, working for Smith's was hard work. It was an early morning start in the very cold winter. I'd ride the bike down to Ilford, sometimes through snow and rain, and I would arrive soaked. The first thing I did when I got on to the site was open up the Portakabin and put the giant water kettle on the gas ring to make the morning tea for everyone. After that it was usually outdoor work, assisting the tradesmen as a general labourer. I was expected to do hard graft, sometimes offloading lorries or mixing concrete by shovelling sand, cement and water into a mixer, then I would take it around the site in a wheelbarrow to wherever it was needed. I hated the work, but I was young and strong and needed the money for America, so I gritted my teeth and got on with it.

The atmosphere on the building site was very macho, with lots of crude joking and ribbing, especially towards me as the youngest. But some of the older guys there were also very helpful and took me under their wing. They taught me how to use a shovel economically so as not to tire myself out within an hour. When I got painful blisters on my hands, which made it excruciating to pick up the heavy tools, one old Irish labourer gave me the remedy. He told me to pee on my hands and let the blisters burst. Sure enough the skin on my hands soon toughened up and I was able to work without pain. I learned a lot from those Irish guys who dominated the London building trade in those days. Some would even sing beautiful songs or recite poetry as they worked. Others told me stories and tall tales about the villages they came from back in Ireland.

Each morning the workers would arrive from 7:30 am onwards, and one of my tasks was to have steaming mugs of tea ready for whoever turned up. Several of the men also brought packets of sausages, bacon, and eggs with them each day. They would leave these in food parcels inside the cabin, planning to cook it themselves for breakfast during the morning break at 10:30am. Within a few days I noticed that each man would cook his own food, one after the other, often arguing about whose turn it was to use the filthy grease-filled giant frying pan. It sometimes even ended up in a fight as some ran out of time to get their food cooked and were left hungry.

I offered a solution to Paddy, the foreman. I suggested that I went to the cabin early, at around 9:30am, to cook everyone's food and make all the tea ready for them as they came for their break at 10:30am. Paddy eyed me suspiciously, probably thinking (correctly, I'll admit) that I just wanted to get out of the cold, but he eventually agreed to let me give it a try.

That was the start of my new position within the building site. I became primarily the cook, tea maker and cleaner of the cabin. I made sure everyone got their food cooked, sandwiches made, and hot drinks provided as soon as they stepped inside. I cleaned up the disgusting cabin from top to bottom, throwing out the old work clothes that had been lying there for years. I scrubbed the stove, walls, tables, and floor until the cabin was spotless. I even bleached the big china mugs and teaspoons that probably hadn't ever had a proper clean since they were new.

It didn't take long for my efforts to be appreciated. Soon I was being greeted warmly and handed food parcels by everyone first thing in the morning, with instructions as to what they wanted. Two well-done bacon and egg rolls for Bill, a full English fry-up for Johnny, or maybe a sausage sandwich for Charlie. I even cleaned out the oven, so that the men could bring in sausage rolls and pies for lunch that I cooked, and served up with boiled spuds, baked beans or tinned peas. Meanwhile I was able to avoid the foul weather and back-breaking labour. It was an agreeable state of affairs for everyone, and within a couple of weeks I had established my job as indispensable. I also did all the dishwashing after everyone had eaten, so the foreman was happy too. He knew I could get the men fed and back to work without all the usual moaning and arguments about access to the gas rings and dirty pots.

Before long I was seldom asked to do any manual work outside the cabin. I had effectively become the building site charlady, and would spend my days keeping the cabin in order, feeding the men or just chatting with whoever popped in for a cuppa. It didn't escape my notice that I had adopted more of a traditional feminine role, and it was a position I was quite comfortable with.

Meanwhile, I'd settled in at Mamie and George's house. During the day we were all out at work, then at night when we all came home, we usually sat in the lounge and had a drinking session. Occasionally, Mamie and George would get drunk and start fighting. In many ways it was just like being back in the Vale.

I had very little time at home alone, so I had few opportunities to get dressed and go out as female. Whenever I was given a window of freedom, like when they went off fishing on a Sunday, I would get dressed in Mamie's clothes and slip out of the house for a short walk. But it wasn't enough for me. I felt like a prisoner, looking through the front window at life on Barkingside High Street passing me by. Girls waiting at the bus stop, mothers with pushchairs chatting and laughing together. I knew I had to either give this up completely, or else somehow transition. I just couldn't bring myself to do the former, and had no idea how to go about the latter. I was still desperately hoping that California and Beth would show me the way, as it seemed clear that living in London with my aunt and uncle was not the answer.

Occasionally, Mamie and George would visit the local pub, the Oak, and I would tag along. George knew the landlord and was given a warm welcome whenever we showed up. They knew he was a big spender and would buy 5-star Mataxa brandies for himself and drinks all round for those at the bar. We usually only had a few drinks and then it would be home again, picking up takeaway food on the way.

One night at the Oak, George introduced me to the landlord Mike, explaining that I was his nephew and would soon be on my way to California. That night Mike seemed to take a real interest in me. We chatted for a long time over the bar when George left us alone and did his usual round of the other customers, telling jokes and flirting with women, or shaking hands and joking with the men.

I sensed something about Mike as we chatted, but I couldn't quite put my finger on it. He seemed very engrossed in our conversation and very friendly. That in itself was quite strange for London, where people were notoriously stand-offish, even unfriendly. Mike was probably three times my age at the time and I was flattered to receive the attention of an older man. He told me I was welcome to come back any time for a drink on my own. He said he would look after me, make sure I didn't get into trouble and would get me home safely. Looking back, and bearing in mind I was only sixteen, I should have realised this was a little unusual, but I was naive and just thought he was a nice guy. When George rejoined us at the bar, Mike repeated the same story to him, offering to look after me if I fancied getting out for a night at the pub by myself. It was all very friendly and on the way home George was happy to believe his mate was only looking out for me. And for me, it would be good to know that I'd have a friendly place to go wherever I got a bit bored at the house. In hindsight it shows how naive I was, and how unworldly George was, too.

A week or so later I duly went over the Oak for a drink on my own. We had eaten dinner at home, and then George and Mamie said they wanted to watch something on TV. I told them I fancied getting out for a quick drink at the pub. There were no objections and soon I had showered, changed and walked the five minutes to the pub.

Mike and his staff greeted me enthusiastically as I approached the bar and ordered a drink. That night Mike spent a lot of time chatting with me in between serving customers. I was perched on a barstool and the drinks flowed, most of them freebies. It felt really nice to be away from the smothering atmosphere of the house and I enjoyed the banter with the barmaids and Mike. Before I knew it, the bell was being rung for last orders. I was having such a nice time so I ordered myself another drink and was pleasantly surprised when Mike added another freebie alongside it. I was still sat on my stool with a drink in front of me when he started ushering the other punters out of the bar at closing time, 11:30pm. I tried to get up to leave too, but Mike insisted I finished my drink. Before long the pub was cleared and the doors locked. I was the last customer and still had a drink on the bar but there was no pressure on me to leave. Yet another drink appeared before me, which I felt obliged to drink as the barmaids cashed up, washed the glasses and said their goodbyes. Mike and I were now alone in the empty bar with the main lights switched off and the doors bolted shut.

I decided it was time to excuse myself. The hospitality was lovely but I felt I'd better leave as Mike would be wanting to get to bed. I tried to get off the barstool and almost fell over. Mike immediately came over and held me up. Embarrassed, I started apologising, saying I was obviously a bit drunk. But Mike seemed really relaxed and told me not to worry. I should have a coffee upstairs in his flat above the pub, maybe a bite to eat, too. He said he didn't want to send me home pissed after he'd promised George that he would look after me.

The next thing I knew, I was being helped upstairs and ushered into a living room. I sat in the comfortable armchair that was offered to me and Mike soon returned with a coffee and a sandwich. There was also another man there who I'd never seen before. Mike introduced him as Paul, his friend who lived in the pub and worked in the cellar. I sipped my coffee and wolfed down the sandwich, still feeling uncomfortable that I was causing Mike inconvenience, but also pleased that such a nice guy seemed to take a genuine interest in me. It felt great that I had come to London and made friends with someone like Mike who seemed so sophisticated and different from everyone I'd ever met before.

After the coffee I was still feeling drunk but also incredibly tired. I was dropping off on the armchair when Mike suggested I needed to get an hour's sleep before going home, and then I would feel much better. This seemed like a good plan to me at the time – I definitely didn't want to go home this pissed.

Soon Mike was helping me into a bed in the next room. I must have fallen asleep right away, but I woke up not long after, and realised with surprise I was naked in this bed. Even more surprisingly, I realised I was not alone.

I jumped up from the bed and put my feet on the floor. I felt confused and tried to find my clothes and piece together what had happened and how I'd got there. Mike sat up next to me, and had his arm around my shoulder, telling me it was okay, I'd just had too much to drink and had taken a nap. I looked beyond Mike in the dim light and saw that Paul was also in the bed. It was only then that the penny dropped and my stupid brain began to comprehend the situation – they must be queer! How the hell hadn't I realised that, I asked myself.

I actually had very little comprehension of homosexuality back then, other than school yard stories. As kids we had joked about 'poofs', but I didn't really understand what poofs were. I'd never met one, and wasn't sure if they even existed. So, I still couldn't reconcile the fact that Mike was probably one of these 'poofs', but the evidence was apparently laid out before me and I was in complete shock.

Mike sensed my concern and began to soothe me by rubbing my back and telling me everything was okay. My first reaction was fear, and that soon turned into anger. I pushed him away. "What the fuck is going on, Mike?" I challenged. But if I'm honest, my anger was more contrived than real. I was more curious than anything else.

The truth was, after I thought about it, I hadn't been harmed in any way, and I still thought Mike was a nice guy. I didn't feel physically threatened, and I certainly didn't want to fight or fall out with him. I had a decision to make in my head. I could grab my clothes and storm out, as my working-class heterosexual upbringing almost demanded that I should, or else I could stay a while and explore this very strange and unusual situation. I forced myself to relax, then I asked Mike to get me another drink. He seemed relieved. "Sure, of course," he said, smiling.

I spent the next couple of hours talking quietly with Mike on the bed. Occasionally Paul intervened with a few funny comments that made me laugh, and I soon felt at ease. I was more than curious; I was fascinated by the situation I'd found myself in, and wanted to know all about their lives. What did homosexual people do? How did they live? Mike and Paul didn't disappoint. They were very frank and open and I was amazed at their funny stories and descriptions of the queer lifestyle. But I had to know why Mike had taken me to his bed.

"Did you think I was queer?" I asked. Apparently, he did.

"You were so obvious!" he chided with a grin. I was absolutely gobsmacked that my 'difference' was so noticeable to him. I thought I'd covered my tracks so well. I imagined I was portraying the tough working-class Glasgow yob persona so well! No one had ever challenged it before. This was before the term 'gaydar' had even been invented, but Mike certainly seemed to possess it. This was also at a time when the legal age of consent for homosexual sex was still twenty-one. It would only be lowered to eighteen in 1994, and then to sixteen in 2000. Mike was taking a big risk here – if he had misjudged me, he could easily have ended up in a heap of trouble if I'd run home screaming and called the police.

But of course, that didn't happen. Instead I took the decision to open up completely that night, for the first time in my life. I felt safe explaining my own situation in front of two gay men who I thought could empathise with what I was going through, or who might know of others like me. I desperately wanted knowledge and the benefit of their experience. Was I a poof? Did Mike or Paul also feel they were born in the wrong bodies? Should I just forget about wanting to be a woman? So many questions, and for the first time ever I felt I was speaking with people who would listen without judgement and provide objective advice. At the very least, I thought they wouldn't condemn me for asking. Finally, it just came out.

"I want to have a sex change. I want to live as a woman. Do you think I'm crazy"? Fuck, I'd said it. I'd finally said the words out loud to another living person. I felt liberated but vulnerable at the same time.

We talked for hours, and to this day I'm grateful to Mike and Paul. They tried their best to understand my situation and to provide answers. To their credit they didn't try to take advantage of me, as they so easily could have. Instead they were kind and thoughtful to my dilemma. But it became clear to me that I was unlike them in so many ways. They liked their bodies and celebrated their masculine attributes. They couldn't relate to my hatred of my own physical appearance. We were alien to each other in our sexual identity, but we all shared a wider alienation from so-called normal respectable society. I felt I was among friends with whom I could be honest. It was fantastic.

The other revelation I experienced that night was the fact I was homophobic. Bizarre, right? It doesn't give me any pleasure to say that. But I have to admit it was true. I had been brought up in a climate of homophobia. That wasn't even a word I would have known back then, but it describes perfectly how I felt in my ignorance of gay people's lives. My family, my school, the church and everyone I had grown up with abhorred and ridiculed the very idea of homosexuality. In my world up until then, homophobia was universally accepted and ingrained in my own thinking. Looking back now, it would take me years to overcome that in myself, and in fact it was a major contributing factor in postponing my own transition. If that's what I thought about Mike and Paul, imagine how much I loathed myself!

To my shame, I only visited the Oak once more after that night. I felt very self-conscious, and worried about what others would think if I spent time chatting with Mike. The truth is, I was scared of being identified with him as queer, so I stayed away. I still had a lot to learn about myself. But one thing was clear: I was still homophobic.

I eventually returned home to Mamie's house at around five in the morning. I let myself in quietly with my key and went to bed. The next morning I quickly got my explanation of my late return in before I could be challenged. I told George that Mike had invited me to carry on drinking at the pub after hours, and that he had only allowed me to stay because I was George's nephew. He seemed satisfied with that, and pleased that his influence had allowed me the privilege of experiencing the legendary pub 'lock-in'.

That winter I carried on working diligently at CJ Smith. By now I found the job easy and I really enjoyed looking after the workmen. They were only too happy for me to do all the chores they couldn't be bothered with. I cooked the food, made the tea, dried their work clothes on the heaters when it was wet, and generally kept the place clean. Only occasionally was I asked to do any physical work outside the Portakabin.

One day, I was told the pavement outside the site needed to be dug up for cable laying. It was a short shallow trench, about 15 feet long and 3 feet wide.

Someone must have been off sick that day because Paddy told me to go and help Steve with it. Steve presented me with a large and heavy pneumatic drill. "Keep the blade inside the chalk line drawn on the tarmac, and squeeze the trigger gently." Okay, I thought, this is going to be a disaster. But once I understood how to work the drill, I really enjoyed myself. It was a crisp sunny winter morning and the power of the machine cutting easily through concrete was really satisfying. Steve and I started at opposite ends and cut along the lines, then we would fill a wheelbarrow with the smashed up rubble using a shovel after digging down about three feet. Quite a few people walking along on our side of the road would stop to watch us, especially children. I quite enjoyed the attention. Look at me! I thought to myself. Everyone is fooled, I'm like a proper construction worker digging up the street, and they think I know what I'm doing. It was great fun.

A funny thing happened that afternoon when we had almost completed the job. I was having a rest, sitting on the side of the trench with my feet dangling inside, when a young well-dressed woman with a clipboard approached me.

"Do you drink lager?" was her opening question. I replied that yes I did, sometimes. I was confused as to why a complete stranger had approached me in the street with that opening line.

"Would you be willing to answer a few questions for a survey I'm conducting about alcohol branding?"

"Yes, sure," I replied, feeling a bit self conscious. But I thought I'll play along with it. It might be a laugh and she seemed nice.

It turned out she was a genuine market researcher. She was looking for people who fitted various demographic profiles to complete her survey. I was, according to her, a typical "young working-class male". If only she knew!

However, I was happy to help so I allowed her to ask the questions, and she wrote down my answers. After ten minutes or so she seemed satisfied. She counted up her scores and then smiled. "Your profile is suitable and fits what we need for the actual taste testing. Would you be willing to come along to this address tonight to sample some alcoholic drinks? Don't worry about transport – we'll pay for a taxi to and from the location, and we will also pay you £50 for your participation." I laughed, thinking this must be a wind-up, but she was serious! She handed me a voucher with the address for the taste testing and a contract to sign. I signed it in a flash, giving a false date of birth.

Meanwhile, Steve had been eagerly watching all of this, waiting for his turn to take the test. But she just thanked me and turned to leave. "What about me?" Steve shouted to her. "Don't I fit the profile"?

"Sorry," she replied. "We have enough people now," and she walked off.

I had such a laugh back at the site later on when we told the rest of the guys what had happened. Steve was livid. "Why you? You lucky bastard, the one time you actually go out and do some real work and this happens! I don't fucking believe it!" he kept saying. But it was all good-humoured, and the rest of the guys were laughing at him and taking the piss.

I did go to the tasting that evening. I ended up sampling dozens of beers and lagers, giving them scores from one to ten. There were around twenty other people there, and by the end of the night we were all having a great time. There was one girl I teamed up with early on. She was called Rose, she was Irish, and like me had travelled to London on her own. She was a few years older than me and worked as a nurse at Goodmayes Hospital. Neither of us could believe we were getting paid for a piss-up and we had a great giggle about the situation all night. At the end of the evening we arranged to meet up for a drink at the weekend.

I met Rose again on the following Saturday in Ilford. We went for drinks and chatted and got on just as well as before. But it soon became obvious that she was looking for a more physical relationship than I was. It was my usual problem – I wanted a girl as a friend, not a girlfriend. Rose, however, was looking for some fun with a boy, and while that's exactly what I looked like. But on the inside, I felt anything but.

We ended up that night back at Rose's flat in the nurses' quarters of Goodmayes Hospital. I sat on her single bed in the tiny room sipping wine while she got undressed and put some music on her cassette deck. She started to kiss me and I could see clearly where this was heading. I was going to be a big disappointment for her. I did snog her back for a while, then I sighed and said I had to get back because I was very tired, I'd drunk too much and needed to get to bed. I pretended I had the chance of overtime in the morning at the building site and I needed the money because I was saving up to go to

America. A half-truth sounds better than a downright lie, I thought. She seemed a bit miffed but accepted my story.

I crept out of the hospital around midnight and caught the last bus to Barkingside, feeling dreadful that Rose must have felt snubbed. I was also annoyed with myself for getting into yet another awkward situation like this. As usual, I allowed my dreams to take over as I bumped along in the night bus back to Mamie's house. One day, I told myself, after I have transitioned, this shit won't ever happen again. Rose and I will be pals and it will all be so much easier. I just need to transition and get on with living as me. Everyone will accept it, and it will be such a relief. I almost believed it myself.

Rose was just one failed relationship, but there were several more during the winter of 1980-81. One night I was drinking alone in a pub on Barkingside High Street. I got talking to a young good-looking and sharply-dressed guy around my own age. He was called Alex and he was from a Greek-Cypriot family who owned a nearby restaurant. We hit it off, talking about music and films, and seemed to share the same sense of humour. The one thing I noticed about him was that he didn't make derogatory comments about girls. That was highly unusual in those days, and I liked that about him. We arranged to meet up for a drink a few times and had a laugh together.

He called round for me one evening at Mamie's house, and since I wasn't quite ready because I'd got back late from work, he came in and sit in the lounge with Mamie and George while I got dressed. I quickly got showered and changed, and soon I was ready to go.

The next morning Uncle George quizzed me about Alex. Who was he? How did we meet? And then he said something that really surprised me. "Watch out for the Greeks, they go both ways. They'll do men or women, they don't mind either way." He tapped his nose conspiratorially to emphasise the point. "Watch your back, son".

I was totally shocked. I'd never heard any reference to any kind of sexuality from George other than the usual banter about getting a girl, and giving her one. To my shame, I immediately felt worried and exposed. Had George got an inkling about my own sexuality? I felt scared. I had to stop meeting Alex in case his perceived sexuality reflected back on me. I was such a coward – I ditched Alex and never saw him again.

My double life continued to drive me mad and, as usual, I used alcohol to soften the edges. Unfortunately, when drunk, I occasionally went overboard in my attempts to seem manly to others, so they wouldn't suspect the real hidden me. One night, I went to a local kebab shop straight from the pub at closing time. In the time-honoured British tradition, I was very drunk and just wanted some quick food before bed. I waited in line for ten minutes or so after giving my order to the guy at the counter. All the time I was hanging around, other people were coming in, regulars who just ordered their food, got it immediately and left. Eventually I challenged the guy at the counter.

"Why are you serving everyone else and not me?" The guy just laughed at me.

"Fuck off, you Scotch cunt." I walked out, went back to Mamie's house and straight into the kitchen. I grabbed the biggest sharpest knife I could find from the drawer and then stormed back to the kebab shop. I kicked the door open, ran straight to the counter where the guy who had insulted me stood behind the barrier. I grabbed him by the hair and dragged his face down to the top of the worktop and pushed my knife against his cheek.

"Who are you calling a cunt?" I screamed, repeating it over and over. The poor man was terrified. He babbled incoherently and snivelled, looking so scared. That's when I came to my senses and thought what the hell am I doing? This is crazy! I suddenly felt ashamed and truly sorry. I wanted to apologise to the guy for what I'd done. Instead I ran out of the shop and back home. I put the knife back in the kitchen drawer, went to bed and cried myself to sleep. These weren't the actions of a woman, nor even a normal man. This was just ridiculous unbalanced behaviour. I felt mortified and deeply concerned about losing control so easily. There were several other similar episodes during that winter. How I avoided arrest or serious injury was a miracle. But eventually it did catch up with me.

I had worked right through the winter at CJ Smith, earning good money and on the whole enjoying it. By now I had also saved enough money for my trip to California, and had already been to the US Embassy in Grosvenor Square to get my ten-year visa. I had Beth's address in Los Gatos as my destination, and a letter from her family guaranteeing they would support me financially during my stay in the United States. I booked my plane ticket to San Francisco and prepared to leave the UK, possibly forever. The time to start a new life was here at last. What could possibly go wrong?

It was February 1981. I had handed in my notice at CJ Smith and worked out the final two-week period. My boss Paddy wasn't surprised when I told him I'd booked my flight, since everyone at the firm knew I was going to California. I'd talked about it enough. I'd taken this job as a stop-gap, just to endure it and earn some money. But now that I was leaving, I realised that I'd had a lot of good times here. The men had always been pretty good to me, making sure that I'd rarely had to go outside and do the hard graft. I'd looked after them in return, doing the domestic work that made life on the site easier, and often by just offering a friendly ear to listen when they were upset or annoyed with life. I would miss them.

To my genuine surprise a few of the younger lads arranged a farewell drink for me at a local nightclub. It was to be on the night before I flew to San Francisco and several of the guys were going to be there. Charlie had organised it. He was an apprentice carpenter on the site, a big lad and only a few years older than me with blond wavy hair and a real cockney accent. We had hit it off in the first week I'd started at CJ's when he asked me to cook his sausages and eggs for lunch one day.

"Yeah, come on, give them here." But Charlie then teased me by pretending he was going to throw the eggs at me. He was surprised when I just picked up the six eggs from the box one by one and threw them at him one after another. Each egg smashed off his head, chest and back, as I stood there stone-faced.

"You're fucking mad!" he shouted as he ran off. But, he never messed me about after that and we later became friends. He would tell everyone else not to fuck about with me because I was crazy.

I don't remember the name of the club we went to on my final night, but it started off okay. I had a lot to drink because everyone was buying me bacardi and cokes to wish me farewell and good luck. There was a dance floor and I ended up dancing. I remember becoming very emotional at some point.

To my friends I was just leaving to go on a long holiday, but to me it was the end of an era, and hopefully the start of my transition to living as female. Obviously, I'd been secretive about that part so I knew it was very unlikely I'd ever see them again, despite the promises we made to meet up in the future for a drink when I came back. The internal turmoil of my life was never far below the surface, but usually I could contain it, at least when I was sober. But on this night it all bubbled up to the surface. I wanted so much to tell these guys who I'd shared my working life with for the past six months who I really was. To come clean and be honest. I knew they liked me, so surely I could trust them on this last night to accept me if I told them the truth?

But of course, I didn't do that. Fear and self-preservation took over. To numb the frustration I felt, I simply kept drinking. I ended up very drunk and hardly able to walk. At some point I fell over and the bouncers picked me up and tried to take me to the door and eject me. My workmates were gathered round trying to help me and stop me being ejected, and the situation was getting quite confrontational. Unfortunately, at this point my aggressive side surfaced and I must have decided to fight back against the door staff. But I was too drunk to do much. I was punched and kicked, then forcibly dragged out. I remember Charlie coming to my aid, threatening the door staff, but also looking very concerned. He took me aside and tried to calm me down, telling me I was off to America in the morning and not to be so stupid. But I continued to fight back, trying to attack the bouncers who had hit me.

Eventually the police were called and I was detained outside the club. But for some reason luck was on my side. Instead of being arrested, spending the night in the cells, appearing at the court in the morning and missing my flight, I somehow found myself being taken back to Mamie and George's house by the police. Maybe it was because I was underage for drinking and the club didn't want to press charges, or because my friends had intervened, or because just the cops were kind enough to look after me. I don't know to this day. But somehow I ended up back home and in bed.

The next morning Mamie got me up and helped me to dress. My face was bloodied and bruised, my fists were cut and bleeding and I had a terrible hangover. We barely mentioned what had happened the previous night, other than to agree it was probably a good time for me to leave. George put my suitcase in the car, made sure I had all my documents, passport and money, and drove me to Heathrow Airport where I caught the plane. I collapsed in my seat, half-asleep and still half-drunk. As the plane took to the air I began singing quietly in my head the Led Zeppelin song Going to California, very thankful that I'd made the flight, albeit leaving yet another fuck-up behind me.

Chapter 5 'California Dreaming'

I arrived at San Francisco airport several hours late. The flight had been diverted to Winnipeg in Canada due to a medical emergency on board when a diabetic passenger had slipped into a coma. I was shattered and still hung over by the time I went through US Immigration, but I was also buzzing and excited to be starting a new adventure.

As I breezed through the Nothing to Declare gate I was stopped by a burly customs officer. "Excuse me, Sir. Can you follow me, please?" he ordered. I was led into a small room where several other uniformed officers were sitting. That was my welcome to America. Perhaps it wasn't that surprising, given my bruised face and red damaged knuckles. "Please give me your passport, then put your suitcase on the table and open it." I complied and stood there, feeling slightly worried. What have I done now,? I thought to myself. Have the London cops messaged through to stop me and send me back for a court hearing? Am I just being paranoid?

The customs officer unpacked my case carefully. He found a bottle of whisky, then another, then two bottles of dark rum, then more bottles of whisky. Each time he removed a bottle he glanced towards me with his eyebrow rising higher and higher. Eventually, when he had unpacked the whole case, eight bottles of spirits stood next to a pile of clothing.

"Can you tell me, Sir, what reason do you have for all this alcohol in your luggage?" he asked. I shrugged. It seemed like a really silly question to me, with an obvious answer.

"To drink?" I replied. Wrong answer. He tapped my passport.

"Your passport records your age as sixteen, and you are not legally allowed to drink in the State of California below the age of twenty-one".

The penny dropped, I was still a few weeks from my seventeenth birthday. Apparently underage drinking was taken much more seriously in California. "It's not for me. I'm Scottish and I brought it for my family here. I heard it's not easy to buy genuine Scottish whisky in California, so I brought a gift for them". He nodded and wrote something in his notes.

Next, I was quizzed as to why I was travelling on my own and not in school? That one really threw me. I had officially left school seven months earlier, just as everyone else in my school had when they reached the age of sixteen. In those days very few people in Scotland stayed on in education past that age.

I explained all this but the customs officer wasn't convinced. I could see he looked very suspicious as I stood before him. This wasn't going to plan. I hadn't even got through the airport and already I was in some kind of trouble! Then I remembered I had some letters in my pocket detailing the address where I was staying, and who my American family were, including phone numbers he could call if he wanted to check. The officer took these letters away and I was left to sit on a bench. Eventually he returned and now he was smiling and seemed in good humour. Clearly my story had checked out and the officer was now courteous and friendly. He had called, discovered my relatives did exist, and that they were also upright, respectable members of the community. That probably surprised him, after looking at the mess I was in.

"Please come this way and I'll escort you to your family. They have been waiting for you and were very worried about the flight delay". His whole tone had softened and he helped me repack my case. I was accompanied through to the arrivals area where I saw Beth standing waiting for me with a huge beaming smile. I turned to thank the officer, and he uttered the ubiquitous words I was to hear repeatedly over the next few weeks. "You're welcome. Have a nice day."

* * * * * * *

At last, I was here! America – land of the free. I ran over to Beth as she rushed towards me, and we hugged.

"How was the flight?"

"Bloody awful. Let's go get a drink. Is there a bar here?" Beth looked shocked.

"No, not here. You're too young, we can get a drink at home."

And so I began to get the first inkling, that far from being the free and easy California of my imagination, this was actually quite a restrictive society, especially compared to what I was used to in Scotland and London.

Over the next few days Beth instructed me on what I could and couldn't do while I was living at her home in Los Gatos. She would be out most of the day as she was still at university, as was her friend Cathy who also shared the house. It was a long list of dos and don't s.

Located in the San Francisco Bay area, Los Gatos was just a few miles from San Jose and right in the heart of what would later became Silicon Valley. Cupertino, today's home of Apple, Inc., was just a few miles away. Beth and Cathy lived in one of those wooden panelled walled houses that are so typical of California. They had neighbours upstairs they referred to simply as 'the guys' and whom I would soon meet. Beth warned me never to venture out and walk alone on the street as there were too many 'crazies' around. Everyone drove everywhere, and since I didn't yet drive, I was forced to wait until either Beth or Cathy came home before I could go anywhere. I already felt restricted.

There were only two bedrooms in the house and I was to share Beth's bed. Cathy often stayed over at her boyfriend's place, so I would be able to use her bedroom whenever she was away. I loved Cathy's room. She had a water bed, the first one I'd ever seen, with a large aquarium at the foot of it with beautiful tropical fish slowly swimming around as if in time with the gentle movement of the bed. I spent a lot of time on that bed chilling, and trying to acclimatise myself to my new surroundings.

The morning routine was always the same. Beth and Cathy would get up, shower and dress, have coffee then leave for school. I would do the same, except I would stay in the house, kissing them both goodbye as they left. At first the novelty of the situation amused me. I would watch American daytime TV all day, cook myself some eggs, and feed the cat. Sometimes I'd sit on the porch outside, sunbathe and have a few drinks, but I soon grew tired of drinking on my own during the day.

Sometimes the phone would ring and if I answered I'd often be met with silence as the girls' friends were shocked to hear my strong Glasgow accent. People would often hang up as soon as I started speaking, convinced either that they had dialled a wrong number or that they were talking to some foreigner who couldn't speak English.

On paper my situation looked idyllic. I was living in sunny California with two beautiful women, rent-free in a very nice part of town. I didn't need any money as everything was provided for me, from food to drinks. All I had to do was sit around in the sunshine and chill, listening to music on Beth's stereo. She loved a lot of the same British bands I did: the Kinks, the Stones, Led Zeppelin records were all in her collection. The daytime TV was a particular revelation to me in those days, since it didn't really exist at all in the UK. But still, inevitably, after a few days, I began to get bored.

It was great at night when the girls came home. We would often go out for food, and I discovered 'Jack In the Box' drive-through, where you actually ordered burgers from a puppet that popped up from a box. One night Cathy took me to a charming Italian restaurant where I ate the best pasta I'd ever tasted. Another evening we all went to a Mexican restaurant called Don Quixote's. I'd begun to get my bearings by this time, and I realised the Mexican place was only a few minutes from our house. It was in the 'village' area of Los Gatos, which was a small parade of shops with a grocery store and a bar. I took a mental note of the direction we travelled and the following day, after the girls had left, I decided to walk back down there to explore.

It was true, the streets really were empty. No one walked around in that area, but it seemed safe enough to me, especially after the rough streets of Scotland and East London that I was used to. As I wandered down to the shops I was aware of people driving past in cars staring at me, but I didn't care. What was there to worry about?

I went into a grocery store and bought some bacon rashers, cigarettes and milk. Everyone I encountered seemed very friendly, though they struggled to understand my accent. This led to some funny mime games as I tried to make them understand what I was saying. I also had a good look at the local bar from outside, before I headed back to the house. It looked like somewhere new for me to experience. I wanted to go in there for some fun. Maybe, definitely, some other time, I promised to myself.

Being on my own during the daytime, and my mobility restricted without a car, I soon began to think that California was actually pretty tame and not the wild land of my dreams after all. I was also having second thoughts about this being the place where I could transition. Beth and I were getting along well, but she must have sensed my restlessness at the monotony of my daily routine. She promised that we would go out at the weekends and do stuff, and maybe make a road trip to Los Angeles. That sounded more like it!

One Sunday we took in the sights of San Francisco, which was about fifty miles north-west of Los Gatos. I loved it there. We went to the famous Pier 39, drove up the crooked Lombard Street made famous by countless movies, had a ride in the cable car and all the usual tourist stuff. I suggested we go and get a drink at the gorgeous Hyatt Regency Hotel and Beth agreed. Once we'd found a table and sat down, a very gay waiter approached us and asked what we would like to order. I asked for a bacardi and coke and Beth ordered wine.

"Do you have any ID, Sir?" the waiter asked, smiling. I was slightly annoyed. I'd not been asked for proof of age since I was thirteen years old back in Scotland. Beth produced her own ID and explained to the waiter I was from out of town and didn't have ID with me. He shook his head and smiled politely. "Sorry, I can't serve you without proof you are over twenty-one." I was pissed off – yet another restriction? Beth could see how frustrated I was in such a controlled environment that I wasn't used to. I shrugged and ordered a coke and we sat quietly, sipping our drinks.

"Don't worry, I can get you a fake ID," she offered. "I'll make a student travel card for you tomorrow at the travel agency where I work." That seemed like a great idea. So, with me feeling a bit more hopeful about life in California, we drove back to Los Gatos.

Beth was as good as her word. The following evening when she came home from school she had a plastic printed University of California student ID card with my name on it and a birth date that stated I was twenty-one, four years older than I actually was. I was delighted, and now at last I had some freedom.

Life in Los Gatos got a bit easier for me after that but I still felt as though I was on a holiday rather than living there. I needed to get a job or go into some kind of education, but without a green card this was going to be difficult. One evening we went to Beth's parents' house for dinner and I met her mother Doris - my mother's cousin - and her husband Lenny. They were lovely people, but very out of touch with the UK in their ideas. It was a very strange evening. Lenny asked me about the 'war' in Ireland. How was it going between the British and Irish armies? Would I be conscripted? He seemed to think there was some kind of trench warfare going on at the border with both countries sending over air strikes and firing shells, World War 2 style. I struggled to persuade him that this was not the case, and it wasn't the only time I discovered the level of ignorance most Americans had of anything outside their own borders, at least at that time.

Anyway, that evening Lenny offered me a job in his factory. It transpired he owned a condom factory, of all things, and it might be a way to get me a green card. Beth's brother Charles was also there and he told me he might be able to get me a job at his workplace doing computer filing, if I was interested. I thanked them both and said I'd think it over. But inside I was beginning to realise that if I remained in California with my generous and lovely American relatives, I'd end up just as trapped as I'd been in Glasgow and London. I'm certain that if I'd announced that night to the family that what I really wanted to do was have a sex change, the room would have echoed with the sound of smashed wine glasses dropping on the marble floor as they stood open-mouthed in shock. I was tempted to do it.

A couple of days later I was on my own at home. As usual, the girls had gone to school or work. It was late morning and I heard a knock at the door. I got up from watching daytime TV, went to answer it and was met by the most beautiful man I'd ever seen. He was tanned and muscled, just enough to look natural and healthy, with the typical Californian beach bum's blue eyes and blond hair.

"Hi, I'm Burn," he said with a generous smile. "Don't worry, I live upstairs. Beth asked me to drop by and see how you are. Do you want to hang out with me today?" It took me a moment to gain my composure after the surprise of seeing this adonis.

"Er, yeah, sure," I mumbled. This guy looked like a movie star who had just walked off the set of the TV show I'd been watching. I invited Burn inside and we sat down at the kitchen table.

"Do you want a coffee?" I offered.

"I'll just have an orange juice," he replied, and then went to the refrigerator and helped himself. We chatted for a while. He was an actor and a surfer, just as I thought. Burn was such a friendly and easy-going guy that I felt comfortable with him right away. After a few minutes he pulled out a small metal case from his pocket. "You want a line?" I had no idea what he meant. I assumed there were cigarettes in the case.

"Yeah, sure." Next he opened the case and inside was a small mirror. He placed the case on the table and took a small package from his pocket and began pouring white powder on to the mirror surface. He then took out a folded dollar bill and used it to divide the powder into four lines. Meanwhile, very matter-of-factly, he chatted about jobs he was hoping to get on a cable TV channel, and his boyfriend.

Cocaine. Fuck! Now I felt like I was in my very own Hollywood movie! I'd never tried coke before or even seen it outside of the TV screen. I tried to act cool and relaxed. Finally, a taste of the glamorous California that I'd expected when I dreamed of coming here to live.

Needless to say, Burn was gay. Just like Beth and Cathy were always saying, if a guy is that good-looking, you can pretty much guarantee he's gay.

Burn rolled up the dollar bill into a straw and offered me the first line.

"No please, you first," I said. I'd never tried cocaine before and so had no idea how this was done. Burn seemed charmed and amused by my manners and bent his head down to snort a line. I watched him closely, and when he passed the dollar bill to me I repeated the procedure. Soon both of us were gasping and smiling huge grins at each other. Hey, this stuff was amazing! After the initial buzz of white noise in my head, I felt fantastic. All my fears and worries over recent weeks disappeared in an instant. The curtains of doubt were pulled back and now I could see clearly again. Wow, finally I had a friend, someone I could talk to. We sat and chatted for the next hour or so. I couldn't shut up. I babbled away like someone who's been trapped alone on a desert island for years and finally meets another human being. We had another line each, then Burn put out some more powder and we had that, too.

Eventually, all too soon for me, Burn got up from the table and said he had to go and pick up his car. He told me I could drop by his place later on that night if I wanted. Then he left.

I spent the rest of the day on a high. I went to the shops again and bought myself some cigarettes and beers, which was no problem now I had my ID. By the time Beth came home I'd had a few drinks and felt great. "Let's go out." I said to her, but she said she had a lot of studying to do that night. She seemed to be looking at me strangely, her eyes narrowing.

"Did Burn come visit you today?" she asked. I said he had, and what a lovely man he was. I began to tell her all about our chat, not mentioning the cocaine. Beth just nodded. I'm sure she knew exactly what had happened but she said nothing. Instead she just took her books into the bedroom and sat at her desk to study.

Later that night I was still wide awake from the coke when Beth climbed into bed. I was restless so I decided to go visit Burn and watch some TV. His front door was next to ours and I knocked a few times but got no answer. I could hear the sound of the TV so I knew someone was there. Eventually I pushed the door open and entered. The lights were off but the TV was on. And as my eyes adjusted I could make out various bodies, girls, boys and some whose gender I couldn't make out, lying all over the floor and on the sofa. Everyone was more or less unconscious and oblivious to me. I also saw in the flickering light of the TV several syringes lying on the coffee table. Burn and his friends were clearly into more than just cocaine. I crept out again and closed the door.

I couldn't sleep at all that night. I was wide awake and buzzing the whole time until it was time for Beth to get up and go to school. I felt miserable and exhausted. If this is how the comedown felt, I decided that cocaine wasn't really worth it and that I should stick to alcohol. It was probably one of my few good decisions.

I did hang out with Burn a few more times, but he was very unpredictable. I would knock for him at a time we'd arranged, but there would be no response. Or he would appear at my door unexpectedly, all set for a day trip out to the beach at Santa Cruz, but he'd not told me anything about it beforehand, so I wasn't ready and he'd get annoyed. He was a lovely guy, but those drugs definitely messed with his brain.

One morning, over breakfast, Beth told me she wouldn't be coming home that night at her usual time. Apparently she was going to see a band with Cathy straight after school. Her ex-boyfriend was in the band and she had arranged this night out weeks ago, long before I'd arrived. It was an all-ticket gig and sold-out, so I wouldn't be able to join them. I felt a bit left out but if there were no tickets, then so be it. Beth said that she and Cathy would be home around midnight.

So, now I had the evening to myself. I hadn't seen anything of Burn for a while so I guessed he must be away. This was an opportunity for me to go out to the local bar, which I'd wanted to do for ages. Beth had warned me, of course, not to go out walking on my own, but I'd already done that several times during the day and had no problems. And so, armed with my new ID card, I felt confident enough to go to the village and have a few drinks.

* * * * * * *

At around 7:00pm I walked along the grid street plan of Los Gatos from our house to the village that night, not encountering another person. I arrived at the bar I'd seen on previous visits to the shopping parade and entered, feeling a tad self-conscious. It was a large and dimly lit room with the actual bar area lit up and TV screens showing sport of some kind, I think baseball. It seemed to take an eternity to walk from the door to the stool and I felt as though all eyes were on me. Remember that scene from An American Werewolf in London when the American tourists went into the Yorkshire pub for the first time? It was just like that, only the other way round. I hadn't felt this awkward and self-conscious in a pub for years. I spotted an empty bar stool next to the counter and sat down, trying to look nonchalant. The guy behind the bar came over to me and I was prepared for him to say "Get out of here, kid," but he didn't.

"What can I get you, Sir?"

It was just like any bar in London or Glasgow. I asked for a beer, pointing to a draught pump, and soon I had a glass of some kind of beer placed in front of me. Before I could offer my money, as you would do in a British pub, with each drink paid for as it was served, the barman had placed a beer mat and a paper receipt next to the glass and moved on to serve someone else. Okay, I thought, I'm apparently running a tab, just like in the movies!

After realising I wasn't going to be refused service or even asked to produce my ID, I began to relax. I sipped my beer and had a proper look around at my surroundings. In the dim light away from the bar where I sat were tables and booths. A few people were dotted around, but the place was actually very quiet with no more than six or eight people in there. I lit a cigarette and pretended to watch the TV. I was just happy to be out in a warm social atmosphere rather than cooped up in Beth's house. I ordered another beer, and this time the barman caught my accent.

"Where ya from, buddy?" he asked, smiling.

"Glasgow," I replied. "I just moved here. I'm living with my cousin a few streets away. It's first time I've been out for a beer since I got here." He smiled.

"Welcome to Los Gatos! You're gonna love it here." And so we started chatting. Soon we were talking about Scotland and the so-called 'war' in Ireland came up again. Then another guy came over with his wife to say hi. He had overheard my accent and the mention of Scotland, so he offered to buy me a drink. He told me his family were part-Scottish somewhere in his distant ancestry. It seemed a good enough reason to me, so we ordered more drinks and I settled in for a good evening.

Everyone I met that first night was so open and friendly in the way that only Americans are. It's true, as I've discovered on my travels over the years. From London to Moscow, California to Bangkok: for a man, bars are much the same all over the world. A safe place to chill, get to know the area, see how the land lies, and have a drink. Later on I'd discover it's very different for women. When you enter a bar as a single female, people often make assumptions about why you're there. Sometimes it's just not worth the hassle of going out on your own because of the unwanted attention. It's one of the few things I miss since I transitioned.

As the evening progressed, many different people came in and out of the bar and I was really enjoying myself. I finally felt I'd made some friends. One younger guy in particular, Brian, was really funny and we got on well. He was dressed like a hippy with long hair and faded jeans. He told me he was a big fan of the Beatles so we started a long conversation about the relative merits of British and American bands. Brian also said he was a keyboard player and he knew how to play all the John Lennon songs, as he'd studied piano at high school and loved his music.

This is where I made a mistake. It turned out that casual acquaintances met in a bar should be left in the bar. It was getting late and I thought I'd better get home before Beth and Cathy arrived back, otherwise they would be wondering where the hell I was, since I wasn't supposed to be out and about on my own.

I decided to invite Brian back to Beth's house. She had a piano in the living room and Brian could show me his playing. I didn't think it would be a problem; after all, it was supposed to be my house, too. 'Make yourself at home,' Beth had told me many times. I told Brian I had some proper Scotch whisky at home and a piano. We could go back for a drink, and some music. It seemed like a great idea at the time and Brian readily agreed.

Brian had parked his car outside the bar. This was in the days before drink-driving was seen as a big deal, and we both got in. I directed him back to the house and we arrived a few minutes later. Pretty soon we were inside with Brian's car parked in the driveway. Out came the bottle of Scotch and I poured a long one for each of us. Brian sat down at the piano with a smile and started playing. He was a natural, a very talented musician. He started off with John Lennon songs but soon I was making requests, everything from the Carpenters to the Doors was bashed out by Brian and we sang along, draining the Scotch bottle, having a great old party. It was the most fun I'd had since I arrived. Brian played while I danced around, grabbing hats to wear and doing Mick Jagger impersonations with silk scarves or whatever came to hand. After a while, and with all the booze, I started to feel a bit peckish.

"Do you want a burger, Brian?" I asked.

"Sure, I'd love something," he replied. So I found some ground beef in the fridge and started chopping onions to make beef patties as Brian happily played on. So, there I was, dancing around, flipping burgers on the griddle, wearing Beth's hat and scarf, and singing along at the top of my voice as Brian stood at the piano and started doing Jerry Lee Lewis numbers with wild abandon. We were having a great time.

This, then, was the scene that Beth and Cathy walked into at around midnight as they returned from their night out. Brian with a bottle of her Scotch and a full glass perched on top of her piano, cigarette hanging from his lip and banging out Great Balls of Fire as I fried burgers, prancing around with glass in hand, both singing along at the top of our voices. Beth wasn't happy.

As the door opened, I turned to see Beth coming through. I smiled at her, but before I could say anything I saw she was mad as hell. "What the fuck is going on?" she screamed at me. "Who the fuck is this?" pointing to Brian. I started to explain but she wasn't listening. "Get out of my fucking house!" she shrieked at Brian. "I'm calling the police right now," and she picked up the phone and started dialling. Understandably, Brian was confused.

"I'm sorry, so sorry. Please don't call the cops! I was invited here, I thought it was his house." He pointed to me.

"Well it fucking isn't. It's my house and you better get out right now!" Beth shouted. I tried to reason with her but it was a waste of time. Brian grabbed his things and ran out the door, jumped into his car and roared off.

Beth was absolutely livid. I'd never seen her angry before, but she was absolutely furious with me. "Never, ever, bring anyone back to my home. Do you understand how dangerous that is?" I tried to explain that I'd been to the bar, and that I'd met Brian there and invited him back.

"He's a friend, a really good musician, he can play all the Beatles music". It all sounded pretty lame in the face of Beth's anger. What I'd done wouldn't have been a big deal back in London or Glasgow. But here in Los Gatos, it was clearly a major fuck-up. Beth went round the windows making sure they were all locked tight, then secured the doors and went to bed, slamming the bedroom door behind her. I decided it was probably best to sleep in the living room that night, and curled up on the couch. I honestly couldn't understand what the problem was.

California was slowly turning into more of nightmare than a dream. I felt very limited in my mobility without a driving licence or a means of earning money. I had a home but not much freedom. The only employment opportunities I had were tied to the family. And the Beth who was at home in Los Gatos was far removed from the carefree and easy-going Beth that I'd got to know in Scotland. Now there was a palpable tension between us that hadn't existed before. Here in California, Beth was very much a part of the establishment, hard-working and respectable. I knew if I'd mentioned my dream of transitioning that it would be met with shock and probably embarrassment. The realisation hit me: there was no possibility of that ever happening while I was living under her roof. So, I had to rethink my future. If I was going to stay in California I would need to find financial independence and also my own place to live. It was too much to expect Beth to accept and support my crazy dream while I was living with her. But perhaps, with a home of my own, I could transition and we would still remain close. I decided the only way forward would be for me to work illegally. Many people did that in California, and it was a regular topic of conversation. So, that was dominating my thoughts one evening when Beth came home and suggested that we go to Los Angeles for the weekend.

* * * * * * *

Our plan was to drive down to LA on Route 1, the famous road that hugs the stunning Californian Pacific coast. We would take our time and see the sights, stopping overnight at the beautiful city of Monterey and spending a few hours at Cannery Row having lunch and looking at the location that inspired John Steinbeck's famous novel. Beth drove as I had no licence. It was really nice to be away from Los Gatos and Beth seemed to be much more relaxed, away from the pressures of school and work. She was much more like the Beth I'd first known back in Scotland. At one point after a gas stop she handed me the keys of her car.

"Go on, you drive for a while," she said, with a wicked smile. This was my old risk-taker Beth.

We arrived at Monterey and had dinner at an Italian restaurant. I was blown away with how good the food and red wine were. That started my passion for Californian wine that I've never lost. I also loved how this restaurant projected old black and white silent Charlie Chaplin movies directly onto a blank wall. It was such a clever gimmick back then, and one I was delighted to copy in my own restaurant some thirty-five years later.

We did the usual tourist trail along the boardwalks, in and out of the souvenir shops and down to the wharf. For once my worries about transitioning were banished from my mind as we just hung out together like old times. Later on that night we booked into a motel near Carmel and after a nice meal we retired early to have a cuddle.

The next morning it was a drive straight through to Santa Monica where we were to meet up with Beth's old college friend Rhoda, with whom we would be staying overnight at her apartment. Beth told me Rhoda was a writer, involved in a small way in the movies. I was looking forward to meeting her and seeing Los Angeles, particularly when Beth told me we would be hanging out with some British ex pats that Rhoda was friendly with. She said there was even a British-style pub in Hollywood we could visit. By this time I was desperate to hear British accents and have a chat with people about what LA was like for someone considering working without a green card. I needed to find out if LA was a place I could survive in, and maybe even transition.

We rolled into Santa Monica on Sunday mid-morning. The famous beach looked fantastic. There were palm trees everywhere and the weather was glorious. I felt really positive. This was such a glamorous location and I imagined myself living here in one of those beach houses. It was a therefore a reality check when we arrived at Rhoda's house. Not a beach house, nor even a house as big as the one we lived in back in Los Gatos, but more of a bedsit, very small and with no view of the ocean. But, hey, it was still Hollywood, just about.

Rhoda was a lovely woman, friendly and delighted to see us as she and Beth hugged. "We need to go out right away. I'm meeting some British friends who are really looking forward to meeting you, Ally." She was very enthusiastic and persuaded us to just drop our bags and leave there and then.

As Rhoda drove she asked me where in England I was from. I quickly corrected her that I wasn't actually English, I was Scottish. Oh that's fantastic, she squealed, since one of her friends we'd would be meeting, Rod, was Scottish too. The Brits were playing soccer in a park and that's where we were going.

Pretty soon we arrived at a public park somewhere in Hollywood. I could see a group of guys involved in an organised soccer match. This wasn't just a casual kick-around, both teams were properly kitted out and wearing boots. It seemed like a serious match. We parked on the roadside next to the park and ambled down to the pitch. It was much like any pub league soccer match you might find anywhere in the UK on a Sunday. Wives and children, some in pushchairs, were gathered along the length of the pitch cheering on, and I could hear distinctive British accents from the players as they shouted to each other 'man on' or 'go left', and a lot of familiar British swearing. I immediately felt at home.

It was almost half-time when we arrived, and by the time we'd made our way to Rhoda's friends on the side of the pitch, the whistle blew and the teams came towards the touchline for drinks. We were standing beside a beautiful blond woman who had several children with her. Rhoda introduced Beth and me to the blond woman. "Alana, these are my friends Beth and Ally from San Francisco," she gushed. We shook hands politely, and then Rhoda said excitedly, "Ally is Scottish, just like Rod, and he plays soccer." Alana looked around and shouted.

"Rod, come here, we have a possible Scottish player for the team." I turned to greet her husband who was jogging over. My mouth fell open as I suddenly realised it was only Rod fucking Stewart! Just a few years previously I'd had his posters on my bedroom wall. Now, here he was, smiling at me, shaking my hand, and asking what position I played.

"Right wing, or centre forward," I mumbled.

"Okay, great! Have you got your boots with you?"

"No, sorry, only these trainers I'm wearing."

"That's okay, get changed. Keith over there will sort you out. You can come on for the last half hour." He slapped my back and went back to the players' huddle.

Well, I hadn't expected this at all. I was still utterly gobsmacked that Rod Stewart was standing in front of me and no one else seemed too bothered. He was such a big star at that time and never out of the press in Britain. But here in Hollywood he was just a British ex-pat playing soccer with his mates. I quickly got behind a bush and changed from my jeans and shirt into the football kit that Keith handed me.

Soon the second half kicked off and I watched from the sideline with Keith and a few other Brits. The women were all screaming at the players and taking the whole thing very seriously. Keith seemed to be the coach and I stood next to him and soon got engrossed in the match. Rod was actually a very good player, by far the best on the field. He was fast and skilful with his blond hair flying behind him. The team the Brits were playing seemed to be made up from various European and South American countries, with a couple of Americans. I quickly got on board with the rivalry and was shouting instructions and encouragements along with everyone else.

Then it was time for me to come on. I replaced a guy who sounded like he was from Yorkshire. He was quite a bit older than me, and judging by everyone else on the field, I was by far the youngest player. I ran the right wing and with my speed easily outpaced the opposition. I managed to put a lot of crosses in and ran their poor left back ragged. I can't remember the score, but I know we won. My competitive spirit wouldn't allow me to take even this informal park game easy and I thoroughly enjoyed myself, chasing down every ball. When the final whistle went we were all jubilant on the British side. The wives and other women ran on to congratulate us. I'd had fun and was really buzzing.

After the game it was decided that we'd all go to the King's Head British pub for lunch. I got changed and we all drove down to the bar in a convoy. By the time Rhoda, Beth and I arrived, the others were already at the bar drinking. I walked in and Rod was sitting on a bar stool watching soccer on the TV screen behind the bar, He looked up and gave me a big smile.

"Let me buy a fellow Scot a drink," he shouted warmly across. he then came over and put his arm round my shoulder. "Have a seat, Ally. Tell me where you're from. Is it Glasgow? It sounds like a Glasgow accent." I confirmed I was from the Glasgow area and sat down. He bought me a rum and coke. Then he introduced me to a woman called Mary. She was from Aberdeen and she and her husband were the pub chefs. She asked me if I wanted the roast dinner, beef and Yorkshire pudding, or traditional English fish and chips. I settled on the fish. Mary was very friendly and I thought I must try to find an opportunity to talk with her at some point about living here, green cards and jobs.

Rod was an extremely genuine and lovely, friendly guy. Very down to earth and not the least bit starry. We chatted for a long time about Scotland and London. He was of course a London boy, born and bred with a cockney accent. His Scottish family had moved south before he was born so it was remarkable how much in touch he was with his heritage. He told me about his parents who still had their Scottish accents, and his brothers. He was from a big family and they were Glasgow Celtic fans. He invited me to join his ex-pat soccer team. They played regularly throughout the year and he clearly took it very seriously. I told him that it would be difficult for me to play regularly since I lived in Northern California. Rod just shrugged.

"No problem. We already have a couple of guys from San Francisco, just fly down to LA, it only takes an hour." I just nodded, telling him I'd think about it. The whole situation was still blowing my mind. Rod fucking Stewart! In a British pub in California? Flying from San Francisco to LA every week to play soccer? It was just crazy.

After an hour or so, Rod decided he'd better be going. He wasn't going to stay for food in the pub because Alana was cooking at home. As he stood up to leave I said, "Let me buy you a drink at least, before you go." Scottish custom dictates that if you buy someone a drink, you must allow them to buy you one back, so Rod agreed. I bought us both another rum and coke and we chatted for a little longer about Glasgow Celtic and the Scottish national team. It was nice for me to be able to speak in my normal accent without having to translate. Eventually, Rod told me he had to leave. He got up, we shook hands, and he made me promise that I would try to fly down for next week's game. Then he left. I turned to Beth and grinned. The whole day had been surreal.

After Rod had left, Mary served me my fish and chips. I took the opportunity to ask her how long she and her husband had been in LA and what the green card situation was like for someone like me if I tried to get a job without one. She told me it had been quite difficult for her and her husband. It had taken them several years before they were able to work, but that was a long time ago. She suggested the best person to talk to was Rupert.

She pointed him out to me and said she would send him over for a chat.

I spent at least an hour speaking with Rupert. He was good-looking, in his mid-twenties and a typical product of the English public school system: charming, well-groomed, and posh with the type of cut-glass accent Americans loved. He'd come to the US a year previously and was hoping to break into the movies. In the meantime he was living off his own, or most likely his family's, money. Like me, he had a ten-year visa but no green card or right to work. He'd so far found it impossible to get a work visa and his money was running out. He told me that he expected he'd have to go back to England if he didn't get a break soon. In short, he advised me not to try to work illegally. The only work I would get without a green card would be very low paid and certainly not enough to cover rent. I'd be competing with all the other illegals for work, and that drove the wages down to a rate that was impossible to survive on. Furthermore, not only would my situation be economically unviable, I'd also be risking arrest and deportation, and once deported, I'd find it impossible ever to get back into the US, even for a holiday. It wasn't what I wanted to hear, but on top of what Mary had told me, the truth of the situation was staring me in the face. There was simply no way I would be able to work and transition in LA. The cost of my surgery alone would be very high, and without the opportunity to earn I'd have no chance.

I'd had a wonderful weekend, a real taste of the good life. But I knew in my heart that this Californian path was not going to work for me. That day I resigned myself to the inevitable: if I was ever to transition I would need to go back to the UK and see if it was possible to do it there. Who knows, one day I might come back post-transition and have another drink with Rod. I bet that would surprise him, though I'm not sure he'd still want me to fly to LA every weekend to play football.

That evening we went down to Sunset Boulevard to have a look at the sights, but my mind was already thinking about leaving for London. Later, we went back to Rhoda's apartment. Beth and I were still thrilled to have spent the day hanging out with Rod Stewart, but we both knew it was a one-off. I would clearly not be flying down to play soccer every week. We made up the sofa bed in the lounge and spent the night cuddled up, drinking wine and eating junk food. Already on both our minds was the long drive back to Los Gatos in the morning, Beth's return to the daily grind, and mine to boredom. I made up my mind to tell Beth once we got home that I would be returning to London. I didn't want her to think I was ungrateful for the fantastic welcome and hospitality she and her family had shown to me, but I also had a feeling she wouldn't be too upset that I was leaving. It had a great experience, one I'd never forget, but I felt it was better to leave on a high rather than outstay my welcome and risk damaging our relationship.

The next evening back at Beth's house I broke the news that I needed to go home. She didn't seem very surprised and didn't try to change my mind. She arranged my flight and we said our goodbyes later on that week at San Francisco airport. It would be another six years before I saw her face again, by which time we'd both be unhappily married to other people.

Chapter 6 'I Want To Be Free'

Hammersmith

It was 1981 and springtime in the UK when I arrived home from sunny San Francisco. I was struck by how dirty and depressing London looked as Uncle George drove me back through the city from Heathrow to East London. I looked through the rain-splattered window of the car at the decayed and tired old city. Margaret Thatcher was mid-way through her first term as Prime Minister, and it seemed like she might be there forever. But politics were not high on my list of priorities, at least not yet.

I'd come back for one reason. I wanted to transition and start living as me, as a young woman growing and breathing in London, the most anonymous city in the world, where I could get away with being different for a while during my transformation. I was scared but excited, and my mind was made up. In fact I had no choice – my future had to be here or I would die trying. I didn't know it at the time how prophetic my commitment was. I almost did die several times over the coming years.

When they heard I was back, everyone I knew thought I was crazy. Why on earth would I leave such a fantastic setup, sharing a house in sunny California with two beautiful blond babes? But of course that was part of the problem. It wasn't so much about wanting to be with them, as much as it was to be like them. I'd seen their lives and knew I wanted to be able to live like them, as a woman in my own right. Living alongside Beth and Cathy had made me so envious that it drove me crazy.

Soon we arrived back in Barkingside. I'd brought gifts for Mamie and George, California wine and a beautiful abalone shell ornament from Monterey. We sat back and relaxed as I regaled them with stories of the places I'd visited, and of course the Rod Stewart tale. Mamie and I drank dark rum and cokes, while George was on beers and Metaxa brandy. I detected an undercurrent of concerned curiosity. They were also wondering why the fuck I'd come back from such a seemingly perfect situation. And more to the point, was I planning to live with them again? Mamie told me she was more than happy to have me back living there, but I could sense that George, although he didn't say it, was not so enthusiastic. I reassured them both that I planned to stay in London but get my own place. I'd be out of their hair again as soon as I had a job and a place to live.

* * * * * * *

I scanned the pages of the employment section in the Evening Standard newspaper. I was looking for a job, one that would enable me to pay the rent on a flat of my own. Then, once I had my own place, I would begin my transition. I wanted to stay in London, but also to create a little distance from Mamie and George.

As usual the vacancies were mostly office and secretarial. If I could only learn shorthand, then maybe I'd have a chance of earning decent money, at least that's what the ads would have me believe. But I didn't have the time. So, I went back to what I knew best: construction work.

There was always demand for construction workers in London in those days. Mostly you found out who was hiring through word of mouth, but there were often vacancies advertised in the Standard, too. I saw an ad for a firm in West London, which was looking for tradesmen and labourers. The address was listed in the paper, and the advice 'apply on site'.

So, within a week of leaving California I was travelling the Central line on the tube from Barkingside to Shepherds Bush. The contrast couldn't have been starker. But I was very happy to be back in London, a place where I could both hide myself and find myself in the anonymity of the metropolis. So what if it was dirty, unfriendly and wet? There were opportunities here, and a freedom that attracted thousands of people every year from all over the world. London was not so much tolerant, but indifferent. You could be anything and anyone. No one was too bothered.

I arrived at the building site in Hammersmith, just behind Uxbridge Road. As expected, the foreman was Irish, a man called Peter. The job was renovating a street of terraced houses. I would be employed as a labourer to the tradesmen. The wage was £25 a day, Monday to Friday and double time for Saturday morning. If I wanted the job, Peter told me, I could start the next morning. I agreed the terms and told him I'd see him in the morning. I caught the tube back to Barkingside. That's how easy it was to get a job in those days.

Once back at Mamie and George's house, I told them I'd got a job and I would need to get a flat in West London. We got out that day's Evening Standard again and had a look through the hundreds of flats available for rent. I saw a ground floor flat in Shepherds Bush advertised. It was £40 a week rent, plus one month's rent in advance. I called up the landlady, a Spanish-sounding woman called Mrs Morales. She offered to meet me that evening at the property for a viewing. I got back on the tube again for a repeat of my earlier journey across London.

The flat was on Blythe Road, just off Shepherd's Bush Road. It was self-contained and furnished, with its own bed/sitting room and a separate kitchen and bathroom. The main entrance was shared, but other than that, I would have my own private flat. I agreed to take it that night and paid the deposit and one month's rent in advance, and Mrs Morales handed me the keys. That's how easy it was to get a flat in London in those days.

I returned to Barkingside that night and told Mamie and George I'd got the flat. We agreed that I'd stay for one last night with them, and in the morning I'd go to start my new job. Later on they would meet me at the address when I got back from work. George would drive to Shepherd's Bush with my belongings. I didn't have a lot, and it could all be packed up in two suitcases.

The new job wasn't as enjoyable as my time at CJ Smith. It was proper labouring and there was no Portakabin for me to make my own. It was a much bigger site and the contractor I was working for was a Mr Conolly.

I soon learned that everyone met up in a greasy spoon cafe on Uxbridge Road at around 7:30 am for breakfast. The men were a similar bunch to the CJ Smith crowd. Mostly Irish and a few Scots, with a sprinkling from Australia and Europe. It was a much looser team because the workforce was so much bigger, so it took a while to get to know who was who. At lunchtime almost everyone went to the pub and downed as many pints as they could during the hour break.

My job was to help the tradesmen. I was sent to whoever needed me on that day. I might be carrying the hod and mixing cement for the brickies in the morning, then unloading boards and poles from a lorry for the scaffolders in the afternoon. I honestly didn't care what I did, I just wanted the wages. I decided to keep my head down, grit my teeth and get on with it. I was here for the money and it was good money in those days, all cash in hand at the end of the week. After my weekly rent was paid I was usually left with around £100 to spend on whatever I wanted.

* * * * * * *

I finally had the freedom and privacy to take my first steps towards transitioning. With my first week's wages I went along to Shepherd's Bush market on Saturday afternoon to buy my very own girl's clothes. No more borrowing from female relatives and friends. I was a bit like a kid in a sweetshop, and I bought all sorts of totally unsuitable stuff, including evening dresses, brightly coloured leggings, hats, and make-up.

At first I felt nervous and self-conscious when browsing. A few of the market traders looked at me oddly. I could see they were wondering why a boy was buying female clothes. I didn't yet have the nerve to try anything on for size, so I would just grab skirts, jackets, or tights that I thought might fit me. If any of the traders asked who I was buying for, and occasionally they did, just trying to be helpful, I would say it's a surprise gift for my girlfriend or my mum. Hilarious, now that I think back. What seventeen year old boy would buy a bra for his mum?

When I got back to my little flat with my clothes shopping it was fantastic. I would try everything on and pose in front of my mirror to see how I looked. This was my haven. When not at work I could spend as much time as I wanted as my female self.

I made up my mind right from the start to keep a complete separation between 'him and her.' He would go to work to earn the money for her to live and dress as she pleased in the evenings and at weekends. There would be no crossover. I told no one at work where I lived, so I could be certain there would be no unexpected visitors for him at home, because that was her flat. I'm quite sure my neighbours assumed there was a couple living in the flat. I would occasionally meet people in the hallway as I came and went to work as him, then in the evening I might bump into the same neighbours as her. If it seems confusing, it wasn't to me. Who knows what others might have thought? I didn't care, and fortunately, in London no one really cares – they're all too busy getting on with their own lives.

One problem I quickly identified was that because I could never be brave enough to try any of the female clothes in the shops or down the market before I bought them. I would find that when I got home that half the stuff I'd bought didn't fit properly. I almost always bought my clothes dressed as him on a Saturday afternoon on the way home from work, then, I'd end up giving it away to charity shops.

One particular episode stands out for cringing embarrassment. I decided to go shopping straight from work one Saturday afternoon and saw a nice pair of red ankle boots in a shop window in a shop in King Street, Hammersmith. At £50 they were expensive, but I simply had to have them.

I entered the shop and a friendly-looking black girl a few years older than me came over. "Can I help you, Sir?" she asked, smiling. I was dressed in men's work clothes, covered in cement dust.

"Er yeah, can I see those boots in the window? Have you got a size seven?" She looked confused.

"Those are women's boots, Sir," she answered, her eyes looking surprised. So I quickly used my 'they're for my girlfriend' story. The girl nodded, apparently not entirely convinced, then went to fetch the boots.

The shop was full of women trying on shoes and I felt as though all eyes were on me. When the girl came back with the boots she handed one over to me and I began handling it as though I was examining a particularly fine antique vase.

"Perhaps it would be better if your girlfriend came in and tried them on?" the assistant suggested. "Most women like to buy their own shoes, they know best what they want, Sir." By this time another shop assistant had joined us. She was nodding in agreement.

"Yes, tell her to come in, or at least have a look at them in the window." She seemed concerned. "You don't want to buy her something she might not like." They were both trying to be helpful but I felt exposed, turning red, with my forehead sweating.

"No, no, it will be fine. It's a surprise," I stammered. I took the cash from my pocket and thrust it towards her to signify the deal was done. "Put them in a bag, please." The black girl turned to look at the other assistant in resignation and half-smiled, clearly wondering what does this stupid boy know about what shoes a woman wants to wear? But she bagged up the box with the boots, took the cash and handed me a receipt. As I practically ran out of the door, she shouted after me, "Tell her she can exchange the boots with the receipt, if she wants." I rushed home, relieved to be out of the awkward situation but also dying to try on the beautiful red boots.

When I got back to the flat I discarded my hated men's clothes and took a shower. I quickly got dried and brushed my hair out. I put on a bra and pants, selected a tight pair of ladies jeans and a short low cut black top from my wardrobe. This was the exact outfit I had in mind when I saw the boots in the window, and I knew they would look great together.

I opened the box carefully and took out the red boots. I really loved them, and it had definitely been worth the awkwardness in the shop to have these boots. I tried to slip my right foot into the unzipped opening, with satisfaction, smelling the new leather. But I couldn't get my foot in. I wiggled and pushed my foot, but no, the boot wasn't going on. Tights – that's what I needed! I remembered I had some sheer black popsocks. I quickly tore open the packet and rolled the thin nylon sock over my foot and tried again, telling myself that new shoes are always tight. But, no, my foot still wouldn't fit. I felt like one of Cinderella's step-sisters trying on the glass slipper after the ball.

I was devastated. I loved the boots and they had cost me almost £50 and now they were absolutely useless to me. I poured myself a large rum and coke for consolation and knocked it back as I sat back on my bed looking at the gorgeous boots in disappointment. What an idiot I was. I turned on the TV to take my mind off things, and poured myself another drink and watched whatever was on, without really taking any notice of it.

After a short while, my disappointment began to turn to anger with myself. The anger combined with the courage boost of alcohol soon had me questioning myself. Why can't I just take the boots back and exchange them, I thought. Okay, so the girls will laugh at me with a we-told-you-so look, but the boots were so expensive and I just need a slightly larger size. Surely I can put up with a bit more embarrassment?

My mind was quickly made up – I was going back to the shop. I still had an hour before it closed. I quickly got changed again into the dusty men's clothes. I picked up the repackaged boots, and had another drink for courage just before I left. As I entered the shop the black girl saw me and came straight over. "Don't tell me, your girlfriend didn't like the boots?" She smiled.

Before I could give her my planned story I'd been practising in my head all the way along King Street to the shop, wrong colour, size, she's bought something else, I heard myself blurt out, "They don't fit me, the boots are for me. I'm sorry, but I need a bigger size."

The black girl looked shocked at first, but quickly smiled and took my arm. "It's okay, why didn't you say that before?" She led me to a seat at the back of the sales area, out of sight of the other customers, and sat me down. She took the bag from me with the boots, gave them a quick check, and then said, "I'll see if we have a bigger size." I just sat there, amazed with myself at what I'd just admitted to a stranger.

A few minutes later both sales assistants were facing me with another pair of boots. "This time try them on," the black girl said. Her friend just smiled.

"Hey, it's cool, don't worry." I put the boots on and they fitted. Both girls looked happy and I felt very relieved. In fact I felt suddenly unburdened. Why had this seemed such an awful heart-wrenching disaster only a few minutes before? After all, it's only a pair of fucking boots! I quickly changed back into my men's shoes and gathered up my bag with the correctly-fitting boots and left the shop, thanking both girls profusely.

I don't know what they thought of me after all that. But I learned that it's best to be completely honest in any situation like that in future. It's really not a big deal. Shop assistants don't care. If anything, they are usually more helpful in that kind of situation. The big problem was in my head and my own shame and self-loathing. The bottom line was that I was still homophobic and ashamed.

* * * * * * *

I'd settled into my new double life very easily and I finally felt I was on my way to transitioning. My plan was to build a base from my little flat that would lead to full transition, including surgery. I realised that a full sex change was probably a few years away, but in the meantime I could at least have the freedom to express myself how I felt inside, and whenever I wanted to. I also had to learn how to 'pass' as female in everyday situations.

Whenever I had dressed and gone out as female back in Scotland, I had always chosen carefully where I went. I was terrified of being 'outed' in the street and I avoided all situations where I might have to speak, since I was particularly worried that my voice would give me away. I began to dedicate time to practising my female voice. I had a cassette recorder with a built-in microphone and I would spend hours reading passages from magazines or just mimicking natural conversation. Then I would play the tape back, cringe, then try again, and again. 'Hi, can I have twenty Benson and Hedges, please?' was a phrase I rehearsed a lot. It would be a regular thing, so I had to make sure I could buy my ciggies from my local grocery shop.

I looked quite androgynous when I was seventeen. I had been plucking my eyebrows for several years and I was still slender. My dark brown hair was thick and long, well past my shoulders. My exposure to what I call 'testosterone poisoning' hadn't fully kicked in yet. Both my ears were pierced so I could wear earnings and other feminine jewellery. It was fashionable for women to wear quite heavy make-up. in the early 1980s, so it was easy for me to cover my beard shadow with foundation and a light dusting of powder and not appear out of place. I usually also wore eyeliner, shadow and mascara, with a light pink lipstick. My hairstyle was more difficult to manage. I hadn't yet had the nerve to go to a hairdresser to have a proper female cut. That level of close-up social interaction still worried me, so I taught myself to cut my own hair using two mirrors. This is something I still do today, though of course I don't really need to. I bought lots of fashion magazines and women's hairstyle books. My hair was naturally wavy, so if I backcombed it and used hairspray I could achieve a soft permed look that was fashionable in those days.

The other vital skill I needed to learn was how to 'tuck'. This is the method used by drag queens to hide the telltale penis bulge. You basically fold everything underneath and between your legs, then pull on a tight pair of control pants to keep it all in place. This was quite uncomfortable at first, but after a while I got used to it. Using the tuck allowed me to wear tight jeans and trousers. The appearance was aesthetically very pleasing to me, but I longed for the time when I could have surgery and tucking was no longer necessary.

It was time for me to register with an NHS doctor. I'd been well settled into my new life for several weeks, and I was happier than I'd ever been. I felt confident enough to take the next step, so I found the nearest GP surgery and went along to register and book an appointment. It was a very simple process in those days. I just filled in a form with my name, address and National Insurance number. I also had to provide my previous doctor's details. My GP back in Scotland had been a typical family practice doctor. I hadn't had much contact with them over the years growing up since I'd always been very fit and healthy. I arranged an appointment for the following day, after work.

When I finished up at work the next day, I rushed home to change. I didn't dress in full femme garb; I wanted my appearance to mirror my position on the transition path, namely part way down the road. I didn't really appreciate at that time that subtlety wasn't recognised by the medical profession; they preferred you to emphasise the point by portraying stereotypical behaviour and dress. I wore girls' jeans and a neutral top, no make-up. but feminine jewellery: silver bangles, earrings and a small crucifix. I sat in the waiting room watching the board with the different doctors' names embossed on it, next to corresponding lights. My new GP was male, Dr Moor. When the relevant light came on it would be time for me to go in. I tried to relax as I waited, but I couldn't. In fact, I couldn't have been more nervous if I tried. I lit a cigarette – amazingly, this was normal in doctors' waiting rooms in those days – and waited anxiously.

After a few minutes the light came on with a loud accompanying buzz; it was my turn. I walked along a short corridor and entered through a half-opened door. Dr Moor appeared quite elderly. With grey hair and a suit to match, he sat behind his desk looking at his paperwork.

"Have a seat, Mr McIntyre. What can I do for you today?" he said as he looked up at me.

"I want to have a sex change," I replied. Might as well get straight to the point. There was no visible reaction from Dr Moor, who looked at me but said nothing. "I've felt like this all my life," I continued. I've moved to London and got my own flat because I couldn't transition at home in Scotland. My family would kill me if I told them." Still nothing from Dr Moor. "I've read that it's possible to have sex change surgery on the NHS. Can you help me?"

This might not seem like such a dramatic start to a conversation with a doctor today in the more enlightened times of the twenty-first century, but back in 1981 it was a bombshell. It was almost the equivalent of admitting that I was a dangerous sexual pervert. Looking back, I marvel at my own courage and naivety, not to mention the trust I placed in the NHS.

If Dr Moor was taken aback he hid it very well. He began by asking me why I thought it necessary to have surgery. Was I attracted to other men? I hadn't really given this much thought before. Perhaps I would be attracted to men once I had a female body? In truth, I really didn't know. I was far more interested in my own physical appearance, than in who I was sexually attracted to. It was (and to some extent, still is) a common misconception that people went through sex change surgery in order to align their bodies towards having a sexual relationship with someone else, so that it would appear outwardly like a heterosexual relationship. Most people, including doctors, confused gender with sexual orientation. It remains the case today.

I remembered the phrase I'd read in books or newspaper stories. "I think I'm a woman trapped in a man's body." This statement seemed at least to move Dr Moor to start taking notes. In truth, the statement made very little sense to me. How could I know what it felt like to be a woman? It's like asking what it's like to have green eyes compared to brown. There is no answer; no one knows how another feels. But I knew, at least from what I'd read, that this was the trigger phrase.

What I did know for certain – and I've never once changed my mind on this over the almost four decades since – is that I did not identify as being male. I've never felt comfortable looking male, nor being addressed as male. The whole idea of being a man was abhorrent to me, and still is. I think I just therefore assumed in that binary world that I probably would be much more comfortable being female. I detested the physical characteristics of a man and wanted instead to have a female body, complete with wider hips, breasts, a narrow waist, smooth skin and a vagina. The ability to have a uterus and produce children was more than I thought ever possible back then, but I desperately wanted to get as close to a female body shape as possible. I knew that if I couldn't at least get rid of my male physical characteristics and live as female, then I didn't want to live at all. Is that how a woman feels? It's impossible to tell, even for a cisgender woman (or cis woman – that is, a woman born female at birth and who identifies as female – it is the opposite of transgender woman). So for all of my life, my personal position has always been that I simply never wanted to be a man, rather than 'I felt like a woman trapped in a man's body.'

I didn't feel that this was the time or place to discuss such nuances with Dr Moor. What I needed was a referral to a specialist, and this appointment was the all-important first step. Dr Moor said he would need to look up the guidelines and explore what options were available. He would also need to have my medical records sent to him from my previous GP in Scotland. Perhaps I could make another appointment to come and see him in four to six weeks' time, he suggested. I said I would, and thanked him for taking me seriously.

As I stood up to leave, he cautioned me: "Ally, you're very young to be considering this path. I'll find out what I can, but it's unlikely you would be accepted for treatment until you're at least in your twenties." For the first time he showed some emotion and smiled kindly. "I'll see you in four weeks or so."

I walked out on a high. He hadn't laughed at me and seemed to take me seriously. It was only the first step, but it was the first time I'd actually had the courage to explain my situation to a doctor. I felt a huge weight had been lifted from my shoulders, and I walked back to my flat with a spring in my step and a beaming smile. Little could I have anticipated that a major storm was approaching from a direction I'd thought was well behind me.

A few days after my visit to Dr Moor, I left work at my usual time and made my way home. I couldn't wait to get out of my male work clothes, have a shower and then step into my female life, at least until the next morning. My mind was on these things as I opened the street door to my building and entered the hallway. My own flat was at the back of the hallway, and as I approached I could see someone sitting on the floor with their back resting against my own door. I had a sickening feeling in the pit of my stomach as I cautiously approached the person. No, it can't be. But it was. I recognised the slouched figure, cigarette in hand, the red leather Dr Martens boots. I knew that upturned thrust of the jaw and the confident grin.

"Gerry"?

Chapter 7 'Fade To Grey'

Gerry Francis was a face from my past, my all-too-recent past! It hadn't even been a year since we'd been in the same gang back in the Vale. We had grown up together and lived on the same council estate. He was a year older than me and we were even distant relations. Gerry had been more interested in drugs, alcohol, and women, rather than in fighting. But he was still part of the gang. He was always ready to get involved with whatever we were doing and never one to back down, so he'd earned respect. I also knew his mother and stepdad well. It had been less than two years since his older brother had overdosed on heroin and died. The funeral wake had descended into a massive piss-up involving tears and fighting. I'd always liked Gerry and we'd always been close.

But right here in London, right now, just as I was successfully putting that life behind me, he was not someone I wanted to see.

"How's it going, pal?" Gerry asked with a smile. "Bet you're surprised to see me!" I could tell he was drunk even before I clocked the collection of lager cans sitting on the step next to him.

My mother had given my address to Gerry. I'd called my parents fairly regularly since I'd got back from America, so they knew I'd moved to West London and got a job. But obviously no one knew I'd started my transition from male to female. I suppose my plan had been to contact them about that once I'd completely changed sex, once it would be too late for them to try and stop me.

"What are you doing here, Gerry?" I asked, trying to hide my dismay.

"Oh, I had a few problems back in the Vale," he replied matter-of-factly. "Some people are looking for me so I had to get away. Your mum told me you were doing well in London, so I thought I'd come and join you and give it a try myself." He seemed really happy to see me. "Can I kip here for a while, 'till I get myself sorted?"

This was a major disaster, but I suppose I should have seen something like this coming. You cannot just disentangle yourself from a whole life, community and family without some comeback. I guess I just hadn't been prepared for it happen so soon.

My first priority was to get indoors before my neighbours saw Gerry lying half-pissed on my doorstep. I grabbed him and helped him up, unlocked my door bundled him into my flat.

The first thing I realised, and that Gerry noticed, when we got inside, were the female clothes, jewellery and make-up. all round the flat, on the dressing table and next to my bed. I frantically tried to scoop everything up into a drawer, hoping he hadn't paid any attention to it.

"You got a bird living with you?" he asked.

"No, it's just stuff that the last tenant left behind," I replied. "I've kept it in case she comes back for it." It seemed a pretty unlikely story, but Gerry seemed to accept it.

Inwardly I was cursing myself. I knew I was going to betray 'her', since I was too much of a coward to tell Gerry the truth. I tried to think on my feet to find a plausible cover story, but this was crunch time for me, and I failed miserably. Gerry pulled out a couple of cans of lager from his bag and offered me one. I took it.

I didn't realise the significance of that moment at the time, but that was the end of my first attempt at transitioning.

* * * * * * *

That night Gerry filled me in with all the news from the Vale. He told me who had been 'done' (arrested), who was in prison, who had been stabbed, and who had done the stabbing. Gerry told me that the drug dealers had recently become a big deal in my home town, and this was one of the main reasons behind his sudden departure. Specifically, he owed money. To be fair, it wasn't only to escape his debts that he'd come to visit me in London. My parents had told him that I was living the high life, with a good job and a nice place to live. I'd got away from the gangs and was doing well for myself. Gerry was impressed with what I'd apparently achieved and wanted to see if he could do the same: get away from the shit back home and make a new start. I couldn't blame him for that.

We ended up in the Richmond pub that night, just around the corner from my flat, and the booze fooled me into believing that this was a just a temporary bump in the road. I convinced myself that I'd tell Gerry the truth about my new life at some point. But for tonight, let's put that off and drink. I'd also agreed to take Gerry with me to work the next morning to see if he could get a job on the site where I worked.

We staggered home at closing time. By this point Gerry was almost asleep on his feet. He'd been drinking all day since he'd caught the bus from Glasgow to London that morning. When we arrived at my flat I separated the mattress from the bed base so we each had something to sleep on. Gerry quickly fell sound asleep, and as he snored I gathered up all my make-up. and female clothing from the wardrobe and drawers. I stuffed everything into a couple of bin bags and stashed the bags in the bathroom.

With Gerry around it didn't take long for my transition to become completely derailed. I took him to the site where I worked and he'd been taken on as a labourer. Now we were often working together, going to the pub at lunchtime and again straight after work. Gerry was a very sociable person, so within a week he'd made many friends among the Irish and Scots on the site and we'd regularly meet up with them and others in the evenings after work.

The social scene for the Celtic community was centred around Hammersmith Broadway, and The Swan and The George pubs in particular. There was a huge community of young people who had left Scotland and Ireland to find work in London in those days, and it was rare to hear a London accent among my circle of friends. It was also difficult not to get sucked in to the routine of hard drinking and partying. There were hundreds of young men and women in their early twenties, living away from home for the first time and intermittently earning good money with relatively cheap housing. Jobs were so plentiful that you could work for a week then pack it in and party for a week before finding another job. Squatting was popular all over London in those days. I spent time in several squats but it was a precarious life. The local council was always one step behind us and would regularly break into the squat when everyone was out. They would simply take a sledge hammer to the toilet, sinks and bath to make the building uninhabitable.

Among the colourful characters I knew at that time in Hammersmith was Jimmy McNeil. Jimmy was a lovable rogue from Clydebank, one of the first people I met around the Broadway. He was quite a bit older than me, in his late twenties. He came from a notorious criminal family in Clydebank and his claim to fame (or at least, notoriety) was that he had become, at fifteen years old, the youngest person ever to have been convicted in the UK of armed robbery of a post office. He had served his time in Wandsworth and Pentonville adult prisons, despite being under sixteen when convicted. He seemed to know everyone in Hammersmith and these days was well-liked, even by the local police.

It was through Jimmy that I met Robbie Ball. Robbie was a Fifer who had ended up in London in his early twenties after deciding working down a coal mine wasn't for him. Little did I know when we first met that Robbie and I would later end up travelling the country, on the run from the police.

'Big Paul Boosh Boosh' was another character. He was six feet four inches tall, a giant of a man from Easterhouse, Glasgow. His nickname came from his habit of describing how he dealt with troublemakers at the posh Chelsea nightclub where he now worked as a bouncer: "Boosh Boosh and it was sorted".

Then there was 'Davy Jesus', a real hard man and a former gang member from Gallowgate, Glasgow. He had undergone a religious conversion after he'd discovered his best friend dead and bleeding, apparently by suicide, in the bath of the Fulham flat they shared.

Tragically, this wasn't the first time suicide had touched his life. Quite matter-of-factly, Davy also told me of the time he'd come home from school in Glasgow aged fourteen. He had found the front door of his council house home locked, which was unusual. He pulled up the letterbox flap to look inside and saw the body of his father swaying on a rope by his neck. Davy smashed a window, climbed in and cut down his dad, then phoned the police.

These days, it was Davy's self-imposed mission to look after the spiritual well-being of the young Scots in Hammersmith. He lived a monastic lifestyle in a converted ambulance, eating only vegetables, fruit and nuts. He had a very difficult task trying to bring order to the chaotic lives of the younger Scottish community that was dominated by alcohol and drugs, casual work and often homelessness. He once took Robbie and me out to the Sussex countryside for a camping trip in the middle of a forest. He was trying to show us there was an alternative, more peaceful kind of life away from the chaos of the city. Unfortunately, we had only been there two nights when Robbie and I got involved in a drunken brawl in the local village pub. The pair of us ended up smashing the place up before joining one of the locals in a car (that turned out to be stolen) for a joyride before crashing it in the trees next to Davy's ambulance. Gone was the vegan pacifist; that night we saw a glimpse of Davy's former gangland self. He was so angry with us that he beat us both up, threw us in the back of his ambulance, then roared off at high speed through the woodland track back towards London, passing the police patrol car on the way that was no doubt searching for the stolen car.

But, all that was in the future. After a couple of weeks of living with Gerry, I was still trying to retain some semblance of control over my life. I kept telling myself that this situation, sharing my flat with Gerry, was only temporary. I resolved that once he had found himself somewhere of his own to live, I would get my life back on track and resume my transition. Unfortunately, that plan was totally scuppered one fateful evening.

Gerry and I had got home from work one night, and we were getting washed and ready for a night out at the George. This had become our routine, and every night we went to the Broadway and met up with whoever was around. We would then go to one of the pubs, and often later on to the disco at Hammersmith Palais. One of the characters I remember from the Palais was a young Irishman by the name of Kevin 'Shitbag', so-called because he had a colostomy bag after being badly injured in a car crash. Kevin was so used to his bag filling up that he couldn't smell it, although everyone else could. One night at the Palais, Kevin was enthusiastically performing his John Travolta moves when his colostomy bag split. As he whirled round with his shirt flying, the shit flew out from the bag and sprayed everyone within a ten-yard radius. The screams from the women and swearing from the men were deafening as you can imagine. The club's management thought at first it was a terrorist attack (the IRA were very active in London back then). It was really very funny, but perhaps you needed to be there to appreciate the humour.

Anyway, as Gerry and I were getting ready to go out there was a loud knock at the door. I was in the shower so I left it to Gerry to answer it. I heard Gerry welcoming someone inside. I wasn't too concerned as friends often called round for us. Often they didn't even bother using the front door and came straight in through the window from the side street.

I came into the living room, still drying my hair with a towel, wondering who had turned up. I was very surprised to see Mark Thompson sitting on my bed. Mark was another acquaintance from my past in the Vale. But he wasn't a close friend and hadn't been in our gang. So why was he here?

It turned out that Gerry had spoken with Mark on the phone a few times, and, unbeknownst to me, had invited him to come down and join us in London. Gerry had also told Mark he could sleep at my flat until he found his own place. I wasn't very happy. Things were spiralling out of control; I now had two other people living in my little flat and my transition seemed to be on hold indefinitely. Despite my best efforts, I just couldn't seem to get away from my past. Actually, the real problem was that I wasn't being honest with other people about my transition, because I still wasn't being honest with myself.

Mark was a big guy, well over six feet tall and heavily built. He was four years older than me and had lived on a different council estate in the Vale. I knew him because he'd been friends with Gerry's dead brother. They were both bikers, but because of the age difference I'd never had much reason to hang out with him. He wasn't in any of the gangs, but he was very close to Gerry who looked up to him as a surrogate big brother. I didn't want him at the flat, though, not least because of the lack of space, but more because I felt I'd been used by Gerry. He had abused my hospitality by inviting Mark into my flat without even asking me first. Nevertheless, into my flat he came.

Over the next week or so, Mark got to know our 'team' in Hammersmith, the people Gerry and I hung out with. He found himself a job on a different building site, which gave me hope that he and Gerry would move out soon. My next appointment with Dr Moor was approaching and I desperately wanted to make that date and get my transition back on track. I did see Dr Moor again, but sooner than planned and in completely unexpected circumstances.

* * * * * * *

Things went very badly wrong one Friday night. I was in the George pub on the Broadway, drinking with Gerry, Mark and a few of the other regulars. As usual, everyone had got drunk and by chucking out time we were still drinking. The landlord, Michael, pushed us all outside, still with glasses in hand. This was quite normal, since after the pub closed the party would often carry on outside in the street.

There were a couple of public phone boxes on the Broadway that we all used regularly. Mark decided it was a good time to phone his family back in the Vale. Gerry and I left him to get on with his call as we chatted with two girls we knew, Mig and Francis, by the railings next to the phone boxes.

After a couple of minutes, Mark stuck his head out of the phone box and asked if we had any coins because his money was running out. We rummaged around in our pockets and Gerry gave him a 50p coin. Mark went back to his call. I was still checking my jeans for coins and I found a few 10p coins. I opened the phone box door and tried to hand the coins to Mark, but he was too busy with his conversation to take any notice of me, so I slipped the coins into his denim jacket pocket, trying to catch his attention and pointing to the pocket. I turned back to the girls and Gerry and we carried on our chat outside. What happened next was to affect me for the rest of my life.

Mark ended his phone call and stormed out of the phone box towards us. He began shouting at me. "You fucking thief!" he screamed. "You were in my pocket trying to steal my fucking money!" At first I thought it was a joke, that he was just having a laugh. Why on earth would I steal from him? I'd given him free accommodation and he was living in my flat. Everyone else seemed to think he was joking too. So it was totally unexpected when he punched me full on the face and began raining down blows on me. As my legs gave way I fell onto my back. Before I knew it he was sitting on my chest and I was trying to ward off the punches. I could hear the girls screaming and shouting at Mark, trying to drag him off, but I was trapped under his weight and couldn't get up.

Whether Mark's attack had been premeditated or the result of drunken paranoia and confusion, I never did find out. He was certainly aware that I didn't like him staying at my flat and that I wanted Gerry and him to leave. Could it have been the alcohol that brought to surface the simmering resentment he felt? Whatever it was, his next move was to have grave consequences for both of us. He kneeled on my arms, trapping them, then dug his thumbs into my eye sockets with all his weight. I was blinded, and all I could hear was the screaming of the girls while I was being crushed by the dead weight of his eighteen-stone frame on my chest. I tried to move my head to the side but his hands moved with me and I began panicking. He was trying to gouge my fucking eyes out! It could only have been a few seconds but it seemed like much longer, and my panic caused a huge surge of adrenalin. I bucked my body and tried desperately to heave myself up from the pavement. I reached out my right hand, desperately trying to get a hold on the railings to give me some leverage, but instead I felt a pint glass. It was instinctive; I swung the glass with all my strength towards where I thought Mark's face was, and heard a sickening smash. I felt pieces of broken glass falling on to my face and liquid which I could smell was beer. Suddenly my eyesight returned as he removed his thumbs from my eyes, and the lights from the traffic and the street lights illuminated the scene in front of me.

Mark clutched his hands to his face. A huge ragged flap of skin had opened up on his forehead and blood was flowing freely from the wound. I pushed up as hard I could and finally toppled Mark off me. Once back on my feet, in panic, I began to kick and punch him. By this time he was on his knees, trying to stem the flow of blood from his head. In my adrenaline-fuelled fear and anxiety, I didn't stop attacking him until he was unconscious.

By this time the girls were trying to pull me away from Mark. Gerry had sat down next to Mark on the pavement and was trying to stem the flow of blood from his head. Meanwhile we had attracted a crowd of people who had come running out of the nearby kebab shop to see what the commotion was. Mig and Francis grabbed me and pulled me away from the scene and around a corner.

"You have to get out of here, Ally. The pigs will be here any minute." I nodded.

"Make sure you get him an ambulance, okay?" I said. They both said they would make sure he was all right.

"Don't worry, he won't tell the cops anything. You just need to disappear before they get here. Now fucking run!"

So, I did. Just like the time after I'd attacked my dad back in the Vale, I was in a panic. I just ran blindly with no planned destination. It must have been an hour or so later by the time I finally stopped. I didn't know where I was. Somewhere in Chiswick was my best guess. I sat in a shop doorway and tried to calm down and gather myself.

Once I'd forced myself to sit still for a while, my heart rate dropped, my head cleared and I finally started to think rationally. It had already been well over an hour since my fight with Mark. The ambulance would have taken him to the A&E department at Charing Cross Hospital. I felt a strong urge to go and see him, to see how badly he was hurt. There had been a lot of blood; I was drenched in it myself. But I didn't even know where I was, and the tube trains had already stopped running because it was so late. I decided to hail a black cab. I shouted at the next one I saw and held out my arm. It stopped, but instead of climbing straight into the back of the cab I went to the driver's window.

"I need to get to Charing Cross Hospital. I've got no money, would you be able to take me?" God knows what the cabbie must have thought of me, standing there in the early hours of the morning soaked in blood.

"Yeah, come on mate. Jump in," he said. He drove me straight to the hospital, dropped me off and then drove off without any further questions.

It was about three o'clock when I entered the Charing Cross A&E department. I half-expected to see Gerry sitting there in the waiting room. I was hoping he would be able to tell me how bad Mark's injuries were. But the waiting area was empty, so I went to the receptionist and told her who I was looking for. I said I was a relative and that I'd heard Mark might have been brought in after a fight. The next thing I knew, I felt a heavy hand on my shoulder and a voice from behind.

"You're nicked!" the voice shouted. It felt like a scene from The Sweeney, which was a really popular TV show at the time. In a slightly surreal example of life reflecting art, it seemed that every cop in London had modelled themselves on the Flying Squad officers that were portrayed in The Sweeney. I swung round and pushed the arm away from me. The skinny young cop who had been behind me fell over on his arse in surprise. Before he was able to stand up, a middle-aged man in a scruffy grey suit had got up right in front of me, and in a calm voice with a Glasgow accent, two inches from my nose, said: "It's okay Ally, everything's fine, but you're under arrest."

And so I first met Detective Constable Jim Kinloch. Jim was a Glaswegian who had transferred to London's Metropolitan Police several years earlier. I didn't previously know Jim, but I would later find out that we had many mutual acquaintances from back home, on both sides of the tracks. Jim asked me to go back to Hammersmith Police Station with him to try and sort things out. He didn't try to put handcuffs on me, so I agreed.

Back at the station, Jim told me that I was to be charged with Grievous Bodily Harm Section 18, In England and Wales there are two levels of GBH, Section 18 and Section 20. Section 18 is the most serious form of assault (short of attempted murder) and carries a maximum sentence of life imprisonment. Section 20, on the other hand, implies a lack of intent and carries a maximum 5-year sentence.

Jim informed me that Mark was badly injured and that I should make a statement. Of course I denied any knowledge of what had happened to Mark, saying only that I'd heard he'd been in a fight. I was confident that neither Mark nor Gerry would offer any evidence to the police. That was the way it had always been back in the Vale.

And so, for the first time in my life (but not the last), I was put in a cell for the night. Jim told me he would interview me again later in the morning. By this time I was exhausted after everything that had happened, so I tried to get my head down for some sleep. But before I could, Jim told me the police doctor needed to check me. I was covered in blood after all. So I sat up and waited for the doctor to arrive. Nothing could have prepared me for what happened next.

Half an hour later, it was with utter horror as I looked up at the doctor as he entered the cell. It was Dr Moor! My own GP, who I was due to see a few days later to talk about NHS treatment and a referral for sex change surgery. I was stunned and mortified to meet him again in these circumstances. To his credit, Dr Moor was the consummate professional. He cleaned me up, noting that I had no wounds other than two badly bruised eyes. He also took a blood sample to determine my blood alcohol level, then left without any reference to our previous meeting.

I was in despair at seeing Dr Moor like this. His face had brought everything back to me; how much progress towards transition I had lost since Gerry, and then Mark, had turned up at my door. He must think I'm just just a violent yob and that everything I'd told him in his surgery was nonsense. I was gutted as I sat there alone in the cell. But just when I thought things couldn't get any worse, DC Jim Kinloch pulled down the flap in the cell door.

"My shift has finished so I'm off home now," he said. "I thought I should tell you before I leave that Mark has died of his injuries. I'll see you later tomorrow for an interview, so try and get some sleep." The flap banged shut and I heard his footsteps disappear up the corridor. Fucking hell.

It was a long night for me after receiving that information. I didn't sleep a wink. This is it, I thought. In a few hours' time, I'm going to be charged with murder, or manslaughter at the very least.

At around lunchtime the next day, the flap of the cell opened again. I saw Jim peering through at me. "Do you want a cuppa and a fag?" he asked. "Come and have a chat with me. I'll take a statement and we'll take it from there."

Soon I was sitting in an interview room with Jim and the young PC who had fallen over when I'd pushed him at the hospital. "Okay, why don't you start by telling me your movements from yesterday between eight PM and when I arrested you at the hospital?" I told Jim I would not speak without a lawyer present. Jim sighed. "There's no need for a lawyer today. You can see your lawyer on Monday." I remained silent.

Jim sighed again, then he read from the charge sheet. "You have been charged with Grievous Bodily Harm, Section 18; specifically, that you maliciously wounded the said complainant, Mark Thompson, on the night in question between the hours of eleven PM and twelve AM on Hammersmith Broadway. Do you have any response?" I gave none, though I did note that there was a 'complainant'. That meant that someone had made a statement against me, and that someone could only have been Mark. Jim noted down my non-response, then he said something that really surprised me.

"I'm releasing you on police bail. You will attend West London Magistrates' Court at nine o'clock on Monday morning for a committal hearing. This will go to Crown Court, unless you plead guilty at that hearing. You will then return to this police station next Friday at three thirty PM, and then on each subsequent Friday at the same time until a trial date has been set. Do you understand?" I nodded. "Right, sign here and then you can go. There are some people waiting for you outside."

Now I was really confused. What happened to the murder charge? But Jim just stood up, turned off the tape recorder and handed me the bail sheets and court paperwork.

"How is Mark?" I asked. Jim just smiled.

"He's not a pretty sight; he certainly won't be winning any beauty contests for a while." I stared at him blankly. Had I dreamt what Jim had said to me through the hatch?

"I thought you told me he had died?" Jim laughed.

"Oh that was just my little joke. You didn't believe me, did you?" Jim was still laughing as he opened the interview room and led me through to the front desk of the station. "Right, Ally. Just behave yourself and make sure you show up at court on Monday. You've been lucky this time; you're also lucky I didn't charge you with assaulting a police officer, too." He nodded towards the young constable who was looking on sheepishly.

I went through the door and into the waiting area, where I saw Jimmy, Robbie and Mig. They had been waiting all morning for me at the station, demanding to see me. I was pleased to see some friendly faces. Word had spread that I'd been arrested at Charing Cross Hospital the night before, and a cop had told Jimmy that I was being detained at Hammersmith Police Station. Jimmy and Robbie had tried to visit Mark at the hospital to see what was happening, but he had refused to see anyone. So they came down to the station with Mig to insist I had a lawyer.

I told Jimmy and Robbie that I'd been charged with GBH and that a statement had been given against me. They knew as well as I did that only Mark could have given the statement. We decided we had to get back to my flat right away to see if he or Gerry were there. When we got to the flat, we found that it had been stripped bare of any trace of them. It turned out that Mark had discharged himself from hospital early in the morning and had gone back to my flat with Gerry. They had just grabbed all their belongings and left London. They both knew they wouldn't be safe in Hammersmith once word got out that Mark had grassed to the police. What I still couldn't understand is why Mark had made the statement. Jimmy said that maybe the cops had offered him something to testify against me. It later transpired that Jimmy was correct.

I had missed my Saturday morning shift at the building site, and by now it was too late to go and see the foreman. They were very strict about attendance and punctuality. It was a decent wage and cash in hand, but if you didn't turn up for even one day, without a very good reason, then you usually weren't welcome back. I would also miss Monday morning because of my court appearance. Now, not only was I facing a GBH charge, but I was also almost certainly unemployed too. What a complete and utter fuck-up.

Mig suggested we go to the pub and at least celebrate my release. I'd first met her a few weeks earlier. She had a Scottish accent but had actually been born and brought up in Corby. Her family had been part of the migration of Scottish steelworkers to the Northamptonshire town that had been going on since the

1930s. She had been in The George pub, playing pool with her Irish friend Martina and an older English man called Ted who never spoke much.

I really enjoyed Mig's company. She was wild and carefree, with long blond hair and a pretty face. She was a few years older than me but had decided to take me under her wing. That night after my release from the police station she insisted I go back with her to where she was living in Richmond. I was happy to go along, I didn't feel good about going back to my empty flat after everything that had happened.

"But what about Ted?" I asked.

"Don't worry about him, he's not my boyfriend. He just lets Martina and me live with him." It was true, Ted made no claim on Mig. And so we went back to Richmond later that night to Ted's place. It was a beautiful large house near Richmond Park. I never did get to the bottom of the arrangement between Mig, Martina and Ted, but he was happy for them to live there rent-free, and was also happy for me to stay over whenever I wanted. Ted was an accountant and seemed to earn a lot of money. He was very generous to everyone, including a couple of smack heads staying in one of the rooms. That was where I first tried injecting heroin, but it didn't do much for me. In fact, I felt awful and vomited. So, like cocaine, it seemed I wasn't susceptible to that particular vice either. I was relieved, to be honest; I already had enough issues to deal with, without also throwing hard drugs into the mix.

I spent the night in Mig's bed, with Robbie and Martina in another bed in the same room. She tried to make love to me, but as usual, I wasn't very receptive to sex. We cuddled instead, then at one point during the night she left and got into bed with Robbie as Martina slept. She came back later and we cuddled again and fell asleep. It might sound odd, but she was the perfect girlfriend for me at that time. We got on really well and were very close. But if she needed sex she went elsewhere and neither of us complained. She always came back to me, and we were together that whole summer.

On the Monday morning I was at West London Magistrates' Court at nine o'clock sharp, together with Mig and Robbie. Jimmy had got me a lawyer on legal aid from Davis Hanson. I asked him what kind of prison term I could expect if found guilty. He told me that GBH could mean anything up to a life sentence, but in my case, he would expect three to five years. I wasn't exactly encouraged. However, this was only a magistrates' hearing and the police didn't object to bail. I was free to go until the trial, which would be fixed at a later date and was likely to be several months later. In the event it would be ten months later.

* * * * * * *

After the hearing I went straight to the building site to see if I still had a job. I didn't. As I said, there were rarely any second chances on that site if you missed a shift, and I'd missed two. It was what I expected.

So, I'd really messed up. A friend from the Vale had had his face sliced open by my handiwork, and now I was facing a long prison term. On top of that I'd lost my job, which meant I couldn't pay my rent. But most of all I'd lost my transition. I had completely wrecked my plans and I felt I had little more left to lose. I was at rock bottom. Fuck it, I thought to myself. I had my death wish back. Bring on oblivion – time to party!

I went back to my flat, packed a bag and left. I didn't really have a plan as to where I'd go. Maybe I'd stay at Ted's, or at a friend's flat, or else I'd just sleep rough in the park. Robbie felt the same so we teamed up. We got to know all the hostels in West London and occasionally we went up to the city and stayed at the Centrepoint hostel. If we had enough spare money we occasionally booked into Terry's Hotel just off Hammersmith Broadway, which was more like a boarding house. It was in 'Terry's' that I first got to know Hammy.

* * * * * * *

Hammy was like the daddy of Hammersmith Broadway. He was in his fifties, grey-haired and scar-faced. Originally from the East End of Glasgow, he had been in London since the 1960's and everyone respected him.

Soon after meeting Hammy, he asked Robbie and me to deal with an Australian guy in the next room to his, who was becoming a nuisance, begging for money and making too much noise late at night.

"No one really knows him," Hammy explained, "and I don't trust him, so just make him leave!" Hammy was so highly regarded in West London that if he asked you for a favour, it was generally a good idea to agree. It was far better to have Hammy as a friend than an enemy.

The next morning, Robbie and I kicked in the noisy neighbour's door and burst into his room while he was still in bed. We told him to pack his bags because he was leaving. He seemed to think we were joking, so Robbie pulled out a knife and began playing with it. I had a meat cleaver, which I made sure he could see. "It's time to go, mate," Robbie said with a smile. The guy began to protest, still not understanding the seriousness of the situation. I knew Robbie had a short fuse when he felt he was being disrespected. I reached down and grabbed the guy by the hair and began pulling him out of bed, hoping to persuade him to leave without any further fuss, but he pushed me off and jumped up on the bed, standing in his Y-fronts, ready to fight. The scene was almost comical.

The next I knew, something flashed past me and struck the guy in the face. Robbie had thrown his knife at him. He soon followed up and grabbed the poor guy by the throat with one hand while he punched him with the other. There was a bleeding wound next to his eye, and the sight of his own blood finally convinced the guy that we were serious. We bundled him out of the door and he took off down the corridor and out onto the street, never to be seen again. Hammy was appreciative.

The summer of 1981 is still remembered today for the riots that took place in cities and towns across England. Unemployment had reached levels not seen since the 1930s and racial tensions were as bad as they had been in years. In a speech that year, Enoch Powell warned of an impending 'racial civil war', and the Brixton riots took place the following month, followed within a few months by similar disturbances across England. The whole country seemed to be slipping into anarchy and I actually embraced it. For me, most of that summer passed by in a haze of alcohol and drugs. We made money by any means possible to keep the party going. After the first week I didn't bother checking in at the police station, as my bail conditions required. So now I was officially on the run from the police.

* * * * * * *

One way to make money was the pool hustle Robbie and I used. He was a very good player and we would enter a random West End tourist pub separately as strangers. I'd get on the pool table and at some point Robbie would challenge me to a game for ten pounds. He would let me beat him quite easily, then he'd up the bet to twenty quid and I'd beat him again, then again. Eventually I'd say I didn't want to take any more of his money so I'd sit down with a drink. Robbie would then appear to be desperate to win back some money, so he would challenge anyone else in the bar. By playing it carefully and looking like a very average player, he'd win and lose a few more twenty-quid games, before ramping it up to a hundred a game. Then he would turn it on and easily beat two or three punters and walk out with the cash. It wasn't subtle, and on more than a few occasions people would figure out what we were up to. If things turned ugly we'd simply fight our way out of the pub. Neither of us feared a fight. So long as we kept the money, it was just an occupational hazard.

We also worked if there construction jobs going for cash in hand. At that time there were countless small building firms renovating properties all over London. It was easy to get a few days' work here and there to tide us over. And as soon as we got some cash together we would jack in the job and go out clubbing with Mig and Martina or whoever else was around. Big Paul Boosh Boosh would let us into the fancy Chelsea nightclub where he worked for free, and there we would simply steal drinks off the bar or tables. If anyone objected we'd just face them down. No one wanted to fight with a couple of Scottish nutters. We felt invincible.

Sometimes we ran out of luck and would wake up in some strange flat or squat, absolutely skint. That was when Andy's Cafe on Shepherd's Bush Road came in handy. Andy was an old cockney, and had apparently been a bit of a gangster in his younger days. He let us run a 'tick list', which meant we could eat there all week and pay him at the weekend. He must have been feeding half of Hammersmith, but he never wrote down what was owed; he kept it all in his head and knew to the penny what the tally was.

Andy's Cafe was where I met another of the many colourful characters from that period in my life, Jacky. He was the only person I've ever known who had a receipt for every item in his house, just in case the police came calling. One of the best shoplifters in London, Jacky once stole a crystal fish fountain from the centre of a display in Harrods, just to prove that he could. Another Scot, he was kind to me and also fed me when I was hungry.

Unfortunately Andy's Cafe wasn't open on Sundays, so then we'd go to the nuns' convent along from Hammersmith Broadway. The convent had a heavy wooden door with a hatch that opened right up onto the street. We'd ring the bell and one of the sisters would open the hatch. We'd explain that we were good Catholics down on our luck and the nuns would pass us, through the hatch, a free packed lunch of sandwiches, a drink, and fruit.

During that summer of 1981 I tried to put my transition and my transsexual feelings completely out of my mind with the help of alcohol and drugs. But there were at least a couple of occasions when they came right back to me. Once evening when we had ventured up the West End to look for a bar with a pool table to hustle. We walked through the crowds of tourists on Leicester Square and I noticed a black transwoman. She was about twenty years old, dressed in a short white skirt with a red blouse and sandals, pulling along a tartan shopping trolley. I clocked her right away; no one can spot a transwoman quicker than another transwoman. Unfortunately for her, I wasn't the only one who spotted her. A group of drunken young lads were teasing her, asking for a kiss and laughing at her. They crowded around her and wouldn't let her pass. They tried to pull her hair off, thinking it was a wig. This scene had of course attracted a lot of attention from the tourists, and soon there were dozens of people gathered round to watch the sport. The transwoman tried to maintain her dignity and walk away, but they wouldn't allow her. She threatened to get the police but it made no difference and the torment continued. Then, a police van did arrive, alerted by all the commotion. I watched in interest to see what would happen, but as I feared, the police predictably went straight for the transwoman and ignored her abusers. She tried to explain what had happened but before she had a chance she was pushed face down to the ground. Her wrists were cuffed behind her back, and her ankles were also cuffed together. Then they attached another pair of handcuffs between her legs and wrist and left her hog tied on her face with her skirt up around her waist, as the crowd jeered and laughed at her. The cops left the poor woman like that for at least five minutes while one spoke into his radio, then they lifted her into the back of the van like a sack of potatoes and threw her shopping trolley in after her, slammed the door closed and drove away. I was sickened and angry, watching the reaction of the crowd and the police. How could they be so cruel? And why hadn't I tried to help her?

On another occasion, I was at Charing Cross Hospital A&E. One of the contractors Robbie and I worked for had fallen through the floor of a building we were demolishing. He was injured, but not badly; at least, not so badly that he couldn't open his wallet and pay us, so six or seven of us followed him to hospital to make sure he didn't forget. As we arrived I looked around for a public phone so I could call head office and tell them what had happened. I saw a girl with long auburn hair sitting at a waiting area and approached her to ask if she knew where a phone box was. As soon as she turned to me I knew she was transsexual. I was a bit wary of what the group of guys who were with me might say if they noticed. She politely told me where the phone was and I thanked her. I turned around but no one else in our group seemed to be aware of anything unusual. I smiled at her, desperately wanting to sit and talk for a while. Of course, now I understand that would have been the last thing she needed! But, I did learn something: I realised it was just me being hyper-sensitive to her situation, something that would help me later on and prevent my own paranoia about being 'read' getting out of hand. I didn't know it on that day, but I was to return to Charing Cross hospital a few years later, as a patient in the Gender Identity Clinic.

Before long, I received a warning from Hammy. He told me that he liked me, and he liked Robbie, but together we were too dangerous for each other. He said we should split up or we were going to end up killing someone. Coming from Hammy this made me think seriously. He had been a razor man with a South London gang when he was younger. Before that, he had chased wars, starting with World War II as an underage British Army recruit. After seeing so much carnage at an early age, he seemed to have acquired a taste for it that he couldn't live without. In the 1950s he went to Canada so he could take part in the Korean War. And when that ended he went to Australia to sign up for the Australian Army and served in Vietnam.

Since then, Hammy just seemed to take his own personal war around with him. He was afraid of nothing and no one, and his exploits were legendary. But, strangely, a nicer man than Hammy you couldn't meet; he cared for everyone in the Broadway community, gave money and help to anyone who needed it. I still don't know why, but he later took me under his wing, protected me and even gave me a home when I needed one. But the warning he gave me was probably well-judged. He also warned me that Hammersmith Police had been going round the pubs looking for me and asking questions. There was now a warrant out for my arrest as I'd jumped bail. Hammy suggested I should either hand myself in, or else get out of the area for a while. I chose to leave, and since Robbie also had a warrant out for his arrest, he decided to come with me.

* * * * * * *

We left London by way of the M4 motorway, hitch-hiking with backpacks. We had hardly got more than a few miles past Heathrow Airport when a police car pulled up beside us on the hard shoulder. A burly policeman wound down his window and peered suspiciously at Robbie and me.

"Where are you boys going?" he eventually asked. My heart sank. Caught at the first hurdle. We knew there were arrest warrants out for both of us. Robbie was cool under pressure, as usual.

"We're hitch-hiking to Bristol to visit friends" The cop looked at us doubtfully. We hardly looked like your typical outdoor, tourist types. When you're wanted by the police, you soon learn that you give off a scent, no matter how casual or indifferent you try to act. There's something about a fugitive that police have a sixth sense about. This cop knew something was suspicious, but he wasn't sure what it was. Perhaps he thought we were just carrying a bit of weed in our bags. He decided to take it to the next step, getting out of the car. His fellow officer stayed inside.

"Names, addresses, dates of birth," he barked. I'd learned long before that it's usually best to provide at least partial truthful answers to the police. It usually satisfied them to know who we are, and if we were providing this information willingly and honestly, then they would probably assume we had nothing to hide and would hopefully pursue the matter no further. Why would a fugitive from the law stand there, bold as brass, and provide details of their identity?

We gave him the honest answers. If things looked like turning bad for us then I was ready to make my escape. No cop would keep up with me if I decided to run. The answers we supplied were processed through the police radio, by the officer in the car. After a few minutes the burly cop turned back to us, this time speaking in a much friendlier manner.

"You know you really shouldn't be hitch-hiking on the motorway. It's dangerous, not to mention technically illegal." We expressed our surprise, grateful for this insight and thanked the officer for his words of wisdom. "Get in the back of the car, I'll take you to a safer spot where you can hitch a lift more easily," he said. Oh shit, I thought, is this a double bluff? If we refuse he'll have grounds to renew his original suspicion. But if we get in, as trusting genuine hitch-hikers with nothing to hide, he'll have us trapped. And he may really know that we're on the run.

I looked at Rob and we communicated to each other without saying a word. Let's go with the flow and take our chances. We climbed into the back seat of the police car.

As we sped along the M4 it soon became clear the cops had believed our story. We relaxed, chatted and laughed. Soon we turned off at a roundabout and the car stopped. The burly cop leaned over the back seat pointing to a spot on the slip road. "You will have a good chance of a lift here," he said with a smile. He got out and opened the back door for us, made sure we were safely on to the grass verge with our bags, and bade us good luck. Rob and I were still slightly shaken as the car sped off. We grinned at each other with relief. That was too close for comfort!

That incident with the police was to be repeated with variations several times in the weeks ahead. With national warrants out for the immediate arrest of both Rob and me, it's difficult to fathom how we managed to evade capture, without really even trying. Sometimes even with the help of the police.

We travelled to Bristol, our first stop. On our first night we looked for a pub in the city centre with a pool table to try our hustle, but there were no takers. Bristol didn't have gullible tourists with plenty of money to spend, like London did. So we gave up on that idea and instead went looking for some hash. We couldn't find anyone selling; perhaps understandably, since we were strangers there.

Eventually we were directed to St Paul's district. As we walked into the council estate area it became noticeable that almost everyone on the streets was black. In fact the further we went, the more obvious it became that we were very out of place as two young white guys. People were hanging out of windows to stare at us. We eventually found a pub that was buzzing with music, and went in for a drink. After a bit of a stand-off we got into conversation with a few people and discovered that the locals were wary of us because they thought we might be plain-clothed cops. In April 1980, the previous year, there had been riots in St Paul's and there was still a lot of suspicion in the air. However, once we had purchased a bag of weed and began smoking it we seemed to get accepted. I think the Scottish accents probably helped, too.

Later on when the pub closed we were invited to a 'Blues'. It was in a community centre, everyone was very friendly and it turned into a great night. There was a DJ and a band playing everything from reggae to gospel music. Bottles of rum were on every table, and we danced and sang along with everyone else. It was a great atmosphere and it made me realise that the West Indian communities were not so different from the Scots or Irish. By the end of the night, when everyone was leaving at around three AM, the older guys who seemed to be in charge asked us where we were staying, because it was time to close up the centre. When we told them we had nowhere to go, they told us to just sleep there and let ourselves out in the morning. Such trust and friendliness from complete strangers!

We ended up staying in Bristol for only a week. After finding a cheap boarding house on Coronation Road, we explored the city. However, it soon became clear that we would struggle to earn any money. There were few building sites that were taking on casual labourers, so we decided to move on. We decided on Liverpool as our next destination. I had an idea that we could take a ferry to the Isle of Man and perhaps find some work in the hotels and bars during the summer season. Also, I had an aunt and uncle, Jessie and Jim, who owned a small hotel there. Maybe they could help us find our feet.

We hitched up the M6 to Liverpool to catch the ferry, but unfortunately arrived too late that day and missed the last sailing. Our only option seemed to be to sleep outside the closed terminal and wait for the first crossing in the morning. So we settled down in the darkness with some cans of beer and a bit of weed to smoke. As the night went on we could see shapes moving all around us. We appeared to be surrounded by people who seemed to be getting closer and closer, like a pack of wolves. It was getting quite disconcerting, and we shouted out to the shapes but received no reply.

Suddenly, out of nowhere, a police car turned up, blue lights flashing. It stopped next to us and two cops got out with torches. We were asked the usual questions: name, address, what are you doing here at this time of night? I explained that we'd missed the ferry, and we gave them our names. We fully expected to be arrested on the outstanding warrants. Weirdly though, once again, we got lucky. The cops told us the terminal area was dangerous at night since there were a lot of junkies and homeless people hanging around and they would rob us as soon as we fell asleep. They told us to get in the car and they would take us somewhere safer, which turned out to be the Salvation Army hostel. That was twice so far that our luck had held out and we'd managed to avoid being arrested.

After a decent night's sleep in the hostel, we made our way down to the docks the next morning and caught the ferry to the Isle of Man. During the crossing Robbie and I talked and laughed about the lucky escapes we'd had. We were amazed at the charmed lives we seemed to be living.

As the ferry docked at Douglas we were still on a high from the good fortune we'd enjoyed so far, and we were laughing and joking and in high spirits as we went through the terminal. We felt invincible, as though nothing could touch us. But then, two men in plain clothes approached as, obviously police. Shit, I thought, it was too good to last.

The cops led us into a side room and locked the door. Then it was the old routine. They asked for our names and addresses, and the purpose of our visit to Douglas. I thought this time we're done for. These weren't uniformed cops; these guys seemed far more serious and business-like. As they went off to check out our story, I busily stuffed cigarettes and matches down my socks and discarded a small amount of weed, preparing for a possible search and detention. When one of them came back to keep an eye on us I had a sudden brainwave. I told him who my uncle was and the hotel he owned. I said we were going to work there for the summer, and that he could check that out if he wanted. Not surprisingly in such a small community, the cop actually knew my uncle. He seemed surprised, then went off to make a phone call to verify my story.

"Your uncle has no idea you were coming here, does he?" Robbie asked, clearly worried. "He'll deny all knowledge, then we're fucked." I said let's just wait and see. A few minutes later the cops came back and now they were much friendlier.

"I've just spoken to your Uncle Jim. He said he's expecting you." I turned to Robbie and smiled. Three times lucky! We were soon released and walking along the seafront to Uncle Jim's hotel.

Jim and Jessie seemed surprised, if not exactly pleased, to see us when we arrived at the hotel. Jim had been canny enough to realise that we'd been detained on suspicion by the cops, so he went along with the story he'd assumed we'd given. It was the first time in years I'd seen them both, and it was to be the last time. But thankfully family ties were important, and they saved us that day.

Just as we had done in Bristol, we only stayed in Douglas for a week. It turned out all the seasonal jobs had been taken a long time ago and there wasn't much chance of making any money. So, after enjoying the hospitality of my aunt and uncle long enough, I didn't want to abuse the situation by taking up a room they would otherwise have let to tourists. We said our goodbyes and caught the ferry off the island to Ardrossan in Scotland. I'd decided I was going home to the Vale with Robbie. There we would find out the situation regarding the statement Mark had made to the police. And if possible, we might perhaps persuade him that it would be a good idea to withdraw it.

I thought we'd surprise my parents, so Robbie and I arrived at their house without warning. We were welcomed in. I hadn't seen them for a year and we had a lot to catch up on. Out came the whisky bottle, as usual, and we all got drunk as we caught up on the news.

I told my dad that Robbie was going to go see Mark, to talk about his statement. I couldn't go as I'd be accused of interfering with a witness. Meanwhile I'd round up my old gang and let them know what had happened with Gerry and Mark, since once word got out they had grassed to the police, they wouldn't be safe in the Vale either.

I was quickly right back in the thick of things. It was as though I'd never spent a year away. I was thinking and acting just like a gang member again. My plan was that if Robbie couldn't persuade Mark to drop his statement, then I'd gather my old team together and we would make sure he didn't turn up for the court hearing, one way or another. However, there was a problem.

My dad told us we couldn't go anywhere near Mark. Apparently, when Dad had found out about the fight and the police statement, he had gone to visit Mark himself. He had waited in his car outside Mark's house until he saw him leave, then he'd followed him and persuaded him to get in the car, then took him to a local pub for a drink. During their conversation Mark admitted that he'd been promised criminal injuries compensation if I was convicted. Just as Jimmy had predicted back in London, it was basically a bribe from the police to ensure he testified against me, and Mark had taken the bait. Nothing my dad said would make him change his mind. Eventually my dad gave up, left Mark in the pub and drove home. But as he arrived back at the house he was met by a patrol car and several policemen who arrested him for kidnapping a witness and trying to pervert the course of justice. It was ludicrous, but Mark's family had seen him get into my dad's car and called the cops. They kept my dad in the station all day until Mark finally arrived home drunk later that night and confirmed that he hadn't been kidnapped. Dad had been lucky, but the upshot of all this was that it would be impossible for Robbie or me to get anywhere near Mark since he was now being protected.

On reflection, I'm glad I didn't see Mark on that visit, because I was so out of my mind with the loss of my transition and the confusion and madness of testosterone and alcohol, that with Robbie at my side I'd have probably killed him if we'd met.

Robbie and I decided to return to London a few days later. There was nothing for me in the Vale. I'd met up with a few old friends and made them promise to put the squeeze on Mark on my behalf. They agreed enthusiastically – no one liked a grass. But we couldn't achieve anything else by staying in Scotland, and besides, I was missing Mig. In the back of my mind I hoped maybe it would all blow over in the coming weeks. We'd been away for a month, and maybe the police weren't actively looking for us any more. That turned out to be wishful thinking.

We arrived back – in London in the middle of the summer of 1981. I was still wary of the warrant out for my arrest, so we decided to avoid Hammersmith and instead arranged to meet up with Mig at The Fox pub in West Kensington. It was great to see her and catch up with all the news. We sat at a table away from the bar but within sight of the door, so I could see who came in. After a few drinks I relaxed. It was Saturday night and the pub was really busy, and everything seemed fine. Towards the end of the night I went to the bar to buy another round of drinks. As I stood with my money out trying to catch the barman's attention I suddenly became aware of someone standing tight up against me on my right. I turned towards the man, and I saw DC Jim Kinloch smiling at me.

"Hi Ally, I've been looking for you. It's lucky I bumped into you, eh?" I looked to my left and there was a tall man in plain clothes pushed up against me on that side, too. He was obviously a cop. "Don't even think of running," Jim said, "my other mate is also right behind you". I could feel someone at my back and realised I was completely boxed in by three cops. What he said next surprised me. "Do you want a drink?" He seemed very relaxed. "Go on, what are you having? I'm having one anyway, then I'm taking you back to the nick, so you might as well." So, I had a pint with three cops pressed against me. It was a bizarre situation. I didn't dare look towards Robbie and Mig in case the cops noticed and grabbed him too. My spell on the run was finally over.

Back at Hammersmith Police Station, Jim asked me where I'd been all this time, and where was Robbie? As usual I had no answer. I declined to make a statement and Jim accepted that. He didn't realise he'd been standing only a few feet away from Robbie back at the pub, and hadn't noticed him.

"Okay, you'll be detained here over the weekend," Jim explained. "And then you'll be taken straight to the magistrates' court on Monday morning. This time the police will be objecting to bail as you absconded and broke the terms of your previous conditions." I resigned myself to being held for the weekend and then likely to be remanded in custody. I'd never been held in detention before, apart from when I'd previously spent the night in the cell. I was gutted.

The following day I lay in the cell reading newspapers and was bored stiff. The cell door flap came down and a cop shouted in: "You have a visitor. Your sister is here from Staines to see you. You've got half an hour." I was bewildered. Carolyn certainly wasn't in Staines; she was in Scotland, so what the hell was going on? I just nodded. A few minutes later the door opened and Mig breezed in with a quiet smile. The penny dropped. She had told them she was my sister and her passable Scottish accent had been enough to convince them. The door banged shut again and we were left alone. We hugged. It transpired that she and Robbie had seen what happened to me the evening before, and had slipped out of the pub. Mig had brought me some money, cigarettes, and food. We sat together and ate. I had a sad feeling this would be the last time I'd ever see her, and that turned out to be correct. It was a melancholic scene as we smoked and held hands. Eventually it was time for her to leave and we kissed full on, much to the surprise of the cop, who must have wondered just how close I was to my sister!

"We'll make sure your lawyer is at court in the morning," she said. Then she was gone.

The next morning I was taken in handcuffs to the court. Upon arriving I was met by two police officers from Shepherd's Bush police station and arrested in the cells. I was told another matter had come up and I was charged, along with Robbie (in his absence) with two further counts of assault on two men. This related to a party we'd been to at an address in White City. I could barely remember the incident but it came as no surprise. We'd been involved in dozens of fights all over London. I just nodded and said I'd be making no statement, and that I'd just go to court.

The hearing was very brief. My lawyer asked for bail but it was denied, as expected. I'd be remanded in custody until the Crown Court trial. Then I was taken back to the cells. Later on that afternoon all remand prisoners were gathered up and put in the 'sweat box' prison transport bus. The bus travelled all over London collecting prisoners from many other courts, and it was early evening before we reached our destination.

It was around seven pm when I arrived at Ashford Youth Remand Centre, an old Victorian prison near Heathrow Airport. I went through reception with the others and was then told to strip and given a quick medical. I was then given a sheet, a blanket, a plastic wash bowl and a large jug with a handle. The jug, it turned out, was for slopping out – the manual removal of urine and faeces from prison cells when they were unlocked each morning. I was then escorted up some stairs to a cell on a wing. The door was open and I walked in.

As soon as the door slammed behind me and the key rattled in the lock, any bravado I'd shown disappeared. Tears streamed down my face and I cried like I had never done before. I could hear moaning and it took me a few minutes to realise it was my own. It was like a dam bursting. I was finally able to look at my situation clearly for the first time in years, rather than through a fog of alcohol and drugs. I couldn't bring myself to lie on the bed, so I just curled up in a ball on the floor and wept for hours. At some point the lights went out and I began to hear other kids crying and sobbing. Some screamed in terror. This seemed to go on all night, or at least until I eventually drifted off to sleep.

* * * * * * *

I spent six weeks on remand in that place, locked up in the cell for twenty-three hours a day. The only time I was allowed out was occasionally for meals, but more often than not they were brought to us. We were supposed to get an hour's exercise every day, which involved walking with hundreds of other boys in the yard, but that rarely happened.

I quickly realised that it wasn't safe to leave the cell anyway, since the yard and dining hall were dangerous places where fights often broke out, and I didn't yet know anyone else in here. To use the toilets we had around ten minutes first thing in the morning during slop-out when forty boys on the wing shared three cubicles (all without doors). Within this short window of time you had to shit, otherwise you had to do it in a bucket inside your cell and live with it until the morning. The slop-out sinks were always blocked so the floor was covered in a lake of urine and shit which you had to wade through. And if you did manage to get a cubicle, there was never any toilet paper. I was told the screws stole it for their own homes.

The whole time I was there I made no friends and spoke to hardly anyone. I felt completely detached from it all. Being completely sober I was looking through clear eyes for once and I realised that I simply didn't understand the male attitudes or reactions to being in this place that most of the other boys shared. Strangely no one really bothered me, and I was generally unnoticed. It was as though they could sense I was different. I was neither accepted nor rejected; I was simply overlooked.

One day the boy in the cell opposite to mine died. His body was taken away in the morning while everyone else was locked down. I never found out why he died, though I overheard others saying it was due to heart failure brought on by fright. It wouldn't have surprised me; it was a scary place. Quite a few of the inmates were mentally ill. It was obvious looking at them, and at night you heard them screaming like caged animals.

If the place sounds barbaric, it was even more so when you remember that everyone in this place was technically innocent. No one had yet been convicted of anything and most of them were young teenagers. But in the short time I was there, I saw many of them turn into hardened thugs. I was struck by the realisation that, far from being rehabilitated by the penal system, these boys were going to be far more of a menace to society when they were eventually released. It was truly awful.

It's difficult to find the words to adequately describe the hell of being in Ashford. The experience was deeply harrowing. The worst aspect of it all, looking back now, was the behaviour of the screws who took great delight in taunting, bullying and physically assaulting what were, after all, just children. Several of these prison officers were sadistic and cruel. They were actually, to my mind, child abusers, there can be no other description of them. Not all the screws joined in with the violence, but in turning a blind eye they were just as guilty by enabling it.

* * * * * * *

It was during my time in Ashford that Prince Charles and Diana were preparing for their show-piece Royal Wedding. Once a week when I was taken back to West London Magistrates' Court for my bail application I would see all the decorations going up and the painters at work through the tiny window of the prisoner transport vehicles. It was surreal watching it all as we drove through the centre of London, being there among it, watching the bunting being hung and the street furniture being painted, but also being a million miles away from it all. When they did get married on 29 July 1981, I never even knew until a few days later when I managed to get hold of an old newspaper. One thing I remember reading was a story saying how everyone in Britain watched the ceremony, even all the prisoners spending time at Her Majesty's prisons. Well, not in Ashford Remand Centre we didn't!

* * * * * * *

One day at court, completely out of the blue, the judge agreed to grant bail, subject to a surety of two thousand pounds, which my dad eventually put up for me. One of the conditions of my bail was that I would live at his address and not return to England until my trial date. I was effectively deported to Scotland. I also learned that day that Robbie had also finally been apprehended and arrested too, for the double assaults. As expected, he had also denied all knowledge of the incidents and was now on remand at a London prison.

Within a few hours of the bail money being put in place, I was out and on a bus back to Glasgow. I felt numb. If that was a taste of prison, then the short sharp shock had been effective. If that had been the end of it, I would probably have willingly faced up to my transsexuality, told my family, and never gotten into any more trouble with the law again. Unfortunately, it was only a temporary reprieve; I was still due back at The Old Bailey for trial, which had been set for May 1982.

For the next ten months I lived in dread of having to return and face trial. I knew I would almost certainly be going to go back to prison; the only question was for how long. Three to five years was what most people thought, including my lawyer.

* * * * * * *

I decided to use the time to try to analyse and understand my feelings. Was I really a transsexual woman? Perhaps I was just gay, or a transvestite? This was before the internet, of course, so to research who or what I was involved reading books. There was very little media coverage of LGBT issues in those days, save for the occasional sensationalised story in the News of The World or other tabloids. In fact, in those days the term 'LGBT' hadn't even been invented. Back then it was just 'LGB', with transsexual people being added in 2004.

I quickly went through everything I could find in the local library in the Vale, but I found little. I then started visiting the Mitchell Library in Glasgow which had a lot more information, but usually only in dry medical textbooks. I needed to speak to someone who felt like I did. But where could I find them?

I decided to approach my GP. My doctor in the Vale was female and had known me since I was born. As I sat explaining my situation to her one afternoon I could see the shock in her face. When I'd finished she was literally speechless. Eventually, she said she had no idea what to do with me. I certainly couldn't have a sex change in Scotland. I sensed she was hoping I'd go away, preferably back to England. Finally, she suggested I see a psychiatrist and told me to wait for a letter in the post. She quickly ushered me out of her room like a bad smell.

I didn't work during that period before my trial. It seemed pointless to start a career in the knowledge that soon I'd be in prison. I stayed mostly sober and completely off drugs and I even began attending night school to try and make up for my wasted school years. I also made sure to avoid the local gangs, and if I went out to socialise it was always on my own in Glasgow city centre.

One day I discovered a gay bar. The Vintners pub was on Clyde Street in Glasgow. I only heard about it by chance one evening as I was having a quiet drink on my own in The Maggie pub on Sauchiehall Street. I overheard some guys talking about walking into this pub, only to discover it was 'full of poofs', much to their amusement. I took note and decided that I must check it out.

It was a few weeks later before I found the opportunity. It was a Saturday night and I walked down to Clyde Street where The Vintners was located. I walked in and the place was booming with disco music. It was very dark and a thick cloud of cigarette smoke hung in the air. The clientele was mostly men and hardly any women. I got myself a drink and sat at the bar to observe. During the evening a few men spoke to me casually but I didn't really engage with them. I felt a bit out of place since everyone else seemed to know each other. Then I saw her, through the smoke. She looked fantastic with long blond hair, a white mini-dress, black tights and heels. I knew instinctively she was trans of some kind. It was amazing just to see this in a Glasgow bar. It's possible after all, I thought to myself. If she can do it, then so could I. I longed to approach her for a chat but she was surrounded by men and seemed so confident. I thought she might just be a drag queen and laugh at me. So, I just watched her from afar.

I never did get to speak to the trans girl in The Vintners. I visited the bar several times over the next months but I saw her only once more. I did make a few other friends there, however.

Chapter 8 'Say Hello Wave Goodbye'

One man in particular, Jim, was always friendly to me and insisted on buying me a drink whenever he saw me. He was much older than me, and while I knew he was gay, he wasn't at all camp. Jim was in his late thirties and very intelligent and thoughtful. He had shoulder-length brown hair and gentle brown eyes. He seemed interested in me but was never too pushy. He introduced me to a few other gay venues, including the Waterloo Bar in Argyle Street. I enjoyed his company, but for quite a while it went no further than that.

Then one night he invited me to meet him at a 'straight' pub in the West End of Glasgow, Tennent's Bar. Without the loud music and the smoky fog of The Vintners, we were able to have a proper conversation. I liked the fact he was just as comfortable in a rough working-class pub as he was in a gay bar. I definitely felt more comfortable away from the overtly camp atmosphere of the 'gay scene'. Jim and I became good friends, and not long after that he became my first boyfriend.

At this time, both my parents were working, and my sister Carolyn had left home, so I had plenty of time on my own to dress as a girl at home and occasionally go out. This was the first time since my London flat that I had really been able to wear what I wanted. I could do it every day, and when my parents went on holiday I was able to dress as female for two weeks without a break.

During this period I also began to analyse how I felt when I dressed as female. When I first started years earlier it had felt exciting. There was always an element of doing something taboo that appealed to my risk-taking nature. I would try on all sorts of outfits and stare at myself in the mirror from different angles, practising different poses and trying to look natural. Being naturally slim, the clothes did hang on me well, except for my lack of breasts. It was much better when I padded a bra with old tights, and after a while I got so used to these 'bumps' in front of me that I hardly noticed them. Now, it wasn't so much a sense of thrill or excitement that I experienced; it just felt right. There was always some sadness, though. I knew I looked okay, but under the clothes and the padding I always knew there was a male body, and I simply didn't want it. I can't say I despised it completely, as some transsexual women do, but it was just incompatible with who I felt I was.

I would stare at my naked reflection in the mirror for hours, trying to see where the boy ended and the girl started. It was weird looking at my body as if it were someone else's. Sometimes I actually admired the lean muscular shape of 'him', but of course, that wasn't really me. So then I disliked me for having this body, but felt sadness that 'he' would have to die for 'her' to live. I also associated all the things that were wrong with my life with 'him', and all the parts that were right were 'her'. This is a very difficult concept to explain, but if you are a transsexual person reading this, maybe you'll have an idea of what I mean. Or maybe not. As I have learned over the years, we're all different.

My main achievement from all this introspection was that it reaffirmed for me one hundred per cent that my gender was not male. I was, as far as I could tell, female. And now I had a boyfriend who treated me as female both socially and sexually. It felt like a comfortable situation when I was with him. I confided in Jim that I wanted to have sex change surgery. His response was casual and offhand. He would smile and tell me I didn't have to do that, and that I should give it more time. Even though I was eighteen by now, he thought I might have a different viewpoint when I was older. He did try to reassure me by telling me he would still love me whatever I decided. His easygoing attitude was definitely what I needed at that time. Jim never pressured me to do or be anything. I also told him I had to face a court case in London for assault and GBH, and that I was probably going to prison. I'm not sure he believed me, but I felt I needed to prepare him for my likely sudden disappearance.

But for now my life was in a kind of suspended animation. I was probably going to prison soon and that was no place for 'her'. It would have to be 'he' who went, and she would have to hide inside his body until I was released. It sounds a little crazy even as I write the words now, but that was the only way I could rationalise what the future held for me. I was still traumatised from the six weeks I'd spent on remand. I regularly had nightmares about it, and I still do even now, from time to time.

As my trial date approached, I became more and more stressed and depressed. I couldn't sleep but I had to face it and get through this part of my life. I had no option but to hide my real self until I was released, whenever that would be.

The way the legal system worked out, I was to go on trial first at the Old Bailey for the double assaults. A further date for trial on the GBH charge would be set later. And so, after my enforced absence from England, I arrived back in London some ten months after my release from Ashford Remand Centre.

My trial began in early May, 1982. The trial itself was all a bit of a blur. I arrived on a Monday morning at court at the appointed time and met my barrister, Ms Peters, for the first time. We met in a side room and discussed the charges and evidence. Ms Peters informed me that Robbie, my co-accused, would be standing in the dock beside me. He had made no statement to the charges except to deny all knowledge of them. He had also decided not to take the stand and give evidence in his own defence, which meant that I would be the only one testifying.

The trial lasted for three days. In my mind it was my fake male persona that was sitting in the dock, while secretly the real female me hid, but she gave me strength to get through whatever happened. Much of the time was taken up by police statements and the evidence of one of the men Robbie and me had allegedly attacked. For some reason, the second alleged victim didn't appear in court, although his evidence was presented by the prosecution.

When it was time for me to take the stand I admitted I knew the location where the assaults had taken place. It was a friend's flat and I had been there many times. I recalled many violent incidents at the flat and I admitted that I had often been involved in fights with various people who had turned up at drug and alcohol-fuelled parties. I also admitted that Robbie and I had sometimes stayed there when we were homeless.

I was asked categorically if I'd attacked the victim. I conceded that I may have, but that I honestly couldn't remember. He was probably just one of many I'd fought with that summer. One thing I did remember, however, was that I'd given him some money and drugs the day after I'd supposedly attacked him. This was confirmed by the victim himself, much to the amusement of the court. The judge pondered why, if he was so terrified of me after the alleged assault, had he been happy to come to me and borrow money and drugs the following day? The reason soon became clear, it transpired that the victim had been found by the police, lying in a park in a state of drug overdose. When he had recovered enough to give a statement, he apparently told them we had forced the drugs on him, to avoid getting prosecuted for possession.

Truth be told, there had been many more incidents in other locations, bars and nightclubs, that I could remember much more accurately, where I'd definitely been involved with violent assaults. I felt if it wasn't this particular case I'd been charged with, it could easily have been many others. I therefore came to terms with the fact that whatever I stood accused of in the Old Bailey that day, I was certainly guilty of much more. But, by this time I was just resigned to accepting my fate and getting the trial over with. I deserved to be punished.

The jury took only a couple of hours to consider the case before returning to find both Robbie and me guilty. Now it was down to the judge's summing up and sentencing decision. To be honest, by this stage I was in a state of apathy, and not really paying attention to the court proceedings. However, when I was told to stand to receive my sentence I distinctively heard the judge say "a term of borstal training". This was unexpected. I'd been given no indication whatsoever that I might be sent to borstal instead of a full adult prison! But, even as I was processing this information, my barrister stood up and interrupted the judge and invited him to deal with the other outstanding charge against me, the GBH on Mark. She explained that, to save the court any more time and public expense, the term at borstal should cover the GBH charge too, if I was prepared to plead guilty to it, there and then. The judge agreed that this made sense and asked if I was willing to enter a guilty plea to the outstanding GBH charge. Ms Peters approached me in the dock and leaned over.

"Take it, take it, this is a really good result for you," she whispered to me while nodding vigorously. I trusted her judgement and agreed. I was to serve a minimum of six months to a maximum of two years. Robbie was given fifteen months in prison (he was too old to be sent to borstal) and we were taken down to the cells.

And so I was sentenced to 'Borstal training', something I was dreading. Named after the original Borstal Prison in the Borstal area of Rochester, Kent, this was a form of youth custody that had been introduced in the late nineteenth century. By the 1980s, however, the borstal system was notorious for its brutality. But, by pleading guilty to the GBH, it at least meant that I had no more outstanding charges against me. I couldn't pretend I didn't deserve it; I'd been going steadily off the rails for years.

Although I was potentially facing up to two years in custody, I was to serve a minimum of 6 months to a maximum two years. The actual length was determined by how well a prisoner (or "trainee" to use the official term) behaved. I never heard of anyone getting freed after only six months, though. A term of eight and a half months was considered standard. In fact you were even given a provisional release date based on that term as soon as you arrived at the borstal. It was then up to you to behave and impress the screws. If you did well you could get several weeks knocked off; but if you were defiant to all discipline, you might end up serving the full two years. Eventually, I would do eight and a half months, with no time added and none knocked off.

There was some flexibility in the system that I benefited from straight away, but I wouldn't know this until later. On the day I was sentenced, I was seen by a member of the prison service who handled the administration process immediately after sentencing. I was interviewed by a kindly middle-aged man in a secure office just off the cells, deep in the bowels of the Old Bailey. He began first off by asking if I could read and write. I replied that I could, then he gave me a few simple literacy tests to check that I was being truthful, which I passed easily.

Then, unexpectedly, he asked me how I felt about my situation. That was the first time I'd ever been asked this question by anyone in the system and it caught me off guard. He also asked about my family, and whether they had been in court. I told him that my dad, Aunt Mamie and Uncle George had been there, but that my mother and sister couldn't be there because they were in Scotland. I told him that the whole family was very supportive. I also said, truthfully, that I was very upset that my actions had caused them so much pain. By this time my eyes were welling up with tears and genuine emotion, but I was determined not to weep openly in front of him because I was scared he would laugh at me, or at least tell the other screws. I remembered I had to keep 'her' hidden, it was 'him' that was sitting here. The officer seemed decent, but I still didn't trust him. However, as we spoke I felt a lot better just to have a civil conversation with someone. He surprised me by asking if I felt uncomfortable or scared around the other prisoners. I told him I didn't, but I'm sure he wasn't convinced of that.

Looking back, I'm also sure that he was probably gay. I think he recognised something in me that was different to the rows of other prisoners waiting outside. Finally, he said goodbye and wished me good luck. I could tell he was sincere. I didn't know it then, but he wrote something in that report of our interview that would prove extremely helpful to me over the next few months. I'll always be thankful to him.

Soon I was back in a six by three feet mustard-coloured Victorian cell as I awaited my transfer to the Borstal Allocation Centre at Rochester. Even in these circumstances, I appreciated the history of this building. How many thousands of people, I wondered, had sat in this same cell over the decades? It must have seen its share of murderers, terrorists, bank robbers, perhaps even Oscar Wilde, I mused.

* * * * * * *

Rochester Borstal Allocation Centre was an old-school penal establishment. It was a Victorian prison built along the same lines as Ashford Remand Centre, with traditional landings, wings and tiny cells. The slop-out system still applied here. After my horror at experiencing six weeks on remand the previous year, I was dreading this. But, actually I was surprised to find out that once I got there, it held no fear for me. I'd been toughened and pre-conditioned to the shock by my time in Ashford. Boys from courts all over the country were sent here to be allocated to the borstal that was deemed most suitable for them, according to their crimes. The age range was wide, from thirteen to twenty-one, which meant there were little children incarcerated alongside grown men.

It was time to keep my head down and my nose clean. I'd made my mind up that it was 'him' that would serve this time, and that I'd hide and protect 'her'. With that mindset, I would take no shit from anyone and could be me again within nine months.

Within a day of arriving at Rochester, during 'association', the time when we were allowed out of our cells to mingle with the other inmates on the ground floor wing, I was approached by a very tall and skinny black afro-Caribbean boy, Mick. He asked me menacingly for some 'burn', the borstal slang word for tobacco. As he leaned over me, a group of his friends crowded round us both in an attempt to intimidate me. I knew I had only one chance to set out my stall. If I caved in now, I knew I'd be taking shit from everyone from that day onwards until my release. I got right in his face and whispered close enough so that only he heard: "You're getting no burn from me. If you want some you'll have to try and fucking take it."

I smiled at Mick, and gave him the 'Glasgow stare' focusing my unblinking eyes directly at the bridge of his nose. He smiled back. We understood each other. He turned to his friends. "He's a fucking mad Jock." He put his arm round my shoulder. "Hey, it's cool, man, what part of Scotland are you from? There's no pressure relax. Do you need anything? Hey Joseph, give Jock a burn," he told one of his friends. Joseph gave me a roll-up cigarette and that was the end of the matter. From that day onwards I was called Jock by everyone, which I didn't mind. But crucially, I never had any more trouble. Mick Camile actually ended up becoming a good friend. He was eventually sent to the same borstal as me and we shared a dorm. He looked fearsome but was actually a pussycat.

The borstal population that I experienced was heavily represented by black boys, most of them from West Indian backgrounds who lived in London. As I mentioned before, I'd had surprisingly little contact with that community, despite living in London. Almost all my friends and the people I'd worked with were Scottish or Irish. I'd discovered over the previous couple of years that a rough Glaswegian accent was often enough to command respect in England, or at least to deflect trouble. Happily, it worked with Mick and his pals.

The discussion among the boys at Rochester was all about where we would be allocated. The borstals to fear were in Portland or Dover, as they were supposed to be particularly brutal. Many of the boys had already served a term of borstal and were back inside again, so they knew the lay of the land. If you had been convicted of violence then you would usually be sent to a closed institution. It's just like it sounds: cells, prison wings and high security fences. Only those who had committed minor crimes of dishonesty, theft and burglary would be allocated to an open borstal, which were far less brutal. Open borstals usually consisted of farms and workshops, the inmates sleep in dormitories and there is no high security fencing. Given my convictions for GBH and assault, I expected the worst.

After a few days I was sent for an interview with the allocation officer. He asked if I would like to be transferred to a Scottish borstal, to make it easier for family visits. He was referring to Polemont, which was notorious as being one of the toughest borstals in Britain. Thanks, but no thanks. I'd take my chances in England where my Glasgow accent would be more useful.

A week or so later a notice was pinned up outside the screws' office with the names of all the boys and where we had been allocated. We all crowded round to look and I saw my name next to 'Gaynes Hall'. I'd never even heard of it! But the other boys congratulated me, saying: "Nice one Jock, you got a result there."

Gaynes Hall, in Cambridgeshire, was an open borstal. Why I had been sent there was a mystery to me, not to mention to the officers at the institution. But, the ways of the British penal system are a mystery never to be challenged nor understood. I firmly believe it was down to the report that followed me from the kindly allocations officer I'd met after my sentencing at the Old Bailey. Gaynes Hall had an education program that was attached to Huntingdon Technical College, and I remembered him advising me that I should complete my education whilst in Borstal, and that he would recommend that I be given the opportunity.

By the time I arrived at Gaynes Hall, I was mentally prepared as to what to expect. In fact I was probably overly aggressive in my determination not to be bullied, and this didn't go unnoticed by my fellow inmates, or 'trainees', as we were officially referred to. It seemed I had already acquired a reputation as someone not to fuck with. As it turned out, this attitude wasn't really necessary. Most of the screws were more like social workers, and most of the other boys were generally kids convicted of car theft or burglary. I'd arrived there half-expecting to fight my way through the eight and a half months to my target release date. In reality, it was nothing like that. I had no fights at all while in Borstal, and the only law-breaking I was involved in was helping one of the screws steal some coal from the boiler room, for his own home. I was paid with a pack of cigarettes.

When we first arrived at Gaynes Hall, we were given a talk by the governor. "If you ever want to leave," he explained, "the main road is up there, and on either side there are fields. Just keep walking and you're out." There were no walls or fences to keep us in, but we all knew that once out, you were classified as an absconder.

This meant a minimum of six months added to your sentence when you were caught, and you would never be trusted in an open institution again. It was silly to escape, but many boys did. They just walked away and were never seen again.

I was allocated to Arial House, Number One dorm out of three, supposedly the toughest. The other houses were Jupiter and Neptune. Gaynes Hall had been an RAF special operations base base during World War II, and the borstal boys lived in the same semi-cylindrical Nissan huts from that time. We were twenty boys to a hut, ten beds along each side and a boot room at the end. It was cramped inside; you could easily put your arm out and touch the bed of your neighbour.

The borstal ethos was very much military-inspired. Lots of scrubbing of floors and walls, keeping your bed space spotless and arranging your kit for inspection at a moment's notice. It was also based on the group punishment system. If one boy had a speck of dirt on his polished boots that was noticed during inspection by the screws, then we would all suffer. Punishments might include missing TV time or being given a route march. This of course led to self-regulation and bullying among the boys.

On my first day I was shown an iron-frame bed, which was to be my home for the duration. The bed next to mine was occupied by a gentle black kid who had just arrived from Luton. He introduced himself as Alex and he recognised my accent as soon as I spoke, since his mother was from Glasgow. Alex was my closest friend right through my time at Gaynes Hall. On that first day, he offered to be my back-up in any fight, if I would be his. This was not unusual, and a lot of people teamed up together with strangers on their first day in borstal to keep each other safe in what could be an unfamiliar and sometimes hostile environment. It was unusual for that hook-up to last for eight months, but ours did.

The following week Mick, the tall, skinny black guy I'd met previously in Rochester, arrived in our dorm. He was delighted to see me, as all his friends had been sent to other borstals and he was grateful to see a familiar face. He also became a good friend, too. Surprisingly, since I'd had very little contact with that community previously, almost all my close friends in borstal were black. It was good for me to get an insight from these guys about their culture and the racism they experienced. It really opened my eyes.

The next eight months passed really quickly. I entered the education program and completed the business course, which involved double-entry bookkeeping, English, arithmetic and store keeping. The course was designed to enable us to get a job in the stores department of a factory when we left Borstal. Unfortunately, it was all rendered obsolete within a few years by the introduction of computer technology, but I was quite happy at the time; it was certainly better than working with the pigs on the farm.

This was the first time since my six weeks in Ashford remand centre that I hadn't had any opportunity to dress as female. I was curious as to how I would handle it, since I'd been dressing as a girl whenever I'd the opportunity since I was a little kid. Now I had no choice but to spend at least eight months without my female life and clothes. How would I cope? Would it destroy me or kill off my desire to transition? It turned out not to be such a big deal after all. I discovered the female clothes were not as vital to my inner self as I'd believed. They were just an outward expression. In fact, when I finally had a full sex change years later, I would go from wearing jeans and T-shirts pre-op, to wearing jeans and T-shirts, post-op. Same old, same old.

I had cut off all contact with friends and family just prior to my trial. Very few people knew where I was and I wanted no visitors except Aunt Mamie in London. I told everyone to forget about me until I contacted them again. I'd warned my boyfriend Jim that I was going to prison for a while, but I didn't offer too many other details. I fully expected him to move on and find someone else, and that was fair enough. I couldn't expect him to wait for me.

As well as military cleanliness and discipline, physical fitness was encouraged in borstal. We started off with a one-hour induction workout, in the old-fashioned but effective gym, that had many of my fellow inmates collapsing and vomiting. I still remember the five-minute step-up exercise. It sounds easy, but with two twelve-inch steps and no stopping allowed, it was absolutely exhausting. My legs turned to rubber and I couldn't control my breathing as I gasped to get oxygen into my lungs. We weren't allowed to stand still, so this meant continually running on the spot, even as we waited for our turn on the apparatus. There was no fancy modern equipment in the gym. Everything was done by using benches, wall bars and climbing ropes. It was simple but very effective training. At the end of that hour I collapsed along with almost everyone else. I was certain I would have a heart attack. But, being young, I recovered quickly. My first attempt at doing the full gym training circuit took me thirty-five minutes to complete. But within a few months I was going round the same circuit in less than ten minutes, while hardly even breaking sweat. The borstal system might not turn out rehabilitated young men, but if nothing else, they were definitely much fitter and much harder to catch when they went back to crime. It's a sad fact that most of the boys who completed borstal did in fact go straight back to crime. Seven out of ten would reoffend and be reconvicted within a year of being released.

Bullying did exist in the borstal. It was hardly surprising, given that there were kids ranging in age from thirteen to twenty-one living on top of each other. The currency of the borstal, just as in every other prison, was tobacco. And it was usually tobacco that was behind any trouble. The allocation for each inmate was a quarter ounce per week. This meant that if you smoked, you would probably run out of cigarettes halfway through the week. If you've ever tried to stop smoking, you'll know how bad-tempered and angry it can make people. So, the anger and frustration was built into the system and I saw many fights over the theft of a cigarette or simply older kids taking the tobacco from younger ones, and then the revenge attacks. It was all so needless. If the prison authorities had simply allowed the inmates to buy whatever tobacco they needed, they could have saved a fortune in smashed-up furniture, court time for violent assaults and hospital care for injured prisoners. It seemed clear to me, though, that there was no joined-up thinking within the British penal system. The often repeated phrase you heard was: 'There's only one rule in prison, and that is that you mustn't break the rules." The fact was, there appeared to be no formal written rules; everything was decided on the whim of an officer or the governor.

As for sexual activity, I saw very little of that in borstal. Of course, no one would dare admit to being gay, or in my case transsexual. A few people were known for being willing to do almost anything for tobacco, including oral sex. But that was seldom spoken about and not considered as 'real' homosexuality, just people getting by. It wasn't unusual for boys to dance together at night in the dorm. The Madness song Baggy Trousers was popular at the time, and everyone joined in when it came on the radio. Several of the screws did take an unhealthy interest in boys showering, and would stand staring at them under the pretext of preventing fights. But on the whole, the borstal officers were far better than the sadists who had been employed at Ashford Remand Centre.

My only personal experience that was in any way close to sexual contact was from Alex. When I came back from the gym and a shower, I would lie on top of my bed face down resting. Alex would sometime ask if I wanted him to rub some of the coconut oil that he used for his afro-style hair, into my back. I really loved that, and he seemed to enjoy it, too. But no one dared suggest we were queer, or nonces. I still think of him every time I smell coconut oil.

I quickly discovered what the term 'nonce' meant in practice. I think it's widely assumed that a 'nonce' in prison slang is a sex offender or queer. The word is thrown around a lot, but actually its use is far more arbitrary in prison, and was generally only applied to those who were physically unable to defend themselves from the charge. A man could be a convicted rapist or child molester, but if he was big and strong enough, he would not be labelled a nonce by the other inmates. Conversely, a weak or scared prisoner might routinely be called a nonce simply because he was unable to defend himself from the charge.

My overwhelming memory of borstal is positive. When not in classes, we spent many hours sunbathing or playing volleyball. We even had a full-size snooker table that we could use most nights when there was a screw available to supervise.

There was also a lot of solidarity among the boys. One time I had my cigarettes stolen from my pocket. It wasn't that surprising, given there were so many pick-pockets serving time. I was pissed off, but had no idea who had done it. When word spread through the dorm, every boy came up to me and gave me one of their own cigarettes. I was really touched.

Another time, one member of our dorm, Smithy, was off work with a rotten cold. The medical officer reluctantly gave him permission to stay in the dorm, but also prescribed no solid food for the day and banned him from the canteen. This was a usual thing with the screws, a crude attempt to discourage any shirking as they saw it. But every one of the boys brought back to the dorm a portion of his own meal to give to Smithy. He ended up with a mountain of food and fruit.

The worst part of the borstal term was the last few weeks. When your release date is months or years away, it's easy to forget about the outside. But once that big day is close, you begin to suffer from 'gate fever'. It happened to everyone. People would start to lose their temper and get moody. It's also a dangerous time because many people lost time for silly incidents, like swearing at a screw, and as a result had their release date pushed back a few weeks.

I was no different. I was desperately watching the days go by on the calendar during the final few weeks. I found myself getting irritable with everyone around me. One day in the classroom, Kular, a boy from Bradford, was teasing me about my accent and trying to copy what I was saying. It was harmless fun, and I liked Kular; in fact we had been friends for months. But for some reason I just flipped and threw a book at him. The heavy hardback smacked him on the forehead, almost knocking him out. His nose started bleeding and the female tutor, who had been bussed in from the local college, went into panic mode and ran out the classroom, fearing a riot. Within minutes several screws came rushing in and grabbed me. I was heading for the block and a governor's report, which probably meant losing some time. But, as I sat outside the governor's office, Kular arrived and sat down next to me.

"Don't worry, I'll tell them it was an accident," he whispered. We were called in to see the governor and Kular repeated his story, saying that he'd asked me to pass him the book and it had accidentally hit his nose. It was just an accident, he said, smiling. Naturally, I agreed. Even the tutor agreed, saying she had panicked when she had seen the blood. The governor looked doubtful but let me go without any punishment.

Finally, my time was up and I was due to be released the following morning. I was taken to the stores and I tried on my own clothes for the first in nearly nine months. Nothing fitted. I'd lost weight and was as lean and fit as I'd ever been. There was a rack of clothes to pick from and I found a pair of trousers and a jacket. I was given a rail warrant for travel to London, and the address of my probation officer. I would be released on licence for one year and would be required to check in every two weeks with the probation service. I was all set. In the morning I'd also be given my resettlement grant, which I think was fifty pounds.

I returned to the dorm for my last night, and all the other boys came up to me one after the other to say goodbye and wish me luck. Some boys from other houses also came across to do the same through the window, since they weren't allowed to enter a different dorm from their own. It was actually quite emotional for me. I'd seen this scene many times before when others had left, and now it was my turn. The tradition was to give each member of the dorm a burn (cigarette) and also give away anything that may be useful, like my radio and my tobacco pouch and lighter. I gave everything to Alex. He was due for release himself a few weeks later, and we promised to keep in touch. Eventually it was time to try and sleep. I doubt if I managed more than an hour, and I was up and ready at five o'clock the next morning. The screw came to collect me at half past seven to take me to my train at St Neots station. I was given my ticket and money, then driven to the station. The screw shook my hand, told me not to come back, and then I was left on my own on the platform.

* * * * * * *

Chapter 9 'Wherever I Lay My Hat' (That's My Home)

The train journey to London was quite disconcerting. Everything seemed so big and fast after being confined in the small borstal community for nine months. Even just seeing female passengers on the train was strange, after spending so long in an almost exclusively male setting.

I decided to go straight to Hammersmith. My probation officer was there, and since that had been my address when I had been arrested almost two years earlier, that was the limit of where my rail warrant could take me. My plan, such as it was, was to try to meet up with an old friend and get word of where there was a job going, or a squat to live in.

I headed for the Broadway. Two years earlier, if I'd stood there for no more than half an hour I'd see dozens of people I knew. But now it all seemed so different. There were lots of people hanging around, and I could hear the same Scots and Irish accents, but I recognised no one. Then I saw Hammy, daddy of the Broadway. Thank god, a familiar face at last! Hammy was standing outside The George pub with a can of Special Brew in his hand.

I rushed over to him. "Hiya Hammy! I just got out this morning. Where is everyone?" I asked. He seemed to take a few moments trying to remember who I was, then it clicked. Hammy shook my hand and offered me a can of beer.

"Where the hell have you been, Ally?" I explained I'd been in Borstal, since he clearly hadn't heard. Why would he know? If you went into prison or borstal you just disappeared, and meanwhile the people hanging around the Broadway were always changing with people coming and going. Life had simply moved on. I told Hammy I needed a place to live. I needed to check in with my probation officer and for that, I needed to provide an address. I only had fifty quid to my name, so not enough for a flat deposit. Hammy suggested I try a squat he knew about, down on King Street. The squat was run by 'Kojak' and my old friend Francis. They had hooked up together. Kojak was a Belfast man, hard as nails. His head was shaved, hence the nickname. I didn't know him very well, but Francis vouched for me.

The squat off King Street was basic, to say the least. It was an old town house on three floors. It had electricity and running water, but the bathroom had been smashed up by the council's anti-squatter squad. I was told I could move in and have a room on the top floor. It had an old mattress but that was it. Once I was working I was expected to contribute food, booze and drugs to the house. Everything was shared in a communal fashion. I gratefully accepted; it would be a place to sleep until I found a job and was able to save some money for a flat deposit. Then, I figured, I could move out and get my transition back on track.

The next day I went to check in with my probation officer. I told him I was looking for work and would sign on the dole. I had an address at least, which I provided to him. However, he looked concerned when I told him where I was living. "I know that address, it's a squat. You can't live there, you'll be breaching the terms of your licence". I told him it was all I could afford. I had no money until I could find work, so where else could I go? He wasn't interested. He told me I'd need to find a secure address within a week or he would seriously consider having me recalled to borstal.

That night I went looking for Hammy again. I needed advice. I told him about my predicament.

"What can I do?" I asked. Hammy sighed.

"I suppose you'll have to come and live at my place," he replied. It turned out Hammy had recently been given the keys to a council flat. Apparently he'd been on the council waiting list for over ten years and had forgotten all about it, until they sent him a letter with the offer of this flat. He had moved in a few weeks before with his new girlfriend, a Scottish woman called Brenda. I could have one of the bedrooms if I was happy to share the space with Jimmy and Paul Boosh Boosh. He told me that Jimmy and Paul were seldom there because the house was a bit out of the way, so I'd mostly have the room to myself.

"Okay, that's great!" I said with huge relief. "I really appreciate this, Hammy. Thanks mate." Then he told me the bad news.

"The flat's in Catford." I'd never been to Catford. I knew only that it was in South London.

* * * * * * *

I caught the train to Catford that night with Hammy and Brenda. We took an overground British Rail train which seemed to take ages to get there. I didn't know South London very well at all. The flat was on a council estate, a block with a main entrance and stairs up to the second floor, where Hammy and Brenda lived. It wasn't the location I would have chosen, but beggars couldn't be choosers. I had to have some kind of permanent address to keep the probation officer happy.

I'd only met Hammy's girlfriend Brenda for the first time earlier that day. She seemed quite distant, but also extremely volatile, shouting and crying a lot. She was also very drunk. She was about the same age as Hammy but looked older, with unkempt blond hair and ragged clothes. She was more like a homeless bag lady than what I'd have thought was Hammy's idea of a girlfriend. I didn't know it then, but Jimmy told me later that she was actually the alcoholic daughter of a retired senior prison officer who had worked in Barlinnie Prison in Glasgow. This was what had attracted Hammy to her when they had met by chance in a pub in West Kensington. They had got talking, both having recognised each other's Glasgow accent. Hammy was delighted to learn who her father was. Small world; it turned out that he knew, and had a serious grudge against, her father, going back to when he had served time in Barlinnie many years before. He didn't tell her, but he saw Brenda as an opportunity to get back at her father. Hammy didn't share this information with me either, so I had unknowingly wandered in to the middle of his crazy and prolonged plan of revenge.

Right from the start, I didn't feel comfortable in the flat. Brenda clearly had no awareness of what was going on, nor even where we were living. She spent her time drinking from early morning until late at night. She and Hammy would go out to the pubs in Catford, and he would treat her with disdain and open contempt. It was very awkward. She was obviously unwell and would visit the doctor or a chemist almost every day. But she had nowhere else to turn, so she just accepted the abuse.

As it turned out, I had the bedroom to myself. Jimmy and Paul rarely appeared and only used the bedroom to store some clothes and some personal belongings. They preferred to spend most of their time back in Hammersmith. I would have left too, if I could. But I had to maintain a permanent address. So, I decided to stick with it for a while, get a job and try to save enough money for a deposit on a flat.

I managed to find myself a job at Safeways supermarket in Catford. I was working in the warehouse as an Assistant Storekeeper, making use of the qualification I'd picked up in borstal. It was a shirt and tie job, and easy work compared to the building sites, though the money wasn't as good. But at least I was finally earning a living again, making some friends and managing to save a bit of cash. I usually finished work at five o'clock, but I was reluctant to go straight home as the atmosphere in the flat was so toxic. I just kept telling myself it would be worth it in the end. Once I had got some money together I'd be out of there and I could resume my transition. In the meantime I'd try to keep myself to myself.

It was quite noticeable that we were not popular in the area where the flat was. This was a very tight-knit white working-class area, where everyone seemed to know each other and we were outsiders. It was nothing like Hammersmith, where everyone came from somewhere else and people were thrown together in a big melting pot of outsiders. Several times I was stopped in the hallway by neighbours asking us to keep the noise down. Since I wasn't there most of the time, I could only presume they were referring to Hammy and Brenda shouting at each other when I was out at work. People clearly assumed they were my parents.

Another time the police came to the door because of a reported disturbance at a phone box. Hammy managed to get rid of them but then blamed Brenda for causing trouble. I didn't know what that was about, but I learned later that Hammy would call Brenda's father in Glasgow and taunt him, telling him graphically that he was screwing his daughter. It was an evil wind-up and poor Brenda was often in tears when I came home.

Although I'd known Hammy for a few years, I'd never lived with him before. It soon became very uncomfortable, even scary. He would often wake up in the middle of the night, screaming orders and warnings as if he were reliving all the wars he'd fought in during his younger days. Sometimes he'd get up and start smashing things up in his sleep. He would also hit Brenda and I'd have to try and calm him down. He would look at me aggressively, as if he'd no idea who I was. He would be sweating with his jaw jutting out and clenching his fists. I'd try to get him back into bed, sometimes giving him some alcohol to calm him down, and all the while neighbours would be banging on the walls or thumping the ceiling below our feet. What was particularly chilling was that the next morning, Hammy would have no recollection of these episodes.

It eventually came to a head one night between Hammy and Brenda. I'd been asked to work late and didn't get back to the flat until around nine o'clock. As I swung round the stairs onto our floor, I was confronted by a thick pool of blood covering almost the entire landing. There was so much blood I thought someone must have died; surely no one could lose that much and survive? I tiptoed round the dark slick and pushed open the door to our flat, fully expecting to see a body lying there.

It was dark inside the flat; all the lights had been turned off. But I could see a faint glow coming from the kitchen. I looked in and there was Hammy, sitting on a kitchen chair with a can of beer. The gas oven was on, with the door open, there was a blue flicker coming from inside and the room was very warm. I could see Hammy's face and it looked quite peaceful and relaxed.

"What the fuck happened out there?" I asked. "What's all that blood, and where's Brenda?" Hammy just flicked his hand dismissively.

"It's okay, she's gone. I cut her throat," he replied matter-of-factly. "I've had enough of that cunt and her old man." That was all he would say. Later on he admitted an ambulance had been called by someone and she'd been taken away. He didn't know or care if she was alive.

I never did find out exactly what had occurred that night, but the next day the blood had all been cleaned up by our next-door neighbour. I know this because she angrily told me she'd had to do it and wasn't best pleased about it. There was also a police calling card behind the door when I got in. It stated something along the lines of: 'We called today while you were out, in connection with an investigation. Please call us on this number as we need to speak to you,' and it gave the phone number of the local police station. I guessed that at least Brenda was probably still alive – the cops would hardly be leaving polite little notes if she had died. I also noticed the note wasn't addressed to anyone in particular, so she probably hadn't given them any information. When I showed the note to Hammy he was oblivious and indifferent. He'd already forgotten about Brenda. The neighbours, however, had not.

Now, every time I left for work or came home there would be a group of women hanging round the main entrance. They told me pretty directly that we'd better fuck off out of the estate. I tried to ignore them at first, then I tried explaining that my 'dad' had a bit of a drink problem. But they weren't interested. They gave me a clear warning: "Fuck off out of here or else you and your dad are going to get a kicking from my old man." Sometimes they even had their kids with them and would still be just as abusive. I didn't know from one day to the next what I might come back to. Hammy was constantly off his head on booze, and I had no idea what he was getting up to while I was at work. I'd frequently come home to find him drinking with strangers he'd only just met that day. I think he just enjoyed the company. He'd sometimes even invite homeless people to stay the night.

It was quite bizarre. I even found myself thinking nostalgic thoughts and missing the peace and quiet of the borstal.

The end came a few days later. I came home after work at around six, and passed the usual gaggle of women and kids shouting abuse and sniggering as I came in through the main entrance. I quickly went up the stairs to our landing and pushed open the front door and walked in. I almost fell over as I slipped on something. Bizarrely, there was a load of raw fish on the floor behind the door. Someone had posted half a dozen whole fish through the letterbox and they were well past their freshness. The whole flat reeked of rotten fish. I went into the kitchen where Hammy was sat in his usual chair with his feet in the oven keeping warm, and a can of Special Brew in his hand.

"Do you know anything about the fish at the door"? I asked. He clearly didn't; he just looked at me curiously. He was drunk but not completely hammered. He got up to look, and at that moment the front door came flying in, almost smashed off its hinges.

Two men were standing at the door, one with a baseball bat and the other an iron bar. They spoke with local South London accents. One of the pair spoke to Hammy.

"You and your family have got half an hour to get out of here," he said menacingly. "And don't think about coming back. Now fuck off before we bring back a load of our mates." They left and walked down the stairs. I quickly shut the door, but the lock was broken so it didn't make much difference. I turned to Hammy, but he wasn't fazed.

"Fuck them, let them come back," he said calmly, walking back to the kitchen and reaching for another can. I wasn't so confident.

"Hammy, we need to get out of here. There's only two of us. Let's get down to the pub and call a cab to Hammersmith. We can come back later with a team and find out who they are." But Hammy was adamant he wasn't leaving. He'd take on whoever came through that door. I was still trying to persuade him to leave with me five minutes later when the argument became immaterial.

The door burst open again and a group of about eight guys came charging through. We clearly weren't even going to get half an hour's grace. They had probably been listening to our conversation from the landing below. I tried to throw a punch but I didn't even land a blow before I was comprehensively beaten up. I lost sight of Hammy as I was smacked around from all sides. These guys seemed like professionals, calm and methodical. Within five minutes I was lying dazed and bleeding.

"Don't fucking be here when we come back."

Then they left as quickly as they had arrived.

So, here I was again, back in crazy town. Trouble and violence seemed to follow me wherever I was. I went to find Hammy, who was sitting in the kitchen covered in blood. His eye was split open and he'd lost some teeth. He was as defiant as ever, threatening dire retribution, but he suddenly looked very tired and old to me. Still he refused to leave the flat. I told him I was going. I would get to the pub or a phone box and call a cab to Hammersmith. I told him I planned to come back for him in the taxi, we would then get to our friends in West London and come back in the morning mob-handed. I told him this to persuade him to come with me, but I didn't seriously believe it myself. I knew he wouldn't leave if he thought we were running away. But, after all the stuff with Brenda, then the shitstorm that had just happened, I just wanted to get away from Catford and from Hammy.

* * * * * * *

I drained a can of Hammy's Special Brew and descended the stairs. When I reached the main entrance a crowd of women and kids were shouting abuse at me, telling me to fuck off. I pushed my way past them and got out onto the street. I looked left and right and saw there was a gang of men between me and the phone box. I started to walk up the street, away from the crowd. I figured I could go down another street and then double back later towards the phone. The important thing was to get away from the gang of men. I had a screwdriver in my jacket pocket from work, which I gripped tightly in my hand, hidden from view. I walked quickly, without breaking into a run; I didn't want to show any fear or provoke a reaction from the mob. However, I'd only made it a few yards before I heard the scuffing of boots running towards me from behind.

One of the things I learned that night was that sometimes stabbing someone in the guts doesn't always stop them dead in their tracks. It's not like in the movies. The guy I stabbed that night was not the first, but he was the first I wanted to seriously maim or kill, because I knew if I didn't stop him, he would try to kill me with the encouragement of the mob ringing in his ears. I held an eight-inch slot-headed screwdriver tightly in my hand as I started running away from him and a gang of his mates. I was a fast runner, but since I took off from a standing start, he quickly caught up with me as I was fleeing down the street. I sensed he was right behind me, and just at that point I stopped and turned to face him. I braced myself, and held out the screwdriver in front of me, aimed squarely at his gut. He ran straight into the blade and it pierced his abdomen fully eight inches. He didn't even seem to notice; in fact his momentum carried him on, knocking us both flying. We got up, I still holding the bloodied screwdriver, he oblivious to it and still roaring threats. I turned and ran, while he – by this time joined by several friends who had caught up with us – gave chase.

The most remarkable thing about that night was that he didn't even know he had been stabbed until later that evening. According to his police statement, it was only when he was back home later on that night, sitting in his armchair, that his wife noticed blood dripping from the bottom of his trouser leg. That's when he pulled up his shirt and noticed the neat half-inch hole in his stomach and the trail of blood running down his beer belly to his blood-drenched and seeping trousers. It was only then that he panicked and decided to go to A&E.

Anyway, back to the chase. I had twisted my ankle as I fell, and was easily overtaken and grabbed by several men. They were demented with rage and started swinging punches and kicks at me. I had a man on each side, holding my arms, so I couldn't protect myself, while others were punching at my face and head. This was bad enough, but then one of the women came towards me with a broken bottle, telling the men to hold me still so she could smash it into my face. I began to really fear for my life and that's when I found a surge of strength. I pulled and writhed around until my arms were free and managed to get away. I knew from the pain and weakness in my ankle that I would soon be caught again so I made a calculation to run into the garden of a nearby house for help. I'd seen through the curtains that the lights and TV were on, so I knew someone was there. I banged loudly on the door and screamed at them to call the police, but no one opened the door. I then decided to smash the lounge window with my fist to get the attention of whoever was inside. Thankfully this worked. A middle-aged man opened the front door to see what the commotion was and I ran past him and into the house, shouting at him to call the police.

I will be always grateful to that unknown man. Not only did he call 999, but when my pursuers tried to force their way past him to get at me, he held them off, and with a lot of effort was able to close the front door on them. The next thing I remember was sitting on the bottom of his stairs with the phone in my bloodied hand, speaking to the emergency services. I asked for an ambulance to be sent, and handed the phone back to the houseowner to provide the address. I didn't ask for the police; I realised as a borstal boy out on licence, I would be the one blamed for what had happened and recalled. In the event, however, a police car was sent anyway.

As we waited for the ambulance to arrive, the man stood guard over me and shouted to those outside that the police were on their way. After a few minutes it seemed like they had all fled, no doubt because they themselves didn't want to be around when the cops arrived. I opened the door carefully and it looked clear outside. I thanked the man for his help and told him I was leaving.

"But look at the state of you!" he said. "The ambulance will be here soon, and what about my broken window?"

"I'm really sorry, but it's best I leave before they come back," I replied. Then I pushed past him and hobbled off down the road as fast as my injured ankle would permit. At one point I heard a crowd of loud voices shouting behind me and I panicked. I ran round a corner, then slid myself under a parked car and lay silently for a while, an hour at least, until everything was quiet again. Eventually I made my way down to Catford town centre and hailed a cab. I told the driver to take me to Barkingside. I needed family help after what had happened, so I went to see Aunt Mamie and Uncle George. I'd always been very close to Mamie, and she had visited me regularly during my time in borstal. It was natural I would run to her.

It was around four o'clock in the morning when I arrived. Understandably, Mamie and George were shocked to see me turn up at their house, completely out of the blue at that ungodly hour. By this time I could hardly move. My whole body ached, I was covered in bruises, my ankle was sprained and my right hand was numb and immobile. I couldn't even get out of the cab by myself, and the driver had helped George to carry me indoors. I explained briefly what had happened, and that we needed to go back for Hammy. George and Mamie assured me that they would go back and look for him, but for now I had to get into bed. Mamie got a basin of warm water and some antiseptic cream and cleaned me up as best she could. She also bandaged my ankle and wrist. Then she gave me a large rum and coke, and I fell asleep.

When I woke up the next morning, I tried to get out of bed but I couldn't move. I'd taken such a severe beating that Mamie reckoned I was lucky to be alive. Mamie also told me that George had driven to the flat in search of Hammy, but had found it empty and ransacked. The police were almost certainly looking for me. I had stabbed a guy, and as a former borstal boy, with my previous convictions, the excuse of self-defence would likely be ignored. Regardless of the facts, I'd probably be blamed, arrested and charged.

George decided it would be best to get me out of London as soon as possible. It would give me some time to try to figure things out, while I could also receive hospital treatment for what appeared to be serious injuries. He decided to put me on the train to Glasgow and so they drove me to the station. It says a lot about the state I was in, that I remember absolutely nothing about the six-hour train journey. But when I arrived at the other end, my dad and Uncle Jake were there waiting for me, and they carried me into the car.

As soon as Dad saw me, he dismissed the idea of taking me home to recover. Instead he drove me straight to the A&E department of the Vale of Leven Hospital. Fortunately for me, the nurse on duty was an old neighbour. Linda was a few years older than me, but her family had lived on the same street as us on the council estate. We were old friends.

Normally when someone came into the hospital with the type of injuries I had, the police would be called as a matter of course. But being streetwise, Linda asked me if I'd like the police to come and see me? I said no. She cleaned and stitched up my wrist. I had no feeling in my hand and she explained that the tendons and nerves had been severed. This injury had clearly occurred when I had punched in the window. All the other cuts and bruises would heal in time, but she advised I'd probably need surgery on my hand, and made the necessary referral to my GP. For now at least, I was free to go home to my parents' house and get some rest. It would ultimately take ten years before my hand regained full movement and felt normal again.

It felt very strange to be back in my old bedroom. I'd left the Vale three years previously. But I was grateful I had somewhere to recuperate. Within a day or two I was up and about. It's surprising how quickly you heal when you're young. My hand still wouldn't work properly, but apart from that I was okay. I tried ringing round a few numbers of people I knew in London to see if they knew what had happened to Hammy, but no one did. In those days before mobile phones and the internet it was very difficult to keep in touch. I decided I would give myself some time to recover fully, then I'd return to London. As it turned out, that trip was to be arranged for me by the Metropolitan Police.

* * * * * * *

It happened about two weeks after I'd arrived back in Scotland. I was in bed asleep when I heard a banging on the front door. It was six in the morning and I knew that could only mean the police. I got up, threw on a T-shirt and jeans, and answered the door. Sure enough, it was two cops from the local station. They had a warrant for my arrest and were taking me into custody. I was wanted by the police in Catford and a couple of their officers would be travelling up to Scotland to collect me. In the meantime I was banged up in the cells at the Vale station.

Later that evening the two officers arrived from London. They came into my cell, formally arrested me and charged me with GBH and unlawful wounding. The Catford cops were actually very friendly. They said I could make any statement and see the charges once I was back in London. But for now, I might as well get my head down for some sleep as we'd be leaving early the next morning, flying down to Heathrow from Glasgow Airport.

The following morning the two police officers took me to the airport. They didn't go into much detail about the incident, simply telling me that I'd be appearing at the magistrates' court later that day. I could make a statement at the police station prior to the hearing, if I wished. They seemed in good spirits and had apparently had a good night out the evening before, visiting the Glasgow pubs. It was their first visit to Scotland and had clearly enjoyed a bit of a jolly. There was certainly no aggression towards me, and in fact they were both very friendly, especially the more senior-looking of the two DCs, who introduced himself as Rob. I had to admit that I liked Rob; he seemed like a pretty cool guy.

The airport itself was going to be awkward for me. I explained that my dad worked there and I didn't want to be seen going through the terminal in handcuffs, if that could be avoided. Rob was very relaxed about it, and said that would be fine. So, we all checked in and walked through to the departures area like three old friends.

Once on the plane, Rob asked me if I wanted a drink. I asked for a beer and he ordered three lagers for us. It was all very civilised and casual. We had a few more beers during the ninety-minute flight to Heathrow. I was quite surprised by all this. What was going on? The only hint I got was when Rob asked me if I knew who I'd stabbed? With my usual caution I denied all knowledge of any stabbing. He just smiled. Okay, he said, do you know the people who had been involved in the fighting that night? I truthfully answered no, I had no idea who any of them were. He smiled again and left it at that.

Once back at Catford Police Station later on that day, I was asked if I wanted to make a statement in response to the charge. I replied only that I'd been attacked by a group of men, and that I had no idea why. I'd suffered severe injuries and these were all detailed by the A&E department at the Vale Hospital. I showed my heavily bandaged hand and wrist and explained I'd tried to seek help during the attack by smashing the window of a house. The owner had called 999, so they should be able to find a record of that call on the night in question. Rob nodded and said he'd already spoken to the householder, who had confirmed that part of my story. Next I was taken to the magistrates' court and formally charged with the offence. I pleaded not guilty and the magistrate remanded me to the Crown Court for trial. DC Rob stood up and said that the police had no objections to bail, so I was to be released on bail pending further hearings. Rob was waiting for me in the lobby when I left the courtroom. He asked if I had enough money to get back to Glasgow. I told him I did.

"Okay," he said, "We'll see you at the trial, then. And don't worry, it'll be all right." I walked out onto the street in a daze. I'd expected to be banged up, remanded in custody until the hearing. What the hell was happening?

I took an overnight coach from Victoria Bus Station to Glasgow, and arrived back in Glasgow the next morning. My family was as shocked as I was that I was free, at least for the time being.

That unforeseen trip to London had a big effect on me. The two Catford police officers had challenged my long-held assumptions about the police. It was the first time I'd ever experienced civility, even kindness from people who I'd always looked upon as the enemy. It was the start of a change in my attitude to authority in general. For the first time in my life, I began to look at the members of the criminal justice system who I'd encountered over the past few years as human.

One of my bail conditions was that I would register with the local probation service in Glasgow. After all, I was still on licence from borstal. And so I was soon invited for my first session with my new probation officer in the Vale. As if to reinforce my newly discovered openness to dealing with authority, I struck gold in the form of my probation officer, a man called Bob.

Bob was a thoughtful and wise man. I was immediately disarmed upon meeting him because he was severely disabled. Bob was around mid-fifties, with straggly unkempt hair. He used a wheelchair, had one arm that didn't work, and was missing an eye. Despite these impairments he was very capable of doing his job, and he was open, friendly and amiable. He came across as genuinely wanting to help me, rather than simply being someone appointed to keep me in line. After that first meeting I not only respected him for overcoming his disabilities, but I really liked him.

During my regular visits over the next few months, I gradually opened up to Bob about my life and internal gender dilemma. He didn't judge, and was as helpful as he could be, considering he'd had no experience of someone like me before in all his years as a probation officer.

One morning a letter arrived, informing me that I had a trial set for a date in four months' time. I was advised to get legal representation and I found a legal aid lawyer in Glasgow to work in conjunction with my London lawyer. His advice was to plead 'self defence' to the charge of unlawful wounding, since there was a clear record of my injuries and of my attempt to call the emergency services. Furthermore, the houseowner whose window I had smashed when I'd sought refuge from the Catford gang had bravely made a statement to the police confirming that I was trying to get away from the people who were pursuing me, rather than fight them. I wasn't very hopeful of getting a not guilty verdict because of my previous convictions, but it was either that or simply plead guilty. So I agreed to go along with the plan.

* * * * * * *

During the period when I was awaiting trial, I also finally received another letter from a place called the Douglas Inch Centre, in Glasgow. The description of their work was in the heading of the letter: 'A community psychiatric centre dealing with adult and juvenile offenders.'

I had been referred to the centre by my GP. It turned out that she had no idea where else to send me when I had told her during my appointment, a year previously, that I wanted to change sex. Somewhat amusingly, she had assumed that it must be a criminal matter, so had referred me there!

Chapter 10 'Who's That Girl'?

I arrived for my first appointment at the Douglas Inch Centre a week later, interested in what their approach to me would be. I wasn't very hopeful as I was shown into a waiting room full of men. I was by far the youngest person there.

As I waited, the conversation was all about football, prison and women. In that order. As I listened to the men, some described why they were here, often in graphic detail. I understood pretty much straight away that whatever this place was, it was nothing close to resembling a Gender Identity Clinic. Most of the men had been convicted of domestic violence, and as I was to find out later, of sexual assault and even rape. It seemed I'd been referred to a clinic group that dealt with assault and sexual offences against women!

When it was my turn, I was called in to see a female psychiatrist, Dr Fiona. She was very business-like and professional. She asked me lots of questions relating to my family, education, and my offending behaviour.

She occasionally slipped in a curve ball about masturbation fantasises. It was all very odd.

I explained that I was actually looking to have sex change surgery through the NHS. By this time I had no embarrassment about coming straight to the point with medical professionals. I'd already explained this to two doctors and also my probation officer. I used the trigger phrase: 'I feel like a woman trapped in a man's body,' and got the expected scribbling-in-her-notepad response from Dr Fiona. By the end of my forty-minute appointment, though, she hadn't directly addressed my comments regarding changing sex. She told me to come back a week later for another appointment.

The following week, Dr Fiona asked me to complete a questionnaire called the Bem Sex-Role Inventory (BSRI). She explained that this is a measure of gender expression and gender roles, framed in terms of masculinity and femininity. It assessed how people identify themselves psychologically. I scored a high feminine score, which reassured me somewhat. It seems archaic now, but these types of psychological profiling tests were the tools used at that time by psychiatrists.

Dr Fiona also asked me questions directly relating to my inner feelings regarding changing sex. What did I think it would be like living as a woman? How would I expect to be treated? Did I feel I was strong enough to go through a transition? Would my family and friends be supportive? (That was an easy one.) I felt quite drained by the end of the appointment, after she had really grilled me with such precise and pertinent questions. I felt I'd been opened up and laid bare, but I also felt a real sense of relief.

At the end of the session Dr Fiona told me that the Douglas Inch Centre was not suitable for my situation, and that I really needed to be referred to a specialist unit. Apparently there was a clinic in Glasgow called the Sandyford, but they were new and only operating a very limited service. There was no place for me there yet since it had a long waiting list. I might have to be referred to the Charing Cross Gender Identity Clinic in London. She suggested, however, that I continue to attend the Douglas Inch Centre in the meantime. But rather than see her, I should see one of the resident social workers, a man called Brian.

* * * * * * *

I was to develop a fantastic relationship with Brian over the next few months. In fact he was to prove pivotal in my eventual transition. One of the most important things he did was to give me a copy of the book Conundrum by Jan Morris. I read it in one sitting that evening when I got home. All the way through I kept saying to myself: "Oh my fucking God!" I'd read chapter after chapter and would be repeating it – OMFG – to myself over and over, at each new revelation. She was writing my story as well as hers, and it was like reading my own diary. How could she know? Then, of course, I realised she knew exactly how I felt, because even though socially and educationally she was a world away from me, we were sisters. I understood that I had more in common with Jan Morris than anyone else in the world at that point in time. She was the first person I'd ever encountered who could articulate my own feelings. But I also understood that even Jan Morris, with all the privileges of money, class and status, had not found her transition, nor her eventual surgery, easy. Without her advantages my own journey would likely be even more challenging. But at least I knew it was possible.

Eventually, Brian prepared a psychiatric report on me based on Fiona's advice and his own observations. The report categorically stated that I was diagnosed as suffering from 'gender dysphoria' and was most likely a 'classic transsexual' woman. The terms 'classic transsexual' actually dates from medical textbooks from the early twentieth century. It became an unpopular term during the 1990s onward because some people in the psychiatric field felt it sounded elitist. These days gender clinics like to talk about a 'spectrum' of trans. At one end there might be people who fantasise about being the opposite gender but will never have any treatment; and at the other end is a tiny minority of people (about 1%) who will begin hormone treatment that lasts for the rest of their life and will have sex change surgery (that's me).

Brian's report recommended that I be referred to a suitable gender identity clinic for further investigation and treatment. I was delighted to agree with his findings and recommendations. It felt like validation for me. This report would be very helpful when I finally accessed a gender identity clinic. But for now, it was my first official step towards transition. However, there was one problem. A big one.

Brian's report recommended that the report be presented to the court at my upcoming trial. I was horrified. I knew that a report like that would follow me for the rest of my life, not just in my medical records but it would become part of my prison records. And if I was convicted at the trial in South London, then this report would be made available to the prison authorities and would dictate how I would be treated and where I'd be sent to serve my sentence. To be frank, prison officials are not known for their discretion, and this report could potentially make my life a living hell in a male prison.

Brian gave me the choice. If the report was accurate and reflected my situation correctly, then ethically, it should be submitted to the court by the Douglas Inch Centre. But if I chose to refuse to allow the report to be submitted, then why? If it was the truth, what was I afraid of? I couldn't keep running away from it forever. He told me that if I genuinely wanted treatment and surgery, then there would inevitably come a time when I would have to expose myself to all the negative fallout that might come with it. It was unrealistic to think I could somehow go back to London and continue my part-time transition in a tiny London flat, without the authorities and my family and friends knowing about it, and then one day suddenly appear, fully-formed like Venus emerging from the waves, sex change complete, and ready to start a full-time female life.

He was testing me, but of course he was right. I realised I'd previously been trying to do this in a bubble, safe from the ridicule and embarrassment of admitting I was transsexual. I was still ashamed of myself. It was more than that, though. I knew what might happen to me in the prison system at that time. I'd probably be segregated with the sex offenders, then subjected to physical abuse from the screws as well as the other inmates. For sure, none of the people I'd served time with previously, whom I might meet again during this sentence, would want to have anything to do with me. It was make or break time for me. If that report was submitted there would be no turning back. Declaring you are transsexual to the authorities, to your family and friends, can never be unsaid. I decided to allow the report to be submitted.

Of course, this meant that the genie would be out of the lamp. Never again would my transition be solely under my control. But, especially after reading Conundrum, I knew that I would need help and would have to trust others to help and allow me to achieve my goal. That was a big step for me – I'd never really trusted anyone before.

The months until my trial passed quickly, and with Brian's help I prepared myself for the court date. I knew that in all likelihood I'd be found guilty and sent back to borstal at the very least. I was prepared for that, but this time I'd face it honestly as me (her) and not hide behind the violent persona that I'd cultivated over the years to keep me safe.

I had reached out to people since I'd returned to Scotland and been met with surprising kindness. First from the two Catford cops, then Bob at the probation office, then Dr Fiona and Brian from the Douglas Inch Centre. I felt confident that there would still be support for me when I was eventually released. With that optimism and hope, I boarded the train to London the Sunday prior to my Monday morning court date.

It was the autumn of 1983 and I travelled to London on my own. My family thought that I'd surely be sent down again, so it wasn't worth wasting any money having anyone travel with me. I'd arranged for Jimmy to meet me and accompany me to court. I had even bought a one-way ticket, so confident was I that I'd not need a return ticket.

I arrived at court on time. Waiting to see me was my previous barrister from the Old Bailey trial, Ms Peters. I was very pleased to see a familiar and friendly face. That's how Crown Court barristers were often assigned in those days: on spec and frequently unprepared. If you were on legal aid you just accepted who was sent along on the day by your solicitor. And then you usually had a hurried ten-minute meeting to discuss the case prior to walking into the dock.

Ms Peters and I had our quick meeting in a side room, just the two of us. The first thing she did was extract a file from her stack of papers. It was the Douglas Inch Centre report.

"Do you want me to present this?" she asked. I said yes, and she simply nodded. Ever the professional, Ms Peters didn't comment one way or the other, but she did smile and simply squeezed my hand. We quickly discussed the merits of my case and the 'self defence' plea. She had spoken with the prosecution and said there might be a deal to be done. She left to start her negotiations, and I went back to sit on the public benches with Jimmy in the lobby to await my call to court.

Shortly, I saw Rob, the Catford detective constable who had come up to Scotland to take me back to London months earlier. He saw me sitting there and came over for a chat. He was very friendly, asking how I was, and how my parents were. He started reminiscing about the night out he'd had in Glasgow, and the plane trip back to London when we'd shared a few drinks. Then he glanced over at his colleagues and said he had to go, but he wished me good luck.

"Don't worry Ally, you're not the worst in this case, mate!" He smiled and was gone. Jimmy and I just stared at each other, both wondering what the fuck had just happened.

I was called into court not long afterwards and entered the dock. From my position I could see the guy who I'd stabbed sitting to my right. He looked very uncomfortable as he stared straight ahead. Ms Peters approached me.

"I have a proposal for you," she said quietly. "The alleged victim in the case does not want to give evidence. He's here only as a hostile witness. In these circumstances, the judge will continue with the trial, unless you agree to plead guilty and accept a non-custodial sentence." My heart leapt. Non-custodial?! That meant I might be walking out of here today, rather than sitting in the prison transport sweat box back to borstal! How did this happen? I didn't even want to know right at that moment. I wanted just to accept the deal before anyone changed their minds.

"Yes, of course I'll plead guilty!" I whispered. Ms Peters smiled and turned to the judge.

Since I pleaded guilty, there was no need for a trial. Instead, the judge spent the next half hour summing up and going through the evidence from the police statements. The incident was described as a violent fracas in which both parties had probably been at fault. DC Rob's evidence was read out, describing how I'd been attacked at home, then in the house of an innocent bystander. The hospital report of my injuries was read out, detailed by my old friend, nurse Linda. The victim's statement amounted to that he 'didn't remember much of the night as he'd been at the pub earlier.' It was the A&E staff who had called in the police after seeing his stomach injury, and that was consistent with a stab wound. Then my previous convictions were read out, and it wasn't a short list. I stood wincing at the details. I wasn't proud of it.

Finally, the judge announced he was going to be lenient in the circumstances, as I had been cooperative and my previous crimes had never involved dishonesty of any kind. He indicated that I had an immature relationship with alcohol and a self-identity that had led to much violence in the past, and this was something that I would need to learn to deal with. He also noted that I'd been receiving and accepting help from the Douglas Inch Centre in Glasgow, and appreciated the informative report that he'd received in that regard.

I felt my face burning. Was he going to mention my transsexuality in open court? Jimmy would faint if he did! Instead though, he just held the report in his hand and looked at me straight in the eye.

"On condition that you attend, and accept treatment from, the GIC at Charing Cross Hospital." He didn't say the words, but of course he was referring to the Gender Identity Clinic. "I am minded to bind you over to keep the peace for one year. Do you agree?"

"Yes, Sir," I replied and nodded vigorously.

That was it. I was free to go. I thanked the judge and left the dock. Once outside I hugged Ms Peters. She had struck gold again for me! I was certainly very fortunate to have her as my brief. But I still had to ask her: "How did all that happen?"

Ms Peters explained that the victim that night, whom I'd stabbed, had a much longer criminal record than me, and a series of lengthy prison terms for violence behind him that made me look almost angelic in comparison. If the trial had proceeded, all his previous convictions would have been presented in court, along with the witness statements that presented me more as victim than attacker. It might even have led to a police investigation of his own actions. Between that and his reluctance to give evidence (he was old school like me when it came to that sort of thing), Ms Peters had managed to persuade the prosecution to deal with the matter as a fight between two equally guilty parties. The police had thankfully agreed (thank you, DC Rob!) and so the deal was struck.

I was incredibly relieved to be walking away from this. But I still had one more question: "What about the Douglas Inch report?" Ms Peters told me that the report had been entered into open court and would remain part of the official record. In other words, the state knew I was transsexual from that day forward. I had agreed to attend a GIC and my probation officer would be instructed to ensure that I did.

I thanked Ms Peters again and I told her she would never see me again in this situation. Jimmy and I caught a cab back to West London and had a celebratory drink that night before I caught the overnight bus back to Glasgow. I sensed Jimmy wanted to ask me about the report, as we relived the day's events in a pub near

Victoria Station, but he never did, and I didn't offer. It would have been too much to explain, and I knew I was leaving this world behind me that night. We parted as friends. Jimmy was always loyal and I loved him for that.

Chapter 11 'New Gold Dream'

Glasgow

I was now finally free to get on with my life. For the first time in years I had no more court cases on the horizon to cloud my future plans to transition. And crucially, what I did have was the support of the Douglas Inch Centre to guide me through the NHS gender reassignment process. I'd even been ordered by the justice system to receive treatment. This order not only compelled me to enter a medical program to address my gender dysphoria, but it also obliged the NHS to provide the resources to deliver that treatment. Finally, things seemed to be back on track.

Within a few weeks of the court case I moved out of my parents' house in the Vale to begin my new future. I'd found a bedsit in the West End of Glasgow, the most cosmopolitan and bohemian area of the city, which included a large student population. My accommodation wasn't as private or self-contained as my flat in Shepherd's Bush had been, but at least it was clean and inexpensive. I had a room on the top floor of an old town house in Doune Gardens, Hillhead, overlooking the River Kelvin. My floor had four separate bedsits and I shared a bathroom with my neighbours. I contacted my old boyfriend Jim to let him know I was back in town. He helped me move my belongings in and we resumed our relationship. Everything seemed to be in place and now I could restart my transition.

Brian from the Douglas Inch Centre had told me that I should begin living as female while I was waiting for my first Gender Identity Clinic appointment. This would count towards my 'real-life test', the minimum two-year period that would be essential to me accessing NHS hormone treatment. It was also one of the terms of the judge's court order. I was determined to do things by the book this time, so if I wanted to get a job, then it would have to be as a female. I would need to live, dress and present myself as female twenty-four hours a day, seven days a week. The GIC rules were non-negotiable.

At first this all seemed perfectly acceptable to me, and I was comfortable with the arrangement, even though I knew it would be difficult. My main problem was that I didn't have much money. I'd just paid a month's rent deposit and a month in advance for my bedsit. My savings were almost used up. I had no income and I would have to find a job as soon as possible to cover my rent.

I had bought myself a new wardrobe of female clothes, mostly second hand stuff from charity shops, and prepared to restart my female life. The clothes were important to the GIC process. In those days the psychiatrists (who were almost exclusively male) believed there wasn't any nuance or overlap between the genders. There was no spectrum – it was binary: you were either male or female, and if you were claiming to be female, then you'd better dress like one, with a dress or a skirt. I was to come up against this fairly primitive thinking many times in the future. But I'd make it work somehow, I was absolutely determined to. A clear path to transition was finally laid out before me, and I was happy. At least I wasn't sitting at Her Majesty's pleasure in a twelve-by-six feet cell in Pentonville. I'd been given a break and I was determined to take advantage of it. Unfortunately it didn't work out that way.

Within twelve months I would be a married man.

So, why did it all go wrong? Well, the first thing I came up against was that I was unable to obtain any official ID in my female persona. When I tried to register with the local Social Security office I was told I could only use my birth name and birth gender. There was simply no provision for someone like me to use a female identity, much less change any official documents such as my passport. This meant that I was only able to work or claim unemployment benefit in my male gender; meanwhile, at the same time, in order to satisfy the GIC requirements, I could only dress and present myself as female. I did try to get some casual work in pubs as a barmaid, but with no success. Glasgow in the 1980s was simply not ready for someone like me. I could pass as female okay in the street, but not in a close-up environment like serving in a bar or working in an office. During one job interview the manager literally laughed in my face. As he stood behind the busy bar with customers all around, he said, "We're looking for ladies," and smirked at his customers, leaving me feeling humiliated.

This scenario was repeated several times over in restaurants and hotels where I applied for work, and I soon felt that I was up against a brick wall. I'd been told I had to construct a female life in every aspect, but at the same time I was forced to do it without any official female ID documents or previous work history.

This was the first time that I truly understood how the class system was rigged against people like me. In order to live, I needed to earn; I was working class, I had no private income or wealthy family to ease my passage. In fact, my family and friends would have killed me if they knew what I was doing. In the end, in order to pay my rent, I had no choice but to register for unemployment benefit in my male name, in order to claim housing benefit so that I could pay my rent. The problem was, this immediately compromised my 'real-life test'.

* * * * * * *

Given these circumstances, the only work I could get was voluntary, working with the elderly at Whiteinch Community Centre lunch club in Glasgow, five days a week. Even in that job, while I could dress as female, I still had to be registered as a male volunteer. Fortunately for me, the community centre was so desperate for people that I was taken on and the female manager turned a blind eye. For me, however, it was to prove an eye-opening experience. While I was definitely accepted as female there by the pensioners and the other staff, I was given all the worst jobs and had to put up with a lot of sexist comments and the occasional bottom-grabbing from cheeky old men. It was a welcome to my life as a woman!

Despite these trials, I did enjoy my time working with the pensioners. During the mornings I would travel all over Glasgow's West End in a black cab. The driver and I would collect our lunch guests from their homes, often walking them gently with sticks or walking frames to the taxi, then back to the Centre. None of these people seemed too bothered by my appearance; they were just pleased to see a friendly face and I felt welcome among them. Then, after we had collected everyone, I helped to cook lunch and serve it up. I was also responsible for calling the numbers in the afternoon game of bingo, which was great fun. I used to call the numbers in a deliberately confusing way to wind them up: "Two fat ladies, forty-seven!" I would cry, or, "Kelly's eye, number ten!" It pissed some of them off to begin with, but before long they went along with it, and it helped to liven up the sessions. I often sat and chatted with the pensioners afterwards and listened to their stories. I wasn't officially supposed to, but I even accepted a few invitations to go and visit them in their homes for a cuppa. I imagine that would never be allowed now, but I enjoyed it and they were delighted to have some company.

Throughout this period I was still living a reluctant double life. Whenever I dealt with authorities such as Social Security, the local council, or the tax office, I would always have to use my male identity. The same applied when dealing with my family, since I still didn't feel able to come out to my parents. I always kept a range of male clothing to wear whenever I knew I would be meeting them. I knew it would devastate them to learn about my transsexuality. But it was more than that: as well as being hurt emotionally, they would almost certainly be angry and there was every chance they would attack me physically if they knew. But at least I did manage to tell my sister Carolyn.

One evening I'd arranged to go to the cinema with her. After the film, I said I wanted to have a serious chat with her about something. We drove to a park and sat in her car in the dark with the rain lashing down.

"Well, what is it?" asked Carolyn impatiently. She was never one to beat around the bush.

"I'm transsexual," I said. "I'm going to have a sex change. I want to live as a woman".

Unexpectedly, and rather annoyingly, Carolyn said nothing. She just sat silently and stared out at the rain. I stumbled on with my explanation, trying to convince her I was serious. I told her about my feelings growing up, how I'd borrowed her clothes, about my life in London, how I'd begun a transition there, and about the Douglas Inch Centre where I was finally now receiving help. Carolyn was impassive, silently trying to process everything I'd just told her. Eventually she turned slowly to face me.

"You wore my *clothes*?" she asked accusingly. I admitted I had done, for years when we were growing up and sharing a bedroom. She seemed to think about this for a while. "Okay," she said. "Thanks for telling me, I had no idea. I don't know what you want me to do about it, though."

And that was it. My big revelation, the day I'd been building up to for years, the moment when I finally came out to someone close to me, passed with hardly a comment. Carolyn started the car and drove me back to my bedsit. Barely a word passed between us before we said goodbye. We never discussed it again until almost twenty years later.

Meanwhile, back at my bedsit I was beginning to get to know my neighbours. I had kept myself to myself in the first few weeks, hardly interacting at all with them other than a passing 'hi' on the stairs if I met one of them.

They were three guys: Ben, Stewart and John, all around my age. They seemed friendly enough and didn't seem too bothered about my androgynous appearance. Ben was the oldest, in his late twenties. He was unemployed and spent most of his time smoking cannabis and listening to music. Stewart was training to be a chef, so worked odd hours, but he seemed nice. John was a student at drama school. He mostly kept to himself but was friendly enough. Later on, the other three of us used to joke about him. ""John seems like a lovely bloke, but maybe he's just a good actor?" But we could see he was passionate about his art, and he would later became very famous as a BAFTA nominated actor and star of film and television. He was John Hannah.

One night Ben banged on my door. I opened it and he told me I'd missed my friend Jim earlier. Apparently Jim had turned up expecting to see me, and when he didn't get a response to his knocking, was about to leave when Ben had gone out to the landing to ask if he could help, or maybe take a message for me. The upshot was that Ben had invited Jim into his bedsit and they spent a few hours listening to music and drinking. It was clear from the way Ben was addressing me and describing this encounter with Jim that he had used male pronouns when speaking about me, and so Ben naturally did the same, as he spoke to me, now. That killed off any chance I had of keeping my female identity intact at the bedsit. Before long, Ben had spoken about me to our other neighbours, Stewart and John, as 'he'. I was outed.

As I went to bed that night I felt sick and wanted to move out right away, the next morning if possible. I felt Doune Gardens had become tainted. Everyone now thought of me as male there. I was really upset with Jim at the casual way he had just unthinkingly killed off my female life. I was also upset at how readily, despite my feminine clothes and make-up., this had been accepted. Obviously I had not been 'passing' as well as I'd hoped. I was due to meet Jim for a drink the next evening at the Grosvenor bar. I planned to let him know how hurt I felt at the casual way he had treated my gender identity with complete strangers.

I arrived at the bar and saw Jim sitting with his old friend Bobby. I immediately launched into him for misgendering me to strangers and disrespecting everything I'd told him. He was taken aback, but didn't really take it seriously. He apologised but couldn't really see the problem. It was little more than amusing to him.

Then Bobby chimed in. "You're not transsexual, there's no such thing. You're just fucking queer like the rest of us and looking for an excuse." I looked to Jim to support me. We'd had so many long discussions about my situation that I felt he would be as angry as I was about Bobby's ignorant comments and would jump in to defend me. Instead he just smiled apologetically, put his arms around me and said, "Come on, I'll get you a drink."

Finally, the penny dropped. For years, Jim and Bobby had just been humouring me, in fact patronising me. Pretending they understood but all the time thinking I was just young and misguided. I felt betrayed and stupid to have entrusted them with so many of my inner thoughts. But, with hindsight, their attitude was not so unusual among the gay male community back then. It was a prevailing belief that transsexual women were simply homosexual men who were too ashamed to admit it.

I couldn't stay. I stormed out of the Grosvenor on to Byres Road. I was wearing a long ankle-length hippy skirt with a cheesecloth top and a long cardigan. As I looked down at my padded breasts, my long painted nails, I had a sudden paranoid realisation that everyone who passed me only saw a bloke in a dress, and by this time, one with with mascara-streaked cheeks from my tears. I was pathetic. What a fool I was! How stupid did I look? I was a joke and everyone was probably laughing at me behind my back. I could never live as a woman.

I needed to get away and go home, but then I realised, back at the bedsit they were no doubt laughing too. Distraught, I began to trudge back to Doune Gardens feeling sorry for myself. On the way I stopped off at the off-licence and bought two bottles of wine. The guy who served me called me 'hen' and asked if I was okay. I ignored him, presuming he was probably just taking the piss, too. I grabbed my wine and flew up the stairs and into the sanctuary of my room. Here I was, back with my old friend, alcohol. There was a quiet knock on my door. It was probably Ben; he really was becoming a pain. I ignored it. I drank both bottles before I fell asleep on top of the bed. At some point in the night I remember waking up and hearing Leonard Cohen music coming softly through the wall from next door. *Famous Blue Raincoat*, my favourite track.

My relationship with my housemates changed after that. Ben started knocking on my door almost every night, inviting me in to his room for a smoke or a drink. At first I declined; I simply didn't want to build relationships with people who treated me as male. But Ben was persistent. He didn't give up easily and his natural good humour finally wore me down. Besides, I was getting a bit lonely sitting in my room and listening to the music and laughter coming through the wall. Ben's room was the epicentre of the house's social scene. He rarely went out, so was almost always around when someone else in the building wanted some company.

Through Ben I got to know everyone else from our floor and the ones below. Most nights we would end up sitting around the floor on giant cushions, smoking weed and having a few drinks while we listened to his high-end Hi-Fi system. There seemed to be a continuous stream of neighbours and friends dropping in for a smoke, and late at night Ben would cook up a meal of whatever food we had to share.

I continued with my voluntary job and made some new friends among the other volunteers. One in particular was 'Little Ed', a typical working-class guy a bit older than me. We got on really well and he always made me laugh. I continued dressing as both male and female depending on my mood or the situation. I was still waiting for a referral to a gender identity clinic through the Douglas Inch Centre, but nothing seemed to be happening. My appointments with Brian the social worker became fewer and further between, as he said there was not much he could do for me. I would just have to wait.

* * * * * * *

The winter of 1983–84 dragged on. It was very cold that year and I couldn't afford to put any heating on because the landlord had fitted her own very high tariff meters that needed to be continually topped up with 50p coins. I decided I needed to save some money and remembered the old electricity meter trick my dad had taught me when I was a kid. I removed the cover and carefully examined the wires. This was a different type of meter but I quickly saw that if I reversed the wires I should be able to make the dial run backwards instead of forward. It worked, and now I could use the heating as much as I wanted. My room was always as warm as toast after that. I just had to remember to replace the wires occasionally and run the dial forward for a time, otherwise I'd end up with a negative reading when the landlord's agent came to collect the money from the meter. I showed Ben and Stewart how to do the fiddle and they quickly followed suit with their own meters. When I mentioned it to John he just smiled at me. "Don't worry about me, I'm an electrician – I'm already doing my own thing!" It turned out he'd completed his apprenticeship before starting at drama school.

It was actually very lucky for me that John *was* an electrician. One night I came home from my volunteering work to hear the news from Ben that the meter reader was coming that evening and I better get mine ready for inspection. They had already done theirs. The problem was that it was evening and it was dark outside, and to replace the wires it was necessary to turn off the electricity at the mains switch. This is why we always did it during the day when there was natural light to see by. I began to panic. I had to do this quickly and by the light of a candle. I grabbed a screwdriver and a pair of pliers, and in the dim light tried to extract the wires very carefully. I knew I would receive a serious electric shock if they touched. I don't know if it was because I was rushing or due to the lack of light, but suddenly there was an almighty bang and a flash of blue light. I was thrown across the room and landed with a thump against my bed. I pulled myself together and tried to calm down. I couldn't find the screwdriver I'd been using but I had a sliced cut on my hand between my thumb and finger, doubtless the result of the screwdriver shooting back. I was lucky it hadn't hit me in the face or body. I tried to pick up the candle but my hands were shaking so uncontrollably I couldn't even hold it. Jesus, what do I do now?

Just then there was a gentle knock at my door. Shit! Was it the agent? Then I heard John's soft voice. "Ally, are you okay?"

I pulled open the door. "No John, I'm fucking not." I began babbling, trying to explain what had happened. John just stared at me. I had scorch marks on my hands and my hair was standing on end. I showed him my hands which were still jumping around beyond my control.

"Okay," said John calmly. "Shut your door and go and sit on your bed. I'll be back in a minute. Don't open the door to anyone except me when you hear my voice."

I did as I'd been told and sat on the bed, trying to calm myself down. Within a few minutes John was back. I opened the door and he had a powerful torch and his toolbox with him. He sat on the floor on and got to work on the meter. He completed the job quickly and then turned the mains switch back on. Everything seemed normal; the lights were on and the dial was spinning properly. John quickly replaced the cover and I thanked him profusely before going to see Ben for a stiff drink.

Within an hour the landlord's agent arrived with his cloth bag to empty the meters and do a quick check on the property. I was relaxed by this time and as he removed the coins he seemed quite satisfied that all was in order. Then, just before he left, he had a look around the room to check for any damage.

"What's that doing there?" he suddenly barked. He was pointing to the wall, at about head height. There, embedded four inches into the plaster of the wall, was my screwdriver, that by this time I'd forgotten all about. I looked in genuine surprise.

"I have no idea," I lied. He looked at me suspiciously, then back at the protruding screwdriver for a few moments.

Finally he shook his head. "Just get it out and touch up the hole, okay?" I nodded, then he was gone. I breathed an almighty sigh of relief.

* * * * * * *

As Christmas 1983 approached, I found myself getting more caught up in the life of the house. Money was tight so we on the top floor pooled our resources. We would each take turns to cook a meal for everyone else. We shared money, cannabis and food. No one went without, but it meant there was little privacy either. Our doors were never locked and everyone was constantly in and out of each other's rooms.

By this time I'd met a girl in Partick, called Isabelle. She was a little older than me and had her own flat where I would sometimes go to hang out just for a change of scene. We were just friends and there was no sexual pressure. Occasionally Stewart's or John's girlfriends visited the house and we would all party together. We might have been skint, but we were never lonely or cold. You could see the effect of our electricity arrangement when the weather turned really bad in that particularly snowy winter. As you walked along our street, every other house had a blanket of snow covering their roof, but ours was snow-free and with a gentle cloud of steam rising.

Ben's and my finances alternated weekly. We both had to sign on for unemployment benefit at Maryhill Social Security office every other week. But I signed on a different week from him so we shared our resources so that neither of us was completely broke during our 'poor week'. In those days the government sent out cheques for benefit that had to be cashed at the post office with ID. One week my giro cheque, usually left on the ground floor hallway table, wasn't there. I called the office but they said it had been sent and they wouldn't replace it. It turned out that a previous tenant, a junkie called Mick, had kept a key to the street door when he'd moved out, and came back occasionally to steal the post. One of the downstairs neighbours had seen him.

I didn't want any trouble, especially not with my previous convictions. I'd hidden my violent history from everyone in the house and I suppose they all thought I was soft, gay or just a bit girly with the clothes I wore. But Ben was incandescent with rage on my behalf. He wanted to be my knight in shining armour. He knew where Mick had moved to, so, grabbing me to go along with him, he went up to Mick's flat and smashed the door in, dragged him out of bed with Mick's girlfriend screaming. Ben forced Mick to hand over every penny he had, then as Mick lay cowering on the floor, Ben pulled out his penis and pissed all over him. It was a very strange feeling for me to have someone stand up for me because they thought I was weak and needed protection!

I still saw Jim, my now ex-boyfriend, occasionally, but we had ceased to have any real relationship, sexually or otherwise by then. I could never trust him after the night in the Grosvenor bar with Bobby when they had both invalidated my existence. But we still frequented the same pub in Hillhead. The highlight of the week was visiting the Blythswood Cottage bar, when either Ben or I had been paid. When I did happen to meet Jim, he seemed to assume I was in a relationship with Ben, which of course I wasn't. Ben was just a friend and entirely straight as far as I knew.

Sometimes Ben and I would venture down Byres Road, the student pub area of Glasgow's West End. It was there one night in the Ubiquitous Chip bar that Ben managed to pull a girlfriend. She was a nurse, as was her friend Lyn. I was then roped in because the girls didn't want to leave each other. Ben begged me to come along and make up a foursome for the evening. We went dancing, then for a curry. Later on, the girls came back to our house and suddenly I was left alone with Lyn in my room as Ben had craftily engineered his date into his room. Lyn looked at me expectantly and I realised that, yet again I'd ended up in this awkward situation. We eventually went to bed and had an embarrassing fumble with each other under the covers, but nothing much happened and we eventually fell asleep. The next morning, there were surprisingly no recriminations from Lyn about my sexual inability or lack of desire. We ate breakfast together and ended up as friends. Everyone else thought we were lovers and neither of us denied it. It was easier that way for both of us. Ben's date was never seen again after that night, but Lyn and I stayed together for months.

One night Jim saw me in the Blythswood Cottage with my 'girlfriend' Lyn. He was furious, and kept coming over and acting really camp and dropping hints about our previous gay relationship, clearly trying to embarrass me. But both Lyn and I shrugged it off and laughed at him. Jim didn't understand that our relationship was purely platonic, but I have to admit I did wind up Jim up a bit when I spoke to him alone, telling him that Lyn and I were fantastic in bed together.

The Blythswood was very bohemian in those days, a mixture of students, staff from the nearby BBC Scotland studios, the West End gay crowd, and prostitutes that worked the streets nearby. It wasn't unusual to see a virtually naked woman come in, go to the bar and order a drink and stand chatting with a well-known sports presenter off the television.

I enjoyed my time and the friends I'd met at Doune Gardens, but as the New Year was approaching I still hadn't received any news about an appointment with a gender identity clinic. I still saw Brian at the Douglas Inch Centre, but only very occasionally. He was apologetic, but funding for people like me was very limited and I would have to wait. Clearly the judge's ruling had little bearing on the slow machinery of the NHS.

One night, Stewart announced that he and his girlfriend Anne were going to her firm's Christmas party. She worked at an accountancy practice, and Stewart knew none of her workmates. He desperately wanted some company for the night, so he wouldn't feel out of place. He pleaded with Ben and me to join him, and we readily agreed – a posh night out with free food and drinks sounded just the ticket. Lyn was working that night, so I asked my friend Isabelle to come with me.

I don't remember much about that night except seeing this beautiful woman across the dance floor. I felt a compelling urge to meet her, so I asked Stewart's girlfriend to introduce us. We were soon brought together, and that's when I met Sharon.

My future wife.

Chapter 12 'I Should Have Known Better'

Sharon also worked at the accountancy firm. She had a good job and still lived at home with her parents. She was four years older than me. I loved her smooth skin, soft permed hair and brown eyes. But most of all I loved her sense of humour. She had me laughing so much I was crying. Her life seemed the height of respectability and maturity, next to my vagabond existence in the West End. We chatted all night and danced, both happy to drink in each other's company. At the end of the night she left in a taxi back to the South side, but not before I'd got her phone number and extracted a promise from her to come and see me at Doune Gardens. I went back to Isabelle's flat that night and we stayed up chatting and eating cold lasagna. I told her I thought I was in love with that girl Sharon. Isabelle knew all about my lack of sexual appetite, whether it be with men or women, but she encouraged me.

"Maybe it's not that you don't like sex with women, Ally," she suggested. "Maybe it just needs to be with the *right* woman."

It wasn't until a few weeks later that I saw Sharon again. As promised, she eventually came to visit me at

Doune Gardens one Sunday afternoon. I watched the street below, straining to see her as the time approached for her to arrive. And when I saw her walking towards the house I felt such a surge of love in my heart. I knew this was something different. I barely knew her but I loved her completely from that day. She must be the 'right woman' for me. At last, I thought, now I could have a proper relationship, the same kind that everyone else seemed to be able to find so casually, but had always seemed impossible for me. Now, finally, I could be normal.

Over the next few months Sharon and I were inseparable. We met up on Sauchiehall Street most days after she finished work, and went for drinks or a meal. I visited her house, a tenement in Ibrox, and met her family. They were all very friendly and I got on really well with her mum. I reciprocated by inviting her to meet my family in the Vale. My parents were delighted with Sharon, who they could see was having a calming influence on me. I'm sure they desperately hoped I'd turned a corner and was finally growing up.

I did begin to feel that my employment and financial situation was somewhat precarious next to Sharon's. She had a good job, could afford to go on foreign holidays and buy nice clothes and expensive meals. Meanwhile I was still on unemployment benefit and working voluntarily. I knew that whenever she came round to Doune Gardens she was slumming it a bit, but she never complained. I even introduced her to some of the elderly people I worked with, and sometimes took her along when I would pop in to see them for a cuppa. Sharon seemed to have a good heart and got on well with these people, which was important to me.

This period of whirlwind romance was intoxicating, I didn't want it to end, but I also knew I had an important decision to make. Sharon knew nothing of my transsexuality, which I had kept completely hidden from her. One day I realised I'd not worn any of my female clothes in weeks. They were locked in my wardrobe in the bedsit. When I was with Sharon I wore jeans and a T-shirt. I still plucked my eyebrows and kept my hair long, but in everyday life I was essentially living as male. I had still heard nothing from the Douglas Inch Centre about my referral. What would I do if it suddenly came through? Would I tell Sharon, which would virtually guarantee an end to our relationship, or would I hide it? I knew I couldn't lie to her, so I had to make a choice. She was already wondering why I hadn't got a proper job. How could I tell her that if I got a job in my male persona it would demolish what was left of my attempt to complete the 'real-life test'?

One evening John Hannah told me he had a play coming up at the Royal Scottish Academy of Music and Drama. It was Chekhov's *Cherry Orchard*, and John was in the lead role. Would I like to go along and watch? He offered free tickets to all of us on the top floor. Neither Ben or Stewart were interested but I said I'd go with Sharon, to offer some support to John. I was curious to see him on stage. Becoming an actor was a brave thing for him to do, since he came from the same kind of working-class background as me, where any participation in the arts was seen as frivolous nonsense, not for the likes of us!

I really liked John. He had a similar background to me, and he was not afraid to be different (though obviously not to the same extent!), in that he would often wear clothes that could be construed as unusual. For example, he wore calf-length tiger skin slipper boots around the flat, not something that went unnoticed in those days! And it was quite clear that he was driven and serious about becoming a professional performer. He didn't worry about anyone else's opinion on that matter, nor about what people thought of how he dressed.

The performance itself was a revelation to me. John was absolutely fantastic. If I hadn't known it was him, I'd have sworn it was a different person on the stage that night. He inhabited his character completely. I could see he was going to be a big star one day, if there was any justice in the world. He stood out head and shoulders above everyone else, but at the same time was able to extract great performances from the other actors around him, encouraging by example. Afterwards we went backstage to congratulate him, where he was surrounded by plenty of other admirers. John thanked us for coming and we had a quick drink before Sharon and I left him to his friends and colleagues.

Later that night in a bar on Sauchiehall Street, Sharon and I discussed the play. She had been equally impressed with John's performance. I told her that he would soon be moving out of the house. He was going up in the world and had told me previously that he had an opportunity to move in with a girlfriend to a much nicer place. Stewart would be leaving soon too – as he was getting married – and he and his fiancée were buying a flat together.

"Maybe we should move in together, too," said Sharon. "You know, maybe get a flat?" It wasn't a complete surprise to hear this, since it had been on my mind, too. But I knew if I went down that path I'd be saying goodbye to my transition, possibly forever. Sharon could see I was not immediately enthusiastic about the proposition, but she didn't know why. "Don't you want to live with me?" she asked. She looked hurt. This was crunch time.

"Of course I do," I replied. "I'd love it if we had our own place. I just don't think I can afford it. I'd need to get a proper job".

"So look for one!" she said. "You can't keep volunteering forever. I've got enough money to get us started."

She was right, of course. I was fed up with being skint all the time and I needed a job. I'd been hanging on for ages waiting for a referral that by now seemed as if it might never come. Even if it did come, I would need to prove to the clinic that I was living the 'real-life test', and I already knew how hard that was to do, with no documents or money. Transitioning seemed to be so far away, an impossible dream slipping through my fingers. But here and now I had a beautiful woman I loved. We seemed made for each other, and the hope occurred to me once again that maybe she would be the one who would 'cure' me of my transsexuality. The 'right woman', as Isabelle had put it.

"Okay, let's start looking for a place."

And with that, my second transition attempt died.

* * * * * * *

The place Sharon and I finally chose to live in was another bedsit, above some shops on Great Western Road. It was only a five-minute walk from Doune Gardens, but since it was on the main road, with a posh Hillhead postcode, it was twice as expensive. We shared a kitchen and a loo with five other residents in the oddly-named house called 'Green Pepper Junction.'

To cover my share of the rent and pay my way I needed a job. I saw an advert in Maryhill Job Centre. Glasgow City Council (widely known as the 'Corporation') was looking for tradesmen, in particular, carpenters and painters. I phoned them and got an interview. I knew that if I was offered a job I would need to take it, but I also knew that the record would show I'd applied for a job as male with a male name, and I'd be officially employed and paying tax and national insurance contributions as a man. I was half-hoping that I didn't get the job. But I did. And so I was now employed on a one-year contract as a painter with the Glasgow Parks department.

I'd consciously and willingly thrown away my transition by taking the job. I had decided to trust in love. Sharon and I would have a future together that would hopefully overcome my transsexuality. Looking back, I can see the selfishness on my part. I told Sharon nothing about my gender dysphoria. I was hoping her love and our commitment to each other would overwhelm my inner torment.

* * * * * * *

I started work at the Possilpark depot. My job was to paint Portakabins that had come into our yard for refurbishment. My everyday dress was no longer short skirts and leggings. Now I wore paint-streaked white overalls and black steel-toe capped boots. The area was about as rough as you could find in Glasgow, with high blocks of council flats and half-derelict tenement buildings. The heroin epidemic was just beginning in Glasgow at that time, and Possilpark was one of the worst-affected areas. The streets were inhabited with junkies and alcoholics hanging around the depot, begging for money. We had break-ins most weeks, even though there was very little of value to steal.

As always seemed to happen with me, I soon made friends with my workmates. Having worked on building sites in London it wasn't a complete culture shock. We worked as a team: labourers, drivers and tradesmen on a kind of assembly line bringing in the Portakabins from all over the city for renovation. I was last in the line, and after everything else had been done I painted them inside and out, and then they went back out to the various Glasgow parks where they were stationed.

It was actually quite satisfying work, but it was in this environment that I found myself following the family socialist tradition. Both my mother and father had been trade union officials, and when a conflict arose with my fellow workers about stripping out asbestos material from the units, I got involved with the dispute. The dangers of asbestos were not widely known back then, and most workers just shut up and got on with the job. But a few of us were not comfortable about working in an enclosed area where carpenters were sawing up sheets of the stuff. We approached our trade union rep, but he was dismissive. So, I took it upon myself to find out how the rep could be replaced, checked the UCATT rules and called a meeting to elect a new shop steward. I was elected as the new union rep by show of hands, and the first thing I did was to call a strike until the asbestos was safely removed from our workplace. I got my way. It was my first venture into politics.

* * * * * * *

Back at Green Pepper Junction, Sharon and I were getting on well. We didn't have a lot of money but we were happy with our own little private space. For me, coming from the open-door policy at Doune Gardens, it was very different. Likewise for Sharon, having moved out of the tenement flat she had shared with her sister, brother and parents. It was the first time either of us had ever lived together with someone else, as a couple. We would both get up early and get ready for work, shower, dress, and have breakfast, then kiss goodbye and go to work. She walked to the tube and I walked to Possilpark. Each night when we came home we'd be eager and happy to see each other again. Often we'd go out for food or to the pub. We still used the Blythswood Cottage socially and so kept in touch with Ben, Stewart and John.

Worryingly for me, my ex-boyfriend Jim would occasionally turn up at our bedsit, especially if he'd been drinking. He and Bobby would press the downstairs street door buzzer and gain entry then come up and bang on our door with no prior warning. Then they would both come in, and hang around for a while trying to embarrass me in front of Sharon by obliquely dropping hints about my previous gay/transsexual life. Sharon knew nothing of this, of course, and thankfully didn't pick up on the innuendo. But I found it tiresome and was annoyed that they didn't want my new relationship to last, and in fact seemed intent on actively sabotaging it.

Jim was becoming a pest, and I thought it was now time to leave that part of my life behind me once and for all. After all, I was now living happily as a heterosexual man. I was twenty years old and living with a beautiful woman I loved. I had a proper job, and so did Sharon. With two decent incomes we could afford to move out and buy a flat away from the West End and leave my past and secrets behind. And so I did the obvious thing to try to bring some closure on the past: I proposed to Sharon.

"Let's get married and move to the South side." It was crazy, such a big step, and so casually thought out and executed.

Sharon accepted.

I knew she far preferred that part of Glasgow, since that was where she'd been born and raised, and it was where her mum was living. We began to look for a flat to buy in the Ibrox area. The plan would also enable me to sever my ties with Jim and anyone else who'd known me as female, gay or transsexual. I managed to convince myself that my previous dreams of transitioning and having a sex change were all just part of a phase I'd gone through. Actually, I was running away again, still desperately ashamed of myself, still homophobic and now transphobic. But most of all, I was still not able to face up to myself.

Sharon and I were still living at Green Pepper Junction as we planned our wedding. We decided on a civil ceremony rather than a church, and managed to get a slot at Clydebank Registry Office for October 1984. It was supposed to be a quiet affair, as we were saving money for a deposit and mortgage, but in the end it turned out to be quite lavish. Many of my family came from all over the UK.

I needed a best man, and this posed a bit of a problem for me. The general idea, of course, is to choose a long-time friend, often from childhood. But I'd cut myself off from all my childhood friends when I left the gangs behind me, and the same applied to my London friends. My next social circle of friends were from

Glasgow's West End, but many of them knew me as female, gay or transsexual, and I'd cut them off too, in an attempt to start my new straight life with Sharon. In the end I asked Ed, with whom I'd volunteered at the White Inch community centre. We'd not known each other very long, but he was very discreet and he got on well with Sharon. Thankfully he agreed. But the fact that I was already struggling to avoid my past in my choice of best man should have been a huge red flag.

Our wedding day went according to plan. The registry office was full and we went on to a luxury reception at the Bellahouston Hotel in Ibrox, complete with a posh meal, presents, speeches and a wedding cake. I actually still have a VHS tape of the event, which was professionally filmed by my sister Carolyn's boyfriend. I can't bring myself to watch it now, because I hate any photos or film of me as a man; it makes me feel physically sick.

We had a disco arranged for the after-party at the hotel. I still remember leading off the night with the first dance, Sharon and me in full wedding garb, with Sade's *Diamond Life* playing. After that it was a blur of alcohol and back-slapping. Everyone seemed to have a great night as we danced into the early hours.

Eventually, Sharon and I retired to the hotel bridal suite that had been booked as part of the arrangements. For our first night together as a married couple, Sharon had bought herself a sexy white basque with suspenders and white stockings. It hung on the wardrobe door as she got showered in the en suite bathroom. I, meanwhile, threw off my wedding suit and sat on the bed. An ice bucket containing a bottle of champagne awaited us on the table, but I was looking at the basque. I had to be honest and admit to myself that I desperately wished it was I who would be wearing it tonight. How fucked up was that? This was my wedding night! My new and beautiful bride was about to consummate our marriage vows with me and already I hated being the happy groom, the new husband, the *man*.

What the fuck have I done?

Chapter 13 'Dancing With Tears In My Eyes'

Much of the following three years of my marriage are a blank to me, even now. My mind blocked out so much of that time. It wasn't until many years later when I began to see a therapist for that I learned how people sometimes simply remove or delete distressing memories as a self-protection mechanism. I'm quite certain that this is what I did.

An example of this selective memory erasure is one time when Beth, my American cousin, former lover and soulmate came (with her new husband, Robert) to visit Sharon and me, two years after our wedding. Beth and Robert, who themselves had married a few years earlier, flew to Scotland to have a holiday and catch up with the relatives. Of course, an important part of their trip was for them to come and see Sharon and me at our house. Apparently we spent a whole day together, I cooked a meal for us all, and then we settled in for a boozy night when the four of us played records and partied. It was the only time I ever met Robert, but I have absolutely no recollection of it, even now. The only reason I know it happened, is because Beth reminded me of it almost twenty-five years later! So much of that period is missing from my memory. Not all of it, though; I do still seem to recall some of the edited highlights.

* * * * * * *

Within weeks of our wedding, Sharon and I had found a one-bedroom flat in a tenement building on Brand Street, Ibrox. It was just around the corner from Sharon's mum's place, so it was ideal. We quickly arranged a mortgage and bought it for £10,000. It's difficult to comprehend how low property prices were back then. Still, at the time it seemed quite expensive to us. We moved in, and with the help of family soon had the place furnished. I felt much more settled and secure here, safe in the knowledge that Jim, and with him my past life, wouldn't suddenly turn up unannounced at the door to embarrass me. After all, I was a respectable married man now – what on earth would the neighbours have thought?

Despite the flat being reasonably priced, Sharon and I soon discovered the other associated costs of property ownership. Building and contents insurance, factors bills, life insurance, etc. It all added up to rather more than we'd anticipated. So, since my wage from the Council (the Corporation) was lower than Sharon's, we decided that I would find a part-time job to earn some extra money.

So, I became a uniformed security guard.

The first jobs I was given were on building sites. As the newbie, I was only offered the occasional weekend shift as cover for others in the firm during their holidays or periods of sick leave. The work usually involved twelve-hour stints at a time, on my own. I'd finish work at the Parks Department at 4:30pm on a Friday, go home to Ibrox for dinner, then go to the site and start my shift at 9:00pm, working right through until 9:00am Saturday morning. Sleeping was impossible because I had to patrol the site every hour and clock in at various points along the way. I had a walkie-talkie to report any trouble, as there were no phones connected and of course mobile phones hadn't been invented yet.

One night I arrived for my shift to see the departing officer I was taking over from, just as he was leaving. He told me he usually patrolled with his dog and gestured towards a large iron-barred cage with a wooden hut inside.

"Here's his lead, and his food is inside the office," he explained. "Just walk him round the route with you and feed him at midnight. He might be a bit frisky with a stranger, but he's a lovely dog," he said, ominously, and with that, he left me holding a thick leather pleated lead. To me it seemed more like a rope that you could have used to tie up a ship in the Clyde! I went into the office and changed into my uniform, which consisted of ex-police jackets and trousers. Together with the hat, I hopefully looked enough like a cop to scare off any potential robbers intent on stealing the building supplies stacked up all around the site.

After an hour I decided it was time for my first patrol and went to see the dog. It was dark and he was hidden inside the wooden kennel as I opened the metal-barred gate, calling "here, boy" with the lead in one hand and my torch in the other. Suddenly, out of the darkness I heard a deep growl and a huge black muscular shape charged at me. It was the biggest, fiercest-looking Rottweiler you can imagine! As it pounced I could see its teeth and its slavering mouth illuminated by my torch light. I turned and ran, just managing to shut the cage door in time as the monster threw all of its weight against the bars. Jesus Christ, that was terrifying!

I went back into the office to catch my breath. That was a close one! That dog was better suited to guarding the gates of hell than a building site, and I decided there was no way I was going to try and walk it around the site. I was certain it would eat me before we even made it half-way round the patrol! So I ignored the dog and did the route on my own, every hour.

At midnight, I remembered it was time for the dog's food. I thought I'd just throw it through the bars and let him get on with it. I nervously approached the cage with a huge slab of raw liver that was still dripping blood when I noticed something was wrong. From the light of my torch I could see that the barred cage door was wide open. I could feel the hairs on the back of my neck lifting. The Hound of Hades had got out! It was free, probably watching me and about to pounce at me from the darkness. I simply dropped the meat and fled back to the safety of the office. After a while I realised I was too scared to do the patrols. I'd have to radio into the office and tell them what had happened. You can only imagine the reaction I received, when I reported that I'd somehow lost the guard dog, and the surrounding area should be alerted to the presence of a ravenous beast on the prowl. Some security guard I was!

Other jobs followed, however. My boss decided I would be less likely to get into trouble at Govan Cross shopping centre. My shift was a Saturday daytime, and I was to stand at the main entrance wearing my uniform and act as a deterrent to shoplifters. I turned up at 10:00am bright as a button, hoping for an easier job than the building site. Within minutes I was approached by a scruffy, long-haired man wearing a thin T-shirt and jeans. He looked to me a bit like a zombie.

"Hiya," he said cheerfully. "You're new, aren't you?"

I nodded. "Yes, my first day," I replied with a smile.

"Right, well I'm going to come running out of this door quite soon, and I don't want you trying to be a fucking hero and stopping me, all right?"

He then produced a dirty-looking syringe from his pocket and waved it in front of my face. It was half-full of blood. "That's Hep C in there," he said. "I'm infected, and you don't want to get this needle stuck in you, do you now?"

"Er, no," I agreed truthfully. "Thanks for the warning."

Sure enough, about twenty minutes later he ran past me on his way out of the shopping centre with armfuls of booze and raw meat, closely pursued by a couple of shopkeepers. I made sure I didn't notice any of this as I was facing the other way and studying the fire and emergency instructions on a wall.

I didn't get offered that gig again.

It was an awful job, but I kept turning up as we needed the money, and despite my various misadventures the firm didn't want to sack me as it was difficult to find new recruits. Over a period of several months I worked a succession of shifts around the city, all the time with my priority being my own physical safety. If I did ever catch anyone stealing it was more by accident than design. I tried my best not to be noticed.

One night was almost the last straw for me. Another guard and I had been allocated to the huge and notorious Glasgow council estate at Easterhouse. The job seemed simple enough. The council had installed new central heating systems and bathrooms to two council flats in a tower block. All we had to do was to make sure no one broke in and stole the fixtures and fittings overnight, as the new tenants would be moving in the next morning. If there was any problem we were to radio for help, and either the police or the other guards would arrive to back us up. What could possibly go wrong?

Plenty, as it turned out. Late that night we found ourselves under attack from all sides by scavenging neighbours coming through the doors and windows. The problem was that the radio signal didn't reach far enough to the base. So we were completely on our own as we tried to fight off the intruders. Eventually I decided it was best to make a run for a phone box I'd seen along the street, and call 999. The police turned up within half an hour, met us at the phone box and we all returned to the flats together. But it was too late; everything had been stripped. Radiators, boilers, sinks, baths, even the toilet pans and cisterns had gone, and most of the kitchen units. It was unbelievable.

I called in at the office the next morning and told my boss I was quitting. The situation we'd found ourselves in at Easterhouse was way too dangerous for the paltry wages they were paying. The boss, however, begged me to stay on.

"Please, Ally, don't leave," he pleaded. "We have another job that will suit you. It's in a factory compound, working with a team of eight other guards. You just have to show a presence and prevent any scrap metal lying around from being stolen. It's a former Victorian ironworks that used to be on the site, and it's full of old junk. Easy job – you can drink tea all night, play cards and listen to the radio."

Reluctantly, I agreed to give it one more shot. After all, the mortgage still needed to be paid.

Later that week I started at the factory. Sure enough, it was an easy and comfortable job. The other guys were friendly and actively discouraged any patrols. We sat in an office all night playing cards or having a sleep, if we could. The management didn't bother us. I was doing twelve-hour overnight shifts, Friday and Saturday.

I was there for a couple of weeks before I noticed something strange. I had decided, against my supervisor's advice, to get a bit of fresh air away from the smoke-filled atmosphere of the office. As I walked along outside, not more than twenty meters from base in the dark scrubland surrounding the office, I heard a squeaking sound that seemed to be coming from under the ground. Rats, I wondered? Then it got louder the further from the office I went, and it was also rhythmical, like sawing metal. Unless the rats were keeping up a singsong with a consistent beat to it, then it must be something else. Very odd.

I was just about to turn and head back to the office when I heard muffled voices. Now it was getting creepy. The voices and the rats seemed to be under my feet. I dashed back to the other guards in the office to tell them what I'd just heard. But rather than display any surprise, they all started looking around at each other sheepishly.

"What the fuck is going on?" I demanded. This was getting scary.

What the fuck was actually going on, I soon learned, was that the entire security crew was working in collusion with a team of copper cable thieves working underground throughout the site. They had struck a deal with the local council house estate gang to remove miles of the Victorian four-inch thick copper cable, sell it and split the cash. All we had to do as security guards was ignore what was happening right under our feet.

As I heard this tale I looked around at a lot of frightened guards' faces. None of them knew if they could trust me and were understandably worried what I would do next. Would I report it? Was I a management plant? Worst of all, would I call the police? The security supervisor was called Tommy Teabag, for some unknown reason. He looked at me expectantly.

"It's your call, Ally. Do you want a share of this? It'll be a few hundred quid each, and we can all have a very nice Christmas with that money. The management at base don't know anything about how much of the stuff is in the ground, and the factory owners have no idea either. It's like a rabbit warren down there. It'll take years to get it all out, and we've uncovered tunnels that have been hidden for over a century, all full of copper cables."

I didn't have to think for too long. The security firm was only paying me just over £2 an hour, so we were indeed talking about a lot of money. These guys were all anxious about having their Christmas bonuses stolen away. These were family men with young kids, or like me with mortgages and rent to pay. What would it matter if some copper that no one had thought about in decades went walkabout?

I turned around and put the kettle on. "Cuppa anyone?" I grinned.

That year we had a very good Christmas. Sharon and I cleared a lot of debt, and I left the security firm soon after the New Year started.

* * * * * * *

Now, away from the West End, and with hardly any free time due to my long work hours, my opportunities to even think about my transsexualism were limited. I no longer had any regular contact with the Douglas Inch Centre, and they still hadn't managed to get my referral to the Charing Cross GIC organised, anyway. I tried to force myself to forget about all 'that sex change stuff.' It was all just a fantasy anyway, I told myself. My twenty-first birthday came and went, and I drifted into living my life on autopilot as I went from home to work, and back home again. From time to time, my thoughts would drift to the possibility of living my life as female. But, for now at least, it seemed way out of reach. I had responsibilities.

Chapter 14 'Love Don't Live Here Any more'

There were occasional breaks from the daily grind, and overseas holidays in particular were something that Sharon insisted on, regardless of how short of money we were. In her view, we worked hard and deserved at least one proper sun-drenched holiday every year. The first trip we took was to Crete, and this started my love affair with Greece and Mediterranean history. I love a hot, dry climate and didn't want to leave. So, when the chance arose to visit her brother in Israel, where he'd been volunteering for a few years on a Kibbutz, we jumped at it.

Our plan was to go as guest workers for the summer. My contract with the Parks department had ended, and I wasn't offered an extension (such is the life of a trade union activist) and Sharon had saved up some money from her job.

And so our party of three arrived at Israel's Ben Gurion Airport in the summer of 1986. I say three, because Sharon's mum Mary came along with us. I was quite happy since she was a sweet and kind woman, and we got on well.

The weather in Israel was gloriously hot and I was excited and looking forward to an adventure. I still thought of myself as believer in God in those days, but not a follower of any religion. And to be in the Holy Land, with all its history, was just fantastic. Sharon's slightly younger brother Gordon met us at the airport, together with his Israeli fiancée Miya, and drove us in a Land Rover back to the kibbutz just south of Akko (Acre), near the Lebanese border.

On arrival at the kibbutz we were given an apartment for our use by the elders, within the lush grassy compound. All the facilities, including our food in the communal restaurant, and our medical needs, would be provided too. It seemed fantastically generous and I loved the whole ethos of communal life.

The first thing I realised about the kibbutz was that, far from toiling in the fields as I'd imagined we'd be doing, we were encouraged to chill and relax. There was no particular requirement for us work for our keep. Instead, we'd do a few hours here and there if we felt like it, but as guests we were advised to enjoy ourselves as much as possible, and go out see the country. If we wanted to borrow a car we could just go and sign one out from the fleet of thirty or more vehicles sitting in the car park. Unfortunately I didn't have a driving licence, but the offer was there.

The kibbutz had a swimming pool and a sports hall, even a cinema. Everyone we met was extremely friendly and hospitable. I loved the community atmosphere, and this seemed an idyllic place to live. The only drawback was that with so much free time away from the constant work and grind back in Glasgow, I now had a lot of time on my hands to think about other things. Inevitably for me, that meant my transsexuality, that I'd mostly managed to block from my mind over the past few years.

Despite what seemed like an idyllic lifestyle here in Israel, under the surface the kibbutznics were not all sweetness and light. It had not been easy for these people to carve out a life in this barren landscape that was truly an oasis created in the desert. They were strong-willed, hardy and fiercely patriotic. The founders had fought hard to establish the kibbutz from the start, and were still prepared to defend it through armed resistance, if needed.

One day I watched as Israeli Air Force jets screamed overhead as they flew north towards the Lebanese border. The noise was terrifying. In the distance I heard the rockets and bombs exploding in Lebanon, followed by sickening plumes of smoke that rose from the horizon. Then the planes flew back overhead into Israel. That night on the Arab TV news channel we could pick up, there were reports of death and destruction but, on Israeli TV, there was nothing except a denial to the Lebanese claims that anything had happened at all. When I asked my Israeli friends about this, their response was usually a smile and a shrug of acceptance. There was an incomprehensible disconnect (to me at least) when it came to the suffering of people outside the kibbutz. On one hand the Israelis seemed to be the most generous and giving people I'd ever met. But on the other, these same people could also sit at night with sniper rifles and telescopic sights firing live rounds at Arab children trying to steal watermelons from the fields.

One day Sharon and I decided to go to Jerusalem by ourselves to spend some time together and see the sights of the ancient city. We hitch-hiked from the kibbutz for the two-hour journey, arrived in the early afternoon and booked into a private room at a youth hostel near the Jaffa gate. It was strange having so much time together, just us alone. For the past couple of years it had seemed we'd never had a moment to ourselves between constant work and sleep. Now, with the opportunity to finally relax together it was slightly awkward and we hardly knew what to say to each other! We quickly decided that we should organise an itinerary of things to do and see that would keep us occupied. It was as though we were both worried about having too time to think about being a couple. We did all the usual stuff, visiting the Dome of the Rock, the Shuk street markets, the Wailing Wall and so on, and managed to tire ourselves out. That evening, after a late meal in a restaurant, we were both happy to get back to the hostel and fall asleep immediately.

The next morning we had planned to visit Bethlehem. I'd always wanted to go there to see the spot where Jesus was born. It was located underneath the huge Basilica of the Nativity. We caught one of the numerous shared white Mercedes taxis from the rank close to the hostel and made the short journey there. As usual, given the extreme heat, we were both wearing lightweight clothing, me in shorts and Sharon in a loose cotton skirt, both topped with T-shirts. This had been our everyday gear since we'd arrived in Israel.

My mood was quite contemplative as we walked towards the low entrance to the building, my thoughts turning yet again to transitioning, and what I'd given up to try to make this marriage to Sharon work. I recalled the endless prayers I'd made to Jesus when, as a child, I'd begged him to make me female overnight as I slept, desperately hoping I'd wake up in the morning as a girl.

As I ducked my head down to enter the narrow passageway behind Sharon, an old Arab lady grabbed me and held me back. She held my arm and began speaking to me in Arabic, pointing at my legs. I had no idea what she was saying, but she insisted in holding me back from the doorway. Sharon and I looked at each other in confusion; what was she trying to say? We smiled at the woman and I gestured to her, trying to say, what's up? What's going on? I was getting embarrassed and a queue of pilgrims were lining up behind us, blocked by my detention at the doorway. Then the lady smiled, and from somewhere produced a beautiful wraparound heavy silk embroidered skirt and placed it around my waist, fastening it together with a pin. Apparently it was considered indecent for women to show their legs inside the church. She thought I was a woman! I decided not to argue with her, and once satisfied the skirt was hanging correctly on my hips, she ushered Sharon and me into the building.

And so, when I finally came close to Jesus, at his birthplace, under the rock and with the smell on incense around me, I was wearing a skirt, just like Sharon and all the other women there. It seemed at that moment an uncanny incident as I gazed at the silver star set in the floor glistening in the light of a hundred candles. It was the first time in years I'd worn female clothing.

Was it a mystical sign from above? Actually, with hindsight, and from the distance of miles, years, and a healthy dose of agnosticism, probably not. But that day lingered in my mind for the rest of my time in Israel, and for years after returning to the UK.

There was another incident that occurred in Israel, something that I now understand as 'grief deflection,' that demonstrated to me later the strain I was clearly feeling at the time.

I have never been able to openly express my unhappiness or grief through tears, in the moment, not since I was a small child. I cannot spontaneously cry, no matter what happens to me. Physical attack, the break-up of a relationship, or even bereavement – I face it all with dry eyes and a hard face. I believe this dates back to when I was physically abused as a child by my parents. People probably think I'm just heartless and uncaring, but I learned back then never to show any emotion, as this just made things worse. My dad wanted me to cry as he hit me, because it would prove I was girly and feminine. So, the only power I had in that unequal situation was not to allow the sobs to come. To hide my natural femininity from his ridicule. I know it's probably unhealthy, but I have continued to bottle up my tears until they only very occasionally come forth at a different, unrelated and sometimes trivial upset. It's something I can't control.

In the kibbutz one evening as I sat alone watching TV, a small gecko startled me by running along the wall close to where I was sitting. I instinctively grabbed a cane that was close by and smacked at the tiny lizard, killing it stone dead. As I looked at the beautiful tiny green body of the dead reptile I'd killed, I burst into uncontrollable sobs. The sadness I felt on seeing this tiny life extinguished by my thoughtless cruelty engulfed me in sorrow and despair as the years of my own fear and vulnerability seemed to be depicted before me. The dam burst for the first time in many years and I cried uncontrollably for hours over the gecko. I still feel sorrow now, more than thirty years later, whenever I think of it.

Towards the end of our time in Israel, things were becoming fractious between Sharon and me. I was beginning to have doubts about whether I wanted the path that seemed to have been laid out for us. It all looked so predictable: work, save money, pay the mortgage, eventually buy a bigger place in Ibrox, and repeat for the next thirty-odd years. We had an argument one evening; I don't remember even what it was about, but I stormed out of the apartment.

There were few rules in the kibbutz, but one was that you do not go into Akko after dark. I'd visited the beautiful medieval walled city many times that summer during the day, but it was deemed too dangerous for non-Arabs at night. Ignoring this advice, I walked to the main road and hitched a lift into town. I went to a bar just as night fell and ordered a beer. I was soon approached by some Arab guys, clearly surprised to see me, but anxious to be friendly, despite the language barrier. We had several beers together and then a girl came over to join us.

She said her name was Rachel and she was Israeli. I told her I was volunteering at the kibbutz but had been told not to come here at night. Was it true that Akko is dangerous? I asked. She laughed, then translated to the guys around us what I'd said, and they all laughed too. Their interpretation was that the people from the kibbutz were all scared farmers, too frightened to mix. One young man who could speak reasonable English introduced himself as Masud, and told me that he and his friends would show me around Akko and make sure I had a good time.

And so I spent the next few hours trailing round bars and cafés being introduced to people by my new friends. I wasn't allowed to buy a drink anywhere we went. All the guys wanted to do was talk about was football or exchange cigarettes – my British ones for their extra-strong Arab ones. I'd never seen so many Liverpool or Manchester United fans outside of the UK! Anything I could tell them about their teams (which wasn't much) they were eager to hear. It was a wonderfully enjoyable night with so many happy and friendly people. As a Scot, I was something of a novelty and Masud clearly wanted to show me off.

Eventually the bars began to close and it was time for everyone to head home. I asked my friends if they could take me to a taxi rank, but that idea was dismissed out of hand. "No, we will take you home, don't worry," I was told. Soon there were about seven of us packed into one of the ubiquitous white Mercedes saloons that everyone seemed to use, and off we drove into the night.

The only time I had any slight concern about the warnings I'd been given, was when we left Akko in the Mercedes. Rather than heading towards the main road, the car began climbing up a low hill along a dirt track. I tried to point out that the kibbutz was the other direction Masud tried to reassure me.

"Don't worry, don't worry," he said, "We'll take you home, but first we go to our village for food." Soon we arrived in the Arab village. There were lots of people around and open-air cooking taking place. I was invited into a yard and introduced to Masud's mother, sisters and other relatives, even the children. Everyone here was just as friendly and curious to meet me. I was shown to a place on a large carpet rolled out in the front yard and we all sat in a circle under the trees that had oil lanterns hanging from the branches. Food was produced – flat breads, rice dishes, some kind of meat and baked fish. It was a fantastic feast and though I could not understand the conversation much, it was a great atmosphere.

After some time had passed, I realised that perhaps I really should be getting back to the kibbutz. I'd been gone for more than seven hours and people back there might be getting concerned about my safety. I indicated to my host that I had to go, and asked if someone could please drive me back to the main road. It took at least another half hour but soon I was back in the white Merc surrounded by my happy companions as we sped off back down the hill towards the kibbutz. It must have been around 3:00am as we drove up the private road to the large gate of the kibbutz. I asked them to drop me off there as I intended to sneak in without having to wake anyone up. But suddenly the whole road and gateway was illuminated by bright lights and I heard Israeli shouts and saw several what were unmistakably rifles pointed towards us. The car came to a halt. My companions were still laughing and giggling, seemingly unconcerned by the situation. I was gently ushered out of the car door.

"Go, go," Masud said, smiling. He indicated that I should raise my hands. I followed his instructions and walked slowly towards the gate.

"Hello, er…it's okay, it's just me, Ally. I'm a volunteer, my brother-in-law is Gordon."

A couple of uniformed kibbutznics came out of the shadows towards me, grabbed me roughly and dragged me inside the gate. Oh shit, I could see I had some explaining to do. These guys seemed pretty angry. One of the Israelis shouted at the Merc and I heard laughter from inside as the car door shut and my friends turned the car round and roared off into the darkness.

My-brother-in-law Gordon was duly summoned to identify me. Understandably, he wasn't too chuffed about being woken up in the middle of the night. But once he spoke with the gate guards I was allowed to go back to our apartment. Once inside I got another rollicking from Sharon.

"What the fuck are you playing at?" she screamed. "Do you realise how dangerous it is out there at night? You're lucky you weren't shot at the gates. Where were you, I was worried sick?"

Over the next couple of days I was met by disapproving stares from many in the kibbutz as word of my nocturnal adventure spread. I'd clearly caused a lot of trouble and annoyance. I tried to explain to some of my Israeli friends that I was sorry to have been out at night without informing anyone, and that I hadn't intended to scare or worry anyone. When I tried to say that I'd also had a really nice time, and try to tell them about the village and the people I'd met, I was dismissed as talking nonsense. No one wanted to hear that. Minds were closed, it was dangerous to associate with the Arabs, subject closed.

* * * * * * *

My escapade in Akko cast a shadow over our final week in Israel, and soon it was time to return to Glasgow. Sharon and I had also begun to have regular arguments. Our time in Israel had exposed some obvious flaws in our relationship. Added to this we had money problems. I'd have to find another job since I'd left the Corporation and it wasn't easy to find something that paid enough to cover the mortgage payments. We were becoming dependent on Sharon's wages to survive.

Finally I got a job in the Clachan bar on Paisley Road, west, Ibrox. It was a large pub with three bars and I was in charge of the lounge bar. The premises had been bought by a wealthy Asian businessman for his eighteen year old son Adji, who had no experience of pubs, either as a customer or owner. Part of my job was to show him the ropes (although I had little experience either – I'd just blagged my way in). The hours I worked were evenings and weekends, the opposite of Sharon's work hours, so, conveniently perhaps, we didn't see much of each other.

* * * * * * *

I still loved Sharon, but I didn't like myself, or what I'd become. I felt trapped. Not for the first time I wondered why I couldn't simply be normal. Being transsexual pre-treatment is ugly – it rules your life twenty-four seven. There's no glamour, no enjoyment; it's a curse I wouldn't wish on anyone. It destroys your family, your social life, your love life, your friendships and your mental health. I had been running from it since childhood but it always managed to catch up with me.

The first two years of marriage proved to me that even Sharon's love wouldn't 'cure' me. And, sadly, some people, then as now, think it's a choice. The only choice I could see was whether to continue living in complete misery, or transition so I could try to exist in slightly less misery.

Then, out of the blue, Sharon announced she was pregnant.

Chapter 15 'Crazy Crazy Nights'

The idea of having children was not something I'd ever thought about. Sharon was on the pill, and since we had sex so infrequently it never even crossed my mind. The worry of having the responsibility of caring for a child was terrifying. How on earth could I be part of bringing up a child? I couldn't even hold down a job! I wasn't any good as a husband. How could I be a father when I didn't even feel like I was a man?

Around the same time as Sharon announced we were having a baby, we had begun to visit the Vale quite regularly. I'd made contact with some old friends but kept away from the gangs. My parents were delighted with the prospect of a grandchild, but like Sharon and me, they were concerned about the financial situation we were about to find ourselves in. Once the baby was born, without Sharon's regular salary, my insecure employment at the Clachan bar wouldn't be enough to keep up the mortgage payments on our flat. A solution was needed, and after a few enquiries were made in the right places from my family, I was advised to go and speak to a local councillor who also ran a pub in the Vale, with a view to obtaining council housing.

In those days that was often the way of things – certain local councillors and housing officials could be easily bought. It was a tradition going right back to the family story I remember hearing of when my granny Chrissie had bribed a council housing official with a gold ring to obtain the keys to my parents' first council house, just after I was born.

So I visited the pub and had a couple of drinks with the councillor, a small fee was agreed, and I was soon offered a two-bedroom council flat in the Vale, with the tenancy in my name. We could move in right away and that meant Sharon could rent out our flat in Ibrox for a profit. My parents were happy with this solution as it meant I was also back home in the Vale and they could be involved with me and Sharon and help out with the new baby when it arrived.

So, we moved back to the Vale. I gave up the Clachan bar job, and despite the inconvenient reality of not yet having a driving licence, decided to start a furniture removal business with my old punk schoolfriend, Glen. I bought a Luton Transit van and Glen, who did have a licence, drove it. We called the business 'Anything Goes' and specialised in shifting single items and house clearances. Sharon and I soon found tenants for the Ibrox flat, so by the time she had to give up work, we were just about managing financially.

Things between Sharon and me were not going well, however. She detested living in the Vale away from her mother. She disliked my friends, and most of all she disliked my parents who visited us regularly, often when drunk. I felt caught between everyone. I wanted us to survive financially and living in the council flat seemed the only option. But I was being dragged back into my old criminal male life and I still had to work all the hours I could to bring money home. The fact was, in order to get work in the transport of goods and furniture in the Vale, you had to be part of the community and that meant socialising in the pubs most evenings. I was quickly back in the habit of excessive drinking and regular drug-taking.

After I passed my driving test, we were able to take on much more work and buy a bigger van. Now we did full house moves as well as single items, and I even worked as a roadie for a local band, taking their equipment to gigs all round the west coast of Scotland. I also took on a lease for a Saturday market stall, selling framed art and basket ware, hoping that Sharon would help me run it and thinking it would give her an interest and a chance to get to know the locals, but she wasn't interested. I was hardly home most nights before 10:00 pm and this meant Sharon felt increasingly isolated from her own family and friends. Even when my friends or family came to visit us, Sharon would often just get up and leave the room and go and sit alone in the kitchen or bathroom, she despised them so much. Understandably, this was socially embarrassing for anyone who came to visit. I could see this was not a good situation; neither of us were happy with the life we had now, and it was a far cry from when we'd first got together in the West End of Glasgow. We both felt trapped with each other, waiting for the birth.

Eventually it was time for Sharon give up work. We'd attended the anti-natal classes, bought a cot, pushchair, and all the other paraphernalia associated with having a new baby. Surrounded by well-wishers, I was dying inside.

I had hoped to be with Sharon during the birth, but it soon became apparent that it would to be a caesarian birth, a procedure where I was surplus to requirements. As it happened, a friend of mine, Mickey (whom I'd first met at my wedding reception, because a workmate had brought him along) was also waiting for his partner, Ellen to give birth. Mickey and Ellen had recently moved to the Vale from Ibrox, too.

On the night Sharon's contractions started, and then her waters broke, we rushed up to the Vale Hospital maternity unit, and once there I was ushered into a waiting room as Sharon was whisked away into the delivery suite. Sitting there was Mickey, with a large carrier bag of booze. We acknowledged each other, sat together, and waited.

* * * * * * *

As I sat holding my baby boy I was overwhelmed by love. It's no exaggeration to say I was changed from that moment on. Holding this brand new human being in my arms immediately altered my world view. All the problems Sharon and I were having in our relationship, and even my own personal battle with my gender identity, seemed dwarfed by the arrival of this beautiful new life we had created. Of course our problems wouldn't go away, and soon it would all come back to haunt us, but this moment demonstrated to me the point, the explanation, the entire purpose of life. Producing this little bundle of joy would be the most important thing we had ever done, or would ever do.

It also suddenly struck me, that if my referral to the clinic at Charing Cross had gone ahead as planned, this new life in my arms would not have existed. It might seem obvious, but of course, if you go through sex reassignment surgery you will, upon completion of the process, become sterile. I always knew that but never thoughtfully examined that fact before now. There is no doubt in my mind – if I had been able to access surgery at any point in the previous ten years I would have jumped at that opportunity in a heartbeat, and this child would not have been born. Another realisation came to me with the birth of my beautiful baby. I understood I maybe had some worth of my own? My own chaotic life of shame, violence, lies and desperate unhappiness had, despite everything, contributed to produce something wonderful. That knowledge would never be forgotten and would guide my future thoughts.

We called our baby boy Joseph after my father. If nothing else, I was very traditional when it came to naming children. I loved him deeply and I felt enormously privileged to have a child. I decided that his needs were paramount and that I should focus on what was best for him above my own desires, from now on. I was now twenty-three years old and would try and make my relationship with Sharon work.

Within a few days, Sharon was released from hospital and came home to our flat in the Vale with Joseph. We were now a proper little family. My friends Mickey and Ellen had their own baby boy, born within minutes of Joseph at the same hospital. I hoped that this this shared experience between Sharon and Ellen would develop into a friendship that would give Sharon a stake in the Vale, and help her settle, rather than always be pining for her mother back in Ibrox.

Unfortunately, problems emerged within days of Sharon coming home. To start with, Joseph was not an easy baby. He had what seemed like constant colic and cried a lot, was very difficult to settle and barely slept at night. Sharon and I were soon frazzled by our own lack of sleep due to his screams. Anyone who has experienced a new baby can relate to the situation. Your ears actually physically ache from the noise of a baby's scream which is pitched at just the right level that cannot be ignored. My parents would often pop in and try to offer help and advice, but Sharon only saw this as interference. The fact that my dad was often drunk when they visited didn't help. On one occasion my aunt Chrissie, who had brought up seven children of her own, came round to see Joseph. She advised that I put a half-teaspoon of whisky into his milk to help with the colic and allow him to sleep, an old mothers' remedy she had used many times in the past. I tried it, and it worked. Joseph slept through for several hours. But when I told Sharon what I'd done she went berserk. She virtually accused my family of poisoning her baby.

The ritual of Sharon leaving the room as soon as any of my family or friends came round, continued. Even with Mickey and Ellen when they brought round their baby for a visit. Sharon wouldn't interact with anyone except her mother and seemed deeply unhappy. I managed to speak with our health visitor on my own one day and explained the situation, seeking advice. The health visitor put Sharon's behaviour down to 'baby blues,' a form of depression, and told me confidently that it would pass.

I continued to work with the 'Anything Goes' transport business, as well as the Saturday morning market stall. One highlight of the week for Sharon was when I visited the warehouses to buy stock for the stall. She would come along too since they were all situated near to Ibrox and it was a chance for her to see her mother. It was the only thing that seemed to lift her out of her depression.

One evening, when Joseph was only a few months old, I came home from work. I settled down to dinner, and Sharon broke the news that she had found a flat back in Ibrox next to her mother, and was moving in the next week. She had paid the deposit, and the first month's rent, and had arranged for our furniture in the Vale flat to be delivered there.

I was devastated. Not only had all this been arranged behind my back, I didn't even know if I was supposed to be part of this relocation back to Ibrox, or was she leaving me and taking Joseph? But Sharon had decided. She told me I could visit any time I liked, but she wouldn't live in the Vale a moment longer.

When my family and friends found out, they were all outraged at the way she had acted. They advised me to let her go and get on with my own life. Anyone who could treat me this way was not worth being with. I could understand their point of view, but they didn't understand how much Joseph meant to me. It wasn't just that he was my son; he was the reason I'd given up any future plans to transition. I'd invested everything in our marriage and our baby. He was the reason I was living as a man, in fact a married man and a father.

A few days later the removal firm came and stripped our home in the Vale of most of its furniture. I came home from work to an almost empty flat, with no Sharon or Joseph.

I know it must seem obvious to anyone reading this, and in hindsight, to me too. I was being told in the clearest terms by Sharon to fuck off, it was game over.

But I couldn't accept or understand it back then. I was blinded by my love for Joseph. I couldn't let him go that easily, so I decided I would fight to win back my family, whatever it took, regardless of my shame and any ridicule that came my way from family and friends. I was plainly not man enough in Sharon's eyes. Maybe she had seen through me? I decided I'd fight to get her and Joseph back by proving I could be a man worthy of respect. So fight I did, in the year ahead.

Several times a week.

Chapter 16 'With Or Without You'

Next, Sharon decided we had to sell the property on Brand Street we owned. Looking back, there was no urgent need for this. We had it rented out and the mortgage payments were covered. But she insisted, and I later realised that what she really wanted was to detach herself from me financially. However, naive as I was, I agreed. As it happened, my sister Carolyn had just got a new job in Glasgow a couple of tube stops away from Brand Street and was looking for a cheap flat to buy. So we sold it to her. Another tie between Sharon and me was unfastened.

After Sharon had settled into her new rented flat on Midlock Street, Ibrox, I began visiting most nights and staying over. I desperately wanted to be part of bringing up Joseph. Sharon didn't object. She was a lot happier now that she could visit her mum and family every day. But it was made clear to me this was *her* place, not *ours*. I was only a visitor who could be told to leave at any time. Sharon was in control.

The constant travelling back and forth between Ibrox and the Vale was becoming difficult for me to keep 'Anything Goes' running. Not being in the Vale and able to take a job at short notice made it impossible,. and before long I had to give it up. However, I still kept the Saturday market stall going. I also still stayed at the Vale council flat a few nights a week, despite there being virtually no furniture, to make sure I could set up the stall early on Saturdays.

It soon became apparent that only working one or two days a week on the stall was not bringing enough money in. I would need to get another job, and preferably one in Ibrox or Glasgow city centre so I could maintain contact with Joseph and stay over at Sharon's flat most nights. My prospects were limited; I didn't have many qualifications from school and my work history was patchy, to say the least. But Sharon's older brother Bert gave me an idea one night.

He was a big guy, six foot four, and could handle himself. He had a regular day job as a locksmith, but at weekends he worked as a bouncer in the Glasgow nightclubs and discos. If I was interested, he said, he could put in a word for me. The money was good for such a dangerous job, and I thought it would also give me an opportunity to prove myself as a man with Sharon, and maybe win her and Joseph back.

* * * * * * *

A few nights later I went for an interview at Tiffany's Disco on Sauchiehall Street, where Bert worked. The manager who spoke to me apologised, he said he'd just hired a couple of bouncers and there was nothing for me. However, he did say he had a friend of his, Steve, who owned a lively new bar next to Queen

Street station called the Pig and Whistle, and they were hiring. I should go and see Steve and tell him that Bert had sent me. I walked the ten minutes to Queen Street and entered the very busy bar and asked for the manager. Steve came over to see me, shook my hand, and told me he'd been expecting me since the manager at Tiffany's had called. I could see by the way he looked at me that he was slightly unsure if I was bouncer material. Most bouncers in those days were well over six feet tall and built like heavyweight boxers. I was five foot ten, slim with long hair and plucked eyebrows. I told him not to worry, I could handle myself. Give me a week's trial, I said, and I'll prove it. So he did.

The Pig and Whistle was definitely more than 'lively.' It was the place to be for the young crowd in Glasgow city centre nightlife at the time I started working there, which meant far more people wanted to get in than we had room to accommodate. There seemed to be no obvious reason why some bars and clubs became massively popular, but when they did the cool people turned up and brought along a lot of admirers. This meant there was a fortune to be made by the owners if they managed it correctly. The landlords knew to maximise the profits while their star was bright, because as soon as the next cool bar appeared the fickle youth would desert en mass.

My job was to be part of a team of three bouncers to regulate the door entry, keep out the drunks and troublemakers, and if needed, be ready to get inside if a fight broke out, and help the three other bouncers who controlled the interior. The rate of pay was £50 a night cash in hand and up to six free drinks a night for each bouncer. This was a lot of money back in the eighties for a part-time job, but Steve knew it was peanuts compared to the money he was taking over the bar. My uniform was the standard black trousers, white shirt and a clip-on black bow tie.

As always, there were a few chancers who tried to push their way in and test the new door staff, usually by claiming they were friends of Steve the owner. But I knew Steve had no friends among the clientele; to him they were all just paying punters, so I treated everyone equally and without favour unless I was told otherwise by Steve. So I knew where I stood, and I knew he would also back me up in any dispute.

That first week one of the guys who worked the door with me, Jim, got into a fight and broke two fingers. He was an environmental officer for the council in his day job so he wasn't dependent on the bouncer work, and so he left to recuperate. A new doorman, Peter, was employed and I moved up in seniority. Within a couple of weeks I was in charge of the door team, as the other guy Tony left and was replaced by Martin. High turnover wasn't unusual on the doors because you could pick up enemies easily and become a target. You had to weigh up who was connected to the large Glasgow estate gangs and who were just casual drunks and troublemakers. If you got it wrong you might easily find that someone you had kicked the shit out of the previous evening would come back the next night with a team of up to three hundred gang members. If that happened, not only were you in real personal danger, but you became a liability to the bar and had to get out, sharpish. That's what happened to Tony.

I managed to keep on the right side of those who I needed to respect, and keep out the idiots, for about six months at the Pig and Whistle, which was a fairly long career for a doorman at a single venue in those days. I had at least one fight almost every night I worked there, but somehow managed to avoid any serious injury. Most trouble came because of women, or rather, the men's behaviour in front of their girlfriends. Fortunately I could talk easily to women and that diffused the situation usually. Unaccompanied men would often just accept being told they were drunk and not welcome, but when they were with women it was so much more difficult as they felt the need to impress them, by fighting the door staff. The girlfriends often carried the weapons for their boyfriends, with knifes or razors in their bags, even sharpened steel combs. I had no qualms about searching the women's bags, whereas some of the other door staff were embarrassed to do this properly. I was attacked on two occasions by women who had removed their stiletto heels to use as weapons on me, but I treated them in exactly the same way I would a man with a knife. This was not a job for misplaced chivalry! Calling the police for help was not an option, firstly because by the time they arrived the fracas would probably be over, and also Steve would get really upset if the police had to be called because it gave the venue a bad name that might jeopardise his licence.

* * * * * * *

Meanwhile, back at Sharon's flat we were still not getting on. The one thing we both cared about was Joseph and that's what sustained our shaky relationship. The nights I worked would be long. I'd start off with a few drinks about 7:00pm, to get me focused, then I'd have several more during the evening. Finally, after we'd cleared the bar at the end of the night, Steve would lock the doors and the staff would carry on drinking for an hour or so until 2:00am; this gave us some time to relax, but it also provided a window to allow those customers who had been ejected or refused entry, an opportunity to sober up and go home, rather than lie in wait outside for the staff, to get their revenge on us when we left the bar.

More often than not after a shift at the Pig and Whistle, a few of us would go to a Chinese or Indian restaurant for a meal to come down after the stress. This meant I'd often not get home until three or four in the morning. And I'd sleep late the next day. Between the bar and the market stall in Vale I still worked, it meant Sharon and Joseph were effectively in a different time zone from me, but I still loved the few hours I did get to spend with Joseph.

When I was back in the Vale working the stall, many people, old school friends or family, would ask me how things were, and about Sharon and Joseph. I usually lied, telling them we'd bought a new house in Glasgow and they were there. I couldn't lie to Mickey and Ellen, though, as they had mutual friends with us in Ibrox and they knew Sharon was in a rented flat. I started hanging out with them whenever I was in the Vale and we became close friends. I began to smoke a lot of hash round at their house. His next door neighbour was a dealer, which made it easy for me to get whatever I wanted.

I wasn't short of money at this time, between my work on the doors and the market trading. But I was still incredibly unhappy. I bought my first proper car, a blue BMW. Up until now I'd only owned vans to use for work. I thought the BMW might make me feel happier, but it didn't. One night after drinking a vast amount of alcohol and smoking a lot of dope I decided to go for a drive. As

I drove through the empty streets between Glasgow and the Vale in the early hours I began thinking about where I was going in life. My marriage seemed to be hanging by a thread, my thoughts of transitioning were never far from my mind again, but now I had the additional responsibility of Joseph. How could I ever transition and bring all that shame and embarrassment on to him as he grew up? It all suddenly became too much and I started sobbing. An idea became clear and obvious to me. If I didn't wake up tomorrow would I, or anyone else, really care? So why not end it all now? A car crash would be best, then it would look like an accident and Joseph and Sharon would get the insurance.

I drove around a council estate in Clydebank looking for a suitable wall to smash the BMW into. I soon found the perfect spot in a quiet street that would give me room to get up to speed. There was a heavy sandstone wall at the end of the straight, just as the street bent round a right hand turn. It would look like I'd lost control of the car on the bend. An obvious accident.

I can see now that I wasn't thinking in any way rationally; for one thing, the insurance would never have paid out on a drunk driver, but I was in a fog of misery. I remember putting a cassette tape of the Stranglers into the player as I started my run up. I'd taken off my seat belt and with the song *Hanging Around* playing at full volume I charged at the wall. I managed to get the speed up to 70 mph as I hit the kerb in front of the wall and bounced up, then as if in slow motion I ploughed through the sandstone blocks. The noise was deafening as the vehicle crunched and ricocheted through the wall. I was thrown forward and bounced off the steering wheel.

It could have been minutes later, or even hours; I was oblivious since I'd been knocked unconscious, but I came round and found myself remarkably but obviously still alive. The car had gone partially through the wall and landed nose-down in waste ground on the other side. There were no lights, and it was quiet. No sirens, no one outside trying to open up the car to get me out. Self-preservation took over, and as I gasped to get air into my lungs, the pain in my chest told me there was some damage done to my body. I felt for wet blood but couldn't feel or see anything. I managed to open the driver's door and fell out of the car. It was a drop of a few feet. I made my way to the front of the wrecked BMW and looked at myself in the light of a headlamp that was still shining. What the hell have I done?

The shock of the situation sobered be up and straightened me out immediately. I had to get away from this mess. Remarkably, apart from bruising to my ribs and two black eyes and a broken nose from the impact on the steering wheel, I was okay. I guess that's German engineering for you! I limped away from the scene and made my way down the street. I saw a phone box near some shops so made for that. I called Mickey, whose house I'd left earlier that evening.

"I've crashed my car, can you come and get me?" I didn't tell him more than that, apart from the location. Within fifteen minutes Mickey was there. I got into his van and told him I was well over the alcohol limit so let's not mess around looking at the car, just go! I stayed the night with Mickey and Ellen, who knew better than to ask me too many questions.

The next morning we hired a tow truck and went back to collect the BMW. Several locals were hanging around as we winched the car onto the back of the truck, but we told them we'd only been hired to pick up the vehicle and knew nothing about the crash. I scrapped the car that day and amazingly never heard any more about the incident.

The BMW crash frightened me. I realised I was losing control of my life again. In the sober light of day I didn't want to kill myself, but I realised that, in what was becoming my normal intoxicated state, combined with the depression that was behind it, I could easily have succeeded. This couldn't continue. I simply told Sharon I'd had an accident and written the car off. She never questioned too deeply about what had happened and I bought a new car, a white Mercedes.

* * * * * * *

Back at the Pig and Whistle, I was now, after several months working there, the senior door steward. I got on well with the owner, Steve, and he allowed me to drink as much as I liked while I was working. Steve had another business interest producing records and managing local bands. I'd often ask him to get me a particular record and he would somehow always manage to get me a copy, even if it was years out of production. He trusted me with who was allowed in or not, and he knew if there was any trouble I'd be first in line to defend the doors. I never backed away from a fight and that encouraged and emboldened the rest of the team. I had my death wish back, which was useful for this work. One night, though, I crossed the line.

When working the door as a bouncer, you're not allowed to go out onto the street to carry on a fight. Your job is to defend the area of the premises doorway, and at most a few feet beyond that. If you go any further, then you open yourself up to getting arrested and charged by the police for assault or GBH. I knew that and the police knew that. Most of the customers knew it too.

One night, midway through the evening, two very drunk guys turned up and tried to gain entry. As was normal procedure, Martin and I blocked the entrance and in a friendly manner told the men, "Sorry lads, not tonight, you've had a wee bit too much to drink. Come back tomorrow." This worked most of the time, but with some it was seen as a challenge that they thought they could change your mind if they explained to you long enough that they were actually quite sober. It never works; once you've made a decision, you can never change it or else you'll lose all respect. The conversation was going on for about ten minutes, and meanwhile other customers were trying get in. These two guys were becoming a nuisance, but they wouldn't leave. Eventually, despite our efforts to calm the situation, one of the guys threw a punch at me, hitting me full on the nose. The blood spurted and my white shirt front was soon stained red. This had happened lots of times before, but for some reason that night I lost control. From my vantage position of standing three steps above the guy I launched at him with a kick to the face and ended up in the street outside rolling around the pavement, trading blows. His friend soon joined the fray and I was outnumbered two to one which left Martin no choice but to come out onto the street and join the melee.

These fights are never very decisive; it's all hair-pulling and headlocks with people falling over. Seldom does a clean blow land. It's messy and what usually separates the doorman from the punter is that the doorman is more controlled, more sober, and fitter. But that night I lost control, and instead of making my way back to the safety of the door, I got into a brawl with these two and Martin was forced to join in. At one point we ended up on top of a parked car as I smashed the guy's face into its bonnet. Finally Martin and I got the upper hand and the two guys made off down the street. As we turned to go back to the doorway I saw Steve standing there looking on in horror.

"What are you playing at, fighting out on the street, Ally?" He was livid, much angrier than I had seen him previously. Before I could say anything else he shouted, "That's my fucking car."

In the heat of the moment I hadn't even noticed what car we had been fighting on, and now I looked, it was clearly Steve's silver Porsche that now had several major scratches and dents, a missing wing mirror and wipers broken off and hanging. I started to explain but Steve just turned away and went back inside the bar. I knew I was in trouble, and I knew I was in the wrong. At the end of the evening after we'd cleared the bar, I apologised to Steve for going onto the street. I told him it was entirely my fault and that Martin had been forced to join in. Finally, I said I thought maybe I'd been working there too long and it was probably time I left. Steve didn't try to change my mind. He agreed, it was time for me to go. I would be welcome back for a drink but not to work. Steve also said he'd be happy to give me a reference. But it was time I moved on.

Within a week I'd found a new job in Disco Viva. This was a very different set-up. A classic Glasgow nightclub, the entrance was from a Union Street doorway, then led upstairs into an enormous cavern of a disco on several floors above the ground floor shops. The manageress was a lady called Julie. She was tough as nails and demanded that nothing obstruct the sale of booze and door entry money. The door staff had very little discretion as to who should get in, regardless of their state of sobriety. If the punters could stand up, and had money to spend, they got in. Not surprisingly, this led to a lot of fights and trouble.

The money was good and the staffing levels high for the bouncers. At the weekend we could easily have twenty-five or thirty door staff. The dress code was the same as usual: black trousers, white shirt and a detachable bow tie. An added bonus at the Viva was a shirt allowance. We were given a cash sum equivalent to the price of three new white shirts a week. Unfortunately, while this seemed great at first, I soon realised that anyone working the doors or bar at Viva would need to buy a new shirt for each evening due to the number of fights you were guaranteed to get into. Every night I worked there I threw my ripped and bloodied drenched shirt straight in the bin when I got home.

This was no cosy and friendly set-up like the Pig and Whistle. The management had no thought for the safety of the staff. Anyone could get in, even if they had been involved in a fight the week before. The large gangs loved the Viva as they could do what they liked and arrive mob-handed in groups numbering in the hundreds. The club relied on the high number of bouncers to quell the fights each night. It was a revolving door. You could be threatened with an axe on a Friday night and throw the guy out, then he'd be allowed back in on the Saturday. It was bedlam. Everyone was off their heads on drink and drugs, including the bouncers, but the money rolled in at the bar and that was all management cared about.

After my shift at Viva in the early hours of the morning, I would often cross the Clyde at Glasgow Bridge and walk home to Sharon's Ibrox flat, if for no other reason than to try and sober up before I got there. I both hated and loved that walk. I didn't feel welcome at the flat, but it was a joy to see Joseph, usually sound asleep when I got in. On the walk, I passed a building where the road forked: to the left was Paisley Road West, and to the right was Govan Road. On top of the building was a huge statue of an angel that I often stopped to talk to, and ask advice. What should I do, leave Sharon and transition, or try to make it work? I never got an answer but I always asked.

* * * * * * *

Back in the Vale I'd met a girl, Veronica, through a mutual friend. I didn't feel sexually attracted to her, we were pals, but she seemed like a beautiful person. She'd had an awful upbringing, in and out of foster homes, abandoned by her family, then damaged by abusive relationships with men, and finally involved in a serious accident that left her with a broken back. Her past was so tragic, yet she kept going. I was in awe of her strength. By the time we met she was able to walk again and had been given a council flat in the Vale. We spent some time together. She would often meet me as I finished up at the Saturday market, and we'd go for a drink. Sometimes she stayed over at my Vale flat; we just hung out together smoking dope and drinking.

Veronica knew I was married and unhappy. She was very sympathetic and listened patiently to my moaning. I also felt sorry for her, because she was such a nice person but seemed to be one of life's victims. I knew she would probably end up with someone else who would mistreat her and the cycle would continue. A couple of times on a Sunday lunchtime I would pick her up in the white Merc and take her out to the countryside where we would have a pub lunch. She was so grateful for such a simple gesture; no one had ever treated her nicely before.

I told her I wanted to get my relationship back with Sharon and Joseph, but we were stuck between two locations. Sharon wouldn't live in the Vale, and I feared giving up my council flat tenancy and staying permanently at her flat, since she could tell me to leave at any moment and then I'd end up homeless. It was Veronica who gave me the idea that I could exchange my council flat and move to somewhere where both Sharon and I had no ties. It would allow us to focus on each other and Joseph, rather than always being held back by our families.

A few days later, I brought up the flat exchange idea with Sharon, and surprisingly she agreed it might be a good idea. It would give us a clean slate and a new start. Encouraged, I went along to the council housing office in the Vale and asked to see their house exchange book. This listed people not just locally, but also nationally, who wanted to swap their council property for reasons of work or family. I spent the afternoon pouring over this register and was surprised to see there were so many people in England who wanted to swap their property to come back to Scotland. I had always loved the Cambridgeshire area ever since my time in Borstal there, so I looked for a suitable property there. The closest available was in Norwich. Sixty-odd miles from Cambridge, but I decided to go for it, with the intention of hopefully moving from there to Cambridge later on.

I'd never been to Norwich, and I knew nothing about the place. But it had one big thing going for it, and that was that neither Sharon nor I had any ties to the area, so we wouldn't receive any interference from others if we relocated there. The whole idea seemed exciting to me. A chance to get away from all the things that had hindered our relationship in the past, and which would force us to concentrate on each other and Joseph. I even thought that perhaps I could finally be honest with Sharon and open up about my transsexuality once we had moved. I could even ask Sharon to help me deal with it because I was committed to us as a family. Perhaps by being honest, I thought naively, it might make us stronger.

I returned to Sharon that night with the idea of a move to Norwich. Now that I was actually explaining it to her it seemed quite absurd. I felt sure she would laugh and dismiss the whole idea as ridiculous. But, to my surprise, she listened patiently. We got a map out and looked at the area. I showed her the details of the flat: two bedrooms on the second floor of a small block on the edge of Norwich city with beautiful countryside nearby. There were lots of employment opportunities there, especially for Sharon as an accountant, with insurance giant Norwich Union a major employer in the city. I was delighted that Sharon seemed very receptive to the suggestion. The next step was to contact the person who lived in the Norwich flat, a lady called Margaret, to arrange a visit. I called her and Margaret seemed equally enthusiastic about the swap. She was originally from Glasgow and, now a widow, wanted to return home. We set a date for my visit to view her flat.

I arrived in Norwich at around seven o'clock one dark winter's evening in November 1987. I'd driven there from Glasgow through the wreckage of the huge storm that had hit England a few weeks earlier, with fallen trees everywhere on the way down. I was on my own, as Sharon didn't think it would be good to bring Joseph on such a long drive. She said she trusted my judgement as to whether or not the flat was suitable for us. This was a time before sat navs, of course, so I was relying on written directions from Margaret and I soon got hopelessly lost in the city's one-way system.

Somehow I ended up in a narrow street behind a lot of city centre shop premises. I was driving through mountains of cardboard boxes that the shopkeepers had obviously left out for collection and the street was getting even narrower, and the cardboard was getting caught up in the wheel arches of my car. I ground to a halt, completely lost. As I sat wondering what to do next, I saw the beam of a torch directed towards me and a the figure of a policeman came into view. Oh, shit. I'm going to be in trouble here and will probably get a ticket, I thought. I wound down my window and the cop looked in.

"What are you doing driving here? Do you know this is a pedestrian area?"

I told him I was lost. I was visiting Norwich for the first time and looking for the Heartsease Estate. But, rather than pull out his radio to book me, he just smiled.

"From Scotland, are we?" I confirmed I was.

"Okay, let's get rid of this cardboard." He then walked around the car pulling out the boxes and plastic packaging from my wheels. After it was all cleared, he told me to follow him and drive slowly. Then he walked forward and guided me out of the back streets on to the main road. He then leaned in again and asked for the address I was looking for. I gave him the instructions and he quickly sketched a map for me to follow on to the paper. I was still waiting for the ticket when he said, "Off you go then, take care, and welcome to Norwich!"

I was gobsmacked; this definitely would not have happened with a Glasgow cop! I thanked, him, impressed already by the city. I drove off and found the flat a few minutes later.

My flat viewing went really well. Margaret was a lovely older woman who made me very welcome. She told me all about the local nurseries and schools for Joseph, and various employment opportunities for me and Sharon. I had brought some photographs of my flat in the Vale and she seemed more than happy with those. She already knew the Vale area and where the flat was, so didn't need to bother travelling up to see it in person. If I was happy with her place, then she was ready to go ahead and set the wheels in motion for the exchange. I told her I was very pleased with the flat and we agreed the deal. I left her feeling very positive about this move. I booked into a bed and breakfast for the night and called Sharon to let her know how things had gone. She seemed happy and told me she was looking forward to living in Norwich. I drove back to Glasgow the next morning feeling excited.

As soon as I returned home to Glasgow, I began preparing enthusiastically for our move to Norwich. I sold off or dumped furniture from the Vale flat that we didn't want to take with us. I organised a removal firm to take the white goods and few other pieces from the Vale, and then to collect the others stuff from Sharon's Ibrox flat on the same day. It was agreed that Sharon, Joseph and I would drive down together on the day of the move and hopefully arrive just before the furniture.

We had six weeks to get things organised, since that was the minimum time it took to exchange the tenancies between both councils. I signed the contract in the Vale Council offices, as did Margaret at her local office. There was no turning back now. Sharon also told me she had sorted out her lease with her own landlord, to give enough notice so she would get her deposit back.

Finally, I gave in my notice at Disco Viva and gave up my stall at the Vale market. I sold the white Mercedes and my van, since we'd need all the cash we could get to help us start up again. I bought a cheap runner, a Talbot Sunbeam, to get us down there and use until we got organised. Everything was sorted and we had a date of entry to the new Norwich flat for March 1988, just prior to my twenty-fourth birthday. What could go wrong?

* * * * * * *

A few days before we were due to leave I was at Sharon's flat. I'd already got my clothes mostly packed and I suggested we get Joseph's stuff organised too. We could pack everything and just leave ourselves a few days change of clothes and the basics to get by until we arrived in Norwich. I was a little bit concerned that Sharon seemed to be leaving things to the last minute and I didn't want to be rushing around on the morning we were leaving.

That's when Sharon casually told me she wasn't going to Norwich.

At first I thought she was just a bit apprehensive and worried about the enormity of the move, and that I would have to reassure her. But no, she was adamant and quite matter-of-fact about it. She had decided she wasn't going, and neither was Joseph. I couldn't believe this at first and tried to reason with her. We had to go! I'd signed the contract and couldn't back out. My tenancy at the Vale had already been transferred to Margaret and I had the tenancy in Norwich. She had given in her notice at her Ibrox flat, hadn't she? If we didn't go, where would we live? Sharon eventually admitted she hadn't given in her notice on the flat

"I'm not going, I'm staying here. You go if you want," she told me.

There was no emotion in her statement.

"I'm going round to my mum's now." And with that, she walked out, taking Joseph with her.

Even then I didn't understand I'd been played. I still thought maybe she was a bit scared of the move and leaving her mum, but that she would eventually come round. But after the next few days of trying to get Sharon to change her mind I had to admit she wasn't going.

It had been a textbook exercise in deception by Sharon. It took me a while to realise the duplicity and planning involved. It seemed obvious to others who watched the situation unfold, but it's true that a fool is easily fooled, and I believed what I wanted to believe because I still loved Sharon and wanted a bright new future for Joseph. I simply did not accept that she could have deliberately engineered the outcome. But I have to admit I was conned.

I'd been tricked into taking a tenancy in Norwich, believing we were all going, Now, if I didn't take up the flat I'd be homeless. I had a choice to make. Clearly for Sharon to do this to me demonstrated she wanted rid of me, and four hundred miles away was perfect for her.

I was very confused and went back to the Vale flat to think. It was almost empty now except for the white goods and TV set. I sat on my own as I tried to figure out what I should do. I opened a bottle of Bacardi and poured a drink. After a few drinks I went across the road to the local pub. I sat in there and had several more drinks. Friends and family came over to have a farewell drink with me. Everyone knew that Sharon, Joseph and I were leaving for Norwich. Except now we weren't, and I couldn't even talk about it!

Later that night I decided to get a takeaway meal and go back to the flat. I didn't feel like speaking to anyone, and I still didn't know what to do. That was when I had a sort of divine intervention. As I sat eating my Chinese meal in front of the TV, by chance a program came on, with Richard Holloway, who was the Anglican Bishop of Edinburgh at that time. More importantly, he was also my cousin.

I'd never actually met him before this time, but Richard was often spoken about with great pride in my family as the boy who had done well, very well indeed – he became a bishop! We all knew about him and I was keen to see what the show was about and settled back in my seat. Next, he indicated the woman sitting opposite him, with whom he was going to be conversing for the duration of the show. He introduced her, to my shock, as, Jan Morris.

Jan Morris! The transsexual woman whose autobiography *Conundrum* had been so influential to me and which Brian the social worker had given to me at the Douglas Inch Centre years earlier. I couldn't believe it, the representation of the clashing of my worlds was playing out in front of me on prime time television! My own transsexuality in the person of Jan, and my family in the figure of Richard Holloway. And, here he was, speaking civilly and intelligently about her transition and faith without judgement. And yet the sky wasn't falling in! I knew many members of my family would be watching this programme too. They always followed Richard on TV, where he was becoming something of a celebrity. They admired him, and by him openly endorsing Jan Morris, someone who was exactly the same as me, it occurred to me that maybe they could one day accept me too? It wasn't quite a miracle, but to me it was a sign. I suddenly knew I should follow my heart. I had been boxed into a corner anyway by Sharon.

I decided to go to Norwich on my own and restart my transition.

Chapter 17 'The Only Way Is Up'
Norwich 1988

I arrived in Norwich after a long drive, I'd driven down in the old Sunbeam from Glasgow and managed to get to my new home just before the furniture arrived. It was spring and I noticed the daffodils were out on the Plumstead Road, that my new flat on the Heartsease Estate overlooked. The guys from the removal firm were efficient and quickly placed what little furniture I possessed in the rooms, then left. I was alone in a new city and it felt peaceful but full of opportunity.

* * * * * * *

I decided on that first night that I would absolutely never, ever, lie to any future partner about my transsexuality. My relationship with Sharon had died and still she didn't understand why, but I did. I would not put anyone else or myself in that position ever again. I understood the situation had come from my own actions. It was unfair on both of us. But I also felt I had to respect myself from now on and stop feeling so ashamed of who I was. I knew many people at that time would have a problem with me as a transsexual woman, but in future I would make sure it was definitely 'their problem' and not mine. I cannot be responsible for other people's prejudices or ignorance. This was not a decision I made in anger, but honestly and thoughtfully. Any future partners could take me, or leave me, from now on, but at least they would know who I am when making that judgment. With that decision I was liberated from so much shit, I only wished I'd made it years earlier.

* * * * * * *

Norwich was very provincial compared to the places I'd lived previously, that's the first thing I noticed. But it was also a kind city, people were reserved but still friendly. One of the first things I needed to do the first week was to MOT my old car, and I went along to the closest garage at Thorpe End to book a test. I sat on a wall outside while the mechanic examined the old Sunbeam. After 30 minutes or so the owner of the garage came out to speak to me and he looked very unhappy.

"I'm so sorry," he told me.

The vehicle was in need of hefty repairs and he thought it was probably not worth the expense to fix it. This didn't surprise me, I knew it was an old wreck.

What did surprise me was that he offered to drive me home and tow the car back to the flat for free, because he was worried I'd be in danger driving it. I thanked him for his kind concern but drove the car back to a scrapyard in Norwich and left it there. I was now without a car but that turned out to be the best thing for me as it forced me to walk and get to know the area on foot, or by the bike I'd found, that Margaret the previous tenant had thoughtfully left in the downstairs lock-up for me.

That first summer I explored Norfolk on that old bike, even cycling to Great Yarmouth and all around the city of Norwich. I loved the countryside particularly, and felt the urge to start sketching again. I'd neglected my passion for art for many years and now found great enjoyment in sitting in bright yellow rapeseed fields pencil drawing ruined churches and landscapes. It was the perfect opportunity to regain my peace of mind after the tumultuous previous years.

But I also needed to find a job and restart my transition. That meant registering, yet again, with a doctor.

I started with a GP and found a surgery near my flat. By now I was completely comfortable and confident in speaking about my transsexuality with doctors. I met my new GP Dr Plunkett, a nice middle aged man with a dry sense of humour. I explained my situation, and that I needed a referral to Charing Cross hospital Gender Identity Clinic. Not unusually for family GP's he didn't even know the clinic existed, but promised to find out, and refer me.

Next, I had to find a job. I scanned the local Norwich newspaper the EDP and found a lot of vacancies advertised. I knew from experience that I would be unable to get a job using anything other than the male identity I was saddled with. So I just accepted that. There was a position of assistant storekeeper in a local building firm available that I was suitably qualified for. I called them for an interview and was invited to go along next day. Ironically the firm was called Trans Industrial, and I took that as a classic case of serendipity. I was offered the job, which involved working in the stores and booking out materials to our tradesmen and taking delivery of the same materials from our suppliers. An easy but unchallenging job, but it meant I'd be working in the warehouse and not on site. I'd also have to do occasional deliveries when things were needed urgently, and to this end I was provided with a company car. Or to be more precise, a company Mazda pickup truck.

So, it was all good. Within a week of arriving in Norwich I had a job and a GP. Now I had to check out the local social scene. I had decided to live as female at all times except for working hours where I was prevented from using a female identity. I started my third attempt at transition, a little older and a lot wiser.

* * * * * * *

The fashion in the late 1980's was convenient, there was a lot of androgyny in both 'Modern Romantic' and Goth styles. Both involved make up, hair dye and gender neutral clothing. I preferred the Goth look and went for it big time, black dyed hair, pale foundation and heavy dark eyeshadow and mascara. I wore black leggings, jeans or long skirts and full length duster coats. It was the first time since I was a punk that I could follow fashion and I felt more free to express myself than ever before. It was fantastic, I had no one looking over my shoulder, no family to worry about, and to be honest, it was wonderful to have no responsibilities to anyone except myself. Norwich was a great place for me at this time. I loved the acceptance and lack of aggravation about the city. As an outsider I really appreciated the freedom to be left to myself without judgement.

One day I was driving round the inner ring road to deliver some roofing materials to a job and noticed a black man (that was unusual in itself for Norwich at this time) at one of the major roundabouts apparently directing the early morning traffic. He looked so incongruous with bright yellow washing up gloves and a big smile. He was right on the edge of the road and waving cars forward, then stopping them from the other direction. Every so often the motorists, and even the police, would beep a friendly hello and wave back at him. I was intrigued. Was he part of the police or a traffic warden? When I got back to Trans Industrial I asked my foreman Sid about the unusual black man I'd seen.

"Oh, that's old Marigold," I was told. "He's been doing that for years, everyone knows him, he's completely harmless but he's got some mental problems. We just leave him to get on with it as he enjoys it."

I was amazed at the casual acceptance of 'Marigold' ;there is no doubt if he'd done the same thing in London or Glasgow he's have been arrested. But, here in Norwich, no one was too fussed. I was delighted by this tolerance, it gave me a good feeling about the city and seeing 'Marigold' was one reason I fell in love with Norwich and decided to stay. I never did get round to moving on to Cambridge.

Many years later, when I thought 'Marigold' had passed on, since he'd not been seen for a decade or so, I painted his portrait in oils from memory. When the painting was exhibited in St Margaret's church of art, and the public response was astonishing. The local TV news crew came along to do a feature and the daily and evening papers had front page stories about 'Marigold'. Everyone who remembered him had fond memories and stories to tell, he was cherished as a local legend. My own fame surged overnight as the artist who had captured his image and I was invited to do several media interviews. The story ran for days and then just as the uproar was dying down the local paper ran a headline 'Marigold Lives' and it started all over again. It turned out he wasn't dead, he was now very elderly and living in a nursing home in Suffolk; his family had seen the media interest and contacted the paper to say he was alive. Eventually he was shown photographs of my painting and, thankfully, he loved it. He sent a message to the people of Norwich to thank the city for the kindness it had shown him in the past. The story of 'Marigold' demonstrates why I love the city of Norwich.

* * * * * * *

But, getting back to my story, I had heard from my work mates at Trans Industrial, about the pubs and nightlife in Norwich. There was one club that was mentioned occasionally with laughter and ridicule, the 'Caribbean Club' that seemed to be the only gay venue at that time. I decided I needed to visit.

The Caribbean Club was everything you expected of a gay venue back in the 1980's. Situated unobtrusively on Rose Lane, the ground floor was a piano bar where a delightful old lady would tinkle away all night on the upright, wearing her best frock and full make up. I'm not sure she had any idea of the kind of venue it was, she just enjoyed being there with the attention of all the handsome young men. Upstairs was the nightclub with a disco and a small dance floor. It was dark, smelly, and filthy, your feet stuck to the greasy carpet and the tables were covered in cigarette burns. It was the definition of sleazy – and I loved it!

The owner of the club was Dougie, a wonderfully camp and sarcastic old queen. Dougie lived on the premises with a few other members of staff, he liked a drink or too and it was very rare to see him in daylight, but most nights he would eventually put on a face and make a grand appearance behind the upstairs bar. A lot of the older male Caribbean patrons were of similar age to Dougie, they had lived through the era when male homosexual activity was characterised as "sinful" and was outlawed. Decriminalisation of sexual activity between men only ended in 1967 in England, and even then there were still strict age restrictions. Dougie and his friends often spoke in the back slang code Polari which had been used by the secretive gay community for years and was usually accompanied by nods, winks and gestures. It was an education to watch them and often hilarious.

Chapter 18 'The Sisters Of Mercy'

Liz

The first night I went along to the Caribbean I was quite nervous, I dressed

androgynously and paid my admission fee to enter the upstairs club after having a

few drinks downstairs. I sat alone at a table too scared to speak to anyone. As the

night went on and the drinks flowed I was eventually asked to dance by a few older guys. It seemed to be a predominately male crowd, I only saw two or three women who were butch dykes, and I began to wonder if this was the right venue for me. Then I saw the most astonishingly beautiful girl I'd ever seen enter the club, and make straight for the dance floor. She was alone but completely confidant as she danced expertly to the hi energy disco. She was tall and slender with long blond hair, spiky on top, and had flawless skin with perfect goth make up. She was wearing what looked like a black bin bag for a dress, fishnet tights and black Doc Martin boots. This fantastical creature seemed to be in a complete world of her own and followed the maxim of 'dance like no one is watching'. After another drink I summoned up the courage to go and ask her to dance. She just smiled and we began to dance together, she didn't want to stop and so we carried on moving together for the next hour or so. Eventually I managed to speak to her in-between tracks. The sweat was glistening on both our faces.

"Come and sit down and have a cigarette and a drink please, I'm exhausted." She agreed, and we found a table away from the dance floor. I got the drinks in and we both lit up from her pack of cigarettes.

"What's your name?" I asked.

"Everyone calls me Liz, but I'm really Phil."

The penny dropped. Liz was a gay guy, not even transgender, and I of all people had been completely fooled. I smiled.

"You look fantastic, Liz. I'm Angie."

'Angie' was the female name I was using at that time. We shared a collaborative smile, finished our drinks and headed straight back to the music where we danced till the club closed.

Liz was the first friend I made in Norwich. She (and I always called her she, even today) was the best person I could have met at that time. She knew everyone, all the best pubs, clubs, and cafes to hang out in, and even the best shops. From that night on we were best friends and Liz began to educate me about Norwich. Not only that, once she understood I was transsexual, she took me under her wing and taught me how to properly apply make up, style my hair and what clothes suited me.

Her mum worked in the big Debenhams department store in the city centre and allowed me her staff discount on clothes I bought there.

Within a week or two of meeting her, Liz told me she was being evicted from her flat. So, naturally I offered to collect and store her few bits of furniture and belongings in the pick up truck I'd been given for my use from the Trans Industrial job. As we drove back to my council flat in the Heartsease it suddenly occurred to me, I had plenty of room, Liz was now homeless and faced with the unappealing prospect of returning to live with her divorced dad and his new wife. We came to the same obvious solution at the same time. I asked her if she wanted to live with me, she screamed Yes! and so Liz moved into my spare bedroom.

* * * * * * *

A few weeks after I'd registered with my GP Dr Plunkett I received a letter from someone called Barbara Ross, who identified herself as a Norwich social worker. Barbara had arranged a date to visit me at home, concerning my request to be referred to Charing Cross. At first I thought this was unusual, and perhaps a delaying tactic by my doctor. But, then I remembered Brian, the social worker in Glasgow who had been very helpful, so I agreed to meet her. Barbara arrived at the time and date agreed, and in preparation I'd dressed appropriately in a stereotypical feminine way, knee length skirt, black tights, blouse, padded bra, etc. I dressed nothing like my usual goth girl look of black jeans and T shirt, because I suspected the 'Stepford Wife' look was probably more suitable, as this is what I knew from experience was what the shrinks and doctors expected. It turned out to be an unusual experience to say the least. Upon arrival, Barbara accepted the cuppa I offered and we both sat down on my couch for a chat. Suddenly she grabbed the pendant I was wearing around my neck.

"Is this jewellery important to you?" she asked.

"Errr yes. I like it a lot," I responded with surprise.

Barbara then held the pendant in her hand and closed her eyes. She seemed to be in deep thought. Eventually after a few minutes she opened her eyes and let go of the pendant.

"I can tell from this pendant that you are genuine. And from what you have said, you are serious about going through sex change. I will recommend you are referred to Charing Cross."

I thanked Barbara, but I was feeling a bit confused, to be honest, by her strange behaviour. We chatted some more about my history and then she got up to go. Barbara gave a me a hug and said she would make sure I got the help I needed, then she left. I thought the whole experience was quite weird! But, to give her her due, Barbara did exactly as she promised, albeit with a few delays along the way. I ended up having a relationship with her that lasted almost thirty years. When she eventually retired she was the oldest working social worker in the country and had been awarded an MBE for services to the transgender community. When Barbara died in 2015 I was honoured to go to her memorial service in Norwich that was packed out with transgender folk and their families.

* * * * * * *

Meanwhile, I'd become a fixture at the Caribbean Club, not least because of Liz. She introduced me to a lot of the regulars and Dougie himself. I got on well with Dougie; he could be very cutting and bitchy towards people but fortunately not towards me - he seemed to like me. And before long, like Liz, I was allowed free entry to the club. This was not strictly a big favour to us. Dougie was astute enough to realise it was beneficial to the club to have young and attractive customers, who would encourage the older and more financially endowed clients to come along.

One Sunday lunchtime I decided to pop into the Caribbean piano bar for a hair of the dog drink, after a heavy previous night upstairs at the disco. There were only about three customers in there, when in walked two loud American guys. Julian and Stanley were both in their 30's and originally from Texas. Julian was very tall and muscular with jet black hair and blue eyes; he looked like the author Stephen King in his younger days. He was a drilling engineer working for an oil company and he'd recently been transferred to Great Yarmouth to work on the North Sea oil rigs. The Americans were both gay and had heard about the Caribbean as the only proper gay venue in Norfolk, so they had come along for a look.

Julian, in the direct manner that Americans have, came straight over to me and offered to buy me a drink. I was happy to accept; I always liked Americans, not least because many of my family were in California and New York. We three found a table and sat down for a chat. It turned out that they weren't a couple. Stanley was an interior decorator who Julian had flown over from the States to sort out his new home in Yarmouth. Julian was single and looking for fun, and he had his eye on me,

,offering to take me out to dinner that evening. He knew right from the start I wasn't a cis female, I was wearing no make up or particularly feminine clothing when we first met and he just assumed I was a young feminine gay man, or a queen as was the common expression then. When he discovered I was Scottish he christened me 'Mary'. When I asked why, he said I was Mary Queen of Scots. That was how I met Julian, who was to be my 'on off' boyfriend for the next year.

* * * * * * *

My first few months in Norwich had turned out to be far better than I could ever have expected. I'd made friends, found a decent well paid job, got a boyfriend, and it looked like I would finally get my referral to Charing Cross Gender Identity Clinic sorted. However, I still missed Joseph desperately and there was very little contact from Sharon despite my efforts to stay involved with our son.

The background to this period was AIDS. The subject had become a prevalent topic of conversation in the gay community. The previous year the government had launched its 'Don't Die Of Ignorance' campaign with leaflets and prime time adverts on TV. It was becoming hard to ignore what was happening worldwide, the public in England were becoming scared and open hostility towards gay people was not unusual. The AIDS based homophobia eventually would affect me too.

One morning I received a letter, finally offering me an appointment at Charing Cross GIC a few weeks later. I'd been waiting for so long for this that I was determined not to miss it, even though it clashed with my work hours. I spoke with my foreman Sid, regarding the situation of time off for a hospital appointment. He told me I could just nip up to the hospital and I wouldn't be missed for an hour, he had assumed I meant the local NHS hospital in Norwich. But when I explained I had to go to London and I would miss the whole day he responded by questioning me, why was I was going to a London hospital, what was wrong with me, etc. I obviously couldn't tell him what my condition was, so I made something up on the spot and spoke vaguely about a blood disorder that needed specialist clinic treatment at Charing Cross hospital. I had my appointment card that had been sent to me, and showed it to Sid. There was no reference on the card to what clinic I was attending, just a department number, a phone number, time and date, and it was stamped with the hospital name. Sid eventually agreed I could go but I'd have to lose a day's pay; also I had to take my card to the office to be scanned for the records. I agreed, and began to plan my day in London.

During this time I'd often become the butt of jokes among my workmates, usually about my dyed hair, shaped eyebrows and the obvious traces of eyeliner that I would sometimes display first thing in the morning after a night out. I was the youngest in the workforce and I took the ribbing in good humour as it didn't seem malicious. On one occasion one of the guys, Brian, had quizzed me in front of everyone else about a girl he'd seen on the street outside my flat., "She looked a lot like you," he said, his eyes narrowing. "Have you got a sister?" I felt my face blushing as I brushed away his questions and changed the subject. Everyone laughed, but it just seemed like the usual workplace banter. On another occasion, I'd been asked to do Saturday morning overtime delivering some steel roofing spars that were needed urgently on site. I had no choice; it wasn't a request, but an order. As usual I went out dancing in the Caribbean Club on the Friday night till 3 am. When my alarm clock went off in the morning I was exhausted, but forced myself to get up for the early morning Saturday delivery. I still had traces of last night's make up on my face but I was in a rush so didn't bother with a bath. Liz offered to come along with me in case I needed help to unload with the crane. I agreed thankfully. \it was often the case that when you arrived with a delivery there was no one to help unload, and I was expecting the site to be empty. As it turned out, when Liz (wearing her usual full make up with her long blond hair) and I arrived on site there was a full workforce waiting for me. I told Liz to stay in the cab and I got out to help offload the steel. I was met with not a few raised eyebrows at my appearance, but fortunately that quickly turned to questions and envious glances towards Liz from the crew. Did I pick her up the night before? Had a good night did we? How much did she cost? All the usual stuff. I just smiled my way through it and refused to answer. I'd let them think what they wanted. If only they knew who they were drooling over!

The day of my Charing Cross appointment finally arrived. I got dressed carefully, selecting a long black skirt with a loose low neck grey and white striped top that tied at the waist. I was wearing my new knee length winter boots and full length black trench coat I'd bought from Debenhams using Liz's mum's staff discount. I kept my make up understated and Liz did my hair. I was all set and got a taxi to the train station for my trip to London.

My journey on the train was uneventful, thankfully, no delays or diversions. Once I reached London I caught the tube to Hammersmith. I felt nervous but happy to be finally on the official NHS path to transition. But first, I had a desire to visit my old stomping ground, the place where I'd began my first transition, and also the place where I'd got myself into so much trouble with the police. I felt the need to test myself in the surroundings of Hammersmith Broadway to see if anyone would recognise me. It was a cathartic experience standing on the spot where I'd almost been blinded and had smashed the pint glass into Mark's face. I'd come so far since that crazy night seven years ago. I had many regrets as I thought about the people I'd hurt. It was a reminder just how close I came to killing someone or being killed, and now here I was looking and dressed like any other young woman on her lunch break. I glanced around to see if I could see anyone I knew from the old days, but of course there was no one. The community was fluid, everyone moves on, and so had I.

I walked down past the Odeon and on to Fulham Palace Road that led me to Charing Cross Hospital . I'd been in here many times before when it was my local hospital, but now I was finally attending the fabled Gender Identity Clinic that had seemed so hard to access for many years. I quickly found the department I needed by following the written instructions on my letter. I approached the receptionist and handed over my hospital appointment card, she glanced at it and wrote something down in her ledger. She looked up at me and smiled.

"You will be seeing Dr Green today, please have a seat in the waiting room and he will come and collect you."

I breathed a sigh of relief, it was finally happening. Right up till this moment I'd feared there would be a problem. Someone had made a mistake, my appointment was last, or next, week. Mr Green would be off sick, or there would be a fire alarm. But, no, everything seemed in order. I slid into a seat and pulled a magazine from my bag to read, and waited.

I heard my name called loudly. Or, rather I heard my former male name, prefixed by 'Mr' announced by a neat middle aged man with greying hair, dressed in a smart suit, who was standing by the waiting room doorway scanning the faces of the assembled patients. He looked like a school teacher. At first I couldn't respond as I was caught by surprise, but I did look up, and the man in the suit caught my eye. He repeated the same name in my direction, but now spoken as a question. I felt my face burning, why on earth had he used that name and the male title? Wasn't I obviously dressed as a woman, with make up and feminine hair? There must be some confusion, even the letter I'd received from the clinic referred to me by my female name 'Angie.' But, there was nothing else for it, I had to stand up and be identified.

"Please follow me," I was instructed.

And so I first met Richard Green, world famous sexologist and research director and consultant psychiatrist at Charing Cross Gender Identity Centre. I followed him as he led the way to his office, walking quickly ahead of me. Once inside he closed the door, introduced himself, and invited me to have a seat. There is no need to detail our conversation except to say I was asked the same questions I'd been asked countless times by doctors, social workers and psychiatrists over the previous years. He then spoke at great length about the dangers of female hormone treatment, the blood tests I would have to agree to after I'd had this appointment, and the length of time I would have to wait before I could access hormone treatment, subject to being given the all clear in my blood tests. I would also need to be seen by the other consultants within the department, who were, I was told: Dr Reid, Dr Hohburger, Dr Montgomery and Dr Jabhani. After which, in time, they would decide in conference whether I was a suitable patient for treatment. Surgery, I was told, would probably be many years away and dependent on how I conducted myself during the time I was being seen at the GIC. The two year 'real life test' was outlined very clearly and finally I was warned that if my blood tests showed up any self prescribing of black market oestrogen, then it would put back my case at least a year, and I may well be removed from the clinic patient list. Did I have any questions? I had only one question; it had been burning in my head since I'd first sat down in his office.

"Why did you address me as 'Mr' and use my previous male name when you called me in front of the whole waiting room?"

"Oh, that's because we hadn't met yet, and you hadn't told me how you would prefer to be addressed. How should we address you in future, here?"

I could see the mind games were starting already and Richard Green was a prick. But I bit my tongue; I hadn't come this far to get into an argument. I outlined my title as 'Miss' and my first name as 'Angie', which he laboriously wrote down, even asking what the spelling was. After that he stood up and I understood the appointment was over. I was directed back to the waiting room where I was soon called to provide blood for testing, then it was over. My first GIC appointment. Despite the seemingly deliberate attempt to upset me I didn't mind, I was just happy to be there. I'd half expected that there would be attempts to trip me up and catch me out. I supposed they had to be very sure they were treating a genuine transsexual woman and not a fantasist. I left and made my way back to the train station and home to Norwich, feeling rather satisfied.

I was very tired by the time I arrived back home that night. It had been a long day and mentally exhausting. I had work in the morning so had an early night. The next day I arrived at work at my usual time, I made myself a cuppa and asked Sid if he wanted one. But he didn't, and seemed distracted. I'd half expected to be quizzed about my day in London and how I got on at hospital but nothing was mentioned. Later on that morning, Sid went along to have a meeting with one of the managers. This wasn't unusual, but when he came back he looked troubled. You need to go and have a talk with Richard this afternoon after lunch, he told me. I asked why, but Sid just shrugged. You'll find out when you talk to him. Richard was one of the two partners who owned the firm, I'd very rarely had any contact with him so this was unusual. What was also unusual was the general atmosphere in the workshop. There was no joking and banter from the guys directed at me, and no one even asked about my trip to London. I felt a sense of foreboding. After lunch, as instructed I went along to the offices and knocked on Richard's door. He asked me to come in but didn't offer me a seat.

"Where were you yesterday? I know it was a hospital appointment, but why were you in London? Do you have a medical condition that we need to be aware of"?

I was caught out by the directness of the question.

"Err no, I'm fine. I just had to get some blood tests done," I stammered.

"Well, why go to London for that? I have to ask you, are you gay? Do you have anything to tell me? Because we know the clinic you went to was called a Gender Identity Clinic. Sara in the payroll department called the number on your hospital card and they told us the name of the department. What's going on?"

I had no answer. I was shocked that Sara had called the hospital, but even more surprised that the receptionist at the GIC had identified the department to her.

"My hospital appointments are my own private business," I protested, weakly.

"Ok, I've heard enough. Go and wait in Sid's office please. He'll come along and speak to you soon."

I left and entered Sid's office. It was unusually empty. I sat at the desk and waited. About half an hour later Sid came in with a grave look on his face.

"I'm afraid we're going to have to let you go, Ally. Richard says we can't afford to have someone who is sick on the payroll. We all know about the hospital appointment and the blood tests in London. The word has leaked and the guys don't want to work with someone who has a blood disease in case they get infected too. Everyone knows about the way you dress when you're not here, and that you've been seen going in to the Caribbean club."

I was flabbergasted! A blood disease? They had assumed I was simply gay and probably had AIDS. I recalled all the teasing about eyeliner and looking like my so- called sister. They had put two and two together and made five.

"I haven't got AIDS, Sid, if that's what you think."

But Sid was already looking out of the window and speaking to me like I was a stranger. We had been friendly and shared a lot of jokes and time together over the last seven months since I'd been employed at Trans Industrial. He'd even confided in me about his marriage problems. But now I was a non person.

"We'll pay you a week's wages and you can give me the keys to the pick up now. You don't have to work any notice. You can go home now."

I could see the conversation had ended. I handed over my car keys and walked out of the factory, feeling the eyes burning me as I walked away. This was my first experience of blatant and unapologetic discrimination. I was raging inside and struggling to control my emotions. My first thoughts were revenge. I was still strong and lean, the testosterone that I often cursed was still running through my body. I could easily go home and tool up with weapons, a few knives and a hefty club would be enough. I could go back later and wait for Richard and Sid in the car park and attack them as they left work for home. In the dark it would be easy, I was much stronger, fitter and quicker than these flabby old farts. In my mind, I felt I would be justified too. I imagined the look on their faces as a 'poof' kicked the shit out of them. They had no idea who I was, my history, and what I was capable of. I began formulating my plan on the half hour walk home.

It was fortunate for me that I'd had to relinquish the keys to the pick up truck that day and walk back home. The time allowed some sanity to come back into my thoughts. By the time I entered the front door of my flat I'd begun to question the crazy act of revenge I was planning. I looked around at my home, my female clothes hanging up on the door ready for my transformation back to Angie, for the night out with friends that was planned for later that evening, at the Caribbean. My make up distributed around the furniture surfaces. Liz's stuff was there too, her hair extensions and nail polish, her discarded clothes from the night before scattered on the floor (that I always moaned about). It was time to ask myself a question again, who was I? Was this flat and Angie me, or was I still the Glasgow nightclub bouncer ready to resort to violence?

I came to the decision now that I was calmer, as I started to run a bath laced with sweet smelling bubble bath. I even lit a couple of incense sticks and a candle. I got the bottle of red wine that was supposed to be for later and opened it. I threw off my work clothes and sunk into the warmth of the bath with the bottle and a glass on the side. By the time I'd drank half the bottle I was feeling thankful that I didn't ever have to wear those fucking male clothes again and pretend to be 'the guy who worked in the stores' at Trans Industrial. Revenge was pointless and self destructive.

One of the friends I was due to meet up with that night was Tanya. I hadn't known her very long. We'd been introduced to each other by Liz a few weeks previously. One of my constant topics of complaint was my hair, I was always dying it different colours and Liz advised me that I needed to leave it a while and let it recover or it would start breaking off or falling out. She suggested that, like her, I start using a wig sometimes to give my own hair a rest. She had a friend who owned a theatrical costumier business just outside Norwich and sold wigs; Liz was sure she'd get me a discount. So, off we went for a trip to the sticks to see Tanya. I can't remember if I bought a wig that day, but I did hit it off with Tanya and we began a friendship that was to last till today.

Chapter 19 'Wind Beneath My Wings'

Tanya

Tanya and I had started to occasionally hang out together. She was ten years older than me and originally from East London. I loved her pillar box red hair and the clothes she wore, lots of leather skirts and plastic macs. She was quite outrageous for the times and we got on like a house on fire. She had landed in Norfolk with her boyfriend, on the rebound from an unhappy marriage a few years previously. But the boyfriend turned out to be a nasty controlling creep too, so now she was single with twin teenage daughters, and looking for some excitement. Tanya was drawn to the gay scene for the attitude, music and flamboyance. She was very easy to talk to. When we'd first met I'd told her I was transsexual and intended having a sex change, and she was very enthusiastic about helping me. But, being Tanya, she also saw me as a bit of a challenge. She had an agenda to turn me straight. She was quite open and frank about it and we often joked that if even she, with her raw sex appeal, could not make me a straight man, then no one could.

Meanwhile, after being sacked from my job I had to think about paying my rent. I decided I would need to claim Unemployment Benefit and Housing Benefit for a while, until I got myself another position. I went along to the local Social Security office and filled in the forms. One section of the B1 form asked me to provide the reasons for losing my job at Trans Industrial. I answered honestly, I was dismissed for being gay, and on the false assumption I was infected with HIV AIDS. I also added that I intended taking my previous employer to an Industrial Tribunal for unfair dismissal and discrimination. Looking back it's laughable how naive I was. This was Margaret Thatcher's Britain after all, the woman who had recently introduced Clause 28, which included:

Section 2A "A local authority "shall not intentionally promote homosexuality or publish material with the intention of promoting homosexuality or promote the teaching in any maintained school of the acceptability of homosexuality as a pretended family relationship."

In other words, this was a green light to anyone to discriminate against gay people and their families. The British government and the Prime Minister had stated in law that gay people were inferior and deserved fewer rights than straight people, and could, with the full backing of the law, be discriminated against. So it should have come as no surprise that I received a letter from the Social Security office a few days later telling me I was not entitled to benefits for six weeks, because I had contributed to my own dismissal. I called them up for an explanation as to what exactly my contribution to my dismissal was. I was told it was because I was homosexual, and I should not have forced that lifestyle on to my employer. I was also told in the same phone call that my claim for unfair dismissal could not go forward either, as I had not been employed for the minimum time period of twelve months. And, anyway, discrimination against homosexual people was not included under the Tribunal's remit.

Wow! Ding Ding! Wake up call. At least now I knew exactly where I stood in my own country under a Tory government. It was a realisation I'd never forget.

Fortunately, when Tanya heard about my situation, she thankfully offered to help. She invited me to work a couple of days a week in her theatrical costume shop. The money would keep me going until I received

Unemployment Benefit, so I jumped at the chance. Not only was it a job, but it was a job that enabled me to comply with the Charing Cross 'real life test' rules. I would be working for Tanya, as Angie.

* * * * * * *

Don't misunderstand me, I do not disregard the AIDS panic that spread through the public in the late 1980's. There was a lot to be fearful of, and I don't blame people for being frightened. No one really knew at that time how easily or difficult it was for AIDS to be transmitted. What I did object to was the government's deliberate policy of discrimination against gay people that made it worse. A few months after my sacking at Trans Industrial I was invited to a dinner party that demonstrated the fear and ignorance that was widespread at the time, even among the gay community.

Julian's house in Yarmouth was finally finished. The building work and decoration was completed by Stanley. For the final touches, he had sent for another friend, Brad, to come over from Texas and help choose and organise the fitting of the drapes, carpets and soft furnishing. Brad, I was told by Julian and Stanley, was an artistic genius and highly sought after for his interior design talents. However, when Stanley had collected Brad from the airport, it was obvious that he wasn't at all well. Brad was in his late 20's, and I had been led to believe was a very beautiful charming man, who I would adore (according to Julian). But Stanley called me up from the airport to warn me that he was very concerned about Brad's health and I should warn Julian, prior to our welcome dinner planned for that night.

When Brad and Stanley eventually arrived that evening I could see the shock in Julian's face. Despite my warning he was not prepared for Brad's physical appearance. When we had a quiet moment alone Julian explained to me that this person who had arrived hardly even resembled his old friend. Brad had lost 30 to 40 pounds in weight, his face was pasty, his hair thinning and the hollows around his eyes were obvious. He was sweating profusely, had a hacking cough, and looked like a man of sixty rather than late twenties. We were all thinking the same thing when we saw Brad, but no one dared say it.

Gathered there that night for Brad's welcome dinner were Julian, Stanley, Tanya, Liz and myself. Despite his obvious ill health Brad was cheerfully trying to help out with food preparation. He insisted on preparing the salad, and as we all watched with concern Brad began chopping up salad ingredients as Julian prepared the steaks. At one point Brad, with sweat dripping into the salad bowl from his forehead, announced he had cut his finger on the knife and asked for a band aid. As Julian took Brad off to the bathroom for treatment the rest of us sat round the table making eyes at each other. "So, who's having the salad?" Liz asked pointedly, "cos I'm fucking not!" When dinner was served later on, the marinated salad sat untouched by all except Brad. The dinner conversation was stilted and it was with relief that Brad announced he was jet lagged and needed to get to bed. After he shuffled off to one of the bedrooms, the rest of us spoke in whispered tones. He looked awful, Julian was upset, and Stanley was angry. He should never have agreed to come over in that condition. He had to go home. The party broke up early and Tanya, Liz and I left to go back to Norwich feeling sad and not a little frightened, not least by our own reactions to a man who was clearly suffering.

Later on that week Julian called me to say Brad had left and gone back to Texas. Apparently, when Stanley had taken him to the airport it was pretty much against his will; he wanted to stay and do the job but neither Julian or Stanley would countenance it. As he left the departure lounge he literally left a parting shot by punching Stanley in the eye. I have to admit, like the others who were at that dinner party, we were all relieved to know the spectre had left the banquet, as we all knew it could have been any one of us next, and we didn't want to see it.

My time with Julian was coming to an end. It didn't happen overnight or by either of us making the decision. We just spent less and less time together. I knew he was promiscuous, and whilst in Norwich he was faithful to me, but I had no idea what he was up to in Yarmouth. I'd also stopped having sex with him. This was not a deal breaker for either of us, because he knew I was not all that interested in the first place. I still enjoyed it when he took me out because he treated me like a lady and spent a lot of money on me including buying me expensive gifts. He also enjoyed showing me off. But, it finally got to the absurd stage that when I knew he would be looking for sex after a night out, I'd insist on bringing Liz along with us, then she would slip into the same bed as me and Julian and provide what he needed, as I went to sleep.

I was also getting much more involved with Tanya. We got on really well and I enjoyed working in her shop.

We had a lot of ideas for expanding the business by introducing new product lines and services. Eventually, Tanya offered me the job as full time shop manager for a small wage, and it was agreed we would create other businesses within the shop environment to make proper money from these to split as partners. Some of these new ventures included a Kissagram agency, a mail order clothing and jewellery range called Punk Post, and a couple of kinky leather fashion and bondage ware businesses, Leather X and Skint Leather. We really were quite prolific. Tanya was always the business brains and I controlled the artistic design.

Life was ok for me at this time.; at least I no longer had to pretend I was someone else during work hours, and I finally felt free to dress and live as Angie full time. But financially it was always a struggle. Liz, although she looked fantastic, found it difficult to get work or hold down a job. She refused to compromise her glamour and style and would be seen by employers as too over the top in the everyday work environment, so she was never really able to pay any rent.

One evening Liz and I were sitting in the Caribbean club, nursing our gin & tonics. It was a quiet night and we were wondering where our next drink would come from. I expected an early night because neither of us had a penny and the prospect of a long walk home to catch Cell Block H on the telly seemed to be the plan. But Liz had other ideas that night that would open my eyes.

"Let's go down Mountergate and get a punter!" Liz exclaimed.

Mountergate was the street leading off from Rose Lane where the club was. It was also infamous as the street where the local kerb crawlers patrolled looking for girls who in turn were seeking 'business' with the men driving past. I laughed at what I thought was a joke from Liz. Mountergate customers were, I assumed, heterosexual men who wanted women to fuck. In fact it was an area most gay people avoided for fear of abuse or attack. I looked again at Liz and realised she was serious.

"Don't worry, I've done it before," she said. "Follow me".

We left our drinks half finished on the table, telling 'Hairy Mary' to watch them, and trotted, giggling, down the stairs and across the road, and stood outside the Nelson hotel car park. It was dusk, and I was flushed by the alcohol and excited by the adventure, but I still didn't expect Liz was really going to attempt to pick up a client.

"Ok, watch me and copy what I do," she instructed.

Liz was standing seductively draped against a lamp post, her blonde spiky hair reflecting the light, occasionally squatting down and standing up with the post between her legs like a pole dancer. Every time a car slowed down as it passed she would move towards it asking, You looking for business, darling?"

I was in hysterics watching this performance. It was still all a joke to me. There was no way in a million years I would copy her. It was a ridiculous parody of the 'genuine working girls' and I was fearful of getting a smack in the mouth from one of the punters for taking the piss, or from one the regular girls for annoying their clients. But it was so funny, I was in fits. Then a car stopped next to Liz! I thought shit, we could be in trouble here. But Liz repeated her greeting.

"You looking for business, darling?"

To which the guy in the car replied

"Yeah, what you got for me?"

I was standing back from Liz, almost hiding in the trees by this time, but close enough to overhear the deal being made. I was in a panic, thinking: If this guy discovers Liz is a bloke he'll kill her!

Liz told the punter, "My boyfriend's in prison and I'm skint, darling. Blow job for £15 to help me pay the rent?"

To my amazement the guy agreed and told Liz to climb in, opening the passenger door. Liz then came back to me and told me to memorise the number plate and the car model, and to make sure the punter saw me clocking the vehicle details. " "I'll be back in 15 minutes, wait here for me," she said. I made an exaggerated show of checking his number plate and then Liz climbed in and they both drove off. I was terrified for Liz. I imagined she was going to get murdered when the punter found out she was a boy. I was still in a panic fifteen minutes later when they returned. My relief must have been obvious as I virtually dragged Liz from the car, grabbed her hand and bolted for the safety of the Club. As we got back in our seats I hugged her and told her how worried I'd been. But Liz was very pleased with herself as she nonchalantly handed me a £10 note.

"Get the drinks in, dear," she smiled.

I learned from Liz that night that most men are not all that fussy where they get sex from, and 'straight' men would happily suspend their sexual orientation if the price was right and the offer was there, and inviting enough;any hole would do. It was information learned that I'd remember later!

Liz was to travel on out of my life at the end of that year. She moved out of my flat and settled with a boyfriend, Pete. She got into music and production with him. I only saw her infrequently over the next few years at the club but we parted on good terms. I'll always be grateful for the help she gave me in my early years in Norwich. We were to meet up again almost thirty years later when I was the North Norwich Labour Party women's delegate to national conference in Brighton, where she had relocated. It was a lovely reunion. By this time Liz was a shaven headed gay man. But, to me, she will always be the most beautiful woman I ever met.

After Liz moved out I had room for Tanya and her kids to stay over at the weekends. She lived in a tiny village called Hevingham, about 10 miles from Norwich, and with the lack of public transport she found it difficult to socialise in the city. Her moving in enabled us to go out clubbing together, whilst her twin teenage girls, who were at boarding school during the week, shared my spare bedroom.

* * * * * * *

The next couple of years, I, Tanya, and her twins, Sally & Lilly, became inseparable. It was a strange little family group we formed. Tanya, being ten years older than me in her mid 30's was the matriarch; I was now in my mid twenties and a surrogate 'cool mum' to the twins, who were aged fifteen and just coming through puberty. I always felt closer in age to the twins than Tanya, because like them, I was learning about becoming a woman at the same time as they were. Weirdly, the twins came to me for advice because I had a couple of years experience on them in certain aspects of female life, so I taught them how to apply make up, walk in heels and the dangers of boys. But, importantly, they taught me things too, such as that being a girl sometimes meant you could dress and have fun like a boy, but still be a girl. This challenged my somewhat rigid gender presentation rules that Charing Cross and all the other clinics, social workers, etc, had instilled in me. These were still quite early days for 'gender fuck' and feminism, and the NHS and I were still trying to understand how it was going to play out.

Working in Tanya's shop Willowisp was good fun for me as I was allowed to give my artistic nature full vent. I could also wear anything I fancied, and work on whatever project inspired me. It was not unusual for me to be seen striding through Aylsham, the neat market town where we were located, dressed in 6" stiletto leather thigh boots, full goth make up and electric blue hair with matching fake nails, as I popped to the bakers for my sausage roll lunch. I was actively encouraged by Tanya to go out of my way to shock the locals - all publicity was good publicity as far as she was concerned, but within weeks everyone got used to my extravagant fashion choices and no one gave me a second look other than a friendly nod. That was one of the things I liked about rural Norfolk, no one was really too fussed about anything, and I soon learned I was far from being the only colourful character in the area. Aylsham seemed to be populated by refugees from 1960's London who had migrated to Norfolk to retire, grow their own grass and chill out in communal living arrangements, as well as wealthy farmers, and eccentric but impoverished aristocracy.

A member of the latter group I encountered one day as I drove from Norwich to Aylsham early one morning on my way to the shop. I saw a long haired middle aged hippy guy bent over, vomiting, and gasping for breath by the side of the main road. I pulled over, and Bob, as he introduced himself to me, looked as if he was going to keel over and die there and then. I thought he was having a heart attack, but no, he reassured me, he had simply been trying to jog back to Aylsham after a night out in Norwich. He had no money left for a bus and thought, whilst still under the influence of the previous night's drugs cocktail, that it would be easy to run the ten miles, forgetting that he'd not actually done any exercise in the previous twenty years. I offered him a lift which he gratefully accepted, as I helped him into my car. I noticed his clipped public school accent as we chatted during the journey; another skint landowner I surmised. There were a lot of them around back then, saddled with the upkeep of the family estate and house with the fortune long gone. Property rich but cash poor. I dropped him off at the gates of his dilapidated driveway and thought no more of it. Later on that afternoon he turned up at the shop with a thank you gift for me, a large Harrods carrier bag filled to bursting with home grown cannabis . He never asked why I was dressed like a New York hooker, and I didn't ask where the grass came from. That would have been impolite. That was Aylsham in those days.

* * * * * * *

My relationship with Tanya was eventually very close and deep, but we had to go through an early mutual learning curve to get there. As mentioned previously, she saw me as a challenge. She could easily understand gay and lesbian people, but to begin with, not transsexual women. She herself was not lesbian, but she found herself sexually attracted to me. We both treated it as a joke for a while but it came to a head one night, when, after a watching a band at a local Aylsham pub and drinking a lot of alcohol, we ended up back at her little village house in Hevingham, tired but happy. It was too late for me to get a bus back to Norwich so she offered me a bed for the night. Unfortunately it was her own bed, and she didn't intend us to share it as friends. She came on to me as we lay together with the lights off. I had to explain, please don't take offence, but I wasn't interested. I saw her as a friend, not a lover. This scenario had happened to me so many times with female friends that I probably came over as rude and dismissive, because I was fed up with it. Unfortunately, Tanya was very upset and felt humiliated; it was an awful situation and exactly what I'd wanted to avoid. She pulled the covers off me and demanded I left her house. It was past midnight on a wet winter evening and eight miles from Norwich, but I saw the anger in her face. I quickly pulled on my clothes, which were black fishnet tights, a short leather skirt and a short cream biker jacket and 4" heels. It was going to be a long walk back to Norwich along the A140 which had no footpath. However, I could see no other way out of this. I walked out slamming the door behind me and started off along the road, down the grass verge.

As I trudged on I became increasingly angry. I was being put in a dangerous situation that no decent person would subject a woman to. I'd been passed by several cars, some slowing down to get a look, and I knew I must have appeared like an easy target for any male driver, dressed as I was, walking along in the middle of nowhere, so late at night. And that's when I had the realisation; Tanya had always told me she accepted me 100% as a woman, but I knew for sure she would not have put any of her other female friends, or her daughter's, in the position she had put me in that night. She clearly did not think of me as really female or vulnerable; she obviously still saw me as a man dressed as a parody of a woman. As I walked on towards Norwich I tensed every time I saw headlights on the road, I took off my heels and walked on the soles of my tights, ready to run into the trees if I had to. It was very scary. After about a mile, what I had feared happened. I heard a car coming along behind me, then I saw the headlights picking out the road, and me. I could hear from the engine that it was slowing.

The car was slowly cruising up behind me, and just as it got next to me I turned towards it ready to challenge whoever was driving. I wasn't going to be an easy victim, I'd fight if I had to. Then, with absolute relief, I recognised the car. It was Tanya's Citroen. She pulled along next to me and motioned for me to get in. I thankfully climbed in and before I could start to angrily take her to task, Tanya threw her arms around me sobbing and telling me that she was sorry, I started crying too, and we sat there in the dark for a while holding on to each other, both upset, but relieved that nothing serious had happened to me. Tanya drove us back to her house, where we had a long talk about what had happened. We made up, and from then on had much more mutual respect for each other.

Working with Tanya was very exciting, no two days were the same. She was a whirlwind of action and ideas and I was happily swept along. As part of her mail order Punk Post business we sold a lot of studded leather belts and wrist bands. These were bought in from a wholesaler to resell, but they were expensive and there was not much profit involved. I had a look at the stock and had an idea that we could make the leather goods ourselves if we had the tools. Tanya agreed, and we searched out a supplier of tools and leather hides. We found a company called Bachelor's who had everything we needed. Tanya didn't mess around; we ordered a complete set of workshop tools, buckles, eyelets, and all the other findings that were required, together with a couple of large dressed hides. I cleared a space at the back of the shop and set up a work bench. I had no training, but very quickly learned through trial and error how to make leather goods. I really enjoyed this work and it allowed me to explore my creativity. Before long we were completely self sufficient as leather manufacturers rather than just retailers, the difference in the profit margin was massive, and the leather goods quickly became a major source of income. Also, as manufacturers of leather items we began to get interest from a different kind of customer, those who required custom made restraints, harnesses and cuffs. A whole new world opened up!

* * * * * * *

The other business initiative at we started at this time was a Kissagram agency. Kissagrams had become very popular, and no retirement party, 21st birthday or hen night was complete without a kissagram girl or boy turning up, dressed in whatever theme you wanted, delivering a card, reading the message and dancing with the recipient. We already had a shop full of all the costumes you could ever want, so we just needed performers, and since none of the shop staff were the shy retiring type, we decided we'd do that ourselves. Besides, the money was great so we were all eager. Tanya, me and another very pretty teenager who worked in the shop, Sara, took on the roles as performers. But, it was also the start of me compromising my transition. I was never a natural performer, and I began to use alcohol to control my stage nerves.

One of the most popular kissagrams was for Tarzan. This required the performer to arrive at the party dressed in a gorilla suit, crash on to the dance floor and chase the birthday girl around with lots of grunting and whooping, then strip off the suit to reveal Tarzan in a leopard skin loin cloth, who would read out the kissagram message written on a plastic banana. It sounds naff but it was great fun for everyone and very popular. Obviously, the only one of us three who could decently strip off as a bare chested jungle man was me. So I did it. I also performed as a gay male leather queen, dressed as an American cop with the NYPD hat, sunglasses, and uniform, but I'd strip off to reveal a leather body harness and whip, with which I'd chase the birthday boy around the party before handcuffing him and delivering the message with a big kiss and an erotic dance. To me it was a performance and the money justified it. But, I mostly played female roles, notably as a belly dancer who danced the seven veils and stripped off to a sequinned bra and long silk skirt. This particular kissagram was developed sometimes as a double act that I and Tanya would perform together. It was extremely popular and lucrative. It was a crazy time and we all loved what we were doing, especially the money! Eventually the kissagram performances would develop into stage acts as Tanya became a regular nightclub act, and I even ended up in the pages of Penthouse magazine as runner up in the national Miss Kissagram UK contest. I was even persuaded to perform as a drag act for a few shows but found it completely disconcerting. I felt like a woman, pretending to be a man, who was performing as a woman. A step too far even for me. I'd have to get tanked up with booze to do those bookings and it never ended well.

* * * * * * *

While all the fun and games was going on at Willowisp, I was steadily progressing with my treatment plan at Charing Cross. Every few months I had to see each individual psychiatrist for at least one session, sometimes more. The next shrink I saw after Professor Green was Dr Hohburger, an Austrian consultant who looked as if he'd stepped straight out of a film set. He was elderly, had bushy dark hair, a big beard, dressed in tweeds and spoke with an accent that you would expect from Sigmund Freud. I can't recall much of what we spoke about but he seemed kindly and satisfied with me. I was happy enough to be on the programme and the pathway to surgery so I was relaxed. Next it was Dr Jahbanni three months later. Tanya had agreed to drive and come with me to the appointment. It went ok, I think. All I can remember is the doctor spending an hour staring at my legs while he asked me the usual questions. I had complied with the conditions that the GIC had set for me in the 'Real Life Test'. I was living and presenting as female 24/7 and I had a job in my female name that could be proved with a letter from my employer (Tanya). I also saw Dr Montgomery, who seemed to be quite probing in his questions and not very friendly, but it went ok, I thought.

The final consultant I was to see was Russell Reid, I'd not had a formal appointment with him yet, but he had introduced himself to me several times in the waiting room when I was attending previous appointments with other consultants. I liked him, he was always happy to chat with me and he seemed so friendly and normal, compared to the others. Also, he was obviously gay which made me feel more comfortable about him.

Russell would eventually become crucial to my successful transition, but not at Charing Cross.

The appointment with Russell Reid finally arrived. This would complete my round of the Charing Cross GIC consultants and be the last piece in the diagnostic jigsaw. The defining decision as to whether I would be offered hormone treatment and a future surgery date would depend on this meeting. Russell came into the waiting room and smiled towards me, "Angie? Please come with me". I followed him to his office and took a seat. The appointment could not have gone any better. Russell confirmed that he had recommended I be prescribed hormone therapy subject to ongoing blood tests, and that I was a deemed a suitable candidate for SRS (Sex Reassignment Surgery) as an NHS patient. I didn't hear very much of what he told me after that as I started crying. I suppose it was just the stress of the previous years, I felt as though I'd passed an exam after a long course. He stood up and came around the desk, gently placing his hand on my shoulder and offering me a tissue from the handily placed box on the table.

"I'll give you a few minutes, Angie. Would you like me to ask your friend to join us?"

I nodded, not trusting myself that I wouldn't start inappropriately laughing. I was happy, not upset! Russell left, and five minutes later returned with Tanya, who pulled up a seat next to me. The remainder of what was said was a blur. I could only clearly remember the phrase 'a suitable candidate for SRS'. Fortunately Tanya was taking more notice of what was discussed. One slightly unusual incident occurred as we all stood up to leave the office. Russell handed me a card, explaining that he had his own private clinic, not far away in Earls Court.

"In case you might need this in the future," he smiled.

Immediately after I left Russell, I went along the corridor for my routine blood tests. I was told if these were ok then I'd soon receive a letter explaining what hormone treatment was to be prescribed and instructions for my own GP.

After about three weeks had passed since I'd saw Russell Reid at Charing Cross, I'd still not received a letter regarding hormone therapy. I checked with my GP Dr Plunkett, and he'd heard nothing either. I was becoming concerned, so I called up the GIC clinic. I explained who I was, and asked if a letter had been sent to me or my GP regarding hormone treatment. The receptionist told me she could not see any letters in my file that I should have received recently. Then she gave me the other news I was not expecting; Dr Reid has left the clinic, but not to worry, I'd receive an appointment soon to see one of the other consultants. I was worried! Russell had been my champion at Charing Cross, the only shrink I felt at ease with, and who seemed to understand me.

Eventually I received an appointment letter some three months later. It was to see Professor Green, the head of the clinic. If my last appointment with Russell had gone perfectly, this one was the total opposite;

everything that could go wrong did, badly! And it was my own fault.

It started on the journey to London. Tanya had agreed to come with me and drive us. Released from the hassle of driving, I thought I'd have a drink on the journey, to relax me. I just had a very bad feeling about this appointment and in the same way as I used alcohol for stage nerves I was beginning to use drink as a crutch whenever I felt scared or uncomfortable. I asked Tanya to stop at an off licence and bought four cans of super strong lager which I hid from Tanya in my oversized shoulder bag. I started sipping one can as we left Norwich, intending to take my time and make it last the two hour journey. Tanya noticed and looked across at me, but said nothing. Within fifteen minutes I'd drained the can and opened another. Now Tanya was shaking her head and warning me not to drink the second can. I reassured her I'd be fine. I was still feeling worried and praying the lager would relax me, but it didn't seem to have any effect. By the time we hit the London suburbs I'd drunk all four cans and Tanya and I were bickering. She was reminding me I'd had no food that morning and I was going to get pissed. With the effects of the booze I could not see what the problem was. I was by now feeling very relaxed, in fact so relaxed I was slurring my words and unstable on my legs when we parked and I stepped out of the car. I was dressed in red spandex leggings with white leg warmers on top and a baggy blue mohair sweater. Remember this was the era of Flashdance the movie and I was right on point with the fashion of the day.

I stumbled into Charing Cross hospital with Tanya offering support as we made our way to the clinic. Finally, booked in, we sat in the waiting room. I was on edge, just waiting for Richard Green to come in and address me as 'Mr' again, as he had on my first appointment with him. However, when he did come and call for me he used 'Miss' and my female name, so I began to think maybe this was going to be ok after all. I desperately wanted to know if what I'd been told by Russell Reid regarding hormones and surgery date was still valid, now that he had left the hospital. But before I got the chance to bring that up Dr Green asked me why I was dressed in jeans and not wearing female clothes. I was stunned; I hadn't seen that one coming! I started to explain that I was wearing spandex leggings, not jeans. I asked him if he hadn't seen Flashdance the movie with …. Damn, I couldn't remember her name. But it was immaterial anyway, as he was looking down his nose at me as if I was something the cat had dragged in. Then he asked if I'd been drinking alcohol. Shit, was it so obvious? I thought. Of course it was. I mumbled something unconvincing about having a glass of wine with my lunch, that clearly neither of us could take seriously as an excuse. Dr Green then proceeded to lecture me for ten minutes on the details of the 'real life test' as though it was a brand new idea that I was unaware of. I was dressed in a masculine way, he told me, and if it wasn't for the fact he knew I'd travelled over 100 miles to this appointment he would have sent me packing and cancelled the appointment as soon as he saw me in the waiting room. He then stood up, signalling the appointment was over. I stood unsteadily, but I couldn't leave it at that, I had to ask. "I still haven't received my letter regarding hormone treatment that was agreed on my last appointment with Dr Reid. Can you write to my GP, please?" The mention of Russell Reid;s name brought a sneering look from Dr Green. I was informed that Dr Reid no longer worked at this clinic, and that he, Dr Green, had reviewed my treatment record with the team and it was not thought suitable for me to be prescribed hormone treatment at this time. I would receive another appointment within six months and it could be discussed then. And that was it. He might as well have said, "Your life is in my hands, I control you, and you will do as I say. Now fuck off and be grateful I even spoke to to you today".

I stormed out of the hospital with Tanya at my heels. As I rushed ahead she was asking, "What happened in there? Are you ok? What did he say? But I didn't want to talk about it. I was angry and embarrassed. Dr Green had spoken to me as if I was a stupid little girl. I felt completely powerless because I understood he had all the power in this situation and there was nothing I could do. I was expected to present as a Stepford wife and dress in a pretty gingham dress, to please a man. But I was also angry with myself. If I hadn't got pissed I probably could have handled the situation so much better. What a disaster, two years at Charing Cross GIC thrown away in a few minutes. And what the hell happened to Russell Reid, anyway? Things were bad enough, but they were about to get worse, as my talent for self destruction kicked in fully. I decided I needed another drink. I suggested to Tanya that we find a pub. She protested, "I'm not going drinking in a pub, I have to drive back to Norfolk, and we need to leave soon because the twins are home today!" But I wasn't listening, I told Tanya I'd make my own way home and stomped off towards Hammersmith Broadway, leaving her pleading with me to come back.

I soon found myself sitting in the Swan pub with a double Bacardi and coke in front of me. As I sipped my drink I reflected that this pub was one of my old haunts from when I lived here ten years previously. Was I subconsciously trying to go back? Not just back to the location, but back to living as male, back to being the boy I was? Transitioning was not easy; every time I thought I'd got it sorted something would happen and I'd fuck it up. Back then, life, despite being violent and unpredictable, seemed easy. No one questioned my gender or forced me to live by their rules of femininity or masculinity. As I looked around the bar I remembered the faces of my old friends who I'd spent happy times with in here, Jimmy Mc, Mig, Francis, Robbie and all the rest. Where were they now? And what would they think of me if they could see me sitting here with my make up and painted nails?

I realised I could never go back to that life. Despite everything I desperately wanted to begin hormone treatment and have surgery. That was my path and I'd always known it wasn't going to be easy. Why did I smash my car into the wall back in the Vale if I was so happy as a boy? Today was bad, I had to accept that, but it could be sorted. But, I couldn't take any more self destructive testosterone driven shit, it would kill me in the end. I'd have to make things right with Tanya and the GIC. I finished my drink and walked out of the Swan. I needed to get to Norwich so I got on the tube and made for Victoria bus station.

The day's adventures were not yet over. When I tried to buy a bus ticket I was told the next bus to Norwich would not be until after 11pm that night. I didn't have enough money for a train ticket so I would have to hang around the bus station for seven hours. I found a seat in the waiting area and settled down. Almost immediately I was approached by an older man who asked if he could buy me a drink. WTF? I thought. "No, I'm ok, thank you", I told him. But he still stood there smiling. Then he leaned over and whispered in my ear "How much?" I really didn't know how to respond to this; it was the first time I'd been propositioned as a prostitute! I just shook my head and stared off at the street until he eventually moved off. Should I be flattered? This guy obviously thought I was a woman selling sex at the bus station. What a contrast to the man I'd met earlier, Dr Green, who told me I was not presenting as female. I had to laugh to myself, it was a crazy day.

Chapter 20 'Hanky Panky'

The Scene

One day a regular leather customer, little Steve, came into the shop with exciting news.

"There's going to be a VERY important, VERY private, S&M Scene party in London. It's personal invite only, and some very well known celebrities will be in attendance, as well as the most influential 'Scene' crowd".

His conspiratorial tone implied how sensitive this matter was, and how impressed we should be with him, as the bearer of this news. Much as I had always considered Steve a Walter Mitty type character, we knew he did in fact move in the upper echelons of the British spanking brigade.

He waited for his information to sink in, before continuing in dramatic fashion, "I will be attending, and I've managed to get both of you on the guest list, too."

This sounds good, I thought! This could be a great little earner for the leather business and a chance to make influential contacts. Although I wondered why we had been plucked from the obscurity of a tiny Norfolk leather workshop and trusted to attend a party with the cream of the usually very secretive UK S&M Scene crowd. As it turned out, Tanya and I hadn't actually been elevated to the Scene hierarchy to mingle on equal terms, but we were to be the hired help - we were simply required to do a 'turn' at the party.

I had met Steve a year earlier. He was known vaguely by Tanya. In his day job Steve worked for a local TV company as an engineer, but in his less public life he was heavily into the S&M bondage scene. He used his engineering skills to fashion 'made to measure' stainless steel bondage equipment, like slave collars and shackles and god knows what else. He sold his "restraint equipment" through adverts in various specialist magazines like Skin Two. But, like many suppliers of such unusual equipment, his most lucrative business came through word of mouth. Not unsurprisingly, the kind of people who used Steve's services preferred a personal and very discrete purchasing experience, and were happy to pay a premium price for the right service. Eventually, we were to have several of these "personal" customers ourselves.

It was Steve who had encouraged my entry into the scene as a manufacturer of "specialist leather goods". He had witnessed my leather making skills previously, when he had dropped by the shop for a cuppa one afternoon. I was in the back workshop making Freddy Kruger claw gloves, using riveted leather strips painted silver (Nightmare on Elm Street was the big thing at the time and they sold really well). Around this period I also manufactured studded belts, wrist bands, and harnesses for the Punk Post mail order fashion catalogue that Tanya ran, and I was also dabbling with making things for the gay leather queen scene at the Caribbean Club. Steve seemed very impressed with my work and asked me to make some leather ankle cuffs for him, which he would use on the steel leg spreader bars he produced. "Sure", I replied." Always happy to earn money". Before I knew it I was regularly manufacturing leather bondage gear of all kinds for Steve. The money was so good that we eventually expanded that side of the business and started producing a catalogue of our own designs, hand drawn by me, and marketed through a sister company Tanya and I started, called Leather X. This was my entry into the strange world of the UK S&M scene.

Steve, as we already knew, was very well connected in the 'scene'. I knew he helped arrange the slave girl chariot racing events at the Sex Maniacs Ball. I'd witnessed one of these chariot races previously with some amazement. I'd never seen anything like it before. The girls were dressed in leather corsets, chastity belts, stiletto heels and usually sporting high ponytails at the top of their heads. They were fastened to the chariots by means of leather waist harnesses, usually with their arms bound behind their backs. They had steel bridles in their mouths attached to reins and even wore horse blinkers. In short they were human ponies. The dressing up side of this wasn't so weird to me, it was all consensual and it looked like good fun to wear all that stuff. But, when not actually taking part in races these girls were often left tied to a post, whilst their "masters" enjoyed the other delights of the evenings entertainments. That, I thought, wouldn't be a lot of fun. Tied up like a horse while he was partying? No fucking way! Saying that, as far as I knew, all the pony girls were willing slaves, they certainly didn't complain about their treatment - but, I suppose having steel bridal gags locked into their mouths had some bearing on the lack of protests.

* * * * * * *

There was also a darker side to little Steve. I'd visited him at his home one night to deliver his leather order, whereupon he delighted in showing me some of the heavy steel shackles he was making to order for an overseas client. They were so small I felt only a child could have worn them. I mentioned this to Steve but he simply shrugged his shoulders. Next he showed me his collection of replica medieval swords, "exact in every detail" I was assured, and extremely lethal weapons. "Here, hold it," he offered. I politely declined. Steve smiled at what he thought was my discomfort, before moving on to his Chinese martial arts collection and then to a more up to date weapon in his collection, a fully functioning AK 45. What the hell was he doing with that in Norwich?

I have no doubt, looking back, that this guided tour of Steve's weaponry was a test of my character. He wanted to understand if he could dominate me, or would it be the other way round. Steve watched my reactions intently. Fortunately, my previous life experiences with violent gangsters and psychos that I'd known from Glasgow to London had prepared me for anything Steve had to offer. I wasn't fazed. But I made a mental note about him. Steve was that kind of man, who, perhaps because of shortness of stature, had developed an enormous inferiority complex. This insecurity seemingly had to be assuaged by surrounding himself with the devices of violence and torture that would put fear into others. Of course, on the Scene he styled himself as a Master. But like a lot of the masters, he was really looking for someone strong enough to dominate him! I certainly wasn't scared of him, but I felt he may be the kind of guy prone to intense rage who could flip one day and I'd be reading about him in the newspapers after he's gone on a killing spree. I felt Steve's demonstration was an invitation. It all became clearer later on, when I met his wife, a very pretty but scary Glaswegian woman who spoke with my accent and who obviously completely dominated Steve. He knew my history as both male and female, which fascinated him because it both attracted and revolted him at the same time. He told me that, and once invited me to accompany him to another smaller London party on a previous occasion. I wore the type of clothing he loved women to wear, PVC corsets, slutty make up, fish nets and spiky hair wigs. My irreverent attitude both annoyed and attracted him. I was a bit of a challenge to Steve. These sorts of mind power games are not unusual among the devotees of S&M.

But, getting back to the London party. At these events complete discretion was always expected. The News of the World newspaper had recently infiltrated the S&M party scene by having reporters pose as bondage fans at a West Midlands private party venue, then splashing the details over several pages for the titillation of their readers. This had caused extreme embarrassment to some of those present. I had attended a few of these West Midlands parties as a trader, when Tanya and I had set up a stall selling clothes and various leather strap bondage equipment, ball gags, butt plugs and the like. These nights were usually held in a bar in the Kidderminster area and, far from being nights of debauchery and sexual depravity, they were very civilised affairs. The people who ran and attended the events were typically middle class members of suburbia, holding down jobs like teachers and bank managers. If not for the exotic bondage outfits and the various slaves crawling around on all fours or getting spanked, the conversation at these events would be similar to a typical Ramblers Association meeting.

The Kidderminster press intrusion had spooked the general scene crowd and for the London event strict security was necessary for the peace of mind of some of the more well known scene members. This was going to be a very private affair. Unless you were known to the host or a very close friend of someone who knew the host, it would be impossible to gain admittance.

Steve had got his invite, as a well known and trusted manufacturer of steel bondage equipment, and a long time close friend to the Scene's 'in crowd.' He had only managed to get Tanya and me an invite, on his personal recommendation, as performers for the live stage show that would be the backdrop to the party.

* * * * * * *

Steve informed us there would be a crowd of over two hundred very important guests. The cream of the UK's S&M scene and quite a few from overseas were flying in, too. Masters with their slaves, Magazine proprietors, fashion designers, famous authors, etc. It would be held in a high class West End art gallery owned by the party's host. He also emphasised in the strongest terms how important this party was for him, and how big a favour he was doing us by giving us the chance to attend. He made it clear he was trusting us with access to the inner sanctum of the British S&M elite and we would probably see some famous people we recognised. If we made a good impression we would be 'in' and a lot of bondage leather work would follow as well as possibly future highly paid international stage appearances. His parting words were:

"Don't let me down."

After Steve left, Tanya turned to me with a grin on her face.

"This is our big chance!" she screamed.

Her mind was already racing, planning dance routines and costumes. We didn't have much time to learn a new routine, so we decided to do a belly dance dressed in bondage gear underneath. It was decided to combine a sort of dance of the seven veils, starting off wearing full Egyptian Yashmak costume and then strip down to black satin basques with fishnet tights and chain link bras. I'd wear the blue Star punk wig and she'd wear the red one. I readily agreed. I was always happy for Tanya to take the lead in these matters. She was far better at planning things than me. I was the creative force but she was always the organiser. Without her nothing I dreamt up would ever take place, especially since I tended to get drunk often and put things off. My motto was always 'it'll be all right on the night'. I thought preparation and rehearsal sapped my spontaneity.

Over the next few weeks we put together new publicity material to hand out at the party. We had glossy catalogues of my leather bondage work printed and colour flyers as well as new business cards proudly proclaiming 'Skint Leather' (this was the company name that eventually succeeded Leather X). The dance routine we deliberately kept fairly simple. Just a few basic steps. It used the same routine I performed in my belly dance stripper kissagram. Most of the show work was in the removing of the silk scarves to a strip tease backing track, eventually culminating in the revealing of the kinky outfits underneath and miming a song to a backing track. It should all work easily enough as long as we danced in strict time and kept our synchronised moves spot on. The important thing was to appear professional. We needed a high impact entrance, Tanya decided. If we could get the crowd attention straight away they wouldn't lose interest in the routine before we finished. I agreed, trying to think of something

"I know! Remember in the film Cleopatra, where Elizabeth Taylor is carried in to Mark Anthony's bedroom rolled up in a carpet? We can do that, we will both be wrapped up in carpets and brought on from opposite sides of the stage by slaves, then unrolled to face the audience and begin our dance."

Tanya agreed it was a great idea. We both knew at this kind of party there would be no shortage of slaves to use. So it was settled. We managed to acquire a pair of matching Persian type rugs large enough to use and we worked on our routine and making the costumes. They won't forget us Tanya, enthused.

Eventually, the day of the party arrived. We travelled down in my old Vauxhall. The car was packed with our publicity material, costumes and of course the rolled up carpets. As was my usual habit at the time, I made sure we also brought along a hefty stash of booze (for my stage nerves). We closed the shop early at 4.30 and left directly for London. Unfortunately, and much to Tanya's annoyance, I resorted to the tried and tested coping mechanism that I regularly used to deal with the stress of performing - I opened a can of Special Bru, and began sipping it quietly, as Tanya drove on and the miles passed.

Tanya occasionally glanced over to me with a frown.

"Oh, Angie! Please don't start drinking this early, you'll be pissed."

But she knew her words would have little effect on me. Looking resigned, she shook her head, wearing a worried look.

Looking back I'm amazed the patience Tanya had for me. I was extremely unpredictable once I'd had a drink. My performance could end up a pathetic 'no show' or I could be fantastic and bring the house down. As it happened on this occasion it was the latter, but not quite what we hoped for.

By the time we had got halfway to London from Norwich I'd had several cans of strong lager and was nagging at Tanya to stop for a pee break. Like most drunks, I thought I was in control of my alcohol intake and was still displaying the appearance of sobriety. My self deception told me I could drink at least six of these cans before I became noticeably inebriated. By the time we were in the West End, parked on the street directly in front of the elegant art gallery, I'd had my six cans. But, I had worked into my calculations, that on this occasion, the adrenalin of pre performance nerves would negate at least two of these cans. So, by my warped reckoning I was still two cans short of my safety limit. The self deception of the piss artist is can be very persuasive.

I breezed into the gallery entrance carrying my costume bags and a couple of rolled up carpets, I was brimming with confidence and raring to get on stage. Tanya, seeing me through her own sober eyes, was understandably a tad more concerned. But, ever the trooper, she beamed her best smile and marched in to the building. We were stopped in the foyer by a serious looking man in an expensive suit, the gallery owner. He was a short thin gentleman, who introduced himself as Nigel. I could tell by his mannerisms and appearance that he was very obviously gay, of the sarcastic queen type.

I introduced Tanya and myself by our stage name Marlena Von Mantrap & Angie Leather – Cabaret Artists (yes, we really were billed as that, cringe). I informed him that we were booked for the stage show. Nigel looked down his nose at us, clearly unimpressed. He nodded towards the rolled up carpets.

"Are you flying home tonight or stopping over?"

I explained the carpets were stage props, we were friends of Steve; we would need to stay over and understood there would be accommodation provided for us. Nigel claimed to know nothing about accommodation but reluctantly agreed we could sleep in the gallery, as long as we were very careful not to touch anything. He ushered us quickly inside the building where we found ourselves in a large hall. I could see a raised stage was set up on one side. I was very pleased to see there was also a fully stocked bar adjacent to the stage curtains on one side of the platform. Immediately in front of the stage there were at least 100 tables with chairs filling the remaining floor space. The venue was packed with leather clad slaves and masters of all descriptions. A spiral staircase snaked up from the back of the hall to the first floor. I noticed the walls were strangely bare, for an art gallery. Nigel informed us that the performers were using the upstairs gallery as a communal changing room. When we went up we saw the area was sectioned off with rows and rows of six foot high partitions. We were warned to be careful not to touch these, as all the gallery paintings had been hung on them, this was all the art from the downstairs gallery, removed for safety. That explained the bare walls. Tanya and I found a spot within the maze of partitions to place our clothes and props and began to get changed into the belly dancer outfits with the leather bondage bras and mini skirts underneath.

As is always the case with these functions, everything was running late and so we had a lot of time to kill before we were due to perform. This gave us the opportunity to find four volunteer 'slaves' to carry us, rolled up inside the carpets, on to the stage. It also allowed time for me to hang out at the bar, which turned out to be free. By the time we were due on stage I'd knocked back half a dozen gin and tonics and I was feeling no fear.

Five minutes before our slot was due we lay down on the carpets and were rolled up by the slaves, then carried, me to one side of the stage and Tanya to the other. The rolled up carpets were then placed leaning against the back drop inside the stage wings in readiness for our music intro. As I waited tightly compressed inside the carpet the time dragged on. I could hear the music of the previous act playing on and on, and see the flashing stage lights through the circular gap above me. Were they ever going to get off? By now the alcohol was really kicking in and I was feeling very hot and flustered. The slaves had gone off somewhere and I was trapped. I managed to get an arm out of the top of the carpet and began waving to attract someone's attention, eventually a passing waiter saw my hand, he peered down at me in shock.

"What on earth are you doing in there?"

I told him not to worry, I was fine. I just needed a large gin and tonic with a straw, and asked him politely to get me one . It was testament to the kind of weird night it was that he didn't even argue; of course he would get the strange woman wrapped up in a carpet a drink. He soon returned and passed down the glass to me. There appeared to be some technical problem with the music and the slaves/stage hands had gone to try and fix it leaving me and Tanya trapped in the wings. Thankfully my waiter friend didn't desert me, he stayed around chatting and got me several more drinks while the hitch was resolved.

Eventually, after some forty minutes or so delay, I heard Egyptian belly dance music, it was our intro. I felt myself being lifted off the floor and carried shoulder high on to the stage, then unceremoniously thrown down and quickly unrolled. The bright stage lights blinded me and I couldn't tell the front from the back of the stage. I tried to stand up to begin the dance routine and discovered my legs were numb from the constriction, I could barely crawl as I felt the spasms and pins and needles sensation of the blood returning to my feet. This was a catastrophe! I looked to the side and saw Tanya wasn't in any better shape. We managed to get hold of each other and somehow got ourselves upright. As we tried to get into the routine we stumbled around like some drunken four legged whirling dervish with silk scarves flying. At one point I separated from Tanya as I got feeling back in my legs and began dancing seductively in time to the music, unfortunately, I was still blinded by the lights and I wasn't even facing the audience, but instead a brick wall. As the last part of the music came along we rapidly began throwing off the scarves, silk skirts and bodices, in a rush to get to our big finish. It was more like 'Carry on Cleo' than the sexy dance of the seven veils as we scrambled around ripping off all our clothing to end up standing in just the leather underwear and Yashmak masks. The music stopped and Tanya and me looked at each other. What a disaster, we'd totally screwed that up. We bowed to the audience in silence, this was excruciating, we had to get off quick! Then, suddenly there was a roar of applause, loud clapping and whistling. We looked back at each other in confusion, huh? They like us! Another quick bow and we bolted off stage and ran for the spiral staircase. It wasn't till a few minutes later that we found out what was going on, our fellow artists were congratulating us on our fantastic hilarious routine. Our sexy dancing had been so spectacularly awful that the audience thought it was a comedy act! Only Steve knew the truth and he just grinned at us.

If the night had ended there it would have been fine, but unfortunately there was much more drama to come. Upstairs, within the maze of art clad partitions I struggled to get out of my costume, I was wearing a very tight elastic panty girdle as I still needed to 'tuck' to hide my bulge in those days. I was hopping around on one leg trying to yank the girdle off when I tripped backwards over a suitcase and fell against one of the partitions. As I lay on my back, I looked in horror as the weight of the framed art slowly tipped it over. It toppled on to the next partition, and that on to the next after that. Like dominoes falling one after the other, a whole swathe of expensive art went crashing to the floor to the sound of twisted screeching metal and splintering wood. Next I heard what sounded like a woman screaming. Oh shit, I thought. Have I flattened someone? But it turned out to be Nigel, the gallery owner. Like a wailing banshee, he was rushing towards me his face a mask of rage. I was still half in and half out of the panty girdle as I tried to make my escape scrambling along the floor. I'm certain he would have killed me if he'd got hold of me. Thankfully some of the others, including Steve, managed to hold him back before he reached me. Once I knew he was retrained I thought I'd go over to Nigel and apologise, but he just kept on saying,

"Fuck off, get out, get out of my gallery!"

In my inebriated state I still thought I could offer some help in repairing the damage. As Nigel and the others began trying to replace the dislodged and bent steel bars of one of the wrecked partitions into their sockets, I bent down to lend a hand, hoping he would understand my regret at what had happened and willingness to try to put things right. I was straining to force one section into its hole when Nigel started screaming again. I looked at his pained face and told him,

"You really need to calm down, mate. I said I'm sorry, ok?"

Then he started shouting about his 'fucking finger', I was confused, and that's when I noticed I'd been trying to push the steel bar into place and trapped his hand in the socket. He was shouting "fuck off, fuck off, just please fuck off!" And I decided, yes, it was probably best I did just that. Tanya and I grabbed our bits and pieces and with me still half dressed, we quickly rushed to the gallery main exit and left to the accompanying sound of Nigel's wailing.

We had to sleep in the car that night; both of us had had too much to drink so we couldn't drive. I remember waking up the next morning curled up on the back seat, entangled with Tanya, and covered in silk scarves, carpets and leather underwear. I was wondering if I had dreamt the previous night. That was crazy, but Tanya soon confirmed it was no dream, when she awake a few minutes later.

* * * * * * *

The London gallery was just one example of many 'eventful' nights I had during my brief show business career with Tanya. Another night in Telford I performed my belly dance routine so enthusiastically at a Penthouse Magazine party that I dislocated a disc in my back and woke up the next morning in the hotel unable to move. I had to be driven back to Norwich flat on my back in an estate car. Thankfully there was an osteopath operating from a house round the corner from Willowisp shop, and he sorted me out. I have always had occasional recurring problems with my back ever since that incident, which I discovered was recorded in my NHS medical records by some wag as a 'belly dancing misadventure injury.'

We worked a lot of the Norfolk holiday camps and took unpaid gigs in pubs and clubs, even doing talent shows. I was always pretty unreliable; no one knew what kind of performance I would give, dependent on my stage fright or alcohol intake. One night we were doing a show in a Caister on Sea holiday camp. Tanya was singing and playing guitar, and I had taken a back seat from the stage and was just providing the backing music with a keyboard. Halfway through her set one guy from the audience started heckling her, telling her she was rubbish, and to get off, etc. Tanya put up with this for a few minutes, then tried to shut him up by asking him nicely not to spoil the show for others. But he wouldn't have it and kept on shouting at her. I'd had quite a lot to drink, as usual, and eventually I couldn't listen to him any more. For the first time in years I lost my temper and got violent. I hadn't felt this aggression in me since I'd came to Norwich and transitioned. I was wearing female clothing and make up, but the heckler and the rest of the audience got a shock when I charged over to him and in a very masculine manner and voice told him to 'shut the fuck up or I'll kick you all round the room'. There was a shocked silence for a few seconds as everyone tried to take in what had just happened. This apparently casually dressed hippy woman had turned into a male Glaswegian hard case, right in front of them. I shocked myself! I'd outed myself. Then I heard jeers. People around the heckler were telling me to leave the guy alone. There was actual booing. I was a bit confused, I addressed the audience, "You have paid for a show and this guy is ruining it for you. I'm just trying to let the performer play". But still there was hissing and jeering. It was only then I noticed the heckler was sitting in a wheel chair, obviously severely disabled. And I had just threatened to beat him up. Oh fuck! I just apologised and walked out. The show was over and I'd ruined it and embarrassed myself, because I was too pissed to notice what everyone else could see. That night frightened me; I saw just how close to the surface the old me was. I really needed to get on to hormone treatment as soon as possible.

I was due back at Charing Cross for another appointment soon and I would beg them to get my treatment started. Since my disastrous appointment with

Dr Green, when I'd turned up smelling of booze and was accused of wearing male clothes, I'd had a couple of less dramatic appointments with the other shrinks in the team. To try and make amends I'd dressed as a good girl, stayed sober and been very mild mannered and stereotypically feminine, but I'd not been allowed oestrogen yet.

The kissagram business was still very popular and financially rewarding, but it was changing. We had been one of the first to bring this service to Norfolk, but now a few other businesses were doing the same thing, and on occasion our innocent risqué party fun was being confused by customers as being something altogether more sexually explicit. It was becoming obvious that others were using the business model as a cover for escort agencies.

One night I drove young Sara to an address in the sticks to what was supposed to be a 21st birthday party. She had been booked as a sexy policewoman. The usual format was she would enter the party in uniform and 'arrest' the birthday boy, handcuffing his wrists behind his back before stripping off to suspenders and bra, singing a birthday message and giving him a kiss. All very innocent and performed in front of his family and friends, one of whom would have booked it. But, on this occasion we arrived at the house and it was dark and very quiet. No music playing, no family or friends dancing. It was just one young guy on his own. Both Sara and I felt very uncomfortable, I told him that we usually perform at parties, and that it was only a fun thing for the family to have a laugh. I even offered to refund his money as I thought maybe he'd misunderstood what we did for a service. But, he insisted that since we were there we should go ahead with the kissagram anyway. So, with me playing the stripper music on our ghetto blaster Sara did the whole performance to an audience of one, ending by reading a funny limerick and giving him a small kiss. It was surreal, and I couldn't wait to grab Sara and drive off from there.

* * * * * * *

By now we seemed to be able to make money at will. Everything we tried turned out to be very profitable. It was only the theatrical costume hire business that seemed to be struggling. As well as the kissagrams, we were selling punk clothes and jewellery by mail order, rubber and leather ladies' kinky fashion wear. I was still churning out the heavy duty leather bondage harnesses and restraints and Tanya was still making the occasional wedding dress. The cash was rolling in and we thought perhaps it was time to expand. It was time we moved out of the village and into the city. Locally most of our face to face business was Norwich customers anyway, so we would likely get much more business if we relocated. It was agreed that we'd set up a small shop in Norwich and close the one in Aylsham, and once we were established in the city we'd get bigger premises and bring all the businesses in house.

The other thought that occurred to me was that if we were making enough money then perhaps I could bypass the NHS Charring Cross GIC and go private for treatment. It was well known that you could get on to hormone therapy much more easily if you went direct to one of the independent doctors. And, from there, a fast track to private sex change surgery. I was getting really fed up with performing like a seal for Charing Cross consultants. Dr Green knew I was under his thumb and had to do whatever he decided. If he wanted me to turn up in a gingham flowery patterned dress with tights and heels I had to do it. We both knew that and it seemed to me he enjoyed that power.

* * * * * * *

I'd also not forgotten about my son Joseph. Every time I thought of him the separation was still very raw. I'd made a few trips back to Glasgow to see him. I'd even bought some male jeans and a leather jacket for the purpose. I hated wearing males clothes or presenting as male, but I knew I had no choice if I ever wanted to have access. His mother, Sharon, had instigated divorce proceedings against me, and now, with my new found family stability with Tanya and the twins, I intended to apply for custody. I figured that one day, once I had transitioned physically and legally, I could be Joseph's second mum. I knew I could never have the bond of his birth mum, but at this time she was bringing him up in a tiny tenement flat in one of the roughest parts of Glasgow. We in Norwich could give him so much more financially and socially. He would be entering in to a ready made family with two big sisters, who had met him and loved him, with me and Tanya as parents.

Chapter 21 'Doin' The Do'

In 1990 business was booming for Tanya and me, and with the encouragement of the bank, we were set to expand into Norwich city centre. I decided to take on a shop lease on Silver Road; this was to be my baby. It was a two story retail premises owned by the Co-op, who were a big property landlord in Norwich. The ground floor was to be a traditional ladies' fashion shop, selling regular women's clothes, jewellery and underwear. Upstairs had been used for stock storage by the previous leaseholder, it was just a long grubby undecorated room. I thought this space would be ideal for conversion into a hairdresser's, so we engaged my sister's boyfriend at the time, Albert, to come up from London, where they lived, and do the building work. We called the new business 'Vamps'. Albert did a fantastic job, dividing the first floor space with an archway wall so one half became a beauty treatment room with a massage couch, and the other was fitted with sinks and mirrors to be the hairdressing salon.

The clothes retail shop on the ground floor made sense; we knew that side of the business. But why open a massage parlour and hairdressers when neither myself or Tanya were qualified to cut hair or do beauty treatments? It was a hard question to answer in hindsight. I suppose we thought if nothing else we could rent the chairs out in the hairdressers, and we did do that for a while but it never made any money. I also decided to enrol on a hairdressing course at Great Yarmouth Technical College, and Tanya enrolled on a massage/aromatherapy course. We were looking to the future; we didn't expect to be always involved in kinky bondage leather, and the kissagram business, and Punk Post was already drying up. It was time to go mainstream, we thought, and the bank gave us every encouragement; they were literally throwing money at us.

Once Vamps was up and running we began looking around for other retail premises for Tanya, somewhere big enough to hold the 600 plus hire costumes she owned, but also having a sales area where customers could buy the kinky leather and rubber fashion wear we usually sold by mail order. We had decided to be open and transparent about that side of the business, and not hide it behind grubby plain packaged mail order parcels. The customers could come along and feel the goods before purchasing them. This extended to the bondage leather harnesses and restraints. We had everything on display from leather zipped hoods, rubber dresses, to a wide array of dildos, vibrators and chain ball stretchers. The premises we eventually took on were the whole top floor of a massive Victorian building on Prince of Wales Road. Underneath was a huge nightclub and disco called 'La Valbon', owned by Malcolm, a friend of ours. The rent was high but we thought we could easily manage it. We called it Metamorphose.

A new addition to the Metamorphose shop would be a dressing service for transvestites. A couple of years earlier Tanya had persuaded me to go and visit the Transformation business in London owned by Stephanie Ann Lloyd, to get information on her business model. Stephanie was a post op transsexual woman who had made a fortune from catering to the male cross dressing community, and had premises in London and Manchester where clients could have an 'away day', get their make-up. done and choose from a variety of female clothes to dress up in and have a photograph taken. Transformation also sold wigs and make-up. at very high prices, capitalising on the vulnerability and lack of opportunity for their clients. It seemed like a very hard- nosed, profit driven set- up. I went along with Tanya, as a cross-dressing customer. It was very expensive but friendly enough, despite the obvious aggressive pushing by the staff to get customers to spend more. We had identified how we could provide a better, less expensive, but more humane service to the clientele.

So that was to be the other new part of the business. We provided a make-up. studio and employed my old friend Liz as the artist. We had a huge range of female costumes for the customers to wear, taken from Tanya's hire stock. Everything from French maids, rubber outfits, to 60's mini dresses, but by far the most popular outfit was wedding dresses. We had so many clients come along for a wedding dress day out it was unbelievable. We gave them the works, full make up, wig, white wedding dress and photographs. We even had a coffee lounge set aside on the roof garden of the building where customers, once dressed, could spend a few hours sipping their drinks and watching television. I was to spend many happy days providing the dressing service and I met a lot of lovely people. We even had a Christmas party up there that was packed out, and most days guys from the local gay crowd at the Loft Club (formerly the Caribbean), which was just round the corner, would pop in for a coffee and a chat. We were very open and up front about our business; we didn't want it to be seen as sex shop sleazy. So we paid for adverts in the local press and were interviewed with photos for a feature. We even ran adverts on the local radio!

By now, between us, we owned a costume hire shop, a hairdressers and massage therapy clinic, a ladies fashion shop, a kinky leather & rubber fashion shop, a dressing service, a kissagram agency, and several mail order outlets. We also had three separate business premises and employed a lot of people. It's true we were not making a huge amount of money, but we were having a fantastic time, and presumably the money would start to roll in again in the future. Career wise I had never been happier or more fulfilled. I loved going to work every day, but when the day ended I was prone to depression and using alcohol because I had still not been able to access hormone therapy from Charing Cross. It would sicken me to have to go there for appointments and be treated like a stupid kid who didn't know her own mind, and at the same time be a high flying business woman at home responsible for paying the wages of our employees.

* * * * * * *

During 1990 the Tory party introduced a new policy, the Uniform Business Rate, along with what was to become known as the Poll Tax. It was to be a disaster for small independent retailers. Suddenly our costs were massively increased overnight, and at the same time our customers were hit with the unpopular Poll Tax. Without going over the boring details it signalled the beginning of the end for our businesses, and incidentally cost Margaret Thatcher her job. Not that I cared much about her. Before the year ended the country had slipped into recession and the once thriving high streets all over England began to be replaced by empty shuttered shops and dilapidated retail buildings not economically worth repairing. It was such a shame, so many people lost their businesses and the hearts of the communities were ripped out. To this day the high streets have never fully recovered from that political vandalism.

As the year rolled on, Tanya and I now spent our time firefighting the disaster. Because we had so many different premises and businesses to deal with, it was impossible to give our full concentration to any one area. We had obviously over- extended ourselves. Every day seemed to bring a new disaster. Suddenly suppliers stopped providing credit and orders had to be paid for in advance. Interest rates went up at the bank and credit facilities were abruptly withdrawn or severely curtailed. Confidence in business in general was lost and even companies that we had been dealing with for years began issuing court proceeding at the first instance of payment delay. We seemed to be spending half our time answering one court summons after another. We had to make staff redundant and stop taking any wages ourselves. Of course the answer was to downsize and get rid of some of our shop leases, but at a time of recession there are very few takers, so we were locked into contracts that were quickly bleeding us dry. I had got a car through the business on HP finance, not just for my own transport but to collect stock and deliver costumes. I missed a couple of payments and began to get a lot of hassle from the finance company. They threatened to repossess the car and I was in the absurd situation of having to hide it each night, anywhere but outside my flat. In the end I gave up, I got the car MOT'd and cleaned, then I left it in a pub car park with the keys in the glovebox. I called the finance company to tell them where it was and that was that.

This kind of pressure can destroy the very best of friendships and business partnerships, and we were no different. Tanya and I began arguing and lost trust in each other. Things that had been no more than a nuisance previously became huge insurmountable problems. One of these was the fact I still smoked cigarettes in those days. Tanya didn't like it, but now it became a big focus of disagreement between us. One after another of our business ventures failed, and we had no financial resources to fall back on, so we had to give up shops and sell off stock at a massive loss.

Around the same time as all this was going on, Tanya had swapped her tiny council flat in Hevingham for a large three bedroomed council house in Norwich, so she and her twins no longer had any need to use my Norwich flat when she came into the city. She had asked me not to smoke in her new house, but I selfishly ignored her protestations. I was drinking heavily and worrying about how the business failure was going to affect my transition. There was going to be no money to go for private treatment and I'd have to crawl back to Charing Cross and play their games. Not only that, but once we no longer had our business I'd be unemployed, and I knew how difficult it was going to be for me to gain employment without documentation in my female name. I'd be seen by Charring Cross as failing the 'real life test' by not being employed and solvent as a woman.

* * * * * * *

And then my aunt Mamie died. She was my favourite aunt and the person in the family I'd been closest to all my life. I'd lived with her in London, she had visited me when I was in Borstal, and she was always there for me when I needed a shoulder to cry on. Her death from cancer was sudden and unexpected. A few years earlier she and uncle George had retired back to Scotland to live in the Vale. I'd not seen much of my family in the Vale for years and now I would have to go back for her funeral. The first practical problem facing me was how I would I dress. I could not turn up dressed as female, as none of my family except my sister knew I was living as a woman. Of course, I could make this a statement, and perhaps it was time I was honest and they found out. But, also I knew I couldn't make Mamie's funeral about me; it would be disrespectful to her and the hundreds of mourners who would attend. In the end Tanya found me some male clothes from her costume hire stock, a white shirt and a black jacket and trousers. Wearing these rough and unfamiliar items, I felt as if I was done up in fancy dress for my dear aunt's final farewell, but what else could I do?

I attended Mamie's funeral and stopped over for one night at my parents' house. As expected, after a tasteful send off, it turned out to be a massive piss up. The after party/wake was difficult; not only was the person I felt closest to in my family, missing, she was the reason why we were all gathered. I'd watched her coffin slowly disappear behind a curtain at the crematorium. It was very uncomfortable for me to be addressed as 'he' and 'him' when I was used to being 'she' and 'her' in my normal life back in Norwich. I was up at dawn, and drove back home first thing the next morning. I was desperate to get back; despite the business problems I missed Norwich so much. It was where I was 'me' and the Vale seemed like a foreign country.

I arrived back at Tanya's new house in the afternoon after driving non stop from Scotland. I wanted to be with her and the twins, and get those horrible male clothes off. I parked my car on the street, grabbed my suitcase and walked inside. Tanya was there waiting for me as I dropped my suitcase on the lounge floor. Before I'd even sat down, the first thing she said to me was "this is now a no smoking area, if you want to have a fag then do it outside". Looking back, it was a reasonable request; I knew she hated my smoking habit. But I was just too tired and emotional to deal with it at this time. I simply picked my case back up, said nothing to her, and turned around and walked out the door. That effectively was the end of my relationship with Tanya. I drove back to my flat and our odd, but happy, little family arrangement of the past 3 years was over.

Chapter 22 'Hey, That's No Way to Say Goodbye'

Life immediately after Tanya was quite lonely. I found myself becoming depressed with my lack of money, a social life, or future prospects. It's funny how quickly fair weather friends disappear. I'd invested everything into our business ventures to the exclusion of all other relationships, and now I was left penniless, with few friends and in debt. I'd mostly lost contact with the local gay scene. When the Caribbean Club had closed down, because poor old Dougie had died, there was no obvious way to meet new friends. I'd lost the custody battle with Sharon; she had Joseph and I was only allowed access visits, but without the financial means I couldn't afford to travel up to Glasgow very often. I had to sign on for unemployment benefit, but at least I had a roof over my head. Thankfully I'd always insisted on keeping my council flat and resisted moving in with Tanya.

I needed a job, but there were few options available for a failed, skint retail entrepreneur who looked like a girl but had male documentation. As before I had to park my female persona during working hours to try and get employment. I told myself it was only a temporary situation, but I had to do something because I could not even afford the travel costs to visit Charing Cross for my next appointment.

I applied to Commercial Union for a job as a trainee financial adviser. I would, upon passing my training exams, become a mortgage and pensions adviser. I despised the work. My purpose was to take the leads the company supplied and turn them into business. In short, persuade people to switch their pension pots to Commercial Union and with any luck then also persuade the clients they needed life insurance policies, ideally connected to switching their mortgage too. The day of my exams I was, along with another dozen or so trainees, to go through a final seminar with the trainer. He discussed all the likely questions and wrote the answers on a huge white board .After that it was time to take the exam paper. The trainer and invigilator handed out the forms, wished us good luck and the exam started. It was impossible to fail because the huge board with all the answers had been 'accidentally' left in full view of where we were sitting. This summed up the duplicity of the whole financial advice industry for me. Nothing was ever explicitly expressed but we were expected to cheat and lie our way to business any way we could. The only saving grace for me was that I was officially self employed on a small retainer and received no wages. My earnings would come from commission and I had the freedom to speak to the clients as frankly as I wanted. Not surprisingly I was completely useless at this kind of business, being far too candid. It was almost never in their interests to switch their savings or polices and I was too honest to tell them otherwise. I never made a single sale, and looking back, I'm quite happy about that.

* * * * * * *

Meanwhile, socially, I wanted to meet new people, so I scanned the adverts in Gay Times and sent off a few replies to those I found interesting. I was not that concerned about finding a relationship, I just wanted some fun company to bring me out of my melancholic situation. This was how I met Michael, who lived in Norwich, was about ten years older than me and a solvent alcoholic - a rare combination. He had a good job in a printing firm but socially was very insecure and drank like a fish. He would visit my flat a couple of times a week, bringing along a huge carrier bag of alcohol, cans of super lager and vodka. We would spend the night listening to music and drinking. Eventually I would cook him a meal, after which he'd fall asleep. There was never any sex involved. Very occasionally I'd get dolled up in a nice dress and he'd take me out for a meal, but that was as far as it went. I was happy enough because I got free booze at least, and some sorely needed company. But he was never going to be the one who would sweep me off my feet, pay for my surgery, and live happily ever after with.

That improbable scenario was the only way I could see of finding a future female life unless something drastic changed. I needed a sugar daddy. I received an answer to one of my Gay Times letters from a man, Jonathan, in London. He was looking for a feminine, possibly transsexual, partner. He owned a large house in Chelsea and worked within the Church of England. He was obviously very affluent and well educated. We spoke several times on the phone and exchanged photos, then I agreed to travel down to London to meet him at the Regent's Palace hotel. The plan was that we would have dinner then go out to a nightclub, I could stay the night at his house and we would take it from there. I spent all morning getting glammed up, make up perfect, and bought a new skirt and top. I took the train to London and arrived at the hotel bar for our rendezvous exactly on time and feeling excited. Could he be the one? When Jonathan arrived I recognised him immediately and I beamed a smile to him with a little wave. Unfortunately, he didn't look particularly enthusiastic to see me. He bought himself a drink (not even offering me one) and came and sat at my table looking troubled. After some small talk, he abruptly said. "I have to go, I'm sorry you are not right for me," got up and walked out! Even for the gay community, which can be brutal, this rudeness shocked me! I was left feeling completely stupid, out of pocket, and trying to figure out if I could get a train back to Norwich that night.

On another occasion I invited a guy who I'd met via the Gay Times adverts to come and visit me. As before, we had exchanged photos and had a few chats on the phone. His name was Johnny and he seemed like a good laugh, and very sociable. He was only slightly older than me and certainly not sugar daddy material. Johnny was a working class gay lad from Leeds. I met him off the train at Norwich station and we went for a drink. There was no chemistry between us but I liked him a lot as a friend. He was really looking for a feminine boyfriend and I was not happy at all about being a boy, or even being called a boy, so we were never going to hit it off sexually, but we did have a great night out. The next morning we were chilling on my balcony in the sun and discussing what we were both looking for, and how hard it was to meet the right person. I'd suggested, only half joking, that I needed a kind older guy who was financially comfortable, and who was looking for someone younger to take care of. This is not an unusual scenario in the male gay community, the young pretty queens often attract a lot of admirers and older men who are happy to have a platonic relationship with them and help out financially. I'd had a couple of much older admirers myself in the past. But what Johnny casually said next was a real wake up call. He said, "Yes, but most of those older men are looking for late teens to early twenty year olds, aren't they?". I understood at once that he was right, of course. He didn't say it unkindly, he was just stating a fact, and I realised that without noticing it I had become too old for that kind of relationship. A young feminine queen's sell by date comes along pretty quickly, just like a cis woman. And if all you have to offer is a pretty face the appeal is time limited, with other, younger and prettier rivals always coming up to replace you. I was twenty seven, and in the gay scene that means getting a bit long in the tooth. I was quite shocked, but it was obvious that it was time for me to properly evaluate myself and take myself more seriously. Just what or who was I looking for? And, more to the point, who, in the ever decreasing pool of possible partners, was interested in me? It was a depressing thought.

One night I decided to go out for a drink in the city. I would normally never go out on my own to a pub as a woman but I was bored and there was a Children in Need charity telethon on the TV and I knew this particular pub would be packed with people raising funds, as it had been advertised in the newspaper. I'd likely not attract too much unwanted attention, it would be a good atmosphere, and I needed cheering up. I arrived around 10pm, got a drink at the bar and found a spare seat at a table. There was a pretty girl about my age sitting there, with, I presumed, her boyfriend. He had a huge fibre glass whale on the bench seat next to him, which must have been three metres long. I guessed it must have been something to do with the fundraising effort, but I didn't ask. As time went on we watched the telethon on a giant screen and I got chatting with the girl, who said she was Maria. There was also a karaoke machine on the go and everyone was enjoying themselves with the drinks flowing. The guy with the huge whale was really drunk, but he was at least good fun, running around with it on his head and singing songs on the karaoke. Maria and I were in fits of laughter at his antics and we both joined him to sing a few songs. I felt great; it was good to get out and just have a laugh for a change. Eventually it was time for the pub to close and I was still sitting with Maria. The guy with the whale had fallen asleep next to us and I told her she'd better wake up her boyfriend. She looked surprised. "He's not my boyfriend. I thought he was with you!" We thought we'd better give him a shake anyway because the bar was emptying. He woke up with a start.

"The pub's shutting, mate. Time to go home," we told him. But he insisted he wanted to get us both another drink. He said he was the manager of the wine bar round the corner, and we should go with him to get after hours drinks there before he closed up. It sounded unlikely, but I looked at Maria and she intimated with a nod she was up for it. In the end we, and another five or six people the whale guy invited, walked round to the wine bar he'd spoken of. As we arrived the staff were at the door waiting to leave; they handed the keys to whale guy, we all went in and he locked the door behind us. He gestured to the bar and said "help yourselves" before going to sit at a table with his whale next to him. It was all a bit weird but we all went behind the bar one by one and got ourselves a drink. Then we put the juke box on and the party continued. But not long after that the wine bar manager had fallen asleep again on one of the bench seats with the giant whale on top of him. Seeing the manager sound asleep, the others soon drank up and let themselves out until there was only me and Maria left, with the sleeping whale guy stretched out. I said to Maria that maybe we should go too. This was a surreal situation, she agreed. "You call a taxi. Can I go back to yours?" So I used the bar pay phone and pretty soon a tax arrived outside. We grabbed a bottle of wine from behind the bar and left the whale guy sleeping, as we locked the doors behind us and posted the keys back inside. We arrived back at my flat, both of us giggling and excited by the strange shared night we had experienced. Maria asked, "Can I stay the night? I've missed the last train to Yarmouth." I said of course, and we settled down with the wine. I can be pretty dense sometimes and I didn't see the signs of where this was going. I was just happy to have the company. "I'll put a pizza in the oven. I'm starving. You?". Then, unexpectedly, Maria kissed me.

This was not the plan when I went out that night! I'd had a great night and a good laugh, and now it seemed I'd accidentally pulled. I had no idea if she had recognised I was transsexual but I didn't want to blurt it out and ruin the night. In the end I said nothing. I kissed her back. We chatted, drank the wine and ate the pizza, then, when I could not keep my eyes open any longer, I said," I'm going to bed, you can have the couch or share my double bed, but I have to sleep". I went into the bedroom and without getting undressed lay on the bed. Maria followed me in and we had a nice cuddle but nothing more and fell asleep; we were both pretty drunk. I woke up early, Maria was still in a deep sleep. I untangled myself from her and went to the bathroom and had a wash, shaved (yes, I still had to shave in those days, yuk!) and applied my make up. I was ashamed she would see me as male bodied, whether she realised or not. Once I'd sorted myself I made myself a coffee and sat in the lounge waiting for Maria to awake. This was a very uncomfortable situation for me. I'd never been in a situation with a woman, romantically, when I was presenting as a woman, and she didn't know any of my history. I hated it, I felt stressed and worried. It seemed even worse that it was a woman who I really felt attracted to. I'd probably lose the possibility of any kind of relationship with her once she found out.

Eventually I heard Maria rise from her slumber. She got up and came through to the lounge where I was sitting."Do you want coffee?"I asked. "Yes please, a strong one," she replied. I made the coffee while she went to the loo and sorted herself. When she came through we sat together at the table sipping coffee. After a short period of awkward silence, Maria grinned at me. "Sorry about kissing you last night. I'm bisexual. I didn't mean to upset you. Are you ok?" I replied, "Yes I'm fine. I enjoyed the kiss, but do you realise I'm transsexual?" Maria looked shocked. "What do you mean, are you lesbian?" I explained my situation, with Maria's eyes getting bigger by the minute. When I finished we both looked at each other and started laughing. It was the most joyous laughter between us as we shared the absurd situation, recounting the guy with the fibre glass whale, the wine bar, the karaoke singing, the bottle of wine we'd nicked and the taxi ride back, and now this, the revelation. With the afterglow of the previous evening's booze it all seemed hilarious. But there was to be no romance; Maria had a boyfriend back in Yarmouth. They had apparently had an argument the evening before when they were out drinking in Norwich. She had stormed off and left him and that's how she ended up alone in the bar when I'd met her. Now she felt the need to get back to him, as she knew he'd be freaked about her not going home last night. I was slightly sad that we wouldn't be getting together again because I really liked Maria, but I was happy that she wasn't upset with me, thinking maybe that I'd tricked her into my bed.

The weird night with Maria made me realise I probably preferred a woman as a partner. I had thought of myself as bisexual, but actually I was really non sexual or asexual. I didn't feel I was equipped for physical sex with anyone. As Boy George was to say later, "I'd rather have a cup of tea". But a female partner felt more comfortable to me. At least we had things in common to talk about.

Men often seemed so selfish and sex obsessed that it was impossible to have a proper conversation, and while gay men were often good fun, a sexual relationship with one usually left us both feeling unfulfilled. I felt so frustrated with my body. Hiding it wasn't enough; I needed to change it to have any chance of feeling comfortable with myself, and meeting someone to have a relationship with was something that I deeply craved. But right now I felt stuck in the middle, not one thing or another. Would I ever be happy? Would changing my body be the answer? I still wasn't sure, but I still felt I had no option but to carry on towards surgery and hope it was the solution I needed.

* * * * * * *

I recalled the night a few years previously when Julian, my American ex boyfriend, had sat me down and told me it was his considered opinion that I should not have a sex change. In fact he'd arranged that I should speak to his friend Kerry, a transsexual woman in Texas who had gone through the procedure and regretted it. He'd arranged for this friend to call me at home and speak with me. I was very surprised that Julian had done this behind my back, and maybe a bit annoyed. But, I agreed after the effort he had gone to that I would take the call and speak with her. One Sunday evening at the appointed time Kerry rang me at home. Julian was with me and anxiously listening to the one side of the conversation he could hear. It was a wasted effort; nothing Kerry could say would dissuade me. She detailed all sorts of medical and social problems she'd encountered. The loss of family and friends, the limitations on getting a job and the resulting poverty her life had become. It all washed over me, and I argued that for me it would be different. We spoke for over an hour. At the end Kerry said she knew it was pointless trying to make me change my mind; she laughed warmly that she had only agreed to try as Julian had begged her to. "I guess you have to go your own way. I wish you well, girl, and good luck." It's something I understood myself in the years to follow, that no one can tell a transsexual woman not to transition. It doesn't EVER work.

* * * * * * *

Shortly after the night with Maria I sank into despair. Everything had caught up with me. I stopped going to work and my contract at Commercial Union was cancelled. I quickly ran out of money and sold my car. Eventually I had to sign on for Unemployment Benefit again. I was getting bills every day, my rent arrears in the flat were building, my phone was cut off, and the council threatened me with eviction. I wouldn't open the door to them. Or to almost anyone else. I stopped seeing any friends, and before long no one called. I was seriously ill with depression but didn't understand it at the time. I went out only to buy alcohol, sneaking to the shops early in the morning. Every Monday I would buy a pound of sausages and a big bag of spuds, which would feed me for a week. The rest of my money went on booze, which I drank alone, sitting in front of the TV. I developed what became known later as 'brown envelope syndrome'. I sat sweating with my stomach churning every day at the time the postman was due. Every letter was a bill or a demand to contact the council. I was a mess.

When I'd first moved into my Norwich flat I'd had a neighbour. He was called Eric (or more often by the other neighbours 'Mad Eric'). He was about the same age as me and his balcony was adjacent to mine on the second floor facing the main road. I'd tried making casual conversation with Eric but he usually ignored me. He always looked angry and even on warm sunny days he would wear lots of layers of clothing, topped off with a leather coat. He seemed to have no friends or family and I presumed he had some kind of mental problems. I always said hello despite rarely getting a response. One morning he began banging loudly on my flat door. He was kicking and punching the door as hard as he could and screaming that he was going to kill me. At the time Liz was with me and we both were woken by the racket. We crept to the door and you could see the hinges were in danger of giving way as he pounded at it, shouting something about ramming a bollard up my arse. Bizarre! Eventually he stopped and we heard his own door slamming closed. We waited for an hour or so, frightened to look outside but when we did it was all clear and quiet. Later on that same day, when late evening came, we heard a lot of crashing and swearing coming from Eric's flat. We looked across at his balcony and we could see him dragging all his belongings out and then throwing them over the railing. Everything went; we watched in amazement as his bed, sofa, TV set and white goods from the kitchen were all hurled down to the communal garden two floors below. Everything was smashed to pieces and several neighbours from below had come outside to watch the spectacle as Eric huffed and puffed with the effort until finally there nothing left to throw. The police arrived not long after and Eric was led away peacefully; all the violence had left him and he looked broken as he quietly slid into the back of the police car. In the depths of my own despair I began thinking often about Eric that night. What he had done was even becoming a reasonable response to my mind. I felt like doing the same thing. If I smashed everything up maybe someone would come for me and lead me away to a place of peace and safety.

Looking back, it was clear that I was suffering seriously from stress and anxiety. Everything that had happened, the loss of all our businesses, the collapse of my relationship with Tanya and the twins, the divorce and loss of Joseph, and to top it all the death of Mamie. Not to mention the constant stress of living as female with a male body and no hormone treatment. It's hardly surprising I went off the rails. It actually affected me physically as well as mentally. I started to lose my balance for some inexplicable reason. I'd be standing in a shop or walking down the street when I'd keel over and land in a heap. It was a very strange experience.

Fortunately, Tanya didn't give up on me completely, and the twins would still occasionally visit. They were the only people I was willing to see. By this time, I'd also missed an appointment at Charing Cross because I had no money for the travel, and I hadn't contacted them to explain, preferring to put my head in the sand. They sent me a letter basically saying if I still needed treatment I would have to go back through my GP for a new referral as they had no option but to discharge me from the clinic according to their rules.

* * * * * * *

One day Tanya called round to see me and told me she was very worried about me. She said I needed to get back into the world. She had spoken with a friend who ran a beauty toning salon, and there was the chance of a 'cash in hand' job if I was interested. Then she explained the job was only available to me as male. I would not be working in the salon, I'd be assisting at the slot machine arcade underneath that was owned by her husband. Tanya urged me to make the phone call and take the job, if for no other reason than to get my sanity back. I was so far down that I felt I had nothing to lose. It would give me a reason to get out of the house at least. I made the call and spoke with Martin, the guy who owned the arcade, He said I should come down and try out for a day and see how I got on. I'd be working with Mary, and she would tell me all I needed to know.

I started work one morning at 10 am in Diamond Mine Arcade on Magdalen Street, Norwich. Mary, who was there to meet me, was an ancient Chinese woman, a long time friend of the family who owned the arcade. In fact the owners were a big showman family who also owned arcades in Great Yarmouth and all around the Norfolk coast. I liked Mary immediately; she was a no nonsense person, she stood at five foot nothing and was intensely loyal to the family. She handled the money in the booth, and my job was to keep an eye on the customers and the machines. If someone was fiddling or trying to smash the machines I had to spot it and remove the culprits. It could be a little tricky sometimes because we were always told never to call the police in to deal with trouble, as that could cause problems with the licencing committee. I had to deal with everything on my own without using violence, if I could avoid it. Shades of working as a bouncer in Glasgow, again.

If it wasn't for Mary I'd have walked out the first day. My hands were shaking from alcohol dependence and although she must have noticed she didn't say anything to me. In fact at lunchtime she told me to go and have a drink at the pub next door, the Cat & Fiddle. I gratefully agreed to her suggestion, and when I came back after a couple of large gin and tonics I felt better and able to get through the rest of the day till 5 pm. I made it through and Mary said as I was leaving, "see you tomorrow". That meant I had the job. It was only part time and a big come down for me, the once owner/manager of so many shops and businesses, but I was happy just to have a purpose again. There was no pressure on me to buy and sell stock, keep the employees happy and come up with the wages every week for others. It was actually a relief to be back at the bottom again with no one expecting too much from me. I was able to cut down my drinking after a while, but I still drank every day in the pub next door at lunchtime. I felt I was in disguise, as no one knew me as a man in Norwich. I sometimes saw people I recognised from my retail days but they looked through me. It was impossible to see I'd once been the woman who owned Vamps the hairdressers or managed the clothing shop. 'Angie' was dead. I joked about it with Tanya and Liz and a few others from the old days. I said she had fallen down the stairs at the flat and broken her neck.

It wasn't all plain sailing at the beginning working in Diamond Mine. One day I was tested by a young 17 year old kid. He was notorious for coming in and losing all his money then taking it out on the machines. He would start punching them or slamming them against the wall, loudly shouting that he'd been robbed. This was the reason I was there; I had to calm him down and get him to leave without any further trouble. The problem was that I'd almost forgotten how to act like a man, it had been so long. I completely over- reacted and went for him aggressively. Rather than try and talk him down I grabbed him by the throat and marched him to the doorway. He was struggling and trying to remove my hand but I held on very tight, restricting his airway until he complied. By this time Mary had got into a panic, and was trying to get me off him, shouting "Ally, Ally, let him go!" That was the name I'd reverted to using, 'Ally.' I figured I could be either male or female with such an androgynous name. When I reached the door with the kid I threw him out backwards and he landed on his arse. I quickly pulled the glass doors closed and locked them. He flew back at the door and bounced off as I motioned to him I was going to call the cops, making the universal pretend phone in hand sign. He carried on for a few more minutes banging and kicking at the glass then he walked away. I was relieved, and frightened. Why had I reacted like that? But Mary was happy to see the back of him. She had been swearing at him in Chinese, as she always did when things got tricky. She pulled me back to the booth, "we have tea - is ok, is ok". But a half hour later he was back, this time with two policemen. He'd bumped into the local patrol officers and told them he'd been attacked in Diamond Mine, now they were here to get to the bottom of the matter. Of course I denied everything. This was just like the old days on the doors in Glasgow. I told them I'd never left the premises, that we had video proof,and that I'd only asked him to leave and then escorted him to the door. There was no proof I attacked him; I was only defending the business. The cop nodded at me, then he brought the young guy before me and said, "Show him your neck". I looked in horror as I saw my full handprint on his throat, all five fingers outlined in a burning red outline that was going blue and purple with the onset of bruising. The cop came in to the arcade and pulled me aside. He spoke quietly. "We know who he is, and we know he's trouble, but don't you ever do that again to anyone or you will be the one getting arrested, understood?" I nodded and said no more. By this time Mary was shouting and swearing in Chinese at the cops, trying to shove them out the door. One thing about her she was fearless, despite her size. Soon the cops had had enough and left.

My time at Diamond Mine settled down after that. I still drank, but much less, and Mary was a calming influence on me. I didn't like the work, and I didn't like presenting as male. But it was at least a routine and I gradually began to regain my mind from the previous insanity. I worked daytime most of the week but I had one evening shift on a Friday when I worked right through from 10 in the morning till 10 at night. It was during my Friday night break one night when I popped next door to the Cat & Fiddle for a G&T that I saw across the room Tanya's twins. They were waving at me, and as I waved back I saw this amazing pair of bright blue eyes looking back at me. There was a girl with the twins whom I'd never met before. I was literally mesmerised by her gaze. It was the classic 'eyes meeting across a crowded room' moment. I had to go over and speak to them, and I was introduced to 'Alice' a friend of the twins from college.

Chapter 23 'A Couple Of Kooks'

Alice

The night we met in the Cat and Fiddle was not about the conversation we shared. I cannot remember anything we spoke about, only those eyes. We were drawn to each other by something that I can only describe as love at first sight, corny as it sounds. It had never happened to me before, and has never happened since. I can only confirm that such a thing does actually exist. It was definitely her eyes that drew me in.

* * * * * * *

I had to go back to work, and Alice was going out clubbing with the twins, so I quickly arranged to meet her the following Sunday lunch time at the Red Lion pub by the river. It never occurred to me that she wouldn't come. We both just knew she would, despite the fact I knew nothing about her, not even her name, nor did she know anything about me. The whole date thing was concluded in a chat that lasted no more than a few seconds as both of us were oblivious to everyone else in that crowded pub.

The first thing I noticed when we met on the Sunday was that she was younger than I'd thought she was in the pub. Alice had long thick black hair, flawless skin and was very slender. But, without make up she looked very innocent and vulnerable. I asked her how old she was. She replied "Almost eighteen." I was a bit surprised. I was twenty seven, so I was nearly ten years older than her. On that first date we had a couple of drinks in the pub and then went for a walk along by the river. It was a gorgeous warm day and I felt relaxed and comfortable with Alice, but I really needed to have a talk with her about my gender status before things went any further. I knew that could all be a bit weird for her to take in, and at this stage I didn't know how much the twins had told her. I suggested she came back to my flat with me so we could have some food and a proper talk. In the flat she would see all my female clothes, make up, and photos of how I usually dressed and lived when I wasn't working in Diamond Mine. It was only fair to both of us that I was completely open and honest.

So, on that first afternoon I told her I was transsexual. I also told her my plan was to have sex change surgery, and to that end I'd been attending Charing Cross Hospital in the past and was waiting to restart appointments. If I was expecting a shocked reaction I didn't get one. Alice just smiled and agreed that I should go for it, if it felt right for me. She went on to say that she wasn't particularly attracted to men, she'd had a bad experience with a boy when she lived up north, that involved an attempted rape. Her face darkened when she spoke of this and I could see the memory was still strong and still affected her. That incident had made her very fearful of men and she told me she had known instinctively, despite my appearance when we met, that I was not male. She also described how she had had crushes on women and girls at her boarding school. Alice didn't see gender, she just saw people, and she wanted someone who was kind and gentle. When our eyes met in the pub she had felt the same as me, and fell in love at first sight. I loved her directness and honesty and complete acceptance. Even then, I didn't imagine that our relationship would last, but I was definitely interested in spending time with her. I suppose I expected we would end up as friends, as that was what usually happened with any girl I'd had any romantic attraction to. Later that night I walked Alice to her bus stop as she had to go home. She was still a student at City College so had to be up in the morning early, and I had work. So we had a cuddle and few kisses and said goodbye with a hug when the bus came.

As I walked back to the flat I felt I was walking on air. Something had happened between us that felt so good. It was innocent and honest and seemed so different from all the relationships I'd had before. For one thing, every partner I'd had previously was much older than me; it was strange being suddenly the older and so called responsible half. Actually, I was still very immature regarding love, but Alice made me feel secure and able to be completely open. I felt protective towards her, she was so young, but at the same time her single minded attitude was exciting; she had no fear. She knew what she wanted and had no hangs ups or indecision about going for it. I admired her fearless tenacity!

When it came to our relationship, or anything else, Alice didn't know the meaning of 'play it cool.' She always jumped in with both feet, totally committed. She had no 'side'.When Alice loved you she said it candidly, and if she didn't, she said that too, equally honestly. She had no filter. That is very refreshing at first but could also be quite disconcerting if you didn't know her well. People often ask others' opinions about their personal appearance, and as we all know they are actually looking for reassurance or even a compliment. It's how we humans work, we don't say to a friend "Do you like my new top?" and always expect to hear the completely honest, if truthful answer, "No, it's awful, and you look silly wearing it." But if I asked Alice if she liked my new hair style or outfit she would tell me, factually and direct! It was something I had to get used to with Alice. She did make me laugh with her directness!

Not long after we had met I learned from her a little of her history, that she'd had measles encephalitis as a toddler, something than can often kill a young child. Alice had been in a coma for several days and eventually woke up blind and unable to walk. It took several months to regain her sight and mobility and she was left with some brain damage. As the neurons reforged new pathways within her brain to bypass the damaged areas, she developed with a different way of looking at things and a complete honesty in her actions and conversation, which sometimes could seem far too honest. There is not a much scarier situation than when a transsexual woman asks your opinion "Does this look good on me?" Be very very careful with the answer! But Alice had no fears.

I was to become her filter when dealing with the world, often mediating with others who felt offended by the things she said. Upon meeting new people or dealing with figures in authority she could seem quite challenging in her blunt honesty. But, it was a two way street, Alice gave me courage and confidence. With her by my side I always felt stronger. Other than the differences mentioned above ,Alice was perfectly fine in all other ways except in her short term memory, and that was the only thing that bothered her about her condition. She could remember a phone number a stranger had told her five years ago, but not be able to remember what she'd had for breakfast that morning. It's perhaps surprising we got on as well as we did, but we were like two halves that fitted together. We were both different but each of us compensated for the other and we made a good team.

One aspect of Alice's behaviour that caused problems initially is that she was always turning up or phoning me at work. To her mind this wasn't a problem; she wanted to chat with me, so went about it the most direct way. What's the problem? But of course my boss felt I was bringing my personal life to the job and disapproved. Fortunately, Mary soon got to know Alice and she accepted how she was and always stood up for us with Martin the boss.

Socially, Alice and I had a good time when we went out. We both loved to get dressed to shock, wearing a lot of clothes and accessories I had lying around my flat from the days when I had the Metamorphose shop. We both loved to put on the short leather mini skirts, with lots of studded belts and over the top slutty hair and make up. We'd often visit the local pub the Wood House just to see the shocked faces on the older customers who drank in this quiet neighbourhood bar. But even there, Alice soon won them over, as she would sit down at the piano and start playing tunes and songs by ear, taking requests and getting everyone involved. Then after a few drinks we would go up the city, usually ending up in the Loft night club, which had opened up in the same venue where the Caribbean Club used to be. It was now not just a gay venue but open to anyone, but a large group of the old clientele still used it. To me, life with Alice was fantastic, I had a best mate and a lover. We spent as much time as we could together.

But there were clouds on the horizon, with Alice still at college. Her parents, who I'd yet to meet, didn't like her to stay out late. She lived on the outskirts of the city and several times I'd had to put her in a taxi back home late at night after she'd missed her bus. Alice, in her usual candid manner, had obviously told them about me, and I probably didn't sound like a suitable partner for their daughter. Working in an arcade, ten years older, living in a council flat, divorced, etc. And they didn't even know about the transsexual side of my life yet! I'd persuaded Alice that information was for me to share, when the time came.

One evening a few weeks after we'd met, after I'd come home from work, I was having a bite to eat on my own in front of the TV. Unusually, I'd not heard from Alice that day and was hoping that she would turn up at the flat and we could go out. When I heard a knock at the door I thought it was her, though normally she would just have walked in. I got up and answered the door and was surprised to see a strange middle aged man standing there, looking slightly uncomfortable. He told me he was Les, Alice's step dad, and he'd like to come in and have a chat with me.

I was caught on the hop but I invited Les inside. Fortunately I wasn't dressed like a hooker that evening, as I may have been any other night! I was looking relatively normal, having just come back from work. Les looked serious, like a man who had some bad news to impart. He began, "Alice's mum and me have been speaking about you and her, and we have come to the conclusion that you are probably not the right person for her at this time. Alice is a good bit younger than you and she really needs to be concentrating on her studies at college." I didn't attempt to argue, as what he was saying was certainly reasonable. I was pretty much an unsuitable partner for most people, given my gender dysphoria and crazy history, and he didn't even know about that part yet. But, his main reason was the age difference. Alice was almost ten years younger than me and we both agreed she was 'different' and perhaps vulnerable to the influence of someone like me. Perhaps it would be better for Alice if I didn't see her any more? I felt really hurt, and the intensity of the feeling surprised me. The thought of not seeing Alice again would be heartbreaking. In that moment I realised how much I loved her already after only a few weeks. But, I could see Les's point. Reluctantly, I thought her parents were probably right, but I objected to Les's idea that I should be the one to break it off. I couldn't lie to her that way and have her believe I'd just dumped her. My voice was cracking with emotion as I told him I'd not pursue the relationship, I'd back off and not encourage Alice, but he'd need to tell her himself it was over. Les agreed that he would tell her and assured me it would be for the best. In a few weeks she'd get over it as young girls do at that age. It was all very civilised as I led Les to the door and said goodbye. I won't lie; I was very upset and burst into tears as the door closed behind him. That's probably the end of that, I thought. And maybe for the best.

But we had both underestimated Alice's determination to have her own way. The next day I was at work in the arcade when she stormed in and ran towards me in tears and kissed me. She was hugging me so tight I couldn't move from the spot as the customers and Mary looked on in surprise.

"What's wrong, what's happened?" I asked. She had run away from home, she told me. "I'm never going back there if they won't let me see you," she sobbed. I managed to untangle her arms from me and looked across at Mary. I needed to go next door to the pub for my break, I told her. She nodded.

Once in the pub I reiterated all the reasons Les had outlined the previous night as to why we shouldn't be together, it was probably better she found someone closer to her own age, she had to finish college. And, of course, when I completely transitioned would she really want to become the joint target of prejudice and hate that would come my way? My own family would disown me, and her family wouldn't want me as her partner, either. The whole thing was impossible. It was best to end it here before we got any further involved. I admitted I loved her, but I also thought Les and her mum were right. She would soon get over this. But Alice said she had made her mind up. She wanted me, she loved me, and we needed to be together. She didn't care about anything else. She would only agree to breaking up if I told her to her face I didn't love her. Well? The question hung in the air between us. "Of course I love you." It was impossible not to say that when she was looking at me. "But perhaps it won't last, and you don't want to throw away your family for something that might soon be over." I eventually persuaded her to go back and have a talk with her parents. I put her in a taxi and she reluctantly went home. Back at the arcade I called Les and told him where Alice was. As I expected they were very worried; she had stormed out and been missing for hours. I said that she was on her way home and he needed to have a talk with her. I hung up, feeling desolate. What a mess.

The next day Alice returned to my flat. I don't know what was said when she spoke with her parents the evening before, but it clearly didn't work! We repeated the conversation from the night before. Once again, I called a taxi and persuaded her to go home again. This same scenario went on all week. I was speaking on the phone to Les quite regularly now. Eventually he told me that he and her mum would like to invite me up to their house for dinner. I agreed.

I arrived one evening later that week at the address I'd been given. It was a very large house in Taverham, surrounded by gardens, in a very nice area on the edge of the city. I felt slightly intimidated when I saw the house. This wasn't just a private house, this was very posh! Bearing in mind I'd always lived on council estates I felt out of my comfort zone. They must be loaded, I thought. What will they think of me? Alice had never mentioned how wealthy her family must be. But then, she wouldn't, money was of no interest to Alice. I rang the bell, the door was opened by Les, and I entered.

As it turned out I received a warm, and informal, welcome. Alice's mum Sue was drying her hair, still with her rollers in. I could recognise where Alice's looks came from; she was beautiful. Les offered me a drink, a beer if I remember. They were both really relaxed and down to earth people. I sat in their huge lounge and chatted with Les, whilst Sue made dinner. Alice had made herself scarce, and we discussed her numerous unexpected arrivals at my flat and my workplace. I think by now Sue and Les both knew I was not actively encouraging her to rebel against them. It was all down to Alice and her own decisions. I was as much a victim of her forceful nature as they were. Les asked me about my background in Glasgow and then told me a bit about himself and his family. He was far from being posh; he was the epitome of a gritty northerner and part of a large Durham miner's family. We actually had a lot in common. Les had done well for himself, leaving the pits where his brothers and father worked, he had joined the RAF and become an electrician, then a radar engineer, and had ended up as manager of that side of things at Norwich airport. He had a good job and had simply bought a very nice house that reflected that fact. Sue was from a very left wing London family, her politics were the same as mine and I could tell she was very intelligent, and although she no longer worked, she was not just a housewife. The dinner itself went well, and by the end of the evening Alice and I had their blessing to continue our relationship. I believe that none of us present that night thought it would last very long, but it was better not to fight it. In the end, as it turned out, Alice and I were together for the next twenty five years. Sue and Les would become much more like my parents than my own ever were, and they would be fundamental in my eventual transition and surgery. But for now it was enough that Alice and I could continue to see each other.

* * * * * * *

Freddie Mercury died in November that year and the AIDS panic reached fever pitch in the UK press. Alice and I continued clubbing at the Loft nightclub, even though things were getting much quieter there. The regular gay crowd was thinning out as people got sick and just disappeared. I wondered about my own status. I'd not had a test, I was scared to. But even though I'd never been promiscuous with men(I preferred a cup of tea after all!) I knew it only took one sexual encounter to get infected. Everyone was at risk not just from their sexual partners but all their partners' previous lovers. It was a very scary time when there was really no hope for people infected, and HIV was seen as a death sentence. If poor Freddie, with all his money, couldn't find a cure, then probably no one could. It was probably a fortunate time for me to become exclusively a monogamous lesbian.

But the hate crime on the street was building against all gay people. Now we had to worry about the beer boys coming out of the Rose Lane straight club 'Peppermint Park' on a Saturday night. They would chase and beat up the people coming out of the Loft Club which closed at the same time. The Tory government's anti gay section 28 laws were still very much in law and in force, so the bigots, and the police, felt they had been given a pass to attack us. Alice and I were lucky we could avoid most of this violent prejudice, we could still go out and socialise, either looking like a male/female couple or just two girls. Others, including my friend Liz, were not as fortunate and ended up victims of vicious assaults. The ongoing resistance to the Poll tax was still very strong and ongoing at this time; Thatcher had gone but John Major was continuing the nasty policies, and my hatred of the Tory party was set in stone with the suffering it had caused.

As we arrived at Christmas 1991, Alice had previously made plans for she and her parents to go to London for the festive period visiting grandparents. I decided, rather than be alone in Norwich, I would go to Glasgow and see Joseph. It was the first extended period Alice and I had been apart since our first meeting at the Cat and Fiddle. We had a tearful goodbye at Norwich station and I felt empty as the train pulled out. Within a week we were together again, but being apart for that Christmas break had seemed like torture for both of us.

In January it was Alice's 18th birthday and we celebrated with a lot of her college friends, including the twins, at a nightclub in Norwich. Afterwards Alice went home in a taxi; we were both sorry that she couldn't stay the night at the flat, but we'd agreed to abide by the wishes of Sue and Les that she must go home at night. But a few weeks after that evening, when Alice and I had been for a night out, her bus didn't turn up yet again. It was a very cold night, but we stood at the bus stop for over an hour before we finally gave up. I didn't have the money for a taxi so we thought we'd better call Les and see if he could come and collect her. We were both in the old red phone box near my flat at midnight when we called up her parents and Sue answered. Alice told Sue that she'd need to tell Les to come and collect her. …. or … could she stay overnight with me? It would be so much easier if she could. Sue asked to speak to me and asked if it was ok for Alice to stay over, and did I have work in the morning? And if I did would I make sure she got to college on time? I assured her it would be fine, we both just wanted to get in out of the cold and get to sleep. Ok, she agreed. Alice could stay over. Alice and I walked away from the phone box on a high: finally she had been given permission to stay over. It had been worth the wait; we had done things properly and not gone against her parents wishes. Alice stayed that night, and we never left each other's side for the next twenty five years. We were together now.

Chapter 24 'Somebody To Love'

We were happy as clams that that first year together, 1992. We had virtually no money except my meagre wage from Diamond Mine, but it didn't seem to matter. We closed off both bedrooms in the flat and moved into the lounge because that had a gas fire, so we only needed to keep that one room warm. The fridge in the kitchen had packed up ages ago, and the electric cooker only had one ring and the grill working. We slept on the floor on cushions with a small TV set and a record player for entertainment. Most nights we lived by the light of candles and the smell of incense against the warm background of vinyl music - Leonard Cohen, Bowie, The Doors or Cat Stevens - as we snuggled up together to keep warm. Whenever we did have any spare cash we'd get dressed up and go down to the city, clubbing. Our one special treat, if we could afford it, was going to the Griffin pub on Thorpe road for the Sunday lunch. We'd have roast beef, spuds, Yorkshire pudding and all the trimmings. It was a six mile walk there and back, but when you had been living all week on toast and baked beans, this was a sumptuous feast. Nothing has ever tasted better than those Sunday lunches, before or since. We were both as thin as rakes, but blissfully happy.

Alice got a couple of work placement trials through college; she was not expected to gain many qualifications so it seemed like a good idea if she could get a job. The first one was serving in a Spar shop, but she was unable to remember how the till worked. The manager had only spent two minutes running through the keys and then left her to it. It was an impossible task for someone with short term memory problems. They sent her home assuming she was too stupid, but she wasn't. She just needed proper training with someone who had a little patience. It upset her and she came home to me in tears. The next placement was in an old people's home, where she was expected to change the beds and help with serving the food and cleaning. But she was sacked on the first day for spending too much time talking with an elderly lady who was upset and needed a friendly shoulder to lean on and an ear to listen. Alice simply could not understand why spending time chatting with someone who was clearly distressed was a bad thing. But the managers of course were more interested in judging her by the amount of bed pans emptied and floors mopped. Compassion is not cost effective and Alice was not suited to the corporate values expected of her. But I still think she was right to do what she did.

An example of how Alice's mind worked was what happened at Easter of that year. We had been out clubbing on the Friday night. It had virtually wiped us out financially but we'd had a good night. I'd budgeted to keep a few pounds left for the Saturday and Sunday so we could at least eat something and put 50p in the gas meter. I knew I'd get paid some cash on the Monday from the Diamond Mine, so we just had to be very careful till then. As was my usual habit at the time, when we came home I emptied my purse and put the coins on the coffee table so I could see how much money we had, then we went to bed. I was woken up on Saturday morning by an excited Alice kissing me. She was dressed already and had been to the local shop. She presented me with a beautiful chocolate Easter Bunny and a card. I was touched; that was so thoughtful and kind. We hugged, and then I got up and began to dress. That's when I noticed there was no money on the coffee table. Instantly I knew what had happened, but I had to check. "How could you afford to buy me that chocolate bunny?" I asked Alice. "Oh, I just used the money on the table," she smiled. "It's lovely, isn't it? I knew you would like it." She was beaming with happiness; nothing pleased Alice more than giving to someone else.

I was infuriated at first. She'd spent all of our money, that was to feed us for two days, on a fucking chocolate Easter bunny! "Why the hell did you do that?" I asked, exasperated. "We're totally skint now! What are we supposed to eat for the next two days? And if the gas goes out we can't even put money in!" But Alice hadn't thought that far forward, she just wanted to do a nice thing for me. The realisation now upset her, her face darkened and she started crying, "I'm sorry, I didn't think, I'm an idiot" Seeing her tears I melted. How could I be angry at kindness? I knew what she was like; it was really my own fault for leaving the money out without saying anything. I quickly hugged her and kissed away her tears. "it's ok, don't cry, we'll manage, I'm sorry I was angry." After a time I calmed her down. I realised that this was what I'd signed up for when we got together. I knew Alice better than anyone, and I loved her the way she was. And she loved me unconditionally too. It was part of the process of me growing up and taking some responsibility. For once in my life I had to think about someone else, and not just me. Previously in relationships I'd always had my older partners to deal with that stuff.

As the summer of 1992 approached I was filled with new hope and determination to get back to Charing Cross. My mental health was much better with the stability of being in a loving supportive relationship. I had stopped drinking excessively, and though we didn't have a lot of money we were happy because our pleasures were simple. We spent a lot of time walking in the countryside. I managed to buy a cheap second hand car and we often drove out to the sticks for a picnic, then Alice would follow her passion for bird watching, logging every different species and the location date and time. In this type of activity she was strictly methodical and impressively expert. It was just a demonstration to me again how her mind worked. To strangers she might come across as scatterbrained, but if you knew her you understood she was just differently focussed, a bit like those on the autistic spectrum. She needed support and love to enable her to have the confidence to shine.

One day I was at work when Alice arrived unexpectedly at Diamond Mine around lunchtime. She seemed upset and said we needed to have a talk. I told Mary I was going for my break and we made our way to a cafe. I knew this was something serious because her face was dark and she was tearful. Once we'd sat down I asked her,"What's wrong?" She replied, "I'm two months pregnant, the baby is due at Christmas."

Wow! This was a real shock, not least because Alice was on the pill and we were only very occasionally intimate. She wanted to know what we should do, meaning obviously an abortion. My view was that it was up to her, it was her body and I'd support whatever decision she made. I did make it clear that there was no pressure from me not to have the baby, because I loved children and I was sure we would manage ok, somehow. Secretly I was delighted, but I didn't want her to feel she had to go through birth if she wasn't ready herself. I'd sorely missed Joseph, I'd only been able to see him rarely and each time when I had to say goodbye it was heartbreaking. The thought of us having our own family and the chance to be a parent again was fantastic. But I also knew a baby would present problems for me at Charing Cross. To be selected for surgery it was not a rule that you cannot have children, but it was understood it would put you down the waiting list. As would being in a relationship with a female. Charing Cross dictated that, for people like me, once post op I would be expected to become a heterosexual woman and attracted only to men. In fact any male to female sex change candidate who was previously married would be required to get a divorce before the NHS would consider surgery. Bizarre as it would seem today, back then the Gender Identity Clinic were very homophobic and child unfriendly; even they considered their own clients too unusual to be considered good parents. It's almost as if they preferred patients to come to surgery with no ties, and once castrated and sterilised they would be safe, and be incapable of passing on their unnatural genes to their offspring. The transsexual 'perversion' would die with the patient. Nowadays, things are so different; transsexual people are encouraged, pre hormone treatment and surgery, to store eggs or freeze sperm, and I would absolutely agree with that. We should not be forced to give up our reproductive rights as a condition of medical treatment. Thankfully, Alice decided she wanted the baby. I was delighted.

* * * * * * *

The first sign of things to come was when we signed up for antenatal classes. We went along in good faith as a couple, but right away my position was queried in public. Before the rest of the class I was asked whether I was a friend or a relative. I tried to discretely explain to the tutor that, no, the baby would be ours. Despite my female appearance I'd contributed equally to the forthcoming birth. She demanded,"What do you mean?" I tried again quietly to explain that my sperm had been utilised and the baby was mine too. She was shocked, "oh, you're the dad, Ok!". It was not the term of address I preferred, but I didn't argue. During the rest of the classes I was segregated to the role of 'father' or more usually, generally ignored.

To access more convenient GP care, Alice changed her address officially to the flat. She had signed up to my doctor's surgery which was two minutes from where we lived on the Heartsease estate. This meant my own GP, who I'd previously asked to refer me back to Charing Cross, knew that we were a couple. And, perhaps because of that, he didn't seem to be willing to pursue my request. In fact I never did get that re-referral from him at all. Probably, and maybe understandably, he thought he was doing the right thing. Bearing in mind the Tory party's Section 28 of the Local Government Act 1988 was still very much in force, and it prohibited local authorities from 'promoting' homosexuality or gay #pretended family relationships' it's no surprise, really. I also faced open hostility from the health visitor who was assigned to us. When she came to visit us in the flat she would only speak directly to Alice and completely ignored me, or any questions I asked. It seemed Margaret Thatcher had succeeded in her aim of creating a 'hostile environment' for people like us.

In fact this prejudice even extended to the local council housing area office when we went along to register the fact that Alice had moved into my flat as my partner. The housing official simply refused to accept she was my partner, or pregnant with our baby, and would not register her as a joint tenant. He got extremely angry and worked up about the whole suggestion and opened the door of his office and told us to get out. As we left, I paused as I passed him, and I told him he would regret this as I'd seek legal advice as I thought he was acting discriminatingly towards us. In response he went berserk and followed us out into the open plan office, where his colleagues were all sitting at their desks, and tried to attack me and (pregnant, let's not forget) Alice by swinging punches at us. One of his co-workers, a big burly bloke, had to intervene and put him into a headlock to stop him from hitting us, telling him, "I'm sorry, I know you are my boss but I have to prevent you from doing something you will regret." I simply turned to the whole office and said, "You have all witnessed that. I'm going straight to Bethel Street police headquarters now to report this incident." After I had reported the matter to the police, they reluctantly agreed to charging him with assault (he had managed to land a blow to my chest). In the end a convenient compromise was agreed and the housing officer was given early retirement. And in return for dropping the charges, both Alice and I were given £50.00 each compensation by the council. We needed the money so we accepted it. But he effectively got away with a violent attack in full view of dozens of his co-workers.

These days Norwich City Council is very LGBT inclusive. I personally know a lot of officials and councillors who are themselves gay. But it was not that long ago that things were very different. Back then, I was beginning to think it was time to get out of my adopted city and start somewhere fresh to give our forthcoming little family a chance!

* * * * * * *

I can't remember who came up with the plan, but we both agreed enthusiastically with the idea once it was raised, that it would be the right thing to do. Alice and I decided to get married. I hoped it would provide some protection to our unborn child and our relationship. It would show the officials that we were committed to each other and the baby. I knew once married my access to Charing Cross would be very unlikely, but by now my focus was on Alice and the baby, and surgery was put on the back burner. It had not gone unnoticed by me that the health visitors thought I was some kind of transsexual pervert, and Alice, for having the audacity to want to stay with me, must be simple in the head. Also, to be completely frank, another reason for getting married was that we thought we might get some wedding presents or money that we desperately needed for the baby.

The immediate problem was who would marry us? A register office ceremony wouldn't do. Alice had always wanted a proper church wedding, with the white dress and reception afterwards. But, the situation was that she was 6 months pregnant and showing, while I was already divorced and a transsexual woman. We had virtually no money. It was not going to be easy to find a church or a priest willing to accommodate us. I did try though, phoning round several churches in Norwich, but we were politely turned away by them all. That's when I came up with a crazy idea.

* * * * * * *

I'd never forgotten my cousin Richard Holloway, the Bishop of Edinburgh, hosting that TV show I'd watched years ago when he had probably the most famous British transsexual woman, and author of the book 'Conundrum', Jan Morris, as a guest. He had become even more prominent in the media as the years had passed, as a strong advocate for LGBT rights, and was pushing for equal marriage long before any of his contemporaries in the Church of England or the government. It seemed like a mad improbable idea, but I felt we had nothing to lose and I always did like taking a chance, so I decided, fuck it, I'd ask him to perform the wedding. I contacted my mum to see if she had a phone number for him, and when she heard what I was planning she was shocked. "You can't ask our Richard, you're divorced and she's up the duff, it would be a disgrace. He'd never agree to it and you will be embarrassing us by even asking." However, reluctantly, she eventually gave me the phone number.

When we had announced to our respective families and friends that we were getting married it was it was met by most with indifference or even ridicule. In fact the only people who were truly supportive were Alice's parent's Sue and Les. My own parents thought it was laughable, and Alice's real dad, Neil, who was a big shot in IBM computers and lived in Wales, laughed too. His actual word to me, when we phoned him with the news, was 'claptrap'. An unusual form of dismissal, but fitting for him. He'd always seemed to me very unfriendly and snobbish whenever we'd met.

I called Richard, the Bishop, one evening from the local phone box. Alice and I were crammed in together as she wanted to hear what was said. It took a bit of nerve because I didn't know him apart from through our family connection. I started by telling him who I was, and he remembered. I'd been a little kid when he'd last seen me, but of course he knew my parents and my grandparents. He said it was lovely to hear from me, he didn't know I'd moved to Norwich, and he asked how he could help me. I took a deep breath, and said I wondered if he would consider marrying my fiancée and me. I quickly followed up with the details of how she wanted a proper white wedding, but she was six months pregnant, and that I was divorced; I didn't mention the transsexuality at that stage, trusting god and gossip to inform him! I also told him we'd been refused by everyone in Norwich and he was our last hope. Would he consider perhaps a quiet private ceremony in the Vale at the small C of E chapel? Richard said he would have to look at his schedule, and he'd get back to me. Could I call him back the next day? Of course, I agreed, and put the phone down with a sigh of relief. At least he hadn't said, "Eh, who are you?" I called back the next evening at the agreed time, and Richard had some news for me. He said, "Let's not bother with the little chapel in the Vale. Come to my church, Edinburgh Cathedral, and we'll do the wedding there properly". He then suggested a couple of dates within the next month and we picked one. And that was it, easy. We now had a white wedding planned at St Mary's Episcopal Cathedral. Edinburgh. And, it would be performed by the Bishop of Edinburgh. Alice would get her white church wedding after all, and then some!

It's funny how much interest and enthusiasm followed for our wedding day, once it was known that the Bishop and the cathedral would be involved. Suddenly we had good wishes from my family and even Alice's shallow and dismissive dad in Wales was busting a gut to get in on the action, and have the opportunity to hobnob with Bishop Richard. 'Claptrap' indeed! And it was wonderful and generous of Tanya that once we'd told her about the wedding she wanted to get involved too. She was fantastic and offered to make Alice's wedding dress, customised of course to allow room for the bump and not to make it look too obvious in the photos. On the big day the ceremony went very well. We had a lovely service surrounded by family and friends. Bishop Richard made sure we had the full works with the cathedral organist playing our music with gusto as it echoed around the beautiful building. When the service ended we exited the building to the ringing of the bells and on to the cathedral steps for photographs. The spectacle stopped the Edinburgh rush hour traffic as drivers paused or slowed down to get a view of what they thought must be a famous or well connected couple getting married. Alice got her white wedding.

My old friends from the Vale, Mickey and Ellen, had attended the wedding, in fact Mickey had kindly offered to be the best man at short notice. In the time since I'd moved to Norwich they had left the Vale to get away from the increasing drug based gang violence and were now settled in a cottage on the banks of Loch Long in the tiny hamlet of Ardentinny. That was where we would spend our short honeymoon, with them. It was during that week that Mickey, on hearing about the problems we were having in Norwich with the medical authorities interfering over the coming birth of our baby, suggested we might want to move away and come back to Scotland. Not to Glasgow or the Vale, but to a rural location similar to where they lived. It seemed like something to consider. Alice adored the beauty of the Scottish west highlands with all the wildlife and magnificent bird life especially. That honeymoon week we travelled all around the west coast, visiting the deserted beaches and hiring small boats to cruise the glass-like surfaces of the lochs. By the time we were ready to go back to Norwich we had decided that Scotland would be the solution to the council interference and anti LGBT situation we were increasingly under from the NHS in Norwich, because of Section 28. I still loved Norwich but thought it might be prudent to get away for a while once the baby was born and start afresh elsewhere. We could always come back later. I'd already made my decision that my own transition would have to be postponed. The baby and Alice had to be the priority now. We would need to save up, as it wasn't going to be easy or cheap to relocate, but with the help of Mickey and Ellen to scout out a suitable house, and financial help from Sue and Les, we could manage it.

Things came to a head quicker than expected. Two week before Christmas, and one week before the baby was born, I was met one night as I arrived for my regular Diamond Mine shift by my boss Martin and his mother Jean. She was the matriarch of the family and had personally overseen all the businesses since her husband had died several years earlier. She also ran her own arcade in Great Yarmouth. She came straight to the point. "I'm sorry, Ally, especially with the baby due, but we are cutting back on staff, business is bad and we're laying off people all over Norfolk and closing down some arcades. You will finish tonight, I'm giving you two weeks money." And that was the end of that. I wasn't sorry to leave the job but I knew I'd miss Mary. She had become a good friend to me and Alice, and we used to take her out for Sunday lunches and a drive in the countryside. She cried as I left that night. We promised to keep in touch but, as often with these things, never did. That was one less tie that held us to Norwich.

* * * * * * *

A week before Christmas 1992 Alice's waters broke and we rushed down to the hospital. She was admitted to the maternity unit at the Norfolk & Norwich, and after a fairly short labour gave birth to our daughter Cherry. I was present for the birth and it was a wonderful occasion for me, despite the cuts in my hand from Alice's nails as I held her hand and she pushed. Alice never looked more beautiful than that night as she had a bath in the birthing suite afterwards, her face relaxed and dreamy, and I sat beside her holding Cherry.

Now that our daughter was born we had to take precautions to make sure she wasn't taken from us. There was an undercurrent of prejudice within the authorities against lesbian and gay parents reflected in the laws surrounding adoption and the aforementioned Section 28. That was bad enough, but being a transsexual parent was to be placed in an even more precarious situation. I was met with open derision and barely concealed moral outrage from some of those who had knowledge of my situation. As we prepared to leave Norwich for Scotland that spring of 1993, unbeknown to me there was the beginning of a fightback taking place. A year previously a team of transsexual activists had got together to form the group 'Press For Change', a UK-based campaign group focusing on the rights and treatment of transsexual people, whose aim was gain respect and equality for all trans people in the UK. The group eventually led the campaign for full legal recognition for transgender people living in Britain, including the right to marry. Their achievement was the Gender Recognition Act 2004. But that was all in the future. Right now, I felt Alice, I and baby Cherry had to get away to somewhere where we were not known.

Chapter 25 'I'll Stand By You'

Strachur

It was Mickey who let me know about the house for rent in the small village of Strachur, which was located on the Cowal peninsula, overlooking Loch Fyne and about twenty miles north of Dunoon. I called the owner and arranged for Mickey and Ellen to view on our behalf. I trusted their judgement. Mickey phoned me up that night and told me it was a nice four bedroom semi detached house with a large garden set in a small cul de sac. There was only one shop/post office, a pub and a hotel. It was a very beautiful but remote setting about two hours drive from Glasgow. The rent was very reasonable and it seemed an ideal place for us to disappear to and get on with bringing up Cherry away from the hostility we'd experienced. There was also the added bonus that I would be able to see much more of Joseph. I had decided I needed to postpone my transition in an effort to keep our family together, and so to all intents and purposes we looked like any normal young family when we arrived that spring to take over the lease. I'd given up my council flat in Norwich and we'd left behind most of our friends and Alice's family. It was an adventure, but one I felt we'd had forced upon us. Nevertheless, we were hopeful and determined to make it work.

Once settled in Strachur we soon understood one reason why the rent was so low. It was an area that was largely an unemployment black spot; there were very few jobs available locally and most people commuted to Glasgow or Greenock for work. If you didn't have a vehicle you were stuffed, but fortunately we had a decent car. I was not too worried by the lack of employment opportunities; I expected I'd find something sooner or later, and in the meantime it was wonderful just to enjoy the scenery and the time with Cherry and Alice. We spent many days exploring the lochs and mountains all along the west coast. Alice particularly enjoyed the birdlife; we would often see buzzards and golden eagles flying high over the village, and it wasn't unusual to be woken up in the morning at first light with a herd of deer in the back garden grunting away.

* * * * * * *

With time on my hands I was always looking for something to do, and one day as I was tidying up the garden I was thinking how to get rid of the old caravan that had been placed in a far corner and used as a shed. It must have been many years previously that it had been dragged in. The tyres were completely flat and cracked and the exterior walls and roof covered in green moss. But inside it was still dry, so the roof was sound at least. I worked out that it must have been towed in to the back garden from the main road, the A815, that ran past the rear of the property. So, if that's how it came in, it must be able to go out if I took down a section of the fence. It was only a short step from that thought that I realised that if I pulled it to the edge of the road then the caravan could make a nice snack bar. It was a fairly busy tourist route in the summer and there were no other cafes or tea rooms for miles around. There was also a lay-by nearby, so there was plenty of room for customers to pull in and park. I'd found myself a new project and possibly a business, and that meant self employment. I asked my landlord if I could buy the caravan and he was more than happy to sell it to me for £50.00. I got to work inside by clearing it all out and refitting worktops and gas burners to cook on. I installed twin sinks and a large gas water urn. I fitted fridges and lights that I could run from an electric extension wire, either from our own kitchen or from a petrol generator. With the interior finished, I contacted the local council hygiene inspector to come and view the van as a commercial kitchen. She came along and confirmed it complied with regulations and was suitable for the preparation and retailing of hot and cold food.

Next, I decided that I had to do something spectacular and eye-catching with the exterior, something that would literally stop traffic. I eventually came to the idea that I should give it a completely all over bright tartan design. The only way to do that in those days before widely available vinyl graphics was to actually paint on the tartan design by hand, using brush-on commercial paint. I started with the background then built up the layers of different coloured squares of the plaid effect. It took me many weeks and lots of different coloured paints. Each coat had to be completely dry before adding the next layer using masking tape and a three foot ruler and a set square. The design plan had the desired effect, as the locals would all stop and watch me as I worked, fascinated by the effect. They would often ask what I was doing and why; some would shake their heads, others would compliment me on the work. But everyone always smiled when they saw it. After far more hours of work than I care to remember it was complete. I had something that resembled a giant Scottish short bread tin on wheels. If nothing else it was different, you couldn't ignore it! I was happy with the job itself, it had kept me busy, but also the effective result was that I had met all the locals during that time as they passed by and stopped to chat. So, it was a worthwhile project for that alone.

The snack bar unfortunately was never actually sited in Strachur When I tried to arrange a pitch for it I was bombarded by red tape, permission applications, and even objections to the council from the local garage owner who, although he sold no food, hot or cold, managed to persuade them that he was planning to open up a tea room at some point in the future. It was all nonsense of course - his objection was more based on jealousy of anyone else having a business in the village - but the council were never going to rule against a local in favour of an outsider, so I finally accepted defeat. I eventually put the tartan caravan up for sale. It was bought by a cafe owner near the town of Lockerbie who was delighted to have it for the sum of £1000. which was quite a lot of money in those days. The only condition was that it was cash on delivery, and I had to get it to him.

I was very fearful of towing this van 150 miles; after all, it had been a garden shed until recently. But we pumped up the cracked tyres and, remarkably, they held the air. The lights had long since stopped working, so we purchased a light board to hang off the back. Then one day Alice and I, with in hearts in our mouths, hitched up the snack bar to the back of our van, dropped the fence, and attempted to drag it out of the deep earth of the back garden that it had gradually sunk down into over the period of twenty odd years. We weren't even sure if the axle would turn after all that time, but it did. After a bit of rocking back and forth, and to the cheers of neighbours, we managed to slowly roll out on to the main road. With relief, we were all set for Lockerbie and a much needed £1000. We set off gingerly to begin with, and all seemed well as we picked up speed and set off on the long mountain lined road to Glasgow, and then on to

Lockerbie. As we travelled along we were met by friendly waves and cars beeping at us as they passed; the tartan snack bar made everyone smile. We were feeling quite relaxed by the time we approached a very steep incline some ten miles out of Strachur. We were chatting happily to each other as I was driving, and keeping an eye on the caravan through the rear view mirror, as we climbed the hill. We were almost at the top of the half mile long incline when I noticed in the mirror that our tartan van seemed to be getting smaller in the reflection. How can that be? I was musing to myself. Then it suddenly dawned on me at the same time as Alice screamed. "It's come off!!" It was like a Laurel & Hardy film as we screeched to a halt and both jumped out of our van and looked back at the brightly coloured giant shortbread tin van careering backwards down the hill, with the metal A frame swinging from side to side in huge sweeping swathes. Cars were beeping their horns, but this time not cheerfully, as they swerved and braked in an attempt to avoid the scything A Frame. We both looked on in horror as the traffic behind us ploughed onto the roadside grass banks on both sides to avoid the tartan swinging menace. Thankfully, and I really am amazed at this, the snack bar didn't hit even one vehicle, and it slowed to a shuddering halt as it got to the bottom of the hill and veered off to one side as the back end hit a tree. Alice and I looked at each other, the thought passing between us that didn't need saying 'Fuck, that was lucky'. We piled back into our van and drove down the hill to the caravan, seeing angry drivers who were passing us going in the opposite direction after pulling off the grass banks. Remarkably, when I inspected the snack bar I could find no obvious damage. In fact the way it had settled against the tree, with the tow frame facing the road, it was ideally positioned for me to reverse up to it and re hitch. This time after we hooked up again we checked the ball locking bar was properly in place, something we hadn't done the first time in our excitement at getting the caravan out of the garden and on to the road. I started our van and we carefully pulled away again Everything seemed fine, but it was with great trepidation that we restarted our journey. We got to Lockerbie without any further incident, met up with our buyer and received the £1000 cash. He asked if there had been any problems. "No, it was all fine," we lied, feeling extremely thankful to get away with that one. Over the following years I would often take a detour whenever I drove through the borders region on my way to or from Scotland to visit the tartan snack bar in its place, seemingly doing good business for decades afterwards.

* * * * * * *

Another thing to come from the tartan caravan was a job offer. One of the Strachur locals was Frank who owned the local hotel. He was an outsider like us, as he came from Glasgow. He was impressed with the work I'd done on the snack bar and offered me a contract to do the redecorating of the local youth club, inside and out. It was a big job and a good price. I asked Mickey if he wanted to share the contract with me, and he agreed. So we were both gainfully employed on that job for the next few months. I was happy, we were managing to survive in this strange new place, we had met new friends, found work and were bringing up Cherry in the most beautiful location. Of course, it wasn't to last!

We weren't to know at the time, but getting that contract to decorate the youth club had put someone's nose out of joint. A local who I will call 'Pete' was the usual painter & decorator in the area. He was always given whatever jobs were going; he'd been established for years. But Frank had bypassed him by offering the contract to me. Now we had an enemy in the village who wanted rid of us. It began when a fraud investigator from the local Social Security office in Dunoon turned up at our door one day. He demanded entry and then questioned me about working, whilst signing on for unemployment benefit. He had been given information that this was the case. I simply denied it, because it was untrue. It was laughable. 'Have you got proof of this claim?' I asked. But he only replied he'd been given information from a trusted source. I knew it was nonsense so I was quite relaxed. "Come back with proof or take me to court". I was confident that he would do neither. He'd obviously acted on suspicion, probably as a result of false information from 'Pete'. The investigator left and we never saw him again, but it was a worrying development. A few weeks later we got a visit from a female social worker, following up a report that Alice was physically abusing Cherry. She admitted that she had no proof, but her job was to question us about the matter since it had been officially reported, albeit by an anonymous source. I refused to let the woman in. I was very angry because I suspected where the false had report had originated. "Come back with proof and a proper report for my lawyer," I told her. She left, and again we heard no more.

By now we had been in the village for over six months and our medical records had finally caught up with us. There was no computerisation in those days, everything was paper, and I knew from my own experience the time lag was long. This meant the local GP now knew that I had a history and diagnosis of transsexualism. Alice had on her medical record childhood brain damage. Of course, our medical history was supposed to be strictly confidential, and I had no suspicion at all that our GP had leaked anything. But there were others who worked in the surgery who had access to the records, and in the way of typical small village gossip, someone had been blabbing. Our neighbours seemed overnight to turn against us. I would say hello and be ignored. Alice had the same experience, even with people we had previously become friendly with. A visit to the local post office/shop would turn into short, offhand, dismissive and cold behaviour from the owner. Something had definitely changed, and though I had no proof, I had my suspicions. It came to a head one day when my car would not start. It was winter, and the battery began to drain as I turned the engine over. I knew I just needed a short push start and the car would fire up and be fine. This happened to me and my neighbours often; Strachur was extremely cold in the winter. There were several neighbours in our cul de sac watching me trying to start the car. I got out and asked if a couple of the blokes could give a quick push. But they just smiled at each other and ignored my request. I appealed to their decency; they knew without a working car Strachur was an impossible place to live, as you had to drive to the shops, doctor's, petrol station etc. Dunoon, the closest town was twenty miles away. Eventually, Alice had to take Cherry, strapped into her push chair, into the front garden where we could see her, and push the car herself as I turned it over, and three or four men all stood around and watched a woman struggling.

It was, I feared, time to move on. Our past had caught up with us, and between that and me taking the work from one of the locals, we were clearly no longer welcome. I had no jobs on the horizon either by that time. In the winter there was not much decorating work. The only chance to make a bit of money I'd been offered recently was with Jim, the local drug dealer in Dunoon, off whom I occasionally bought some cannabis resin. I knew Jim from way back; he was originally from the Vale and I'd been to school with him. He needed someone he could trust to help him move around his supply on the Cowal. He had even tested me one night. I was in my car with him one evening when we'd gone to the off sales on Dunoon high street for wine. There was a police car outside the shop parked on the double yellow lines, and Jim insisted I pull in behind it. "They've parked there, so can you", he sneered. "Here, hold this for me while I'm in the shop," he said, before handing me a parcel that was about the size of a house brick wrapped in brown waxed paper and tied with string. Before I had a chance to say anything he was out of the car door and away in to the shop. I looked at the parcel he'd handed me and realised it was huge block of solid cannabis; the earthy sweet smell was over powering. Just then the cops came out of the shop and were both climbing into their car. I could see one look at me, parked on the double yellows, and then say something to his partner. I was sweating buckets as I tried to look natural, praying that they wouldn't come and knock on my window. But they soon pulled off and drove away, clearly with more important matters to deal with than my parking. When

Jim got back into the car I was livid. "You bastard, handing me this shit with the cops there, what the fuck do you think you are doing?" But Jim was laughing uncontrollably, he thought it hilarious seeing my face. As we got back to his house he handed me a big chunk of solid cannabis resin, and said, "Sorry about that, mate, here you go. You handled that ok." But I knew I was not cut out for drug dealing no matter how much the money was. I had responsibilities with Alice and Cherry. I told Jim to fuck off. He must have felt bad about that night later on. Because when my car finally packed in a few weeks later, and I was in desperate need of another, Jim gave me a car, a nice Mazda, as though it was nothing. I needed transport so I took it. But I never worked for him.

Chapter 26 'Who By Fire'

Main Street, Vale

Not long after that, Alice and I decided we needed to get away from Strachur. We'd been there for a year and it had turned into a dead end. We were running away again, from my medical records and small village jealousy and gossip. Without friends in the village it would be very difficult to survive, as everyone depended on their neighbours in those small communities. I'd heard about a nice flat that was available back in the Vale. It seemed like failure to be returning back there after all the time and effort I'd put into getting away from it. But beggars can't be choosers, we didn't have a lot of money and I knew at least in the Vale I'd be among friends and family and we'd be safe. Or so I thought anyway.

* * * * * * *

We moved into the two bedroom private let flat on Main Street, the Vale in the spring of 1994. We'd left Strachur with no notice. The landlord was ok about it though. He came round one night and intimated that he knew what had been going on and we were probably best to leave. He even apologised for the actions of some local people without naming names, or what they had done. But we both knew what he was talking about.

Incidentally, there was some payback for 'Pete' a year later after we'd left Strachur. It appears we weren't the only enemies he had made over the years. He was running an unlicensed taxi service with his own car, which is not unusual in the villages of the highlands. Someone in the community usually does that. It's not worth being legally registered and paying commercial insurance and tax because of the very few fares that are available. So people turn a blind eye to it. But one night 'Pete' was called to collect some people from a local bar in his 'taxi'. The bar manager had called him on behalf of the people who required the ride. 'Pete' turned up with his little plastic taxi sign sitting on top of his brand new car and beeped his horn, but no one came out of the bar. After a while 'Pete' got impatient and entered the bar to demand who had called his taxi. Whilst 'Pete' was throwing his weight around inside the pub, someone set fire to his taxi outside in the car park. It was a burnt out wreck within minutes and the fire brigade and police were called to the scene of a 'taxi on fire.' It was undeniable that Pete had been operating illegally and therefore his insurance was void. Karma.

We settled in to the Vale flat and hoped things would be better. I knew I could easily get work here and we also had my parents as baby sitters. The other important thing was that my medical history would never be leaked in the Vale. For one thing, if it happened anyone working in the GP's surgery would know that I would find out easily who had done it, and also no one would ever believe that I was transsexual, so it would be dismissed as a joke. Within days I was surrounded by old friends and gang members, drinking in the local pubs and a world away from the female life I'd left. Many of my old crew were delighted to see me. Things were different in the Vale now. It was not just violence and fighting for the sake of it. There was a lot of money at stake now as drugs, especially heroin, were big business in the Vale. It would have been so easy to slip back into that criminal life, and so difficult to try and fight for my transition. I was older and wiser now, I had experienced how difficult life would be for me, financially, socially and as a parent, son or even friend if I transitioned, but still it was what I desperately wanted to do. But was I strong enough? Alice was still completely supportive of me, whatever I chose to do, I knew that. She had always stood by me without question, and never pressured me. She was my absolute rock.

Within weeks I was forced to choose my path. The first thing that occurred was that a close friend and associate of my old gang was shot. Someone had waited for 'Big Neilie' to come out of a pub in Balloch and had fired both barrels of a shotgun at him from close range. He survived, just. But he was an invalid from then on. We knew who was responsible and revenge was planned. It was assumed I would be part of this. The people responsible were from outside the Vale. In recent years, Balloch and Loch Lomond had become the playground of the Glasgow gangsters and drug dealers. What do you do when you have money to burn? You buy a big 'fuck off' motor cruiser on Loch Lomond and hang out with the other gangsters. The Vale at that time was the most dangerous place in Britain for shootings, stabbings and drug related crime, and many of my old friends had found themselves in the hierarchy, simply by fortune of location. All the west of Scotland gang leaders wanted to be represented in the Vale and Loch Lomond, so it was easy with local knowledge to accommodate them and make alliances. Who was going to look after your Loch Lomond boat if you didn't have local connections to protect it?

The other thing that happened was that my downstairs neighbour , who was a small time dealer in ecstasy tabs, became a nuisance with his dog. I knew who he was, and his family; he was a couple of years younger than me so didn't understand exactly who I was, or more to the point who I once was. He was a kid to me and my friends. But to protect his dealing he had got himself a big Alsatian dog that he allowed to roam the common stairwell of the flats. This prevented him being caught on the hop if the police raided; the dog would hold them up enough to allow time for him to flush his stash down the loo. A reasonable plan, but a very big inconvenience for the other tenants of the flats who had to try and navigate round this dog just to get in and out of their homes. The dog had jumped at me and Alice several times as we used the stairs, and I approached the dealer and told him it was unacceptable. He would need to keep the dog inside his house. He apologised but laughed, telling me I would get used to the dog, and once he knew us it would be ok. Unfortunately he wasn't taking it seriously. A few nights later, Alice, and I, with Cherry in her push chair, were coming in to the flats when the dog flew at Cherry in her pram. Alice and I beat it off and Cherry was unharmed, but we were livid. I banged the door of the little dealer and told him what had happened, warning him again that the dog must be kept indoors. But he was drunk or stoned and we couldn't get any sense out of him. Later on that same evening I was in Mack's bar downstairs on Main Street, relating the situation to some of my friends. I was advised I'd need to deal with it or the guy would continue to take the piss. I knew this but I was avoiding the confrontation. One of my friends, Derek, offered me a weapon from under his coat. it was a heavy duty, grey plastic coated, three foot long electrical cable that was used to connect up electric ovens. One end had been made into a looped handle, and the other was stripped back to reveal three thick bare copper wires that had been fashioned into hooks. It was a vicious whip that would tear chunks of flesh when applied. "Take this, use it on the dog on the way up the stairs and it won't come near you ever again, or do the same to the dealer, and you'll get the same result with him." Derek laughed, and even offered to do it himself, but he said it would be more effective coming from me. I knew he was right. I was in a situation where only personal violence would make an impact. The type of person the dealer was would only respect brute force. I was back in the Vale, after all.

I took the cable, and that night, feeling sick, I approached the stairwell. Sure enough the Alsatian was there, prowling back and forward in the half light. As I opened the barred iron street gate and entered, the dog came towards me growling and barking, and I swung the cable towards its head. As the blow struck the dog, at first it seemed to get even more enraged, but then it paused, and as it came forward again I swung the cable at its left flank. This time the dog pulled back in shock and pain as the heavy cable ripped into the skin with a sickening thud. It was still growling as I moved forward and flayed into its flank again. That was enough; the dog cowered and whimpered as it slunk back and hid in the shadow. I walked past it and up the stairs feeling nauseous. As I walked past the dealer's door it opened a few inches. From the dark interior I heard him whisper at me, "What the fuck is going on down there, is it cops?"'I replied,"No, I warned you about that fucking dog, keep it indoors!" I walked past and went inside my own front door. But Derek was right, it was the dealer I needed to whip with the cable to put an end to this. I was too queasy to do what was needed; I'd lost my aggression and could no longer act decisively. I locked and chained the door because I knew what was coming, and, sure enough, within minutes our front door was being banged loudly with the dealer demanding that I came out to face him for what I'd done to his dog. I opened the door, unwisely, and a samurai sword came flashing through the gap, just missing my face. I struggled to close the door as he struggled to stab me. Eventually I managed to get it closed again as the dealer shouted and screamed at me from outside making dire threats. Alice was upset but angry, and was ready to open the door and attack him, even through he was armed. Cherry had woken up with the commotion and was wailing now from her cot. Eventually he stopped banging at the door and it went quiet.

We never slept that night and I realised I was no longer willing or able to deal with this kind of violence. I knew where this would escalate to, the next stage was I would get my friends to deal with him, and he'd retaliate with his family coming for me. I'd seen it all before; eventually either I or him would end up like 'Big Neilie', blasted with a shotgun one night, and the other arrested and charged with pointless murder. I knew I could not stomach this life any more. What the hell was I doing here, anyway? Fighting with a drug dealer's dog! Norwich might have been uncomfortable for Alice and me at the time we left, but we were never at risk of this kind of pointless violence. Cherry was now almost two years old and we had proved we could take care of her. I asked Alice if she wanted to return to Norwich. She said yes.

* * * * * * *

At this time I could see no way to escape my fate of being born into male violence and crime. Living as a woman was a dream that could never be fulfilled. The state had blocked me through their documents that defined me. The medical profession was a gate keeper who rationed and restricted my female persona. It seemed only money was a key to open my future, but to acquire it I would need revert to being everything I'd sought to escape. My avenues to financial security were limited and gender identification defined, or socially blocked off. I was in despair and could see no future. Alice was the one person who supported me through my desperation and black depression. She, and of course Cherry. Alice's love was stronger than all the guns and swords and beatings. Stronger than the hate, poverty, and casual violence. She was indifferent to the negative forces; her love shining through like a beam of light. She held me in her arms that night and gave me a reason to not give in. Alice is the reason I carried on and probably why I'm alive today, I have no doubt about that. Her unconditional love and support held me up when it seemed far easier to drown and give up. In later years when she was criticised by my friends and family, who couldn't understand my loyalty to her, well, this was why.

* * * * * * *

Meanwhile, things were happening, events I was unaware of. In London Lynne Jones MP and Dr Jane Playdon set up the Parliamentary Forum on Transsexualism in 1994. It comprised the UK's leading experts on transsexualism, in both the legal and medical fields, along with a number of MPs. They began pressing for legal reforms to bring British legislation into line with the rest of Europe and thus end the discrimination from which transsexual people had suffered in the UK. In those days before the internet there was very little opportunity to hear about these important matters.

I called Tanya in Norwich and told her we were coming back, She suggested I call Lilly, one of her twins, as she had a flat that we could borrow temporarily. This was a sign of good fortune. I rented a van from a national hire company that had a branch in Norwich, which meant I could drive to Norwich, unload our furniture and leave the van at their depot without the need to return it to Scotland. I gave the Mazda car, that Jim in Dunoon had given to me, to a friend in the Vale. I wanted to leave behind all connections to crime, drugs and violence.

We arrived back in Norwich penniless and homeless, but relieved to be away from the hard grind of gang violence and drugs in the Vale. We stayed temporarily at the borrowed flat on Philadelphia Lane, Norwich. It was located in what was considered in Norwich as quite a rough council estate, but compared to what we'd left behind us it was an oasis of peace and tranquillity. Eventually we applied for council housing again and were offered a small flat in Lakenham, on the south side of the city.

But for now, we desperately required cash. I needed work of some kind and contacted a few old friends. I was directed to the Jaclyn agency for film and TV extra work and signed up for them. I'd previously done some work with them in the past with Tanya and the twins. It was hardly regular employment but when I did get jobs they were quite well paid. I worked on such TV shows as The Chief with Martin Shaw and Tim Piggot Smith among others, several Lovejoy's with Ian McShane and numerous other shows. Probably the best paid was Growing Rich, a drama series with Martin Kemp of Spandau Ballet, that ran for a while and provided good money. Because I was able to be versatile gender wise I could play men and women, so I suppose I was good value - they got two for the price of one! The craziest job was playing a sleazy Hong Kong drug dealer, dressed in leather and dispensing heroin from a red light area nightclub doorway. This was for a cigarette company, and, hilariously, filmed in the small Norfolk village of Beccles, of all places!

Through this work I met with other extras who were also performers and writers in their own right, and I was invited to join a travelling Murder Mystery performance group. We wrote our own scripts and played undercover at functions from Norfolk to London. It was usually a corporate social where the boss had employed us to wind up his own employees as we played out the scenes of murder that they believed were genuine, until the big reveal at the end. I really enjoyed this work, but it could be dangerous when the public reacted to you as what they thought of as a genuine murderer, victim or police officer. I was even attacked on more than one occasion, which was sort of gratifying, because it meant we had been playing the part so realistically that the audience had completely been taken in. But mostly it was good fun, and a world away from the real life stuff in Scotland that we'd escaped from. The important thing was that I didn't have to provide male or female documentation that differed from my appearance, when I worked with Jaclyn or the Murder Mystery group. Working in the performing arts was rarely well paid, but it was at least open to someone like me.

Alice was unable to get a job, and it was suggested to us by the Job Centre that she should claim benefits for her well documented disability due to her childhood brain damage. This had never occurred to us before, but when we went along to a local disability charity called 'Hand' in Norwich, they told her she had a very good claim and should have been getting disability money for years, ever since she left school. They filled in the forms for her and she was awarded a regular allowance. That gave us a little bit of security at least.

Chapter 27 'A Design For Life'

Over the next couple of years I parked my plans for transition to concentrate on bringing up Cherry and keeping my family together. I'd discovered there was a softening of attitudes from the authorities towards us. There was no longer open hostility from GPs and the council. I was still severely restricted in what work I could do, without the ability to change my gender on documents like my driving licence and passport, but if we kept our heads down then the authorities would more or less leave us alone. Alice and I rejoined the Labour Party whilst we lived in Lakenham and campaigned for a Labour government under Tony Blair in the 1997 election. It was clear his incoming government would be a lot friendlier towards LGBT people.

Around this period I'd started going to local auctions in the hope of picking up some nice object, silver, crockery or small item of furniture that I could resell for a profit. Maybe it was all those episodes of Lovejoy that gave me the bug! However, I soon discovered it was really difficult to make money out of that business. There was a lot of competition and I was not much good as an antique dealer, I didn't have the knowledge, training or the 'eye' to spot genuine collectables. But at these auctions they also usually sold household furniture from house clearances, anything from white goods like fridges, cookers, and washing machines. This stuff often went for very little money as 'untested' so you could pick up a nice fridge, or a hoover, for a few pounds. I had an estate car, so I would travel around the county auctions at Aylsham, North Walsham, Watton, Stalham, and Acle, which were all held on different days of the week. If I picked up a fridge or a vacuum cleaner at each auction I could turn a little bit of profit on each and earn a small wage. Critically, it was an occupation that was self employed and required no I.D.

After a few months doing this I began thinking it was a shame that about fifty per cent of the items I bought were faulty, and I'd have to dump them. I thought I should try and teach myself how to repair these items. So, like everything I've ever learned, I taught myself through trial and error. I stripped down old vacuum cleaners, fridges and electric cookers to understand how they worked and to identify where they were broken. It was often just a simple component that had gone wrong, like a thermostat, or cooker ring, or maybe an off/on switch. Soon I had taught myself to repair almost anything that went wrong with white goods, except where a fridge had lost its gas. This improved the success rate of things I bought to sell from fifty to ninety per cent. I discovered I could actually make a reasonable living from this. My new problem was lack of space. We were living in a small two bed flat with no garage, just a small lock- up shed. I figured that if I had the room, I could take in many more of the white goods to repair, and also store the spare parts I needed. It was something Alice could get involved with too. Once I'd repaired an item she would clean it and even touch up the paintwork if required. We would then sell the items through the local paper. It actually seemed as if we had stumbled upon a decent way to make a bit of money at last. I sold the estate car and bought a large Ford Transit panel van, so now we could buy much more and store items in the van. We even sold fridges and cookers straight off the back of the van, using an electric hook- up to demonstrate to customers that they were working. We could deliver straight to their home, and that made a big difference, because a lot of our customers had no transport. After a time we decided that if we wanted to do this business properly we needed a workshop. I'd heard from one of the auctioneers at Aylsham that there was a workshop available at a farm in Marsham, a village a few miles away. It was very inexpensive and the rent included electricity. I visited the man who owned the farm buildings, who was a Dutch antique dealer from Amsterdam called Cornelius Head. He and I agreed a price and now we had a workshop!

* * * * * * *

The Marsham workshop was a big step up from the cottage industry that we'd been running previously; now we had the makings of a proper business with all the pressures that would entail. The main difference was that, because I was not working from home, I had a lot of time apart from Alice and Cherry, which I hated. Also, now I had the space, I would need to fill it with stock to justify the rent we were paying. The obvious problem with that was that I'd need to spend more time at auction houses, which can be very time consuming, and the hours spent there were hours not spent repairing the stock. A solution to this soon became apparent. For a year or so I'd taken the white goods that were beyond my repair down to my local tip, just south of Norwich. These tips were known euphemistically as 'waste recycling centres' but in actual fact they were just dumping areas; very few things were recycled apart from textiles and bottles. The guy who ran the tip I used was called Rolly, and I got to know him through my frequent visits. One day he asked me if I was interested in buying the dumped white goods that arrived on his site. I considered it, and thought it was perhaps worth a punt, since I now had plenty of room, and though the units were probably less likely to work (since they had been dumped) than the auction stock, I could at least break the stuff up for spares. We just needed to agree a price to see if it was worth my while. Amazingly, the price I was asked for each unit was £2.00. Rolly said I could fill up my transit van every evening with the white goods that had come in and take them away for that price on each item. This meant I could take away up to twenty items a day for £40.00. I knew I could sell one fridge, repaired and cleaned, for £35.00. So I quickly agreed, and that was my first contract with a tip. What followed were similar deals with other tip managers in Norfolk. I eventually had exclusive rights to almost all of the sites; the main ones were controlled by one family and once I had them on board it was a monopoly. My workshop would be filled each night with white goods, I'd spend all day repairing them, or breaking up what was beyond repair, then we would sell them. It was a proper business and it was also recycling, long before it became fashionable.

* * * * * * *

But meanwhile, I had been reading in the press that things were changing for transsexual people It was slow progress, but meeting less resistance as time went on. In 1998, the European Court of Human Rights ruled against two trans women, but only narrowly. They had sued the UK government for breach of their human rights, as it provided them with no mechanism for amending their birth certificates. Kristina Sheffield and Rachel Horsham both maintained that their privacy was breached by having to disclose their birth gender in official and professional contexts in the UK. Their legal contention also stated that by 1998 almost all other European countries had a means for transsexual people to amend their legal sex. The process had begun.

* * * * * * *

With the success of the white goods business, Alice and I decided to move out of the poky council flat in Lakenham. Alice found a nice house in the village of Stalham, ten miles out from Norwich, with a large garden and a good village school for Cherry, who was now almost five years old. The Stalham house had the added advantage of being close to the auction yard where I still went on a weekly basis. We had also decided to build a large workshop/shed in the garden where I could work repairing the stock. This meant I didn't have to leave Alice and Cherry each day as I could now work from home and give up the Marsham premises. We were now, financially at least, quite comfortable. Alice had her disability money and I as her carer was still able to earn a certain amount each week, and be on hand if she needed me. Cherry was happy in the village school and everything, on the surface at least, was rosy.

So why was I not happy? We were being left alone as a family by the authorities, had a nice place to live, and more than enough money. But I found myself becoming depressed. It almost seemed that, with nothing to fight against, the new security we enjoyed became oppressive and boring. I just wasn't used to it! I started having panic attacks. With the basic struggles of day to day living apparently solved, I now had time to think about the transition I had lost. I had managed to put the gnawing pain of living as male to one side whilst my immediate and daily worries had kept my mind occupied.

Now I had too much time to think. To control the increasing panic attacks I began drinking again.

I didn't even need to drive most days now. I could go out just twice a week and collect my stock from all round the Norfolk tips, unload it into our garden workshop, step out of the back door of our house, walk ten feet into the workshop and get on with the repairs. By now I was experienced enough to know what units to buy and how to fix them, so I had very little waste. Almost a hundred per cent of the items I bought from the tips were able to be repaired, cleaned and sold within hours. I had by now regular customers who came to me, second hand furniture shops and private landlords who rented out flats and bedsits. It was the perfect business and we had worked hard to build it, but now it often seemed pointless to me.

I started to begin my day with a couple of strong cans of lager. That would settle me and I'd then work through to lunchtime. In the afternoon I'd relax in the workshop pottering around with minor repairs, drinking, and meeting with my buyers who turned up then. Each night I would go down to the village off sales shop, where I'd got to know the owner, and buy my alcohol for the next day. I'd usually sit in the back of the off sales and pass an hour or so drinking with him. After that I'd buy a takeaway meal, go home and eat that, throw down the day's takings in cash on the kitchen table for Alice, and go to bed, then the cycle would repeat. Without going into detail - to be truthful I don't remember much anyway- I went on like this for a couple of years. I put on a lot of weight, and with the regular lifting of the cookers and fridges I built up a lot of muscle in my arms and shoulders. I knew now that with my weight, physique and ongoing subjection to testosterone (poisoning) that I could no longer even remotely pass as female. I made a point of never looking in a mirror during this time because I knew it would upset me too much. Whenever I was sober I was having increasingly severe panic attacks. I started hiding cans of lager in the work shop, in my van and in my car. It was the only way I'd get through the day. If we had to go shopping, and drive to the supermarket, I knew I had an emergency alcohol supply, if needed, close by. Alice as always was completely supportive, she never questioned my drinking. Although she must have known what was behind it, she was wise enough to know that an alcoholic, which I'd certainly become, would not respond to nagging. I'd have to find my own way out of this self inflicted hell I was living. The only thing that gave me any pleasure during this time was when Cherry would come into the workshop and sit with me. She would tell me about her day and what had happened at school. I adored her. Some days she would insist I went for a walk with her in the woodland next to the house, because she wanted to look for butterflies or hedgehogs. I'd grab a few cans of lager and follow her through the trees and we'd find a spot where I could sit and drink, while she flitted through the trees shouting back to me the things she saw. She was so full of life and innocent pleasure at the wildlife, I'd often sit in tears watching her. I was so proud that we had managed to keep her and bring her up into this beautiful child.

This self destructive life couldn't last, and two days just before Christmas 1998 I woke up and couldn't breathe. I still smoked at this time and I felt I was trying to suck in air through a wet cloth over my face. I was weak as a kitten and felt awful. My head was sore and I felt every part of my body was aching. I'd felt ill for weeks previously but I had always self medicated with alcohol and that got me through the day. But now I clearly had flu or a chest infection. I'd previously got a bad chest infection a few years previously when I was at the very cold Marsham work shop. It had laid me up for nine weeks in bed and resulted in scarring of my lungs, but at that time my fitness had eventually pulled me through. But this felt worse. Now I was very unfit, overweight and I seriously felt that I was dying. I forced down some alcohol to see if that would help, but it was a struggle as I felt the bile in my stomach rising and I was sick. There was nothing else for it, I needed to go to the GP. I'd avoided visiting doctors for years by this time, because I knew they had access to my full medical records, including my diagnosis of transsexuality and my period of transition at Charing Cross. I didn't want to speak about this to anyone, or even be reminded. But today I had no choice, I had to go. I managed to drag myself into the car and somehow drove the half mile to the surgery. I almost fell in the door, and the receptionist didn't even question if I'd made an appointment. I looked so awful that she ushered me straight through to the GP as soon as the previous patient came out. The GP, an elderly gentleman who I didn't know, examined me, and decided I had severe bronchitis complicated by flu. But he also insisted on taking a blood sample and then I was sent off to North Walsham cottage hospital, where they gave me antibiotics and oxygen. Within a day I was able to get up and walk around. I got dressed and checked out; I was desperate for a drink. The hospital weren't happy to discharge me but I insisted, and they made me promise to see my GP for a follow up appointment that afternoon, to which I agreed. I went home and had several cans of Special Bru lager before I felt able to think properly again. It was Christmas Eve, and we were due to visit Sue and Les that afternoon, and to stay over for Christmas dinner, but I didn't feel up to it. I didn't want to spoil Cherry's Christmas day with her grandparents, so I insisted that she and Alice went ahead without me, and assured them that I'd be ok at home resting. Besides, I had the follow up appointment with the GP to go to. After Alice and Cherry had left, I pulled myself together and went along to see the doctor.

I sat in the waiting room for only a few minutes before I was called in. The doctor looked up and asked me to take a seat. Then he did something I'd never seen any doctor do before, or since. He came round to my side of the desk, bent down and put his arm around me. His beard was tickling my face as he spoke quietly to me with his arm gently holding me.

"I'm afraid you are quite unwell, Ally. It would be remiss of me not to tell you the truth," I was shocked by his words, but also by this familiarity.

"The hospital agreed I've got bronchitis and the flu, I'll be ok!" I replied.

"No, you need to listen carefully to me." He then went back round to his side of the desk and took out some notes.

"This is the result of your blood sample. Your liver function test is by far the worst I have ever seen in my long career from someone who is still alive. I'm amazed you are still able to sit there in front of me. When I first saw this, I expected the hospital in North Walsham would contact me with news of your death. I really did not expect to see you again, Ally."

Fuck! What do you do or say, when you get that news from your GP? I was struck dumb. But I knew from the arm round my shoulder he was deadly serious.

I stammered, "Well, what shall I do? Have you got a prescription for me, or should I go back to hospital? "

"No, I have nothing for you except advice, go home and be with your family. Do not drink, not even one, and if you can get through the next few days do not ever drink again. But please, just go home and be with your family." And with that he helped me up from the seat and guided me to the door, smiling. "I'd like to see you in the New Year. Goodbye."

Chapter 28 'No More 'I Love You's'

I went back to the empty house. Cherry and Alice had left for Christmas dinner with her parents. Would I ever see them again? I was alone and feeling sorry for myself. But mostly, I was embarrassed. How had it come to this, and so suddenly? I thought maybe I should call them and let them know, but it all sounded so pathetic and stupid. I'd basically just about killed myself with alcohol - me, who had been so disdainful to my own parents who were also alcoholics. It even looked as if they would outlive me. I was actually worse than them! At that moment never had I wanted a drink more. I knew I had a cupboard full of booze in the kitchen. What difference would it make now, anyway? I felt so bad physically that it would be a relief to be dead. And so I got myself a drink, a can of Special Bru. I came back to the lounge and turned on the record player and lay on the couch.

I woke up around three in the morning. I must have been so exhausted by the previous day's drama that I basically shut down; I'd slept for around ten hours. I saw the can of Special Bru on the side table next to me untouched. . I didn't want to drink the lager; the thought of it made me feel sick. I wanted to cuddle Alice and Cherry so much, or at least talk to them. But I knew they would both be sound asleep at Les & Sue's house. I went to a drawer in the unit next to me where I knew there were photos of them. I took out the albums and the numerous Boots the chemist envelopes and started going through them, each photo a memory of the past few years, There was very few of me, as I hated having photos taken of me as male. I delved further down into the drawer and there were packs of photos of Alice and me before Cherry had been born. I looked like me in those. I was dressed as a female with make- up and my hair long and back- combed. Even further into the drawer were photos of me and my friends before I'd met Alice. I looked so innocent and fresh faced, a slender young woman smiling back at me. I'd not looked at these photos for years. I made a decision. I'd never get back those years since Cherry had been born, but they were necessary. I'd had to protect her by conforming to what was expected of me. But to die now would make those years pointless. I needed to quit drinking there and then, or it was all over. Cherry's and Alice's lives would continue without me, and I wanted so much to see what that future would be. I was still so tired and my joints were aching. I took some paracetamol and dragged myself upstairs to bed. Before lying down I got Cherry's pillow from her bedroom and took it back to our bedroom, then I cuddled up with it, smelling her, and fell asleep again.

The phone ringing woke me up later on that morning. It was Alice asking how I was feeling and asking if I would be coming to Christmas dinner. I said I was coming; a table had been booked in the local pub in Reepham and I was determined to get there. I forced myself to get washed and dressed and drove through the snow covered country roads to Les & Sue's. The roads were empty as it was Christmas morning, and I actually enjoyed the drive. I made it in time to get to the pub along with everyone else. I remember my dinner choice was pheasant, but not much else. I couldn't taste anything because I was still full of flu, but I made it through. Afterwards we went back to the house and opened presents. Watching Cherry ripping off the wrapping paper with such delight and excitement was better than any medicine.

The next day I called Alcoholics Anonymous.

* * * * * * *

I was surprised that the number I called for AA was answered by a human being. It was the holiday season after all, and I was expecting an answerphone message with some information, but a man answered with a cockney accent and he sounded quite grumpy. I told him my situation, including the conversation I'd had with my GP. He wasn't particularly impressed. I suppose he's heard it all before. We chatted for a while, and after a time he softened up and became slightly more sympathetic. He said he got a lot of time waster calls at this time of year from people who had overdone the booze a bit at Christmas, or wanted to make a new year's resolution. I managed to convince him I was serious, deadly serious, and I was sober. I absolutely needed to stop using alcohol and I was desperate to accept any help that was on offer. He gave me information on the local meetings I could attend, and advised me to look out for a man called Mike S. After a forty minute chat he eventually wished me good luck and I hung up. I felt that he meant it.

Mike S was a very tall man, at least six foot six, with a trimmed beard and a fresh healthy face. He was probably in his forties when I first met him at a meeting in Stalham. To cut a long story short, I was very impressed with Mike's personality and his leadership of the meeting. He was no mug, he'd seen it and heard it all before. He'd been there himself. And, after I had attended several meetings and had a few private chats with him, he agreed to think about being my mentor. When I was talking with Mike I felt empowered and strong enough to live sober. But, occasionally, when I'd not seen him for a while, I would get jumpy and slide into desperation. To get through the first few days I had decided, probably foolishly, not to go to my GP for something to help with the alcohol withdrawal symptoms.

I thought it would only delay the inevitable pain. I had the shakes, I heard noises, and saw things that were not there. I was sick every morning, I felt miserable all day. I could hardly speak to Alice or even Cherry; I just wanted to hide my face from them.

When things were at their worst at night time, I drove to the coast and pumped money into the seaside arcade machines, mesmerising my brain with the spinning reels. It didn't matter if I won or lost, I just needed the distraction. I ate chocolate, lots of it! Mars bars, Twixes, and huge bars of Dairy Milk. I often bought huge family sized bags of crisps and ate them all to myself. I drank countless cans of coke, teas and coffees and bought fish and chips, curries and kebabs, often only to throw it away after a few bites. I just needed to try and satisfy a craving somehow for a positive stimulus, a buzz of some kind. Mostly it was just a distraction, something to do with my hands and my mouth that wasn't drinking alcohol.

But after a relatively short time - about ten days - I was physically detoxed from alcohol, according to Mike. I was now only psychologically dependant. Knowing that didn't make it much easier at the time. Temptation is never far from the mind and unfortunately, for an alcoholic, every situation seems like an appropriate time to have a drink. To celebrate feeling better, or to commiserate on feeling bad, whatever. A hot day and a cool beer looks good, a cold day and a nice warming whisky? There is always a reason, and they are all very good reasons. But I knew this, as I'd been warned by Mike and others at the meetings. I somehow managed to stay sober and demonstrate to Mike and myself that I was serious about recovering. This was when Mike gave me his phone number. I'd proven I was genuine and so he told me he would back me up by committing his time to me, I could call him day or night and he would come to me, or we would meet up. He was a rock, and I owe him so much. People like Mike are unsung heroes who casually save lives every day. I went to an AA meeting, or similar addiction group, every day, sometimes two. If I was feeling like slipping and needed a meeting right away I'd drive to one wherever it was. I'd drive three hours to Lowestoft or Essex to be with 'my' people, others who knew exactly how I was feeling and what I was fighting.

It was only after six weeks or so, with the support of Mike, that I felt strong enough to get through more than a day without a meeting. He came round to our house one day and we sat in the kitchen with a cuppa. I was able to relax and joke with him now. I was sleeping at night and waking up feeling refreshed. Mike said he thought I should try to carry on without his on call support. I knew he had others to deal with. I was out of the woods now. He was right. It was up to me from here on. He had got me this far but if I was to stay sober it would need to be because I wanted it. I also knew I always had the meetings to fall back on. I wasn't giving them up, and I still occasionally go to meetings. Mike had never asked me to reveal the underlying reason why I became an alcoholic, It didn't really matter; he was just there for me. I had needed a prolonged period of sobriety to clear my mind, and with his help I'd achieved that. Now, he suggested I contact a local drug and alcohol addiction counselling service via my GP, called NCAS, and go from here to identify the reasons I'd got so ill and alcohol dependent.

It was fortunate for me that drug and alcohol addiction services were still properly funded in those days under the Blair Labour government. Within days I was given an appointment to see a counsellor, coincidentally, at the North Walsham cottage hospital where I'd been admitted at deaths door only a few months earlier.

I was offered a block of 16 weeks of therapy, which enabled me to explore the reasons why I was so unhappy and why I would seek oblivion through alcohol. Of course, it was so bleeding obvious. But with this counsellor I was actually able to be completely honest and open about my hatred of my body, the fear of losing Cherry, the official intimidation that we as a family had endured, and my shame as a transsexual woman, which meant I believed I deserved all the shit that had been thrown at me. I knew I'd brought this discrimination and prejudice, that also affected Alice and Cherry, to our door. It was my fault I felt guilt and shame about my condition. All the counselling and therapy sessions I'd had previously with consultants at Charing Cross had never addressed this inherent transphobia I felt about myself; in fact they had reinforced it by implicitly implying that I was right to feel shame about myself.

I'm sure (I hope so anyway) that therapy ideology has changed for the better now at the NHS Gender Identity Clinics. But back then it was based very much on a moral position and I never had the confidence to challenge it. I was after all a deviant who had to be repaired, to be made normal. It was true that the GIC told me it wasn't my fault, sure, it was an accident of birth, but it was still a fact, and I'd have to deal with that as best I could by hiding it. The ethos at Charing Cross was always about hiding. There was no such thing as trans pride in those days. The ultimate goal was to 'pass' and to live in stealth. I was encouraged that this would be the cure for me. Success would be when I was no longer visible as a travesty of nature. I had to become physically as female bodied as I could, and to reinforce that by having a relationship, preferably with a straight man, to work and dress in an acceptable female way (by their judgement) and most of all to conform.

The counsellor I saw at NCAS challenged that. She was a feminist, and if I was inherently female in mind, as the psychological tests and Charing Cross had told me I was, then why shouldn't I also be lesbian or asexual? Some women were, after all! And sexual orientation was nothing to do with gender identity. Of course I had always thought this, but never dared mention it to Charing Cross. It was encouraging to hear it from someone in the medical profession, at last.

* * * * * * *

Later on that year we got some bad news from our landlord in Stalham. He was selling the house and we were given six weeks' notice to get out. It meant we would lose the business we had created, the workshop and showroom we'd built in the back yard. By this time we even had a customer car park laid out at the side of the house. It should have been devastating to lose everything we'd built, and the money we had sunk into it, but I was not too upset. I'd talked with Alice of course during my period of counselling, I'd told her everything that we'd discussed, and that I had decided I needed to go back to my transition. Living as a man was literally killing me. She supported my decision completely and without reservation. As always, Alice delighted and reassured me in her love. She never wavered, through sickness and health, richer or poorer. She meant it. It was always me who had the doubts, never her. She was solid. We decided it would be better for me to transition and start afresh in the city.

Chapter 29 'Whole New You'

Holt Road

We found a nice bungalow on Holt Road, Norwich. It was near the airport and next to the junior school for Cherry, and we moved in the spring of that year. I still needed to earn a living of sorts, so we had a garage that I used as a workshop, but the white goods business was much reduced now. I was now 35 years old and in this house I would begin my fourth and final transition.

I had to register, yet again, with a GP. I went along to a surgery in the city and explained myself, as I had done to GPs many times in the past. The GP I saw was quite an elderly man, Dr Cole; in fact he told me he was due to retire quite soon. He had no experience of someone with my condition. But perhaps surprisingly, given his age, he was very sympathetic and. as it proved, supportive. He told me that he would seek advice, and if it was appropriate would refer me back to Charing Cross GIC. It took several months, but eventually at the end of the year I was asked to return to the surgery to see a psychiatrist. He was a decent enough man, who seemed willing to help, but yet again was completely inexperienced regarding gender identity. He explained it was the Local Health Authority policy that I would have to see him for three appointments before he could refer me on. Procedure had to be followed after all! So I had three fairly superfluous appointments with him where we discussed my previous life and experiences. I tried to use the time to educate him, because if nothing else it might help others who followed me. He was honest, he knew virtually nothing about transsexuality, but we had some nice chats and went through the motions. And then he told me I'd be referred to the regional gender identity expert. I was intrigued; the Health Authority had a 'gender identity expert' now? That was interesting.

I'd always been slightly annoyed that GIC treatment was under mental health. To me it was primarily a physical condition that needed to be sorted through hormones and surgery. But instead, countless hours of many psychiatric appointments were spent and wasted on transsexual patients, often for many years. My thoughts were that after initial psychiatric evaluation, to see whether I was of sane mind, or a fetishist, then once diagnosed as transsexual through the accepted NHS criteria, I should be referred direct to an endocrinologist for a hormone treatment regime, and a surgeon who was capable of performing sex change surgery. After all, if you had a rotten diseased tooth that was causing severe pain, you would go to the dentist and have it removed. You didn't have to go to a shrink over a period of many years and have dozens of appointments to talk about whether it should be removed. But I knew the score and I didn't complain out loud, keeping my thoughts to myself. I was grateful that at least the NHS had a programme in place for people like me. I waited for the appointment with the regional gender identity expert.

* * * * * * *

At the end of the year we visited Glasgow for the New Year celebrations. it was fitting but slightly sad, because I was saying goodbye not only to the 20th Century, but to my parents and friends that I was close to in Scotland. It was to be one of the last occasions I dressed and pretended to be male. I did it for them because I believed I would probably never see them again once I had fully transitioned. I knew that once they had learned about me, I would never be welcome there again, and that turned out to be the case.

When I finally received an appointment to see the 'regional gender expert' in early 2000, I was very pleasantly surprised, as it turned out to be the social worker Barbara Ross! I thought she had already retired by then, so I was delighted to see her again. It had been over eleven years since she had visited me in my council flat on the Heartsease Estate. Back then she'd held my pendant, told me she knew I was genuine and that she would make sure I received the help I needed. She was absolutely true to her word; it just all took a bit longer than we both expected. Barbara further amazed me by informing me there was now a Gender Identity Clinic in Norwich. It was run by her, and a local psychiatric consultant, Dr Olive. This was fantastic news. I couldn't believe Norwich Health Authority had become so progressive, but it was all down to Barbara's hard work. She was always a true pioneer in the treatment of transsexual people.

So, I began attending Norwich GIC as a patient. It was located in Town Close hospital on Bowthorpe Rd, Norwich. To begin with, the expected plan was that I was to be referred back to Charing Cross. But, when I expressed my previous disappointing experience at that clinic with Professor Green, and described how they had treated me when I was a patient there before, Barbara sympathised. But, she informed me, I had to be referred to another accredited GIC somewhere , to obtain the two independent psychiatric referrals needed for surgery. Barbara then had a suggestion; one of these referrals would obviously come from Dr Olive in Norwich, but if I preferred, the other could come from Russell Reed in London. Would I like to be referred direct to Russell's private Earls Court clinic instead? I didn't take long to answer, of course I would! She made sure I understood that by going down this path it would take a little more time to arrange, but apparently, It would cost the Health Authority the same money. However, if I was more comfortable with Russell, then it would be better, it was worth the additional waiting time, and they would send me there. Norwich GIC had sent others to him previously. I was very agreeable to that plan, I'd waited many years already, so a few more months wouldn't make much difference to me.

It was also around this time that I discovered the internet. Tanya had been telling me for a while that I should get a computer, it was the future, but I'd had no real interest, until one day I was at her house and she gave me a quick demonstration. I had never used a mouse so I was very clumsy about it all. But even in that short demo I could understand that this was going to be massive. I could get information about anything from all over the world, in minutes. OMG, that was amazing! Of course, the thought that was immediately foremost in my mind was that perhaps I could use this technology to understand more about my condition? Just as when, as a young teenager, back in Glasgow I'd visit the Mitchell library and trawl through the medical books looking for any reference to 'transsexual' in the epilogue or index. With the internet I'd have a world of books and information at my finger tips and in the comfort of my own home! This was such an exciting development and the timing was perfect for me.

That same day I went to PC World upon leaving Tanya's house and bought my first computer package on Hire Purchase, and my world opened overnight. I got myself an AOL account and using the old dial up connection of the period began browsing. As well as the web pages full of information, I soon discovered an added unexpected bonus was that I could also find people on the internet who were like me, and talk to them in real time. This was something so astonishing to me at that time. I'd spent my whole life feeling that I was almost completely alone with this condition of transsexuality. And now I could find, and maybe even meet up with, others. Wow!

In those days, there were online message groups called 'egroups' and they in turn, a few months later, became Yahoo groups. One of the first groups I joined was 'Transsexual UK' and through this I began to learn all about what transsexual medical support there was available (or not) in the UK. There were even social groups where people could arrange to meet up, and anyone was able to start their own group. It was mind blowing to me. I found I was able to chat online with the very knowledgeable people who had formed the campaign group 'Press For Change' -Stephen Whittle, Christine Burns, Claire McNab and others. I learned that these brave wonderful people had been campaigning against all odds, hatred and bigotry for years to achieve protection and equality for transsexual people like me, and I didn't even know! Even better, they were beginning to break through the brick wall of ignorance, the government were now speaking with them, and legal cases were being enacted in both Europe and the UK. These were the pioneering warriors who would eventually achieve the Gender Recognition Act in 2004.

At this time there was a strict hierarchy among people who were sometimes called transsexual, transgender, gender variant, or suffering from 'gender dysphoria'. It essentially amounted to a pecking order with transsexual people at the top; they were the people who would seek to take hormones and undergo surgery. Below this group were transvestites and cross dressers, basically straight men who liked to get dressed up for personal pleasure or occasional socialising. There were also drag queens, who were usually gay men. There was very little mention or evidence of 'trans men' those who were born female and changing to female. In fact for many years the only trans man I was aware of was Stephen Whittle.

As a group we were all under the American umbrella term transgender, but this was also highly contentious, as many transsexual people felt they had nothing in common with the others, who they viewed as fetishists. You have to remember we were all at the beginning of understanding ourselves and our situations in relation to others. Like me, most people were quite ignorant of the existence of people similar to ourselves until those groups brought us together. In time, Stephen Whittle would coin the term 'trans' which covered most of us, and cleverly enabled a 'T' to be tagged on to the end of LGB. I admit I was one of those who objected in the early days to becoming part of a group attached to the LGB acronym. After all, we were about gender identity, not sexual orientation. Many gay people objected too. But, I eventually accepted that Stephen and the PFC campaign had made the right call. We were all part of the queer diaspora and there is safety and strength in numbers. In time it would allow such people as gender non binary and gender queer (who no one even spoke about back then) to find a place of acceptance within the LGBTQ family, and together we had much more political power.

* * * * * * *

The six years of living almost exclusively as male since Cherry was born had taken a toll on me physically and socially. I could no longer easily pass as female at this time. Through the hard work and heavy lifting of the white goods business I'd gained a lot of muscle, and I was also very overweight. But I would still need to begin and complete the 'real life test' and live full time as female for at least two years. The GIC rules hadn't changed. The fact I was no longer slender and of androgynous appearance became pretty obvious to me as I started to dress as female again.

One day I decided to experiment. I took a long walk around Norwich on my own, just to see what the reaction would be. I was wearing a pair of cropped white leggings, sandals, a summer top and a padded bra. My hair was still shortish and I was wearing no make-up. I received a lot of hard stares, and at one point a car with a group of young guys slowed next to me, honking the horn and cat calling out of the vehicle at me. It was clear they recognised I was trans. They didn't try to physically hurt me, they just wanted to humiliate me and have a laugh. I didn't respond, I stared ahead and kept on walking till they drove off. But it made me realise I had a lot of work ahead of me. I felt poisoned by testosterone. Only a few years earlier I had 'passed' effortlessly in most situations. The intervening years had been hard on my appearance and body shape. But on the other hand, I couldn't regret those years, I have never thought it was six years wasted, because we had Cherry, and she was more important than anything.

Cherry was actually the next thing I had to deal with. Obviously, she had no recollection of me as living female in her first year. She had only known me as 'daddy' and I would have to have a difficult talk with her. But before that, I needed to speak with Sue and Les, Alice's parents. They would have to be told I was back in treatment and would be transitioning, and after the RLT, I would have surgery. I expected it would be a bit of a shock. But I was determined to carry on this time, after so much had derailed me in the past. I was still not drinking alcohol, and during my GP visits they had taken blood samples and checked my liver, as you would expect given my recent medical history. Within a year my liver function test results were back within normal range, if still at the high end. But I had managed to mostly recover and had a future. I'd definitely dodged a bullet and I didn't want to waste any more time.

Alice and I arranged a meeting with Sue and Les to explain the situation. I wasn't confident that I would have their support. after all it must have seemed improbable that I would be undergoing sex change surgery. I hardly looked the part these days! I was still over twenty stone and muscle bound with the years of physical work. They had only really seen me, since Cherry was born, as male, a husband and father. I didn't know exactly how much of my previous life they had heard about from Alice. It was not something we had spoken about really, but I guessed they were aware of some of it. But, as it turned out, they were both fantastically supportive. I'm sure it didn't come as a complete surprise, but I do understand it must have been difficult for them to get their heads round.

What is true, and this was confirmed in later conversations, was that Sue and Les had seen how unhappy and changed I'd become in the previous couple of years and they had an idea something was wrong, but they never knew the full extent of the pressure we had been subjected to by the Government and the health authorities. Their thoughts and concerns, once we'd explained I was going to re transition, were of course with Cherry, and how we should tell her. It was important that we were all supportive and open.

As it turned out, Cherry had already got an idea of what was going on. She had probably overheard discussions at home and seen some of my female clothes. She asked me about it one night unexpectedly, and I decided to just be completely open. I told her about myself growing up and how unhappy I'd felt as a boy, which had led me to transition and live as female long before she was born. I also showed her some photos from the time I had previously lived as a woman. I explained I would be having an operation soon, to make me more like a girl. I would still be the exact same person, I would just look a bit different, but I'd love her just as much as I did now, and that would never change. She looked worried and I could see there were questions she wanted to ask. I was expecting medical or practical things, like how does the surgery work? Or what should she call me now? But she surprised me by saying, "what are we going to tell Nana and Grampa?" I smiled at this, and assured her that they already knew and that they were ok about it. She seemed satisfied with that, but I did not underestimate how much of a shock this news must have been and I made a point to include her in everything from then on. We would mess around together applying make-up and wearing various wigs/ I wanted her to see it as fun as well as important, and she was always told that nothing had changed between us, I loved her just the same. I only ever had one practical problem after that which upset me grievously.

One day I was dressed as female and shopping in a supermarket with Alice and Cherry, when Cherry ran up to me saying, "Can I get this toy, daddy?" in front of several other shoppers. I could see that we had got a few strange looks by her referring to me in that way, so I took her aside quietly and told her maybe it would be best if she didn't call me that any more. I could see the confusion in her eyes, so I quickly explained I wasn't telling her off, it would just be easier for both of us if she called me 'Ally' from then on, and thankfully, that is what she did.

Since telling Alice's parents, things between us had went remarkably well. They were great and supportive, but now I had my next big test, the family Christmas dinner. It was all very well with Les and Sue, they knew me well, but the rest of Les's family were tough working class northern miner folk, not accustomed to meeting someone like me who was transitioning. I admit I expected a mixed reaction to say the least! His brothers and sisters came down to Norwich for the big meal as usual. I'd met several of them before, but only as male. How would they react to me now? I was really nervous that day as we arrived at the house, but there was no turning back. If they ignored me it would be worse than being openly belligerent. I knew my own working class family in Scotland would have been openly hostile and probably very aggressive. But it was something I didn't want to duck. I was determined not to hide from now on. I dearly hoped people would accept me, but if they didn't I would understand and move on.

We arrived late and everyone else was already there. I was feeling very self- conscious, but as soon as we got in the door Les's sister Mary came straight over to me and gave me a hug, steering me into the kitchen where Sue was cooking and the rest of the women were hanging out. She got me a drink, and soon I was chatting happily with the other women, who it seemed went out of their way to welcome me into their group. Meanwhile the guys were in the lounge drinking beer. The party had split along gender lines, so I still had to face the men, whose group I'd been part of for the previous couple of years. Presently, after a drink or two, the two groups naturally met up and mingled as we sat down to dinner. I walked into the lounge where the table was set, and

Mary's husband Mal came over and gave me a hug and everyone else followed suit. Nothing specific was mentioned about my different appearance, I was made to feel very welcome and still part of the family by everyone. From that day on all of Les's large family couldn't have been more accommodating and helpful to me, always getting the pronouns correct and calling me 'her' and 'she' etc. It was very thoughtful, and I will be forever grateful for their kindness that day and in the future. The only reference made to my transition was when we played the traditional post dinner board games and Les and Mal joked that I had gone to great lengths just to get on the women's team, which won every year.

However, I still couldn't tell my own parents. I knew the reaction from them would be a lot different. The Norwich GIC and Charing Cross had issued some unofficial guidance about how to inform your loved ones and family that you are transsexual, and had started treatment to transition permanently. It was based on a very middle class sensible letter, that explained how you had always felt, how unhappy you had been, and an apology for not telling them before. But you were still the same person, and still loved them, and hopefully in future they would understand and eventually accept the situation. This sample letter was credited with great success, and an insistence that the vast majority of families would come to understand and in time actively support the transsexual person. That may well be the case for most, but it hadn't been written with the Glasgow sectarian working class in mind! Especially my parents. So for now I put it off.

* * * * * * *

As the year 2000 went on and I waited for my referral to Russell Reid, Alice and I discussed the future. We obviously knew that I would soon be on a hormone regime, and with that I would eventually become sterile. But we both wanted another baby, especially me. Alice knew how much I loved children and, though we had Cherry, we had almost lost touch with my son Joe after the custody battle, and I rarely saw him now. I still desperately missed him. We knew that we had a window of opportunity to achieve a pregnancy before it would become impossible, and, without going into too many details, we managed it. Later on in the winter of that year, Alice announced to me she was pregnant. As we approached Christmas and New Year we looked forward to our baby being born in May of the next year. I was absolutely delighted.

The year 2001 was also the year Russell Reid finally got my transition back on track, and there would be no going back this time. I had been attending Norwich GIC over many months in preparation for getting a schedule of appointments arranged with Russell Reid in London. By now I had begun to really lose weight due to giving up booze. I was generally feeling much better within myself as my future looked to be settled and my transition assured. I was advised by Barbara to change my name by deed poll, since the government still didn't legally allow me to change gender on my official documents, but, she advised me, there was a loop hole! If I could present to Russell Reed a legal deed poll change of name document when I visited him, then he could provide me with a letter certifying I was transsexual and undergoing NHS gender reassignment treatment. This letter from Russell could also be presented to the DVLC and they could change my name and gender on my driving licence, and the same information could then be applied to the passport office to change my passport.

Wow! This is what I'd been desperate for ever since I was seventeen and first attempted to transition. I was blown away that I could finally do this. Times were indeed changing. Also, once my driving licence and passport were changed, the DWP would change my name and gender on all official records for tax, benefits and employment. It's hard to express just how massive this was for me. The lack of female I.D. and documentation had severely hindered me all of my adult life.

When the day eventually came for Russell Reid to give me this precious letter that would allow my documents to be changed, he also asked if I'd like another to keep on my person at all times, in case of arrest by the police. He called it a 'get out of jail card'. It was a reminder that there were still big problems for people like me who could be targeted by the police for using a public toilet which someone thought was not gender appropriate. I could also easily be charged with soliciting if a policeman decided I was dressed as female in an attempt to offer my services as a prostitute. Attitudes to transsexual people had changed a lot by the turn of the century, but it was much slower to penetrate the offices of the police and justice system.

With the imminent arrival of our baby, I thought I should let Barbara and the Norwich GIC know. I knew she would find out anyway. Previously, I would have had grave misgivings about telling Charing Cross anything like that, but Barbara was ahead of her time, and she saw no reason why transsexual people should be barred from having children. Our elderly GP, Dr Cole, was encouraging, too. In fact, in his last week before retirement he signed my statutory deed poll for change of name. He didn't charge me the usual fee for this, but called it a gift and wished me well for the future.

It's difficult for most people to understand today how things were then, and it's not that long ago. Being gay was a reason that was often used by the courts to stop people from having any access to their own children. Gay marriage was a distant dream, and gay adoption was thought of as laughable. Can you imagine what it was like being labelled transsexual?

* * * * * * *

As 2001 continued, things in general seemed to be finally going well for us. We had support from Alice's parents, and my Norwich friends were happy to see me transitioning again, because they knew it was the correct thing for me. And now the NHS was actively supporting us as a family, rather than the negativity we experienced when Cherry was born. A wind of change and optimism was definitely blowing in the country. However there had been one slight fly in the ointment. I had been walking along Holt Road early one evening and just as I turned into our bungalow I heard a man's voice shouting 'fucking tranny' towards me. It wasn't the first time. I didn't see who it was, so it must have come from a passing car on the busy road. It was enough to give me a bit of concern. I knew there was still no shortage of transphobia and anti- gay sentiment around, but it was becoming much rarer , so I was a bit shocked it was so blatant. I was even more concerned that whoever had shouted to me must know where I live. I mentioned the incident to Barbara the next time we met.

At the following appointment I had with Barbara at the Norwich GIC, she told me she had been thinking about the incident of transphobia I'd mentioned previously. It was clear she had decided that it was time for me to hear some home truths. Did I understand that relationships rarely survive sex reassignment surgery? If Alice and I managed to stay together post surgery we would be a very unusual couple. Perhaps I should begin to prepare myself for the prospect of having to move out of the family home? I got the feeling that Barbara was as much concerned about our children as me, including the baby that was due. Did I really want to bring the danger and worry to our home that my being transsexual could attract? Of course I had absolutely no doubts about Alice. We had been through so much together already, and I had always been completely honest about my situation with her right from the start. We had no intention of splitting up, it was the furthest thought from my mind. But Barbara insisted it could do no harm in making pre-emptive arrangements, just in case. She suggested that if I were to put in a housing application to the council, in my circumstances, and with the Norwich GIC's support in the form of a letter, then if needed I could get a flat. Would I like to do that, anyway? If it wasn't needed, then no harm done. By this time I was in contact with many other transsexual woman on the online Yahoo message boards, and I had to admit Barbara had a point. Almost everyone I knew online had split from partners and families, sometimes with a lot of animosity and distress. I knew the courts were very hostile to transsexual women when it came to access to their children, never mind parental rights. Being transsexual was also an accepted reason for a partner to gain a divorce on the grounds of unreasonable behaviour, despite it being classified as a medical condition by the NHS, an example of the double standards applied to transsexual people. Can you imagine someone being divorced for the 'unreasonable behaviour' of having cancer or heart disease?

I decided I should be realistic, and so I talked it over with Alice. I asked if she thought this would ever break us up. I told her I had no intention of ever leaving her, and she said she felt the same. But eventually we decided maybe it would be worthwhile taking the offer of help to find a council flat for me, just in case. And, anyway, who knew what the future might hold? The bungalow on Holt Road we were living in was a private let, just like the house in Stalham, and we had had the rug pulled from under our feet there with just six weeks' notice. Social housing was relatively easy to get in those days; no one wanted it when mortgages were so easy to get. If nothing else it would be good to have a secure council tenancy to fall back on. So I put an application in for housing with the support of Barbara and the GIC. Within weeks I was offered a small property in Wroxham, a little Norfolk Broads town ten miles north of Norwich. It was a first floor flat overlooking a square and just round the corner from the shopping centre. The property was allocated to me through a local housing association, and it was described as being in a 'safe community environment'. When I read this I imagined it was some kind of sheltered accommodation, probably with a lot of elderly and pensioners. But, as it turned out I couldn't have been more wrong!

The Wroxham flat was part of what can only be described as a roof garden complex. Built on the first floor, you would never know it was there from street level. But once you climbed a set of stairs, you came through a door into a wide open communal garden space surrounded by neat little houses. The first day I arrived there were groups of people hanging out in the garden area, their front doors left open, as they socialised together with drinks and the definite aroma of cannabis drifting all around. Alice and I walked through the peaceful scene towards my front door on the far side, and as we passed people we were met by friendly smiles and 'Hi's from everyone. 'Are you moving in?' I was asked by a smiley faced girl in her early twenties. When I responded in the affirmative she introduced herself. "I'm Kathy, I live in number nine". I smiled and introduced myself and Alice. Next we were surrounded by others, all very friendly and welcoming. We'd met and been introduced to over a dozen people before I'd even reached my door. Most of my new neighbours were in their late teens or early twenties; this was no retirement community! I loved it at first sight. Once inside, Alice and I had a look around the new flat. It had a large lounge with windows overlooking the street, a decent kitchen and a nice sized bedroom. I was very glad I'd taken Barbara's advice; this was the perfect bolt hole if things ever got too difficult in Norwich.

Within a few weeks I'd got to know most of the people at the Wroxham flats. It was ostensibly a community for people the council felt were, in different ways, vulnerable. Some had been in care for most of their lives, others were ex offenders, there was a handful of people with mental health problems and several drug addicts. I suppose I should have been a little offended that the council had deemed me, as a transsexual woman, to be someone who had a 'problem' that needed to be placed in this safe environment. But in the end it didn't bother me, as the reason I'd taken the flat was to get a secure tenancy and anyway, almost everyone I met there became a trusted friend over the next few years. Some of them I am still close to.

One day not long after I'd been allocated the flat, Alice went into labour. We were at home in Holt Road when the contractions started; we called the hospital and they decided to send an ambulance right away. I followed on in the car and we arranged for Cherry to be collected from school by Sue and Les. It was a much shorter labour than it had been with Cherry. I sat there in the maternity ward until 11pm and everything seemed to have stopped; we thought it wasn't going to happen that night. The nurse told me I might as well go home and wait. They would call me if anything happened, but they expected the birth was going to be at least a day later. Instead of going home I went to Tanya's house to chill out with her and the twins. I'd hardly got in to Tanya's place when I got a call from the hospital to say Alice's contractions had restarted and I should get back as soon as possible. Alice was really strong, and later on that evening she gave birth to a beautiful baby girl. As previously with Cherry, I was present and holding Alice's hands for the duration of the birth. This time she was more relaxed, and she didn't draw blood from my hands with her nails!

After the birth we placed the baby in the hospital cradle next to Alice's bed and then we both snuggled up in the hospital bed and fell asleep in each other's arms. In the morning, after the baby had been checked and given the all clear, we carried her down to the car and drove back to the house. The new baby was beautiful and the spitting image of her elder sister Cherry. We called her Danni, and when I realised she had been born on my grandmother Agnes's birthday ninety nine years before, we gave her the middle name 'Senga' which is Agnes backwards and a Scottish tradition.

Chapter 31 'Changes'

Hormones

It was now time for me to officially begin hormone treatment. I finally had an appointment arranged to see Russell Reed in London. I will admit I had already started self prescribing at the beginning of the year. As well as meeting new friends who were transsexual like myself, online, I had discovered the existence of online pharmacies where you could purchase almost any regular medication without the requirement of a doctor's prescription. I was already receiving parcels from the other side of the world containing Premarin tablets, which could have been of dubious and unknown quality, but which I'd found very effective.

It had been ten years since I'd been promised hormone treatment by Russell at Charing Cross. I was now approaching age 37 and desperately wanted to begin to reverse the poisoning of testosterone. But I have no regrets about those years. I considered myself very fortunate to have two beautiful daughters, who I would not have had if things had gone to plan at Charing Cross, and if Russell hadn't been forced out of the GIC back then. I considered myself lucky compared to many of my trans friends who had got their hormones earlier, but had lost the opportunity of having children of their own. But I also knew that now I had an uphill battle to regain my femininity.

Russell's clinic at that time was in Earls Court, London. On my first appointment with him I travelled down alone on the train. I didn't know exactly what to expect. Would he remember me from Charing Cross? Would he prescribe on that first appointment or would I have to wait? If he insisted on a blood test then he would know that I'd been self prescribing. Would that get me into trouble? I knew it would have been a big problem at Charing Cross. I finally arrived at the clinic and entered. His receptionist smiled and asked me to take a seat in the small waiting room. There were several other transsexual women sitting there, and I could see they ranged from very advanced into treatment to relative newbies. As I sat down, some of the others nodded and smiled towards me. This was a relaxed atmosphere and a world away from the tension filled waiting rooms I'd experienced at the NHS clinic, ten years ago, and just a few miles away. When it was my turn, Russell himself came into the room, called my name and asked me, with a grin, to please follow him.

Russell looked a bit older; his face had filled out and he was no longer the stick thin, rather straight laced character I remembered. He looked far more relaxed and comfortable in his grey casual suit. His hair was also longer and swept to one side in a rakish flourish. In short,

I could see he was a happier man than he'd been at our last meeting.

I began by informing him that we'd met before back at Charing Cross. "Do you remember me?" Russell smiled warmly, and told me of course he remembered me. Whether that was entirely true I wasn't sure, it had been ten years after all, but his manner was always friendly and designed to put people at their ease. I reminded him that I'd been due to start hormone treatment back then, but when he left my treatment plan had been changed by the other consultants. He apologised for what had happened, but things had been very difficult and beyond his control. "Let's concentrate on where we are today, shall we, Ally?" I agreed. Russell then began referring to his notes, asking me to confirm the information he had about me, and I realised he'd actually kept the records from our last meetings all those years ago. He had updated these with new information sent to him from Norwich Gender Identity Clinic. He inquired about Barbara Ross, and asked me to pass on his regards when I next saw her. They were clearly good friends as well as colleagues. Both had the same supportive attitude to patients, as opposed to the traditional challenging confrontational style of Charing Cross. The appointment lasted about an hour, and after some final questions on my physical health, Russell confirmed he was happy to prescribe a three month course of hormone treatment for me, based on my previous diagnosis and the updated medical information supplied to him from Norwich. He also dictated a message to himself on his Dictaphone regarding a letter which would be sent to me to enable me to change my documentation from male to female, as described earlier. And that was it. I walked out on air with Russell's hand written private prescription in my bag. I would be able to convert it to an NHS prescription at the pharmacist, so it would be also be free of charge. Ten years may have passed but Russell had not changed; he was still the kind compassionate man I remembered.

My life was finally coming together again. I was older and a bit wiser now, so I had to plan for the time when I could no longer earn money from the white goods business. That time came quicker than expected. Within six months of being on my hormone regime my muscle strength had dropped dramatically and I was not strong enough to casually pick up fridges on my own, as I used to. When I went to the waste disposal tips to collect items, I invariably had to ask for help now from the site managers to load up, if Alice wasn't with me. That was noted, as well as my weight loss. I'm sure they thought I was ill.

One day, as I drove out of our driveway in the Renault Traffic van I used for business, I heard an almighty bang come from the engine or gearbox. The van trundled to a halt; there was obviously a serious problem. I called the local mechanic I used, and he came out for a look. He concluded I needed a new gearbox, and the cost of buying and fitting that was more than the van was worth. I took that as a sign it was time to give up that business for good. I asked him to take the van away for scrap and that was the end of the white goods enterprise. I had to think of another way to earn money as quickly as possible.

The physical effects of the hormone treatment were less obvious in the beginning. I did notice within months that my skin was clearer, softer and felt much more fragile. It was as if I'd had a thick layer of outer skin removed. I felt the weather more keenly, heat or cold. I also bruised more easily and felt pain far more acutely. Even from my own limited experience I understood to a certain extent how much more fragile and delicate female skin tone and structure is compared to male. If a man punches a woman in the face it's the equivalent of punching a child. Most men don't understand this but they should. A male body has a tough exterior barrier that women don't have, so male violence on a women is like a hammer blow. I even noticed a difference in my body odour. My hair, which had always been very thick, changed too. It became frizzier and more full. Unfortunately, by this time, I had begun to develop some male pattern baldness at my temples and crown, and though I didn't lose any more hair, I didn't regrow any in these areas either. Physically, the most noticeable reaction to the oestrogen was breast development. It started within weeks, and my small boobs began to ache under the nipple as I felt the tight buds begin to develop. Perhaps strangely, I enjoyed this pain because I knew the hormones were working and my body was changing. But it was bloody painful if I walked into a door or something because that part of my body now stuck out much more. My face became fuller as the hollows in my cheeks filled out. The hair on my body didn't decrease but it became much finer. The one area that didn't seem affected at all was my facial hair. I still needed to shave every day before applying make- up, and sometimes shave again in the evening if I was going for a night out. I had been forewarned by the Norwich GIC and people I'd chatted with online that I'd need to start electrolysis treatment to remove the facial hair, or perhaps, if I was lucky, IPL

(Intense Pulsed Light) would work for me. Whichever method I would employ, one thing I soon discovered was that it would definitely be very expensive. Most transsexual woman, me included, do not realise at the start of their transition that facial hair removal will inevitably be the most painful and expensive part of the treatment. It will cost much more than surgery or the price of a hormone treatment, and the NHS will not pay for it. In my own case I estimate I spent somewhere between £25,000 and £30,000 over four or five years, which was an awful lot of money back then. Especially when you consider sex reassignment surgery was around £5,000 and breast augmentation (boob job) was under £2,000. The other obvious effects of the hormones were felt in my genitals. I could no longer achieve erection or orgasm, as the organs seemed to shrink and diminish. This was absolutely fine by me because I had always despised the sight of what was between my legs if I was forced to look at it, and now it became much quicker to tuck and easily hide it.

But by far the biggest change caused by the hormones was not between my legs, it was between my ears. Literally within days of starting oestrogen my world expanded. I felt as if the curtains had been pulled back and the light let in. Rather than viewing life as a small television screen, suddenly I was experiencing it on a panoramic giant screen. Colours were brighter and more varied, and although the 'screen' was all encompassing it was as if I could pick out details that I hadn't noticed before. All my senses and emotions seemed to be heightened. Songs on the radio had more depth and subtlety than I'd previously noticed. I remember at the time I tried to speak to female friends about this experience, but it was not something they recognised and they probably thought my enthusiastic babbling was a bit weird. But of course, they had always been oestrogen fuelled in their interaction with the world and it only felt normal and natural for them. For me it was a happy revelation; I never expected it to feel so good.

But it was also a roller coaster, especially in the first few months when my testosterone levels were fighting with my oestrogen levels for dominance. I did cry often and for no obvious reason. One night, alone, I cried for me. I went through in my mind my previous life, growing up in Scotland. The violence, the poverty, the friends and the enemies, my little dog, my parents who I knew I'd probably never see again. I cried for the boy who I'd been. I felt such pity for him and I was literally feeling sorry for myself, but the sobbing was good; it was therapeutic, it was needed and I felt much better afterwards. My tears at this time were not always self focused. I could simply see an old lady walking past the house and start crying because her coat looked old and worn. A happy child cycling in the park, a moth dancing round the bathroom light, an advert on TV for bread -the list of things that could set me off was extensive and varied. But probably what set me going the most was music. I would play my old Bowie, Lou Reed, and Joan Baez records and every new song brought floods of tears and emotions along with memories. By far the worst was Leonard Cohen. I could hardly get through one side of an album without a box of tissues and needing to redo my make- up afterwards. I could only really listen to music on my own because my sobbing was embarrassing in company. Fortunately, this phase passed and I eventually managed to control my emotions as I learned to regulate my hormone intake.

When it was time to return to Russell Reid some three months after my previous prescription, he asked how I was feeling. I had to check myself, because I knew my enthusiasm must sound a bit manic and over the top. However I explained I was very, very happy with my hormone treatment and I would NEVER go back. He seemed pleased, and concluded that oestrogen definitely seemed to agree with me! Russell also confided in me that I was unusual among his clients, one of only approximately twelve per cent who returned for more hormone treatment after the initial prescription. Most of his clients who presented to him as transsexual women could not handle the side effects. Oestrogen made some people feel ill, or they discovered the effects on their sexual organs, lack of erection or ability to orgasm, etc., to be not what they wanted. Russell said it was a kindness to allow people the opportunity early on to experience the effects first hand of hormone treatment, rather than have them come back for years to multiple appointments, wasting time and money, and possible giving up relationships or losing families in the belief they were transsexual, when they were not. This sorted the wheat from the chaff quickly, and stopped people making big mistakes with their lives. And the physical effects of the three month course of treatment were completely reversible.

I'd been hassling Barbara back at the Norwich GIC by this time, asking when I was likely to get a surgery date. By the end of 2001 I was ready. Would I still have to still complete the two year 'real life test' before I got a date? Who would be the surgeon, would it be Charing Cross for surgery or Leicester where my friend Rachel had just been given a date with Tim Terry? Another Norfolk friend had been told she would have the surgeon Mike Royle at the Nuffield hospital in Brighton. This was the power of the internet. Suddenly transsexual women were in touch with each other and knowledge was power. The doctors didn't like it, because not only were we becoming aware, we were exchanging information about which surgeon was deemed better than another. Web pages sprung up that looked like present day comparison sites with reviews of surgeons, not only in the UK, but all over the world. Many people I knew were travelling to the US and we were also beginning to discuss Thailand and the far east. Thai surgeons had been at the vanguard of sex reassignment surgery, way ahead of what was happening in Europe. But most people were unaware of them until the internet, when the smart Thai surgeons employed good web designers to display what they were doing in English translated pages. The choice was opening up, especially if you were able to fund your own surgery. I was still dependent on the NHS, so my choice was limited to surgeons working in British hospitals, but compared to most of the world we were very fortunate. At least I could get top class surgery in a modern clean environment for free. My American sisters were paying what seemed to me like a fortune that I could not ever afford.

Barbara and Dr Olive told me to be patient. Yes, I would still have to go through the full two year long 'RLT' despite the fact I'd done it all before. These were the rules. And, Barbara asked me, without being unkind, was I fit for surgery? I knew what she meant; I was still overweight. I'd dropped at least six stones since Stalham, but I needed to lose more and tone up the flab.

I decided to turn the Wroxham flat into a gym and workout space. I installed a stationary bike, a rowing machine and an ab crunch frame. I started driving up there every day for a minimum 3 hour workout on my own. I'd play a lot of house and dance music and go through a regular exercise program. It was shades of Borstal circuit training! I also used the Cindy Crawford workout video. My god, that woman was so fit and strong!. Her video was a wonderful help. I followed it every day for over two years.

During my regular workouts in Wroxham I got to know much better the girls who were my neighbours up there. They heard my music playing and asked me what I was doing, because sometimes it would be nine in the morning, or nine at night. I just arrived when I had the free time. Pretty soon I was inviting them in to work out with me. Natalie and Kathy were the two most regular visitors. We'd all work out and have a dance, then afterwards chill out with herbal teas or a glass of wine. These women were all years younger than me but we all clicked. I decided to be honest and tell them I was a pre op transsexual woman. They must have guessed as much and were not bothered; they were even kind enough to say they hadn't realised, but they must have really. In fact they became actively supportive. I made some very dear friendships during this time. These girls would have my back on many occasions in the future. They had their own stories of why they were living in our little rooftop community. Natalie had been brought up in care, her mother and father had split up when she was a baby, her mum had become a born again Christian and joined a commune, her dad had disappeared. Natalie's time in care had damaged her. It was a story I was to hear time and again, physical and sexual abuse, foster parents only interested in her for the funding they received. Natalie was also a very beautiful girl and attracted attention from men with dubious motives, in my opinion. Her boyfriend at this time was a drug addict, a nice enough guy but completely out of control. Kathy had had a similar upbringing, but she had got pregnant very young, and she and her boyfriend, who was an alcoholic, had been given the flat. They had no money because he spent it all on booze. Others included Marie, who when I first met her was an extremely butch dyke lesbian. With shaved head and carrying about 4 stone extra weight, she looked quite fearsome. She had also been diagnosed as schizophrenic. Sarah, another young girl, was often suicidal; she was a self harmer with slash scars all over her legs and arms. But when I explained my own history and journey, they all got on board to help and support me. I was like the focus that united them and enabled them to forget their own problems for a little while to offer me advice and help. I became their project. I have always been lucky with the people I've met; usually they, like me, were looked upon as the lowest in society, whether in Borstal, gay bars, on the streets of London, NHS clinics or even this Wroxham community of misfits. I always met and made friends with beautiful caring people. I naturally gravitated to the girls in the community, but there were men there, too. And one in particular, Markie, became a good friend. He liked to look after all the girls up there. His story was tragic too, Markie was in his mid thirties, he'd been married with two children and living a normal everyday life going to work, paying the mortgage, etc., until one day he was involved in a road accident on his motorbike. His back and leg were smashed up and he was in hospital for a year as they tried to put him back together. During this time he was on morphine for the pain, and by the time he was fit enough to leave hospital he'd become addicted. His addiction eventually cost him everything and he lost his home and family. During the time I knew him he was in daily methadone treatment, but he still topped that up with vast quantities of alcohol. He'd been provided with a flat to get him off the street, but he was still a hopeless addict. Markie was the nicest guy. and very protective of everyone in our little community.

* * * * * * *

Meanwhile, back in Norwich, money was getting very tight. With a new baby and me no longer earning, we were living off Alice's disability benefits, which were not much. I decided to start a wig supply and cutting business. It was something I could do from home and I thought if I specialised in trans clients then I could attract a lot of people from my online presence in the community. I'd heard countless stories of trans girls being treated with contempt when they were trying to buy wigs, or just having their hair cut in female salons. I had a lot of experience from my days with Tanya when we owned the hairdressers at Vamps and makeover service at Metamorphose. I still had contacts with wholesalers and so I opened a business account with Trendco, who were one of the UK's largest suppliers of wigs and hairpieces. This line of business also had the added advantage that when I was preparing for my own electrolysis treatments, for which the operator needed to have at least two days of beard growth, I was still able to see trans customers because they understood why my face had obvious facial hair showing. It's really not easy trying to work at the same time you are having regular facial hair removal treatment. most of the time you either have stubble in preparation for removal, or red blotchy damaged skin as the after- effects of the treatment. So if you are going to treatment once a week, for four days of that week you will not want to be seen in public.

* * * * * * *

The wig business took off in a small way. I did have a lot of customers visiting me, some from as far away as Scotland and Ireland, but the profit margin was very small. What I had failed to allow for in my financial forecasts was that these trans girls were nearly all as broke as me. Usually they were unable to work because of the same problems I had, facial hair removal, name and gender documentation, family rejection, etc. In short, being trans usually means learning to be very poor and lonely. But the upside was that I did meet many clients who became friends. I had a cohort of trans women who were all going through the same treatments as me at the same times, visiting the same clinics and having the same problems. It got to the stage that I became quite well known in the circles we all operated in, and I could turn up to see a surgeon, IPL operator or a psychiatrist and know half the people in the waiting room. This even extended to clinics abroad in later years. In the meantime I still needed a way to make money. My own electrolysis treatment cost £50.00 a session, which was a lot of money to take out of our family budget, with Alice, me and two children to provide for. I needed to think again how to make some serious cash.

2002 began the way 2001 had ended. We were really struggling financially. I felt guilty about the money we spent on my hair removal and trips to London to see Russell. Each appointment could decimate the week's budget. At least my hormone treatment was free. By this time I'd had my driving licence and passport changed to reflect a female identity and name, but that didn't help much when seeking work as female, if I was looking male with beard stubble half the time.

One day I remember we had been on a trip to the coast at Yarmouth, and I had the girls and Alice in the car. I was due hair removal treatment the next day, so I had no make- up, neutral clothing, and beard stubble. For some reason a police car started following us on the road back to Norwich; eventually the blue lights came on and I pulled into the side of the road and the cop parked up behind me. I got out and walked back to him as he got out and met me between our vehicles. He started off by saying, "Do you know why I have stopped you sir?" I said I didn't. Then he told me I'd driven too fast through road works a few miles back. I didn't argue. Next he asked whose car was I driving. I said "My own" He looked quite excited by this comment and demanded to see some proof of ID, as in his opinion this car was not mine. Of course I knew what had happened, the registration had come up as a car owned by a female, me. But I certainly didn't look very female that day. I handed him my female driving licence and he looked at it, stunned. I could see his mind working behind his eyes trying to figure out what was happening here. I just smiled at him. He took my licence back to his car and radioed in to check it, and naturally it matched with the owner of the car and the address I'd given him. I could see he was bamboozled by the whole situation and didn't know what to do next. Eventually, he came back to me and gave me the licence back, mumbling something about taking care while driving through road works, then he offered me a "Thank you for your cooperation, madam," as he turned and left in a hurry.

* * * * * * *

This kind of thing wasn't every day, but it could happen at any time, I was caught between two physical gender appearances in this stage of my treatment. It wasn't the first time I saw people in a quandary when they had to address me; was I male or female? I admit I even used the situation to my own advantage occasionally, much to the disgust of some of my transsexual friends who believed we should never compromise our identities. I had made the discovery that when buying a car, for example, a woman would be treated completely differently from a male buyer. And that's how I occasionally became my own wife!

The discovery came about due to my own problem with my voice. Barbara at the Norwich GIC had arranged for me to attend speech therapy at the local hospital, in an attempt to feminise the tone and pitch of my voice and my pronunciation. I found these sessions very hard going and had my doubts about whether it was necessary. When I was dressed and presented as female no one ever doubted face to face that I was a woman, regardless of my voice. It was only on the telephone where I'd invariably be referred to as 'sir' or 'mate' by whoever I was speaking with. A confused silence would then follow if I had to give my female name and title. Similarly, if I called up a seller about a car I wanted to buy, if it was a man, he would tell me all the information I needed to know and be far more honest about the condition. However, if I started the conversation by providing my female name, then the details would be less forthcoming and I'd be treated like a child. The way to overcome this presented itself by accident one day. I called a seller who had advertised a car I wanted in the newspaper. I asked about mileage, rust spots, gear box, the condition of the tyres and electrics etc. His answers were all forthcoming and detailed, as he answered me as 'mate'. Finally, he suggested I come along there and then for a test drive, as he was sure I'd be happy with it. And besides, he wasn't going to be around again until the next week. An idea came to me. I suggested to the seller I was too busy to come along myself at this time, but I'd send my wife, as the car was for her anyway. Would he give her the test drive instead? Of course, he replied. So, within ten minutes, I was down at the showroom as my own wife to view this car. The man who I'd only just been speaking with on the phone had no clue at all I was the same person. He instead showed me how comfy the seats were, how easy the car was to drive (even for a woman) and waxed on about the colour and room on the back seats for children. It was amazing the difference in approach he had to me as a woman rather than to his perception of me as a man on the phone. I used the situation even more to my advantage when it came to the price. As we haggled over how much the car was worth, I informed him that my husband had insisted I didn't spend any more that the figure I now suggested, which was well under the asking price. He hummed and hawed and even suggested I phone my husband and persuade him that the car was worth more, but I stood firm. "No, my husband will not allow me to spend more than the price I've offered. He told me to walk away if you won't accept that. Sorry, but he'll be angry with me if I offer more. But I really like the car," I said with a smile. Remarkably, the guy folded, and gave me the car for the price 'my husband' had suggested, because he could see how much I loved it. He was doing me a favour because he wanted to see the lady happy.

Confused? I wasn't. You have to have a laugh on occasion, because it's often pretty grim the situations you face going through transition. I was playing a dual role and it worked. I used the same twist on several other occasions. Notably one time when my car wouldn't start, I was the other end of the city from my home and I didn't have breakdown cover. I knew there was a garage along the road so I walked along to it and asked for help. The mechanic insisted he needed the car in his workshop to look at it, and so it was towed in, where several mechanics all crowded round. They put the car up on a ramp and then insisted I needed a new engine fitted, that would cost £1700.00. I told him I'd need to think about it. I knew they were at it. I caught a taxi home, and got 'my husband' to phone the garage, and they caved in immediately, and admitted that after another inspection all that was required was a new starter motor costing £35.00. I could write an entire book on about the subject of how differently men and women are treated. But that's for later.

* * * * * * *

In the spring of 2002 I had been on my hormone regime for a year and was feeling good. My emotions had stabilised and the feminising effects were become far more obvious. My waist had narrowed and my body fat had been distributed around my hips and lower tummy. My breasts had developed into an A cup and with the help of the silicon breast enhancers looking a bit like chicken fillets, that I'd purchased from Boots the chemist, I was wearing a 36 B bra. My muscle strength had reduced by at least fifty per cent. All of this, combined with my regular work outs at the Aylsham flat, lowered my weight considerably. I'd lost eight stone since my near death health scare in Stalham. I was now no stronger than Alice; in fact I was asking her to open tight pickle jars for me, as my wrist strength in particular had gone! Danni was a year old and I loved the fact that she would never know me as anything other than female. Her brother Joe in Scotland knew me only as male, and Cherry, the middle one, was there to see the transition period.

I was still trying to earn a living from the wig business, but it was difficult. The one upside from the wigs was that I had made literally hundreds of friends in the transsexual community. Hardly a day went past without a visit from someone looking for a wig or a trim. Girls travelled from all over the UK to visit me and we often socialised afterwards. Alice and I also had lots of invitations from these girls to go to parties and nights out in Sheffield, London and Manchester. If we could arrange for the children to be looked after by Alice's parents, and we were offered free accommodation, we often went. I had by now converted the back bedroom in our bungalow to a wig studio and built a dividing wall in our large kitchen to convert half of it into a bedroom for Danni and Cherry.

Life was pretty good, my transition was going well and our social life was certainly taking off. The only downside was that we were still always so short of money. I was still thinking of future employment around this time and decided to go on a counselling course. It was run by a very respectable organisation in Norwich and was affiliated to the University; because of my financial situation I was able to sign up for a reduced fee. So I began training as a person centred counsellor. I hoped in time this would provide me with employment, but in the meantime we needed something else urgently to cover my very expensive hair removal costs.

Chapter 30 'Walk on the Wild Side'

'Suzanne & Monique'

I suppose it was inevitable the line of work I eventually entered to pay for my electrolysis treatment. I'd read often enough on the online forums about trans girls making a living as 'escorts'. We had even seen it, especially in Manchester when we had visited the gay village with a hair customer of mine, Debbie, who had become a good friend. By now I knew about a particular breed of men that were in the main attracted to transsexual women. They were called 'TF's' for short, which translated as Tranny Fuckers, or the polite version Tranny Fanciers. I admit I found it astounding that so many, apparently straight, men would be attracted to trans women, specifically over cis women. But a walk round the Manchester gay village on a Saturday night demonstrated the truth of this. Especially a bar called Napoleons, which Debbie had taken us to. The trans girls would dance in the middle of the floor and be surrounded by men ogling at them. Then you would often see the girls pairing off with men and leaving for a short time as they concluded 'business' up a side street.

* * * * * * *

One night I read a message on one of the online forums from a trans woman who I will call 'Nicola' who was openly discussing that she had taken up this line of work to pay for her surgery, She was very professional and safety conscious in the way she operated, advertising only online on a few select web pages. She had financed her surgery in America and afterwards returned to her job as a teacher. I was intrigued, so I sent Nicola a private message asking for more information, as I told her I was considering following her into the oldest profession. Nicola was very kind and helpful; the post I'd read was quite old and she no longer worked as an escort, but she recommended I try it if I needed to earn proper money quickly. I would either be suitable for 'the game' or not; she advised that most girls would find it was not for them. The main thing she told me was to never work on the streets or in bars like the girls I'd saw in Manchester. Only work from a safe address, a flat or a house where you could monitor who was visiting, and if possible, don't work alone.

Unfortunately this is where, perversely, the law makes life very difficult for girls involved in escorting, or

– let's be blunt - prostitution. It's perfectly legal to work as an escort, as long as you are on your own, but it's also a widely acknowledged fact how dangerous it is to work on your own. But if you work with some one else, to keep each other safe, then it becomes illegal as you can be charged with running a brothel, or one of you charged with living off 'immoral earnings.' I thanked Nicola for her advice, and the web site addresses she gave me, and I began to work out out a plan. But first I needed to talk with Alice.

After a lengthy discussion one evening it was agreed. We needed the money, Alice and I trusted each other completely. We decided to try it. I'd only work from the flat in Wroxham and keep this private and away from the children. I'd advertise as a pre op transsexual escort and I'd offer 'full and complete massage' but I'd draw the line at penetrative sex. Alice would work with me when she could, as my maid, so I was not alone.

To be honest, we had no idea what we were doing, and I don't think we ever thought we'd get any punters. In the beginning, Alice and I looked at it as an adventure; we had nothing to lose and we thought, if nothing else, it would be a laugh. I figured we only needed one customer per week to cover the cost of an electrolysis session. One thing was in our favour. The national website, where I uploaded my ad, had no other pre op transsexual girl in Norfolk advertising. It was also free to advertise and so I'd uploaded a few photos of myself. I was wearing a wig and heavy sluttish make up. so it would have been difficult to recognise me. I used the name Suzanne (as always, I invoked Leonard Cohen as my good luck charm). The contacts were made through chat rooms and a Pay As You Go mobile phone that I made sure never left the flat. This was the very early days of online escort advertising and we had no great expectation of anyone actually ringing.

That first evening I tried it, we had arranged for the children to go to Nana's. Alice and I went to the flat, and with great hilarity got dressed up in what we assumed the punters would like. I had a black Victorian lace up corset with suspenders and stockings and thigh high black leather stiletto boots. Alice wore a leather mini skirt, heels, and a low cut leopard skin top. I went to the web page and clicked the button to say I was available that night, and joined in the live chat. We actually had a bottle of wine and nibbles available for anyone who turned up, as if it was a little house party and the vicar was coming round, that's how naive we were! Alice and I were still laughing and joking about the whole situation, saying to each other "how mad are we?" As we made up stories about the kind of men that would turn up, never believing any of it, as we giggled about the absurdity of being prostitutes, … then the phone rang.

We looked at each other in shock. Fuck! It's a punter. Alice said,"You'd better answer it." I said,"No, you're the bloody maid, it's your job." I think we both hoped the ringing would stop, but it didn't. Alice yanked the phone off the table. "Hello, how can I help you?". I was slapping my head in exasperation. "What are you saying?" I was mouthing to her, "He's not calling for a fucking taxi!" But she shooed me away, covering the mouthpiece and telling me to shut up and sit down. Alice asked the client his first name (Brian) and what time he would visit and for how long. It was £50.00 for an hour, and he decided he'd like to come for two hours. So she read back his phone number to him and then told him the address with directions. It should be noted that we were at least aware enough to insist in my advert that withheld numbers would be ignored, and the phone numbers of those who didn't show up would be circulated within the chatroom. This was simply following what we had seen other girls doing, but it turned out to be very important.

About half an hour later a short middle aged man was knocking at my door. I'd watched him approach across the courtyard and made sure he was alone. Alice opened the door and there he was, our first ever punter! Alice welcomed him in and showed him to the lounge where I was sitting dressed as described above. The lights were subtle and I had Bowie on the turntable playing softly. I showed him a seat on the sofa and helped him take his coat off. "Before we go any further, Brian, can you give me the fee, please?" I asked with a smile. He complied right away, handing me £100.00 for the two hours, and then he sat down. I took the cash to Alice who was sitting in the kitchen, then offered him a glass of wine which he accepted gratefully. This was pretty weird; he seemed like a nice guy, cockney accent, with an open friendly face. With my 4 inch heels I was towering over him, so I sat down next to him on the sofa and started chatting. It was all so civilised and English as we talked about the weather and how easy was it for him to find the address. He settled back and relaxed and we spent the first half hour in pleasant non- sexual conversation. I was conscious of the clock on the wall and wondering how I was going to spin this out for two hours. I began stroking his inside leg with my scarlet painted nails, and I could see this was having some effect on him as she shifted his position to accommodate his erection. Next, Brian surprised me by asking about Alice. I said she was 'Monique' my maid (this was the name she chose to use) and that she was there to make sure I was safe. He agreed this was a good idea. "You must get some very funny characters turning up here?" he asked." Oh, yes, we've had a few, but mostly it's nice gentleman like yourself just looking for a relaxing time," I lied, trying to give the impression of vast experience.

Then Brian asked, "Errr… can Monique join us, Suzanne?" I certainly wasn't expecting that! So I said the first thing that came into my mind, that if Monique joined us the price would have to be double. "Oh yes, no problem about that," he agreed, "I have the money here." I told him I'd have to ask her and went into the kitchen, feeling concerned at this turn of events. But Alice was sitting there with a big smile, she'd heard everything, and was already rubbing her hands at the prospect of the money. Nodding away at me. I could see she was trying not to laugh out loud. "Yes, yes, tell him," she whispered. So we both went back in to the lounge and sat on either side of Brian. 'Monique' surprised - no, shocked - me, in her forwardness with him. She asked Brian to get undressed (something that stupid me had forgotten to do) and began stroking his legs and groin area over his pants. His penis was bulging out of his Y fronts by now and I was trying to slow the whole scene down by asking if he wanted another glass of wine. This is how naive I was, thinking that if he came too quickly then what the hell were we going to do for the next hour? Of course later on I learned that this was not my problem; if a guy came in and shot his load right away and then decided to leave, then he still paid for the whole period of time he'd booked. You don't get a discount for an early finish!

The way it went after that was unexpected. 'Monique' stood on the sofa, with her legs on each side of him and forcing her leather mini skirt covered vagina on to his face and grinding away. I did a double take, what the hell? She'd got herself into character fast enough! I positioned myself on my knees on the floor between his legs and began stroking his penis. I had the foresight to have condoms close by within reach and managed to slip one on to him. As I grasped his penis and gently massaged I was preparing myself for giving him a blow job, but before we got to that stage he started thrashing and moaning, his arms flaying and thrusting his groin forward as his penis began jerking and pumping, Brian ejaculated for a couple of minutes into the condom. His face - or what I could see of it behind 'Monique's' thrusting hips -was a mask of pleasure. Eventually he was spent. Monique stepped down from the sofa and sat next to him, while I got some baby wipes and removed the condom and cleaned him up, then sat on the other side. I was eyeing 'Monique',wondering what we would do next. But I needn't have worried. Brian was happy and relaxed and put his head back to rest it. "That was fantastic, girls, thank you, thank you." He closed his eyes.

After a few minutes of silence, I asked Brian if he wanted more wine. But he said he'd love a cuppa, if that was possible. Of course, no problem. I looked hard at 'Monique' "Can you make Brian a cup of tea?" I was trying to remind her she was supposed to be the bloody maid. Eventually she took the hint and went off to get it. Brian sipped his tea as he got himself dressed, and once he was sorted he sat down again and finished the cuppa. "I need to be going, thank you for a lovely night. I really enjoyed that, and I will be back," he said. We both saw Brian to the door and he left with still forty minutes of his time left. We watched silently through the kitchen window as he walked away across the courtyard, then through the door that led down stairs. It was only then that Alice and I looked at each other and beamed smiles and whoops of laughter at each other. "We did it, we fucking did it!" we both screamed, as Alice got the bank notes and threw them in the air and we hugged and kissed as they fell over us. £200.00 for less than two hours work. Wow! I would have had to sell five wigs to five customers to earn that!

* * * * * * *

Within a few weeks I felt confident to work on my own, but still keeping in contact. Alice had been with me the first couple of nights but plainly with two children we couldn't keep that up, as someone had to be at home at night to look after them. Fortunately my friends at the flats, Kathy and Natalie, helped me out. They had obviously noticed that my lights were on at night and a few times had popped by to say hi and invite me for a cuppa and I had to shoo them away. So I felt I'd better be up front with them and I took them into my confidence and explained I was escorting. This was no surprise to them, as they had already noticed a few strange men visiting me. In that small close knit community you couldn't hide much from your neighbours. I was glad I was honest because they offered to help me out. The word spread among the other neighbours that could be trusted and, while they may not all have actively supported me, they kept an eye out for me, as we all did for each other up there. If it was a night I was 'working' I would always call in to Kathy or Natalie before I started and let them know, and if I had to call them then they knew I had a problem, and they should come and bang on my door. But they even went above and beyond that by making a point of saying hello to any men who walked across the courtyard to my door at night, just to let them know they had been clocked. As another precaution I always falsely advised new clients casually that the courtyard was covered by CCTV for security reasons. But the truth is I had very few problems.

Most clients were like Brian, decent blokes just looking for a few hours distraction. I also had several transvestite clients who wanted to spend some time with me and get dressed up themselves. I had no problem with that. You could tell they were usually married men who had very little opportunity to indulge in their fantasies at home. they usually brought with them a plastic bag full of awful female clothes, purchased from charity shops, and often a tatty old wig that had been kept hidden somewhere, like behind the spare wheel in their car. After a while I provided a wardrobe of female clothes for punters, and actively encouraged the transvestite customers because they were no trouble, always grateful and easy to please. Many just wanted to dress up and then sit and chat with me over a cuppa. Of course some wanted more and expected a 'happy ending' to the session. I was happy to oblige.

I can count on one hand the clients who were a problem. This was usually caused by their own fear of themselves. I had a few who arrived very drunk full of bravado and I could tell that they had needed to fill up on

Dutch courage because they were inexperienced and probably hiding their own shyness. I could usually talk these guys round and settle them down, but very occasionally I had to stand up, give a man his cash back and tell him to leave. Once this happened the decision was final. I would not ever change my mind. I had threats but they were usually hollow. One afternoon a guy turned up and he was obviously pissed; he was very macho but wanted to be dressed as a girl. He was visibly shaking with rage. Luckily, Alice was there that day. We tried to get him to chill out and relax but he seemed so angry. At one point he referred to me as 'him' and I asked him politely not to do that, but he started to argue about it, insisting I was a man. Before I even got the chance to challenge him Alice had grabbed his coat and threw it at him, ordering him OUT right now. His money was tossed back to him and he sheepishly gathered it up and departed. Alice took no crap, and she was a tiger when it came to defending me. The only other real troublemaker was a guy who came a few times and was no problem, he liked to chat and have a massage that ended with a blow job. But then he started arriving with no cash. I told him he would need to go to the cashpoint and come back, which he did. But he did this several times, until one day he demanded credit, saying he'd pay double next time. He also demanded on this evening that I use a strap on rubber dildo to fuck him up the arse! This is something I would never dream of doing; it was alien to me and I told him no. But he wouldn't leave. I could see he was getting angry, he was a lot bigger and stronger than me, and I thought he was going to physically attack me. Eventually, just to get him to leave, I persuaded him to go and check his balance at the cashpoint, and said I'd take part payment. As soon as he left I banged on Natalie's door and told her what was going on. She grabbed her boyfriend Shaun and banged on Markie's door, telling him to get over to my flat right now. When the punter came back he was met by the four of us and told to sling his hook and never come back. He was shouting at me, calling me a cunt and promising to inform the cops on me as he left. I didn't see him again, but he sent me some nasty text messages and I put his number on the webpage as 'one to avoid'.

An aside regarding the police. On a completely unrelated incident I had a visit one evening from two cops, one female and one male. They asked if they could come in for a quick chat. So, rather than have them standing at the door, I agreed. They came in and informed me that they were aware I was escorting. But they had just come to see if I was ok and ask if there were any problems to report. I denied that I was doing anything illegal and said there were no problems at all. I got the feeling that they were checking up on whether I was being coerced or the victim of trafficking. They certainly were not trying to get evidence to arrest me, and were actually very friendly. I managed to assure them I was ok and they eventually left. But I wondered how they knew. It was quite reassuring that they were ok about my business, and just concerned that I was not being exploited.

One night, and it also happened to be a night Alice was working with me, a young guy arrived. He was around twenty years old and very feminine looking, but nervous. He wanted to dress as female and talk for a while. Both Alice and I were thinking the same thing, that he would look fantastic with a bit of make- up and the right clothes, so we both took extra effort with him and applied make- up properly, a nice styled wig and even some of our own clothes. The transformation was incredible; he looked absolutely natural and could have passed easily. When he looked in the mirror he burst into tears. As we chatted, it became clear he was actually more likely a transsexual woman. He began describing his early life and feelings, and how much he would have preferred being born a girl. This was such an authentic and honest story that it could have been me speaking when I was that age. I began crying, too. I provided 'her' with some information and useful contacts, Barbara Ross's contact info, and the NHS Norwich GIC address. She was not very optimistic about a future life as female because of the pressure of family and friends. She was terrified of ever being discovered and 'outed'. It was so sad, but I knew better than to push her. It would have to be her choice in the end and I knew it was not an easy road. I gave her her money back as she left later on that evening and wished her luck. I hoped I would see her again in the future but sadly I never did.

I found escort work to be the easiest money I've ever made. I'm not saying that flippantly, but describing how it was for me personally. I had the mindset that I could switch off when I had to do anything that I might normally have found distasteful. I was never emotionally involved and, as I am someone who is basically asexual, it was only ever work. For me it's like when you have to clean up someone else's vomit or shit, and as a parent that's not unusual. You just get on with it because it's your job!

But most clients were pleasant enough anyway. Also I came to the business out of need, not desperation. I needed the extra money to pay for my hair removal treatment, not to feed a drug or alcohol habit, or to pay the rent, and it wasn't because someone else was forcing me to do it, like a pimp, who demanded the money I was earning. I was in control and I could stop any time I wanted. That's not the case with all girls and I understand that. But the laws around prostitution, in my opinion, make it far more dangerous for the girls than it needs to be, and forces them to work on the street. Some 'feminist' viewpoints make me quite angry; the wish to 'save' girls from prostitution based on a moralistic dogma seems to me to be completely at odds with the other feminist view that a woman has a right to be in control of her own body, what she wears, who she has sex with and the right to abortion. Why does this promotion of female empowerment suddenly stop when it comes to whether or not a woman wants to sell her labour, if the job she chooses is in the sex industry? But it's ok for a woman to sell her labour in a backbreaking low paid zero hour contract job cleaning the homes of the middle class elite feminists? Those who push to make prostitution more dangerous and outside the law deny women the legal protections that they should have.   I knew I had a limited shelf life as a 'pre op transsexual' escort. It was the fact I was pre op that attracted the type of men I did. Even though none of them ever saw what was between my legs, they knew, and it fascinated and titillated them. I once made the mistake of advertising myself as 'she male' without understanding what this description signals. Of course I was inundated with request for penis pics and measurements in inches. All very unpalatable to me, who could hardly bear to look between my own legs, far less than take photographs to post online. I knew that immediately after I became 'post op transsexual' my appeal would drop off dramatically, I would have nothing special to offer and I'd be competing for clients with cis women who were far more attractive and younger than me. However, later on when I needed to, I did change my escort category to female dominatrix, once I was more experienced and the hormones and facial surgery had taken full effect. But meanwhile I was happy just to be earning.

I was making enough to cover my hair removal costs quite easily, despite the fact I could only work about two or three days a week because of stubble and after treatment damage to my face. By this time I'd discovered a beauty clinic chain called Saks who offered IPL treatment at a good price, and they had a clinic in Ripon, North Yorkshire, that was specifically favoured by transsexual women. I had a couple of friends who used that clinic and were very enthusiastic about the operator, Mary. She knew what was required for girls like us and offered extended IPL sessions to make the long trip worthwhile. Conveniently, I had a transsexual friend Sophie, who lived in nearby Richmond, and she offered me a bedroom to stop over, so I regularly started to drive up there from Norwich every other week to have IPL with Mary. It was a very painful but effective treatment. Mary would carry on with the session as long as I could stand it, and sometimes this went on for hours. Afterwards she smothered my face in aloe vera cream and I hid my swollen red visage from public display at Sophie's house that night. In the morning I'd cover my ravaged face and neck with make- up as best I could and drive back to Norwich with the windows open and the cold air blowing on me. The results from these aggressive sessions were very encouraging. My face was finally clearing. By the end of 2002 I was really making progress.

* * * * * * *

Now that immediate money problems had been solved, I began to think about how much else I could get done towards my transition during this, probably limited, period of affluence. I had always planned to have Facial Feminisation Surgery (FFS) at some point in the future. My nose in particular was not a pretty sight and was a reminder of my younger days of gang violence when I'd broken it, twice. Some of my friends and hair customers had had FFS done, usually in England, America, or sometimes Belgium. But increasingly people were talking about Thailand, where the surgery costs were so much cheaper. I knew a few girls, both trans and non trans, who had gone out there for boob jobs and were really happy with the treatment and the results. There was one surgeon in particular, Dr Suporn Watanyusakul, who ran the Suporn Clinic in Chonburi, which specialised only in transsexual surgery, from FFS to full sex change. His reputation in the UK was not well established at this time, but he was becoming more and more popular, as many girls went out there and came back with great results which they posted enthusiastically on the UK online forums.

My friends Sophie and Jane, who were both hair customers of mine, had booked for full sex reassignment surgery with Dr Suporn. They judged, correctly as it turned out, that his prices would quickly rise the more well known and popular his work became in Europe and America. They wanted to access his clinic while it was still affordable. They had both booked for the following June 2003, and I admit I was extremely envious. I wanted my own sex change done as soon as possible but the NHS had already agreed to treat me, so it seemed silly to pay a lot of money to go to Suporn, when I was getting surgery free at home. However, I felt I could now probably afford to pay to get my facial surgery done with Suporn if I kept on working as an escort. I thought how good it would be if I could book to go to Suporn Clinic at the same time as my friends, so we could all look out for each other. After all, it is a bit scary going abroad for major surgery on your own. I decided to talk with Alice about it and see what she thought.

I showed Alice the Suporn clinic web page one night. It was full of detailed information regarding the surgical procedures they offered, including before and after photos that looked very impressive. But what really swung it for us was that we both knew some of the girls in the photographs, so we were aware they were genuine and not enhanced. What was not openly listed was the prices. The reason given for this by the Suporn Clinic was that each price was tailored to each client and the amount of work required. The clinic insisted on a full set of high quality digital images of a prospective client's face, side on, frontal, and oblique angle. Based on these photos and other medical information provided, they would come to an estimate of the cost. This price could go up or down a little once the patient was physically examined by Dr Suporn in his clinic. But, at least you had a good ball park figure. Alice suggested before we go any further we should get the photos of my face taken and send them off with a suggestion of which surgical procedures I thought I needed. I agreed and the pics were taken and emailed to the clinic where they would be analysed by Dr Kim, who was the person in the clinic at that time who assessed what surgical procedures were required and calculated fees.

Dr Kim had already made a reputation for herself among the western online transsexual clients. She could be very frank and honest about what procedures she felt were needed. This straightforward and candid approach did sometimes upset some girls. She was widely described as 'very scary' but I believe she was always simply giving an honest opinion. Trans women can tend to be very subjective about their own appearance, and I dare say somewhat delusional on the subject of their own faces (including myself). Dr Kim was not a woman to mince words. A Korean by birth, she was also herself a transsexual woman and had gone through many of the surgical procedures she now advised on. I trusted her judgement and honesty. I felt she had my best interests in mind despite the somewhat brusque comments she made in her emails.

along with the digital photos I sent to the clinic were my suggestions of what surgical procedures I felt were needed for my face. Firstly, my twice broken hooked nose needed straightening. I also thought my brow ridges were too prominent, a consequence of testosterone poisoning. My upper eyelids were quite hooded and wrinkled through years of late nights and a misspent youth. I also thought my very large earlobes would look better if reduced. Finally I would benefit from a lip lift, which would reduce the area between the bottom of my nose and my top lip. This procedure also included a plumping of the top lip through a Botox type filler. Once I'd sent off the email to Dr Kim I sat back to wait for her conclusion and suggestions. It was a nerve-wracking few days waiting for the response.

* * * * * * *

When Dr Kim finally got back to me, her suggestions were as follows:

Forehead Reconstruction- removes prominent male-like bossing around the forehead and eye orbital rims

Rhinoplasty- reshapes and resizes the nose to a feminine appearance. Can correct asymmetry or pre-operative defects

Upper and lower Blepharoplasty- tightens sagging upper and lower eyelid. Additionally, an injectable filler such as Aquamid can be used to remove 'crows feet' from the outer corners of the eye area

 Lip Lift- reduces the distance from nose to upper lip, giving more feminine proportions and appearance. This has the effect of slightly rolling outward the upper lip giving a fuller juvenile effect. It is achieved through a shallow 'v' incision immediately below the nose.

These procedures were suggested and advised by Dr Kim. Of course I could agree or not; it was my choice. She had added the lower blepharoplasty to my suggestion of upper, because quite correctly she pointed it out it would like odd to have wrinkle free upper eyelids alongside untreated lower eye wrinkling. She also advised there was no reason to reduce my ear lobes as they looked fine by her judgement. The fee was £3,600.00, to be confirmed on physical examination by Dr Suporn at the clinic. This price included hospital stay, drugs, all after care and daily clinic consultations for three weeks post op. Dr Suporn would only accept me as a patient if I agreed to a minimum of three weeks post op care. This wasn't a pop in, quick fix surgery plan. I would have to commit to all the post operative care and the time that would take. There was a Mercure hotel near the clinic that Dr Suporn recommended for me to stay in for the duration of my visit, post op. The clinic had an arrangement with the hotel so I would get a reduced rate. All Dr Suporn's patients used the hotel and his staff visited each one, every day, in their rooms, as well as the regular clinic visits. I calculated that with the cost of the surgery, flights and hotel, the whole package would cost approximately £5000.00. Thai hotels were incredibly good value in those days, even without the Suporn Clinic discount.

In those days, compared to the prices being charged by British and American surgeons at the time, this was amazingly inexpensive. Also, none of the western clinics offered or insisted on the aftercare period that the Suporn clinic did, so that made me feel safe in his hands. But what really decided me was the fact that Thai surgeons had a very long and detailed history of transsexual medical surgery. At that time the Thai surgeons were technically and culturally years ahead of anything the west could offer, which was down to the fact that transsexual people have long been an accepted and valued part of life in Thailand. They had the surgical knowledge, experience, and acceptance of transsexual people that could not be matched in the west, where we were often treated as though the surgeons were doing us a favour and we should be eternally grateful.

As we came to the end of 2002 I was feeling very hopeful that I could have the facial surgery I needed. My hair removal treatment was gradually but obviously taking effect. The more treatments I had the less I would need to budget for in the future. If I kept working at the present rate we could start to go into profit each week as I needed fewer treatments. Also, with fewer treatments I had less preparation and recovery days, and thus I could be available for clients more often. But we needed a lump sum up front for the Suporn clinic. I would have to wire the clinic around £600.00 as non- refundable deposit to book my surgery, and then pay the balance on arrival at the clinic. The only way we could do that would be if we borrowed money and repaid the loan over the next year, as I wasn't able to get a bank loan without wage receipts. So we decided to have a talk with Alice's parents, Sue and Les.

It must have sounded like a mad plan to Alice's parents when we approached them for the loan. I had printed off the surgery procedures, with the prices, that the Suporn clinic had recommended, together with the total amount needed for flights and hotel stay. As I was showing them, even I felt this all sounded very self indulgent. They had absolutely no knowledge of how I was earning money at the time except for the wig and hair business, so they also didn't know if we could ever repay a loan. It must have looked like a long shot that they would ever be repaid. But they listened patiently as I showed them the figures, the before and after photos, and explained how much this surgery would mean to me.

Also, the very idea of going abroad for surgery was very new at this time. Les wondered if I might not be better off going to a UK surgeon. What if I had a medical problem, or infection, or the clinic was corrupt and inflated the price? These were all reasonable questions. I could give no guarantee. My plan was based on personal recommendations from friends and online acquaintances, and my own extensive research, none of which was available to Sue and Les. In the end, and to my eternal gratitude, they backed my judgement and agreed to lend me the money. I wired the deposit to Dr Kim and my surgery date was booked for June 2003. With the post-operative recovery period I would be in Thailand for just under a month, and I'd be there at the clinic at the same time as my friends Sophie and Jane.

* * * * * * *

With the surgery date booked I intensified my fitness regime. I worked out every day at the flat for at least two hours, followed by an hour of hectic dancing to House and Trance music, often with the girls at the flats joining me. By that spring my weight was ideal for my height and age, I'd not been this fit since I was a teenager. I had lost over 8 stone or 115 pounds since Stalham. I now only drank red wine occasionally and was very careful with my diet. However, I still smoked. I wasn't ready yet to give that up.

As the summer approached, there was still something nagging at me that I knew I could no longer put off. I would have to tell my parents that I had transitioned. Over the course of the twenty odd years since I'd left home for London, I'd not told them anything about my transsexuality, my periods of previous transition, my treatment, or my legal name change. How much of it they had guessed I didn't know. I had still always kept in touch by phone during this time, as they had kept up regular contact with my son Joseph and he visited them most weeks. During these visits I would often speak with him on the phone. Joseph was a teenager now and he would also need to be told. It was not something I was looking forward to. But I couldn't hide it any longer; after all, the effects of the hormones had had a big effect on my body. I already had breasts that were difficult to conceal, I was half the size I'd been since I last saw Joseph, and by the time I came back from Thailand my face would look different, too. And, if everything else went to plan, I'd have full sex change surgery by the end of that year or in early 2004. My NHS funding was in place and my RLT was due to be completed. It was just a case of deciding which UK surgeon would fit me in, and where the hospital would be.

I decided to follow the Charing Cross GIC advice of writing a letter to my parents and several other members of my family who I'd always been close to. I needed to explain everything in detail. I knew if I tried to speak about it over the phone to my parents they would get angry and probably hang up as soon as I started. My hope was that if I wrote a long detailed letter then they would read it, get mad and outraged, but then go back to the letter in a calmer mood later and read it through properly. Neither of my parents had mellowed with age; in fact they were worse than ever, both alcoholics who spent as much time fighting with each other as other people. They were only united in their drunkenness. My father in particular seemed to have completely lost the plot. He would call me up at odd hours to rant and rave about my sister, calling her really awful disrespectful names like a whore or a stupid cunt, and expecting me to call her and relate this stuff because she wouldn't speak to him. During this time Carolyn was working away as a top civil servant in the MOD, living with her partner of many years in a house in Bristol she had bought. She was the model of respectability. So if that's the treatment she got from my parents, imagine what they would think of me when I told them they had lost a son and gained another daughter?

Chapter 31 'The Letter'

It was time to write the letter to my parents. I began by telling them how sorry I was that I'd not spoken with them before, but that I'd been worried about their reactions. Now I had to be honest. I was transsexual. I explained exactly what that meant, including the medical definition, and the treatment that I'd been offered by the NHS. I reminded them of the times I'd attended the Douglas Inch centre in Glasgow as a teenager, and now I could finally tell them exactly why I was being treated there. I recounted my experience of growing up, feeling different, of my dreams and prayers that I would one day be female. I had not changed in these desires since I was around three or four years old, when I sat knitting little jumpers for my action man. I had hoped I would grow out of it, and when that didn't happen I'd fought against it by trying to become more masculine than anyone else, and that resulted in all the violence and dangerous situations I'd put myself through as a teenager; borstal, the stabbings, the cuts and bruising and hospital admissions I'd both caused and received. I apologised for the worry I'd given them for my safety. I revealed the suicide attempts, which at the time I'd fobbed off to them as accidents.

I had to tell them that none of the distractions worked, I could never run away from myself and in the end I had accepted it. I was transsexual, and the only way I could live was if I let 'him' go, and lived as her. I still loved them and hoped they could at least accept it one day, if not yet understand how I felt. I informed them I was having facial surgery within the next few weeks but I would like to come up to the Vale to visit them when I came back, and have a talk with them. I had the full support of Alice and Cherry, Alice's parents and all my friends in Norfolk. I assured them I was exactly the same person as I'd always been. I hadn't changed, but my appearance would. I was about to undergo some serious surgery under general anaesthetic that would take more than five hours. If by bad luck something went wrong during the operations, then it wouldn't be fair that I hadn't even told them about this beforehand.

The actual letter was much longer than this summary and contained a lot more information. I took three days to write it, edit it, rewrite it again, to make sure I'd covered everything. Finally I asked them to take some time after reading the letter before contacting me; to discuss it between themselves first, even make an appointment with the GP and talk it over with her if they thought it might help. Then I typed it up and printed it off, making sure there was no misunderstanding caused by my dreadful handwriting. I showed it to Alice, and she agreed I had covered everything and been as gentle as I could be, given the subject and the shock it would cause. I inserted it into an envelope and kissed it for luck before putting it in the post box.

We didn't have to wait very long for the response, as a letter from my parents arrived by return post. It began:

"Don't ever DARE come near our house or street ever again.

It went on in a badly handwritten scrawl to tell me I was "a disgusting fucking poof, a cunt and an embarrassment to them and the whole family". If I tried to contact them again they would call the police. Also I was not to contact anyone else in the family, especially my son Joseph, and they would leave instructions to make sure I was banned from attending their funerals. It ended by informing me I was dead to them. and "Don't write or phone EVER again."

My instincts had been right. Although this was the reaction I had expected all these years, it was still shocking to see the vile words and undisguised hatred scribbled across the page of a cheap lined page ripped from a notepad with the serrated edge still there at the top, as if in their haste to get this message back to me they couldn't even wait to trim the paper or correct any of the numerous misspellings.

I imagined them together back in their council house in the Vale as they wrote this, my mother probably pacing the room in her drunken fury, spitting out insults to be included, her eyes narrowed as she tried to conjure up words that expressed her full loathing. My dad sitting, rum glass in hand, his eyes like bullets bulging with anger and outrage at 'fucking queers' and what I'd done. Both fearful their shame would become public knowledge as they hurriedly compiled the reply to me and shoved it roughly in an envelope, out of sight of any passing visitor who might happen to call by and see it, before they had the chance to post it.

unfortunately I had already defied their order not to speak to anyone else in the family about this. At the same time as I posted the letter to them I'd sent similar but personalised letters to six other family members, those who were closest to me as I grew up, and who had meant the most to me. None of those cousins, aunts and uncles ever replied.

I had emailed my sister to let her know I was going under the knife in a foreign country to finally achieve what I'd spoken to her about many years earlier; my desire to fully transition was about to be realised. I was scared but happy, and I hoped I would see her soon. No response was forthcoming from her, either.

I never spoke to or heard from my parents again from that day onward. They never contacted me, or even my children (their grandchildren living in Norwich) ever again. No birthday or Christmas cards for the girls, no phone calls, nothing. I'd obviously, in their view, contaminated my children with my queerness and they were also to be whitewashed from history, just like me. I learned later that my parents, with the connivance of Sharon, had encouraged my son Joseph to believe I was dead and never to be mentioned again.

Strangely, my transsexualism was the catalyst that brought together my parents and Sharon, I suppose in mutual condemnation of me. My ex- wife, who would at one time leave the room as soon as my parents entered it, now became a drinking buddy and great friends with them. I had also written to Sharon to let her know about my transition. I felt she needed to know, as it was only fair that Joseph would be entitled to be told at some point in the future. Sharon had written back with a similar hate filled homophobic rant to me, threatening me that if I ever contacted Joseph I would be sorry, and dismissing Alice as 'my retard wife'. Her letter was so disgustingly abusive of me, Alice and our daughters that I actually snatched it from Alice before she could read it. I didn't want her to see such hateful ignorant comments. It would have upset her so much as she had always thought her relationship with Sharon was friendly. I hid that letter so she would never see it.

I did try to build bridges several times over the next ten years or so, but they would never respond to my messages. I sent them photos of the girls periodically as they grew up, with a note to say they could contact them any time, even if they chose not to speak to me. I gave our address and phone number, but never had any reply.

My mum died first; she had a stroke and collapsed one day. I received a text message from my sister to inform me. Of course, none of us were welcome to the funeral. The following year my dad, by now living on his own, very elderly and suffering bad health, had a heart attack. He was taken into hospital and he too died, alone.

A few months prior to his death Alice, our youngest daughter Danni and I had taken a week long holiday to the Lake District. During this trip I intended to take Danni the further 100 miles journey to Glasgow one day, so she could see the Vale and Loch Lomond where I'd grown up. A week before we left for the holiday I decided to give it one more try, and asked my sister to contact my dad to let him know we would be in the Vale area. Would he allow Danni to visit him? A lot of water had passed under the bridge, many years had gone by and my mother was dead, and it was probably his last chance to meet his youngest granddaughter, whom he had chosen to ignore all those years, and who had now grown into a beautiful young woman. It was time to forgive and forget, I suggested. But sadly no, he refused to see her, and so died, like my mother, without ever seeing his granddaughter. They both took their hate to their graves.

* * * * * * *

I've never understood what this rabid aggressive homophobia was all about, or where it came from. I specifically call it homophobia because my parents never acknowledged transsexuality as something that existed. I was dismissed as a 'poof.' At the time, and over the years since, I was never angry with them. I just felt genuine sadness that they could feel such hatred to the extent that they cut themselves off from one of their own children and two grandchildren. When I was growing up they had always been casually homophobic, but no more or less than anyone else at that time. My dad had always encouraged me to read books and learn about other cultures. He was in the left wing working class tradition of using the local library to educate himself and stood up for socialist principles like the NHS, unions and equal rights. But with my situation there was a blind spot, so maybe it was just personal? I'll never know because we never spoke again after that letter.

When my father died and his will was announced, as expected I and my two daughters were cut out and left nothing. What was a surprise is that he cut out my son Joseph, too. It seems his homophobia, directed principally towards me, also extended to targeting my children to add additional hurt to me from beyond the grave. The whole estate, including a house, car and jewellery, worth approximately £100,000, went to my sister Carolyn, who was relatively wealthy, had no children, and already owned a house. Sadly, much to our surprise, she decided to uphold the document of prejudice and endorse the hate behind it. I think Carolyn fell into my father's trap, she refused to share a penny with anyone, thus alienating herself from her closest family, her nephew and nieces. So the poison of bigotry was perpetuated, just as I believe my father intended.

Chapter 32 'The First Cut Is the Deepest'
Thailand

By early spring of 2003 I was preparing for my trip to Thailand. I'd booked my air tickets and had all the recommended vaccinations that my GP had suggested. I had a transsexual friend, Sian, who lived near Heathrow airport. She had offered me a place to park my car for a month, and she would also drop me off and then collect me from the airport when I came back. I had made arrangements with another friend, Rachel, to do any driving for Alice and the children, including any shopping trips, doctor's appointments, etc. that might be needed while I was away. That was a great thing about the transsexual community in those days. We would all help each other out. It was still novel to meet transsexual women online who had been through all the same stuff growing up that I had. We quickly became friends and we were supportive of each other. On this trip I would be travelling alone, but I'd soon have company, as my other two friends, Sophie and Jane, were already in Thailand having flown there a week earlier.

In an effort to save money I'd opted for the Russian carrier Aeroflot. This meant I would have to change planes at Moscow where I'd have a stopover delay of five hours before I made my connecting flight to Bangkok. My overall travelling time would be eighteen hours. It was the first time I'd used my female passport and I was excited if a bit apprehensive.

* * * * * * *

Aeroflot was an experience not to be forgotten! The flight from Heathrow to Moscow was like being on a factory works outing. Everyone was drunk, and it seemed everyone smoked(you could still smoke on aeroplanes in those days). I was allocated a seat beside a Russian bear of a man, massive with a huge beard, who offered me vodka from his bottle as soon as we were seated. Over the next four hours he tried to chat me up, kiss me, buy me food, and discuss football. I actually quite enjoyed his attention; he was very funny and it made the journey pass more quickly. The in- flight meals were unique! A heavy set middle aged Russian woman stewardess walked along the aisle with a large basket containing packets of salted peanuts. She shouted in Russian "Who wants a bag?"

And if you did, you put your hand up and she threw one at you. This created much hilarity as passengers scrambled over each other trying to catch a bag.

These Russians on the flight certainly seemed to be friendly 'party people' similar to the Scottish. I really enjoyed their company, but upon arrival at Moscow I came across probably the most rude and unfriendly Russians ever! They were all employed by the airport in passport control, the shops and bars. What a contrast. The woman in the airside coffee shop was probably the worst. I entered the empty shop, took a stool at the counter, and looked across at the only staff member on duty, who was reading a book. After about five minutes, she looked up at me and scowled. I smiled, with my purse in hand, ready to place my order. The woman yawned, ignored me, and went back to her book. I gave it another five minutes, then I asked "… err can I have coffee, please?" I received another angry glance, a sigh, then she turned her back on me and went back to her reading. Defeated, I slunk out. I ended up in the 'Irish pub' instead, where I sat at a table with some rather friendlier Russians and an English man. I got chatting and recounted my experience in the coffee shop. The Russians laughed. "that's the legendary Muscovite native rudeness, they pride themselves on their discourtesy," I was told. After encountering two similarly rude and unhelpful women working in the souvenir shop, I had to agree they were world class!

The onward flight to Bangkok was almost empty, so I was able to stretch out across three seats to make a bed and sleep for hours. It was the best flight ever. Upon arrival I approached the passport control with my documents, I was asked only one question,"why are you visiting Thailand?" I followed the advice the clinic had given gave me, and simply said 'medical'. That was it, I was through, my new passport was ok and my Thai adventure had started.

* * * * * * *

As I came out into the arrivals lounge there was a throng of hundreds of people shouting names, some waving cards with names written on them. After a few minutes I saw a tiny Thai woman waving a card with my name and I waved to her. She approached me with a big smile and gave me a hug. This was my introduction to Wannee, a nurse and driver from the Suporn clinic. What a nice welcome! Next a heavily built Thai man appeared from behind Wannee and gave me another hug, then grabbed all my luggage. We left the air conditioned airport building and I got my first taste of Thailand. The heat hit me like a wall; the smells, chattering, and the traffic noises all around me was sensory overload after the sterile atmosphere of the plane and the airport. I loved it; it was everything I imagined it to be and more. However, I didn't have the chance to see much of Bangkok that day because we still had an hour's drive to get to Chonburi where the Suporn clinic was located, some fifty miles away on the coast overlooking the Gulf of Thailand.

I arrived at the Mercure hotel and was met by my friends Sophie and Jane. We all hugged and kissed when we saw each other; it was exciting to be meeting up again half way around the world. Wannee booked me in and I was told I would meet Dr Suporn in the morning. That night we hung out in Sophie's room drinking coffee and ordering room service food. It was only now that it became real. Within days we would all be undergoing major life threatening and life changing surgery.

Sophie was a good bit older than me, in her mid fifties. She had a pretty face and a good figure, and she was very clever. We had a similar transsexual medical history background, but Sophie had hidden hers better and had transitioned much later than me. She was an ex Royal Air Force officer who, once she had left the service, had done really well for herself in business, working for a massive European car parts corporation in the Netherlands. It was a dream job, travelling all around the world and earning a massive salary. She loved her work, but when a new Chinese managing director came in she was ousted for being transsexual, because he claimed it wasn't 'compatible with his culture'. She was a natural language expert and could speak virtually all European tongues, and even now she was picking up Thai in the few days she'd been here. Eventually, in years to come, Sophie would relocate to live in Thailand and work for Dr Suporn, translating and answering the hundreds of international emails and phone calls the clinic received each week from prospective clients all over the world.

Jane was slightly younger than Sophie, an ex computer programmer from Guildford. She was very elegant and quite tall She also had held down a good job for many years, but when she had told her boss that she intended to transition she was gradually undermined and edged out of her position. Both had typical back stories of what often happened in those days to transsexual women in the workplace. Fortunately for both of them, they had left employment with hefty pay-offs and had good pensions, otherwise they would never have been able to afford to transition, pay for private surgery and go back to the UK to basically live a life of early retirement, because it was unlikely they would ever be employed again.

Both of these transwomen also demonstrated the class divide that was still very evident in the transsexual community. Very few could afford to do what they were doing. I was only here myself because I had great backing from Alice and her parents, and of course I had made the choice most would baulk at, and worked as an escort. Over the next few weeks I met many other trans women; the underlying defining reason we were all here in the best clinic of the best transsexual surgeon in the world was because each of us had managed somehow to access the funds. I knew hundreds of girls back home in the UK who couldn't, and that was so sad. But I also knew that we were among the first wave of transsexual people who could actually access treatment at all. The history of LGBT Pride goes back many centuries and we can look back now and identify people who were actually transsexual in that history but had no option of treatment. So I have always felt extremely fortunate.

The next morning I walked around the corner from the Mercure hotel to the actual Suporn clinic. By this time I was feeling a bit nervous about the major surgical procedures I'd signed up for. The building was set on the main road facing the busy Sukhumvit Road. Inside it was air conditioned and modern with comfortable sofas, a free coffee and soft drinks bar and access to the internet. It was a hive of activity, all overseen from the reception desk by Dr Suporn's wife, Aoy. As soon as I entered,

Wannee immediately grabbed and hugged me. She introduced me to everyone including a beautiful young Thai girl, Aey, who was the clinic secretary, but also so much more. Aey had perfect English language and would liaise between the clients and the clinic, trouble- shooting any problems and overseeing hospital admissions and arranging leisure activities. She became my friend that day and we are still in regular contact today. I was offered a seat and an iced soft drink, and told that Dr Suporn would see me soon. There were several other girls there, both clients and staff. Everyone was so very friendly and relaxed and I began to feel at ease.

Soon Aey ushered me into a room where Dr Suporn himself was sitting behind a desk. I was about to meet the great man I'd read and heard so much about. He was wearing a white doctor's coat with a stethoscope hanging round his neck. He looked typically Thai, with a pleasant even- featured face and a warm smile. He stood up, formally introduced himself and offered his hand, before indicating I should sit. I must admit I was in awe of Dr Suporn on that first meeting. I'd heard and read so much about him from his former patients who I knew online, not to mention the first hand descriptions I'd listened to the night before from Sophie and Jane. I expected him to be taller and impressively assured and smooth talking. But the first thing that struck me was how gentle and kind he seemed, very polite and humble but with an aura of authority and strength. From the beginning I felt I trusted this man, who had very compassionate eyes.

It was just as well I felt I could trust Dr Suporn, because after a physical examination of my face and head, he went on to explain the surgical procedures he had in mind for me:

Firstly, Forehead Contouring.

'The shape of a typical male forehead is more prominent over the brows (bossing) and less rounded overall in profile than in a female forehead. The re-contouring procedure removes the bony prominence, to provide a more typically smooth and rounded appearance. This involves a surgical incision horizontally across the hairline above the forehead. The skin is then peeled down over the eyes to allow access to the skull. Then the brow orbital rims bossing is shaved off and filed down to smooth out and feminise the shape.'

In my case, a controlled fracture of the anterior wall to realign (reset) it to a more posterior position would be carried out. 'This procedure is used when the brow bossing is prominent and the air sinus cavities are large (indicated by x-rays) with a thin anterior wall such that contouring would otherwise breach the sinus cavity. It also involves removing the anterior wall of the frontal sinus, and thinning it down to create a less prominent, smoother and more feminine profile. The thinned bone is then refitted, and held in place and reinforced with thin titanium plate and screws.

The bony prominence immediately above each eye is also removed by surgical process, and the surface where it was removed above the eyes is then ground down to create a continuously smooth profile with the rest of the forehead. The removed bone is discarded, and the forehead skin is replaced and stitched in place'. So, not for the faint hearted!

(In my own case Dr Suporn also gave me a little freebie, as while he was performing the above procedure, he removed V shaped sections of my scalp above the temples on each side where the hair had thinned, then stitched the scalp together, thus removing the effects of male pattern baldness caused by testosterone.)

My nose job – Rhinoplasty. This was slightly more straightforward.

'To change the shape and size of the nose to a more feminine profile. The procedure involves aggressive shaving of the bone, straightening the nose, cutting the cartilage, and contouring, then a fine sheet of hard silicone is implanted to improve the symmetry'.

Next - Lip Lift.

Lip Lift would involve a small incision at the base of the septum. My lip would then be brought up nearer to the nose. This shortening has the effect of rolling the upper lip outwards, giving the upper lip a more feminine 'pouting' appearance. This procedure exposes the upper teeth slightly which is another typical female appearance characteristic.

To finish off - Upper & Lower Blepharoplasty

This is a typical cosmetic surgery procedure that tightens sagging upper eyelids and under- eye bags. It basically removes wrinkles. An injectable filler would also be used to remove 'crows' feet' from the outer corners of my eye area.

When all this was explained and set out in detail with the use of a surgical skull model by Dr Suporn and Dr Kim (who had joined us) the procedures become very real and quite frightening. This was serious shit! Thankfully, craniofacial, aesthetic plastic and reconstructive surgery was Dr Suporn's stock in trade; this was not a little aesthetic facelift. He was experienced in rebuilding the faces and smashed skulls of road traffic accident victims. Dr Suporn certainly knew what he was doing and I trusted him.

The fearsome Dr Kim, when she joined the consultation, was very professional and open about exactly what would happen, how long the procedures would take and the recovery time and pain involved. It was not sugar coated, and at the end of the appointment I was asked if I still wanted to go ahead, and if I had any questions. There was absolutely no pressure. I could take my time to think about it. But I had no doubts. I asked for the consent form and produced the balance of the surgery fee in US dollars, cash. Dr Kim smiled at my eagerness, and said she would recalculate my fee based on the physical examination and medical evidence I'd provided. I should take a seat back in the main clinic and they would call me back in soon.

I went back out and hung around the clinic with the other girls and staff who crowded round to ask how it went with Dr Suporn. An American girl, Kayleigh, told me she'd had similar work done four months previously. Her face and forehead looked flawless, with no scars, which was encouraging. Then a Thai girl who was visiting, Dang, pointed to her head. "Same," she smiled. I was amazed; I didn't even suspect she was transsexual, she looked absolutely amazing, very beautiful. Even Aey pointed to her nose. "You will have my nose, it's very good, yes?" And she was right. I ended up with a lovely nose exactly like Aey's and a few others. We all joked it was 'the Suporn nose.' and I started noticing it everywhere around the clinic.

Eventually I was asked to come back into the back office to see Dr Kim. She had my file before her and a calculator. She had reassessed my fee and decided after personal examination it would be approximately £500.00 less than the original quote I was given. I was delighted and impressed by the integrity of the clinic. To be honest, if they had asked me for an extra £500.00 I'd have paid it! Next, some blood was taken from for an HIV test. Fortunately this came back negative, and that was another worry off my mind.

* * * * * * *

This summed up the Suporn clinic; they were pure class. This was the start of a long association I had with Dr Suporn over several years. He and his family became friends. My daughter Cherry would come to Chonburi in the future and Dr Suporn would take her to his beach house where she hung out with his older daughters. I visited his city house and played with his youngest daughter Eeb, who was only a toddler back then.

I, like many of Dr Suporn's former clients, could stop by the clinic any time in the years following surgery for any advice or even surgical repairs, free of charge. Even if you were only in the country for a personal holiday he would send staff to collect you from the airport and look after you. Once you had surgery with Dr Suporn you became part of his worldwide family for life. A rather different relationship from what you would get from a British surgeon!

I had a few days to wait before my admission to Aikchol Hospital, which was only two miles from the clinic and was where Dr Suporn operated from. It was a beautiful modern private establishment that I got to see first-hand as I went along for the ride when Sophie and Jane were admitted the next day for their sex change surgery. After they were both settled into their rooms I returned to the Mercure hotel, alone. There were other girls visiting the Suporn clinic at the hotel, some just looking for advice, and several who were post op and recovering. I met a girl from England, Kim, who had had her sex change surgery on the NHS at Leicester the previous year. She was a beautiful petite girl in her mid twenties. I was quite envious; she would not need any facial surgery, she looked stunning. Unfortunately her surgery had not gone to plan in England, the vaginal canal that had been created was twisted and had become constricted. She needed a complete restructuring, as she had only a few inches of depth. It was heartbreaking for her. The NHS had said they could not justify any more funding, and so she'd come to Dr Suporn for help. Sadly, he was not hopeful, and had told her it would be very expensive to repair with no guarantee of success, and she had very little money. She left a few days later to try other surgeons in Bangkok, so I never found out what happened in the end, but it was worrying to hear how the NHS had abandoned her. There was another girl I caught a brief glimpse of one day in the Mercure, as she plodded along the corridor outside my room in her dressing gown. Her blonde hair was tousled and her face looked tired. I said 'Hi' and she smiled as she headed back into her room. I asked Wannee about her and she said she had travelled alone from the USA and her name was Shauna.

She was only a few days post op and had just been released from the hospital. I decided to pay her a visit.

* * * * * * *

Shauna was to become my best friend in Thailand. I tapped on her door that evening after dinner to see if she wanted some company. She opened the door a crack, then invited me in. I'll be honest, and hope she won't mind me saying it, but she looked awful, really drained and exhausted. I guess the last thing she wanted at that moment, while she was still recovering from surgery, was a chatterbox like me turning up. But there I was - I had decided she needed company, whether she liked it or not! It turned out we had more in common with each other than anyone else at the Suporn clinic. Despite my Glasgow accent and her deep southern Alabama drawl, we just about understood each other that first night. We both smoked too, which was quite rare among the Mercure girls.

Shauna was a working class southern girl from Alabama, very pretty, slim with feminine features, She'd grown up in a rough environment, with a large family that did not understand her, just like me. We'd both seen a lot of violence and crime in our early days as part of everyday life. We had the same sense of humour and laughed at the life we were both part of now, sitting there in Thailand. It had been a long journey for both of us. We had got the money we needed from wherever we could and were both driven and street smart from an early age. Although she was tough she was compassionate, and worked as a nurse back in the States. This was a woman who'd travelled to the Cambodian border so she could buy ice cream for the refugee orphan children. Shauna could make me laugh no matter how low I was feeling, which was good because I needed that after my surgery.

Soon it was my turn to check into the hospital. I said goodbye to the girls at the Mercure and skipped breakfast,.Dear Wannee came to collect me and drive me to the hospital. On the way she could see I was nervous so she began singing to me.

"You are my sunshine, my only sunshine
You make me happy when skies are grey
You'll never know dear, how much I love you
Please don't take my sunshine away."

Soon she had me singing along. Her Thai accent and huge smile was infectious, and I couldn't help but laugh.

I was taken to the Suporn ward on the eighth floor. The private room was very pleasant and modern, and had a great view of the sea and coastline. Through the French windows I could access my own balcony with a couple of chairs and a table. It was very much like a hotel bedroom apart from the medical equipment and numerous white uniformed nurses. I had a TV and a selection of food menus.

The nurses at Aikchol Hospital were employed by the medical facility and not by Dr Suporn, so they had very little English language. The staff nurse in charge of the ward seemed quite hard-faced and businesslike. Very soon after I'd unpacked my case and settled into the room, she told me that I should take a shower and wash my hair, and then get dressed in the pink hospital gown which was like a pair of loose fitting short cotton pyjamas. Someone would come for me within the hour. As I waited on the bed I felt quite scared again. I sent

Alice and the girls a text telling them I loved them. I can't deny, as I thought about the surgery I was soon to undergo, I was beginning to think "What the fuck am I doing here?"

Suddenly the room door opened and a trolley rolled in, followed by two male porters and the hard faced nurse. She indicated that I should get on the trolley and lie down. I startled babbling that I'd rather walk, but 'hard face' insisted "not possible, rules." So I eventually climbed on and they started wheeling me along a maze of corridors, down a lift and along another long corridor. We finally arrived in a very modern bright operating theatre and I was left for a few minutes while the nurses checked the paperwork. My heart was thumping and I almost felt like jumping off the trolley and telling them I'd changed my mind. I closed my eyes and tried to force myself to relax. Then I felt my arm being softly stroked; I looked up and it was 'hard face'. She was gently massaging my arm and shoulder, her fingers were so soft and gentle. I looked at her and she just gave me a quick smile as she continued talking to the other staff as her hand was moving softly over my skin. It felt like a soothing balm, and soon I was feeling relaxed and calm. It was such a small act of kindness but it meant so much to me at that time. Then Dr Suporn's gentle smiling face was above me. He explained I would have the pre-anaesthetic shot that would let me have a very nice sleep. I hadn't even noticed the cannula that had been inserted into my arm. Dr Suporn smiled again saying, "I will see you very soon," and then I was out.

It seemed only a minute later when I looked up and again Dr Suporn's face was above me, smiling."It's over and complete, Ally, you have a very good result. I will come and see you on the ward tonight." Five hours had passed. I felt no pain at all and once more I was looking up at the corridor lights on the ceiling as we repeated the trolley journey in reverse, back to my room.

Once back in my bed I was hooked up to a saline drip on a stand in one arm, and a morphine drip with a button control in the other. There were two drain tubes coming out of each side of my head which fed into plastic containers that were strapped to my chest. I had a plaster cast shield taped above the bridge of, and covering, my nose. There were tubes coming out of my nose too. I put my fingers to my face and could feel the hard nylon stitches around my eyes and my hairline. I also had several steel staples inserted into the side of my head above my ears. I asked 'hard face' for a mirror, but she just said "Later" and walked off.

I drifted in and out of sleep for the next couple of hours, and each time I awoke I looked across and there was 'hard face' watching me. She never left my side all evening. At some point Dr Suporn came to see me, his gentle fingers holding my chin and running over the shape of my forehead. Taking my temperature and listening to my heartbeat. He seemed satisfied. I asked him who the nurse was, the one I'd been calling 'hard face'. "She is Beam," he told me. I slept soundly that night and woke up at seven.

For once Beam wasn't sitting on the chair. I was alone. Now the pain was kicking in but it wasn't in any specific area; I just felt as if I'd been hit by a bus. I ached all over and felt very fragile. I pumped the morphine button and almost immediately felt the benefit. I decided

I had to sit up, and I was desperate for a cigarette. I thought perhaps I could sneak out to the balcony before Beam or someone else came back. I pulled myself up and the whole room swam around. It took me several minutes to stop the feeling of nausea, but then I got my feet on the floor. I took a cigarette and my lighter from the bedside cupboard and attempted to stand. I felt so weak, but the nicotine addiction was strong and I persevered, eventually shuffling myself across the room and through the glass doors to the balcony, dragging two drip stands with me. The fresh air felt wonderful on my face. I lit the cigarette and took a deep drag. It hit the spot and tasted so good. Then I heard a crash and my vision seemed distorted, everything was side on, even the table and chairs. I was just trying to figure out what had happened to my vision when I heard a scream behind me and feet and legs appeared before me, also horizontal, and that's when I understood I was actually lying on my side. I'd collapsed and it was me who was the wrong way up, not the world. Strong arms grabbed me and I was lifted up and gently carried back to bed by a porter and Beam. She was definitely scolding me for leaving my bed; I couldn't understand the Thai words but the meaning was clear enough! The drips and tubes were all checked and I was examined to see if I'd damaged anything but it all seemed ok. "Stay bed!" she ordered. That was clear enough. I must have snoozed after that because it was lunchtime before I was aware of anything again.

By late afternoon I was feeling ok and almost back to normal, till aching but not nauseous. I had a meal and a coffee and felt much better. It was early evening before I saw Beam again, when she came in with Dr Suporn as he examined me again. No mention was made of my sneaky cigarette, and I guess it was in her interests as much as mine to forget that had happened. Once Dr Suporn left I asked Beam to forgive me. I said that I was sorry but that I hadn't been thinking and just needed a smoke. She may not have understood the words but she got the sentiment. She sat by my bed and stroked my arm again as she gently told me to "please call for porter" if I wanted to go for a cigarette. I agreed, "I will next time". "You very bad girl." was her parting shot as she left, but she was smiling. Beam was particularly tactile, but it was a common trait among the Thai nurses to touch, hold and caress patients. This was something that would have been frowned on in the UK, but it was so normal and human in Thailand, and I appreciated it.

That night I was able to get up and visit Sophie and Jane, who were in different rooms along the corridor from me. They were both confined to bed and unable to get up for five days post surgery. Both seemed very happy, blissful even. Their operations had gone well and Dr Suporn was happy with all of us. Wannee was buzzing around making sure they had everything they needed to hand - laptops, hairbrushes, make up. I was sitting with Sophie when I asked Wannee for a mirror, as I'd still not looked at my face. She handed me a yellow plastic make- up mirror and I looked at my reflection. "Oh my god!" was my first reaction. "What has gone wrong ?Wannee? Sophie?" I called, "look, look, it's awful what have they done to me!" I had two black eyes, my nose was swollen and huge, and my forehead and eyes were covered in stitches, making me look like a very bad version of the bride of Frankenstein. But the worst was the shape of my head. It was pear shaped. My cheeks and jowls were all puffed up, bruised and yellowish. I burst into tears. I could never go home like this, my girls and Alice would be horrified at the sight of me. It took Wannee, and later on Dr Suporn, to convince me that everything was ok and the swelling was normal. After the surgery I'd had, the fluid all drains to the lowest point, and in a day or two it would go and my face would regain its shape. Of course they were right and even I sort of knew that, as I'd been warned beforehand, but that first look in the mirror was still a shock. I understood why Beam had not given me a mirror when I first asked.

* * * * * * *

In less than a week we were all back in the Mercure for post op care and recuperation. My swelling had gone down and I was healing fast. Both Sophie and Jane would have to continue with catheters inserted to pee for a while, but rather than hang around in the hospital they wanted to be back among the other girls, so they each carried little shopping bags with them, and the catheter tubes snaked down from under their skirts and drained into airtight bottles contained within them. It was quite funny and normal to see girls walking around the hotel with these bags over the next few weeks. Shauna was much better by now, as she had had her surgery a week ahead of us. That cohort of girls was due to go to Pattaya for a week's break away from the clinic. I asked if I could go too, and as my face and head were due to have the staples and stitches removed the morning they were leaving, it was agreed that if there was no infection or bleeding I could go.

All was well with my ongoing recovery, so we all set off one morning in the clinic's mini coach for Pattaya. There were four of us patients, including me and Shauna.

Aey came along for the ride and Natta, the Suporn main contact in Pattaya, drove. She was beautiful; an ex contest winner of Tiffany, the huge transgender beauty pageant that dominates the city's calendar every year. Natta was a very tough cookie. She had been a street lady boy in her teens, working the bars in Pattaya and Bangkok to earn the money to pay for her surgery. Anyone who knows those girls and their reputation will understand how hard their lives are and how few make it out. Natta was strong, she scared everyone and was great to have on your side.

* * * * * * *

We booked into the massive Royal Palace hotel just off Boys Town, the gay red light district famous for its bars, and just along from the infamous Walking Street area. As usual with the clinic, everything had been arranged; Dr Suporn had a deal with the hotel and we got beautiful large hotel rooms for a big discount price. Natta gave us a lecture about what and who to avoid, the tricks and scams that westerners get caught up in, and some emergency contact details if we did get into trouble. We would also be having visits each morning from Suporn clinic medical staff who lived in Pattaya, just to make sure everyone was ok. And we had phone numbers for any emergency medical help if needed. They thought of everything!

After the stress of surgery both Shauna and I were looking forward to some down time and pampering, and this was the town where you could get anything you wanted, as demonstrated by our first night when we entered Boys Town and were accosted by the pimps keen to provide to us whatever we were looking for.

"You want boy? Boy with big dick? Look!" He pulls down his shorts and proudly shows an erect giant penis." No, no," we laughed. "Ah, ok, you want girl? Pretty sexy girl, big breasts, or small breasts, here, see" as a selection of girls was paraded before us. Again, we laugh. "No, no. We're just looking for a bar." "Ok, ok, you want lady boy? Pretty girl, big dick, over here, we have for you. One each, yes?"

And so it went on, We knew from Natta not to get involved with anything like that, and indeed she had her friends in Boys Town watching out for us. We sat in the open air bars and watched the circus surrounding us, the pool bars where they played for money, the boxing bars where lady boys would fight any western tourist and easily beat the hell out of them, the film shows and the live cabaret. It was an amazing sight, but always we were aware of the underlying poverty. Late at night there were plenty of young Thais who were sleeping on the street in shop doorways. The drunk tourists, Russians, Brits, and American sailors, were all out for a good time and this often ended in a fight which the Thai police quickly turned up to stop, fining people on the spot.' Thai justice, the best justice you can buy' was the motto.

As I've mentioned before, no one can spot a trans woman better than another trans woman, and it was true in Pattaya as well. Shauna and I were often approached by lady boys in cafes and bars where we would get into discussions about surgeons and surgery techniques, and the best prices in Bangkok. One night in a pharmacy we got talking with a lady boy who wanted to talk about her recent sex change surgery and to recommend her surgeon. She lifted her skirt in a quiet aisle to show us the handiwork. It was very good! Others told us where to get the best injectable oestrogen or boob jobs. When we told them we were Suporn girls they were impressed. Suporn was the best sex change surgeon in Thailand and that meant the best in the world, most agreed. We – me in particular - felt a real affinity with these Pattaya girls. I was in the same line of business and Shauna was no stranger to the work, either. We were working girls like them. They also made me realise how lucky I was that I didn't have to do what they did just to survive.

* * * * * * *

One day we went for a Thai foot massage to a hotel salon which had been recommended to us by a street girl. It was the most fantastic massage I'd ever had, all without leaving a comfortable leather armchair. The cost was only a few dollars, so we settled a high tip on the girls and were welcomed back several times before we left Pattaya. Another time we decided to pamper ourselves in one of the many beauty parlours. I decided to have a facial and eyebrow wax, while Shauna had a pedicure in the next seat. The beautician had just smeared the hot wax onto my forehead and eye area and was about to place the cotton waxing strip on when Shauna noticed what was happening and screamed "stop!!". I'd actually forgotten I still had soluble stitches all around my eye area which, if Shauna hadn't stopped the waxing, would have been ripped out by the beautician. It was a close call. But I suppose it demonstrated how well I'd healed in only a week or so. I'd forgotten! The girl gently washed off the hot wax and moisturised my face, and I settled for a manicure and nail polish instead.

The week in Pattaya soon came to an end. Shauna and I had had a lot of adventures which would bind us together from then on, but we were both quite happy to get back to Chonburi and the more relaxed atmosphere of the Mercure. Every morning all the post surgery girls would have a visit from Wannee to ensure there were no problems. With me it was just a simple facial examination, but for the girls who'd had sex change surgery it was slightly more detailed. We were all in and out of each other's rooms and any false modesty was soon discarded. If I happened to be in Shauna's or Sophie's room when Wannee came round to inspect the surgery sites then it was no big deal. Wannee would say to those girls "OK, on bed, pants down, legs open!" then she would address the vagina on display with a 'good morning' before examining the surgery in more detail. After that we all became very close. We had seen each other in the best and worst of situations and it cemented our camaraderie.

The clinic arranged for us to visit zoos and crocodile farms, or to go on shopping trips to buy jewellery. There was always something going on and the clinic made sure no one was bored during the after care period that they had insisted that we sign up for when we booked surgery. It was probably the reason why Dr Suporn's clinic became the gold standard for transsexual surgery. He had very few complaints or problems because the extensive aftercare package picked up any problem.

Soon it was Shauna's time to go home. We hugged and said a tearful goodbye as she left for Bangkok airport. We would keep in touch. I was sorry to see my best friend go, but we always kept in touch, and we were to meet up again later on, when we shared a room in a Bangkok brothel. But that's another story for the future! I was due to go home with Sophie and Jane the week after. My face had almost healed completely and I was very happy with the results. Both the other UK girls were delighted with their surgery, too. I was a bit jealous that I'd not had my sex change surgery here at the Suporn clinic, but at least I knew my NHS surgery was imminent when I got home. I flew back to the UK in July 2003 and knew I had been changed forever, and not just physically. The Thai experience was wonderful and one I'd come back for time and time again. I now had a whole new family.

* * * * * * *

I arrived back at Heathrow airport and was collected by Sian, who took me back to her house for my own car. I then drove back to Norwich and a first meeting with Alice and the girls since my surgery. I was soon reassured that I still looked like me. The surgery didn't make me unrecognisable from my former self, it just achieved what it was supposed to do and subtly feminised my features. The proof of this is that I continued using my passport with a pre facial surgery photograph for the next nine years without a problem. It did take me a few weeks to believe that my new face wasn't a very fragile facade that could easily be damaged. I think that was a subconscious fear because I knew what had been done and the plates and screws that held everything in place.

Within a week of my return Danni tested my nose. It was a sunny afternoon, she was only just over two years old at this time, and we were all out in the back garden messing about with Sue and Les and kicking a football around. The plastic football rolled towards Danni and she managed to swing her leg and get a great connection on it, thumping it straight at me. It smacked me straight in the face, bringing tears to my eyes. Everyone had the same thought - is the nose ok? I sat down and wiped the tears away, feeling the shape as Sue and Alice looked on with concern. But it was fine. Poor Danni was really upset but I reassured her I had a tough old nose, even stronger than before.

I believe the surgery did change my appearance to casual observers much more into the female spectrum and away from androgyny. Personally I was very happy with my nose because not only did it look straight and more feminine, but I could also breathe more easily with the removal of scarred and battered cartilage caused by previous breaks and damage. I now had a complete hairline rather than the gaps on each temple that I'd had previously. I have very rarely been misgendered since having that surgery/ I can think of only two occasions, and both were based as much on my voice as on my appearance.

I remember one humorous experience a few months later, when I had to change my name and gender on an old building society savings account that I'd previously not got around to altering since my I.D. documents were changed. I approached the counter in the branch and asked to speak to someone about changing my name and identity on my account. The woman at first assumed I'd got married, and began getting forms out relating to that. I stopped her and said gently, "No, it's actually a bigger change than that." She looked confused, so I thought it was best to just come out with it. "I am transsexual, and I'm going through transition leading to physically having a sex change, my documents have already been changed and I just need the name and gender on my savings account corrected."She looked a bit flustered but then her training must have kicked in as she seemed to understand. "OK, yes, I'm sure we can do that for you today. What is your female name and what will your new male name be?" Now I was confused! I replied, "Sorry, you misunderstand, I'm not changing sex to male, I'm changing to female." She looked flustered again. "I thought you **were** female and changing sex to male." It took a few more minutes and examination of my passport to explain it all before she finally understood, and then the process was completed easily enough. But as I walked out I felt quite chuffed that I'd had to argue and convince her that I wasn't born female! Thank you, Dr Suporn!

* * * * * * *

Within weeks of returning to England I went back to escorting at the flat. I felt increasingly more confident of my appearance and a few of my regulars were very flattering. But I still advertised as pre op transsexual. I had a quite a few transvestite punters now and they were the best. All they wanted was to spend a few hours 'dressed' and chatting with me. I was making enough money to continue my IPL hair removal and repay my debt to Sue and Les without having to take any dodgy dangerous punters, and we were living comfortably enough at home. I was also still seeing Russell Reed in London regularly. He had already agreed to be one of the two referrals I needed for sex change surgery; the other one came from Dr Olive at the Norwich GIC. I was probably becoming a bit of a pest to Barbara Ross, by constantly asking when my surgery date would be. The Local Health Authority had agreed my funding, so it was now just a case of where and which surgeon was available. Eventually Barbara came back to me and said I could go to the Nuffield hospital, near Brighton, early in 2004. I was delighted.

* * * * * * *

But, while I seemed to be doing ok, I had friends who weren't as fortunate. Here I recount a story I wrote in about the summer of 2003 just after I'd returned from Thailand.

Debbie Fox

The last time I was with my friend Debbie we never laughed quite as much as we used to. We had a good time together as always, but not the crazy giggling that usually characterised our get- togethers. We'd decided to go to the Euro Pride Mardi Gras in Manchester together. Debbie lived nearby and invited me to stay over. I'd only made up my mind I was going the day before, and I'm glad I went now.

I called Debbie from a motorway service station on my way to Manchester to tell her I was running late. I said I'd see her in half an hour and she said she'd put the kettle on. As usual, I got lost after coming off the motorway at Bury. I couldn't get my brain to read the map and directions to Debbie's new home. In a daze I headed towards her old house because I knew the way there, but eventually I had to call her again to come and get me from a petrol station opposite where she used to live. We both laughed as we acknowledged that the hormones can turn your brain to fog sometimes, and the simple task of following directions becomes an impossibility.

Debbie, with her usual good humour, drove out to meet me so I could follow her back. I can't remember now if we first hugged at the petrol station or if we stayed in our cars and hugged when we arrived at the car park behind her flat. It seems important that I should remember this but I can't.

After we parked we gathered all my gear and went into the block of flats where Debbie was living. A woman neighbour was leaving as we entered and she stopped to chat with her. It was typical Debs; she'd only been living here a short time and already knew all the neighbours. She was proud that she had fitted in easily in her new home and life. I could see it, and I was pleased for her.

She showed me round her new flat, which was actually no more than a bed sitting room. She had decorated it beautifully, though. I could see all the little feminine touches she'd done, the curtains, the wall mirrors, the plants and pictures as you came in the front door. She'd even painted flowers on the tiles in the kitchen and bought saucepans to match. The best thing was her bed, which was on a platform five feet in the air so she could utilise the space under it better. She also had her wardrobe under there, and her PC with an office chair.

I was impressed with how she had made a big effort to make this a home; she told me several times how happy she was to be able to finally live as herself. I remembered the old house she had shared with her partner, where I'd stayed a few times. That place was 10 times bigger than this tiny flat, but we both agreed that at least the flat was hers. This was a fresh start, a new beginning. Debbie had decided after years of heartache that she must transition, but her partner and family were dead set against it. I encouraged her that in time her family were sure to come round and accept her. (I was one to talk! Of course I didn't mention how badly news of my own transition had gone down with my family in Scotland). We laughed, but I thought about my own parents who had angrily disowned me completely, and how much hurt this condition causes.

We spent the next couple of hours getting ready to go out, as you do. We both tried on different clothes and tried different hairstyles while we sipped at the bottle of wine I'd brought. These times are always the best, I think, as they are when you really get to know someone and feel comfortable with them. Getting ready to go out is almost better than actually going out. We did our make up together at the same time in the same kitchen mirror. We were both using tinted moisturiser, and we laughed at the pre IPL and electrolysis days when we used to have to plaster our faces with heavy foundation. Now we spent almost as much time doing our make up to look like no make up. We complimented each other on our hair, she was just beginning to grow hers long enough to look really good, and I'd had mine permed since we last saw each other a few months ago. I told her she looked great and I meant it. She had a nice slender body and good legs. She was all sun-tanned and healthy looking.

Debbie refused to believe she looked passable, though. She thought she needed Facial Feminisation Surgery. I told her she could get it if it meant that much to her, but really it's what's inside that counts. She joked about how our mutual friend Nikki would put her hand over the bottom half of her face and say she looked great, only needing the chin and mouth bit done.

Finally we were ready and it was time to go. Debs had worked out the travel arrangements, which were that she would drive us to the local tram stop and leave her car while we got the tram into Manchester. I'd never been on a tram before and I normally hate public transport, but if Debbie said it was safe I believed her. So we managed to squeeze on to a packed tram heading for the city centre. We found a seat together and chatted all the way in. I was a bit dubious about using public transport on a Saturday night but it was no problem. We both seemed to pass completely and I soon relaxed.

We finally arrived at the gay village, via a straight pub (I guess we both wanted to prove to ourselves we could use straight bars if we wanted). We did the usual round of bars and clubs and danced everywhere we went, even in the street. Debs loved to dance. We ate chips in the fast food place next to Napoleon's bar and Debbie tried to matchmake two young gay guys who were sitting near us. Typical Debbie, she saw they were made for each other and went out of her way to facilitate it. They went off together smiling soon after.

We went into Napoleons for old time's sake and danced with the trans girls. Debs caught the attention of TF and danced with him. He wanted more from her but Debbie refused to leave the club, she so loved to dance!

Everywhere we went Debbie started conversations with strangers. She always amazed me at how she could do this and everyone always responded positively to her. She'd done the same thing previously in Norwich when visiting me, one night when we got a taxi into the town centre. The driver was the most awful unfriendly macho homophobic bastard you could imagine but within minutes he was chatting away happily to Debs while I looked on in amazement.

Eventually the night ended and we went for the last bus back to Bury at 3:30 am. The crowd on the bus were not as friendly as the one on the tram coming, but Debbie was relaxed. A lot of guys were drunk and arguing but no one bothered us. I thought we must be passing OK. You get worried when you are out with another trans girl because it multiplies the likelihood of being read.

We were only a few minutes from our stop when disaster struck. This guy walked down the bus to get off. As he came up behind Debs he started playing with her hair and saying, " Your wig's not very good, mate." It was clear he had "read" Debs, he was drunkenly aggressive, challenging her to respond, and calling Debbie 'he' and 'him,' looking for a fight. For the first time that night I felt vulnerable. I was afraid for Debs. I looked at her and she looked back at me and I could see the hurt in her eyes. She said nothing and we both ignored the guy. Fortunately we soon arrived at his tram stop and he got off laughing.

It took the shine off the night, because we both realised how close we'd come to trouble and no one on the bus had made any effort to step in to help, as they would have if Debbie was a 'real girl'. We got back to

Debs' place soon after and had a cup of tea and a nice chat, sitting on her settee with our arms round each other reliving the night till I couldn't keep my eyes open any longer and fell asleep. Debs then phoned Nikki in Thailand; she told me about that in the morning.

The next day (Sunday) we got up at 10 am. Debs made me tea and toast. We decided to go back to Manchester city centre to do a bit of shopping then go to the Euro pride again. I drove my car to collect hers and we went in tandem to the city and parked in a multi-story. We walked through the city together with Debs hanging on to my arm. She's never done this before but it seemed right and I was happy to be close to her. We spent ages in Primark looking at clothes, and Debs, thoughtful of others as usual, bought a couple of belts, one for her and one for a girl at work who she thought would like one. Then we went back to the village and looked for our friend Cathy on the union stands but never saw her. We had a giggle looking at the leather and dildos on sale at some of the other stands then watched a bit of the free music concert while we had some takeaway food in the open air. I decided to take a photo of her and called her name just as I clicked. I wanted a keepsake of this time and I knew if I asked her to pose she wouldn't, she never liked her photo taken. I asked her to take a photo of me and she did, but her eyes looked far away and uninterested.

I suppose it was then that I first realised we hadn't had quite as many of our usual giggling fits as we always had when we met up. It had been a great weekend, but that was missing. We had always had a chemistry between us whenever we had been together in the past, which made us start giggling uncontrollably for no reason. She was the only person I ever did this with. She always made me happy and I really looked forward to being with her.

We walked back to the car park and again she held my arm along the way. Debs offered to lead me back to the motorway because she knew how dizzy I was when it came to directions. I agreed, so although I would follow her out of Manchester we said our goodbyes in the car park. We had a hug and a kiss, then both climbed in our cars. I followed her for 5 or 6 miles to the motorway. I remember laughing at her because she was still dancing, even in the car, to the music from the radio. We came to the junction where we would part. I pulled up beside her at the lights and we mouthed our goodbyes and waved at each other. The lights changed and she was gone!

That was many years ago and the last time saw Debbie Fox. I'm still shattered about what happened the next day. I can hardly begin to say what I feel, but I thought I'd write down our last times together as a memorial. I'll never forget Debs.

My dear friend Debbie Fox took her own life the day after I said goodbye to her in Manchester. She'd been unable to negotiate with her ex-partner any access arrangement to see her infant son, and her parents had refused to accept her transition. They buried her using her male name.

* * * * * * *

Just before Christmas 2003 I was told by Norwich GIC that I would definitely have my surgery at the Nuffield hospital, Brighton. I was pleased, having half expected it would be changed to Charing Cross, and I wasn't keen on going back there.

This news also reminded me of a transsexual girl, Anne, that I knew from another GIC and who had recently asked me for a favour. She had been given her date for surgery at the Nuffield hospital with a certain unnamed surgeon. Would I drive her down there, and then collect her post surgery, a week later? I said of course I would! This would give me the opportunity to see the hospital where I might be going, and to meet a surgeon that I'd perhaps have, too.

Anne was another girl at odds with her family. She was younger than me, in her late twenties, but had transitioned in her home village, much to the anger and disgust of her parents and neighbours who did not agree with her decision. However, at least they hadn't thrown her out of the family home. She had transitioned and completed her real life test whilst living with her parents, who still called her by her old male name and referred to Anne as 'he' and 'him'. They suffered Anne in silence and offered no assistance at all. This is why she needed a lift to Brighton from me.

Anne was a lovely person, very independent of mind. It took me a few years to appreciate what she was doing at the time. She never wore make up or dressed in a particularly feminine way. She would not be bullied into wearing a dress at a GIC appointment, for example, as I had. Fortunately, things were beginning to change in the NHS GICs and she had not been thrown off the patient list. I appreciated that at least my local Norwich GIC was also more flexible about such things, probably because it had a female, Barbara Ross, in charge. Barbara didn't believe much in stereotypical women's behaviour, dress or appearance, either. Of course she was correct, but I admit it took me several years to believe I wouldn't be penalised for an unfeminine appearance. Such was the fear instilled from being conditioned for years by Charing Cross.

Anne had her own path laid out. Once she had had her sex change she planned to go to North Carolina and drive a huge truck for a living. She told me this several times and I admit I doubted whether it would ever happen. But that's exactly what Anne did.

On the day I drove Anne down to the Nuffield she was excited finally to be getting her surgery, and I was really happy for her too. We parked at the hospital and I walked in with her. My first impression was the drabness of the place. It felt more like an old folk's home and smelled like it too. There were no staff to greet us and we hung around for ages before someone finally turned up at reception to book Anne in. We were directed to her room, which was at least private, but it was very grubby with no home comforts. I suppose I'd been spoiled by my time at the Aikchol Hospital in Chonburi. … but still.

At least Anne was happy enough, and she had no complaints as she threw her gear into the bedside cupboard and bounced on the bed to test the comfort. We knew the surgeon would be along soon to see her and get the consent form signed, so I hung around for the chance to meet him. After a time the surgeon appeared. He seemed pleasant enough as he spoke with Anne, often referring to a nurse who was with him. He didn't ask who I was or speak to me, but just ignored my presence in the room, so I didn't have a chance to mention that I'd perhaps be his patient one day. He wasn't rude, just busy. And as quickly as he'd arrived he was off, before I had the opportunity to even say hello. Once she was settled in, I kissed Anne and wished her good luck, and told her I'd be back to collect her in a week.

A week later I arrived at the Sussex Nuffield to collect Anne. She walked out very gingerly. I carried her case and she carried a large doughnut seating ring. Unlike my friends who'd had their surgery in Thailand when I was there, she was far from blissful, but at least happy it was over with. She settled into the back seat of my car, resting on the doughnut, still clearly in pain. "Are you ok?" I asked. " Yes! Please just get me home."

On the 130 mile journey back to her village Anne was clearly not very comfortable as she tried to adjust her position constantly. She had taken her dose of painkillers already, but before we even got to Essex she had taken another dose. She was very unhappy, and I suggested we stop at the service station so she could stretch her legs and get a coffee. At this stage I was seriously thinking I might have to drive back to the Nuffield because Anne was in so much pain. But we had a coffee in the restaurant, and Anne insisted we press on. She just wanted to get home as soon as possible. We arrived at her village. Her mum reluctantly came out to help her inside. I said goodbye. Anne hardly even noticed me, she was in so much pain, so I wasn't upset not to get a thank you. I could see she had much more on her mind than polite pleasantries.

A day later I was not surprised to hear from Anne that she had a problem. She had been trying to dilate her neo vagina as per instructions, twice a day for at least an hour, but the pain was too great. She dosed herself up with painkillers and tried again but eventually gave in, it was too much. She fell asleep that night and woke up with her sheets covered in blood, Panicking, she called the Nuffield, but her aftercare had been assigned to her local health authority, and there was nothing they could do except to advise her to call an ambulance. Anne was rushed to her local NHS hospital where she was met by A&E staff who had no idea or experience of a post op transsexual woman. They put her in a bed and a surgeon managed to find the area of the bleed and stitched it. Anne had an infection which led to necrosis and the eventual removal of some tissue, but no one could say where she had acquired it, whether it was in Sussex or the local hospital. There could be no blame assigned.

As soon as Anne's condition was stable they discharged her home, to the care of the district nurse who came by once a day, but she had absolutely no experience of sex change surgery either, although she tried her best. Eventually, months later, Anne would have to undergo more surgery to repair the damage done by the inexperienced surgeon who stitched up her infected wound. The whole saga was awful, and I could not help thinking that this could end up being my own NHS experience. It was a far cry from what I'd seen at the Suporn clinic, and their aftercare.

* * * * * * *

I don't want to come across as overly critical of the NHS transexual medical care at this time. During this period I had a friend, Rachel, who went through sex change surgery at Leicester with the same surgeon who had left my friend Kim in Thailand with a big problem.

Rachel was delighted with her result, and I visited her in the Leicester hospital, which was clean and modern. It seemed to be hit and miss the treatment you received, and as we were always reminded, every surgery carries risk. The outcomes were sometimes fantastic, other times less, so. But, one thing I was certain of, the prolonged period of aftercare that Dr Suporn insisted on was really important.

It was 2004, the year I would finally have my sex change surgery. I would also turn forty that year. It had been a long journey. I estimated that since my first transition in London twenty three years previously, when I was seventeen, I'd have lived sixteen out of twenty four years as female.

I'd now had successful facial surgery and I was accepted as female wherever I went. Against all the odds I had a partner and children still living with me. I'd obviously lost all my family in Scotland, but I could manage without them . What I really wanted now was to complete my surgery; I felt I'd waited long enough. So when I got a letter from the Norwich GIC informing me in January that my surgery would finally take place in March, in the Sussex Nuffield hospital, with the surgeon Phil Thomas, I was delighted. Mr Thomas had a very good reputation amongst the girls I knew. I thought he was a good option for me.

I was given a date to meet with Mr Thomas at Charing Cross hospital in February for a preliminary physical examination before finalising the surgery date. The only concern I had was that the technique that Phil Thomas used apparently required that I first have electrolysis in my genital area, as that skin would possibly be reused as the lining of the neo vagina. If that was required in my case then I would need to know about it as soon as possible because it would cause a delay, not to mention the pain involved.

The day of my meeting with Mr Thomas arrived and I drove down to Charring Cross, yet again. The place where I'd experienced so much hope and heartache in the past. I had a long list of questions I'd written out to ask him regarding genital hair removal, what surgical technique he was going to use, and particularly aftercare. Would he provide me with a full record of the procedure he'd used and what should happen if there was any difficulty once I was back home? I wanted this information to pass on to my local NHS providers if I had a problem, because I had real concerns about that lack of planning, after Anne's experience.

Mr Thomas arrived to see me as I sat in the GIC waiting room. He was a middle- aged man, dressed in a suit and carrying a doctor's black bag. He introduced himself and asked me to follow him, as he looked for a room where he could examine me. After trying several doors we ended up in an empty treatment room he found. It was just us two, and he pulled the curtains round the bed and told me to hop on the treatment couch and pull down my pants. The whole examination seemed hurried and lasted less than five minutes. Afterwards I produced my list of questions. I had expected we would go to a private office so I could go through my concerns. But, Mr Thomas was obviously in a hurry to be somewhere else and didn't have time to sit down and discuss those things with me. He apologised for the rush, but said it would be OK, and that I shouldn't worry, as I could discuss matters at the Nuffield hospital in March when I was booked in. Then he said goodbye and he was gone. I felt quite uneasy about this meeting. After all, this would be about the biggest surgical operation that one could undergo and I felt it needed at least some detailed discussion, especially the hair removal question. If it was decided I did need that, then it would be too late to arrange to find a local electrolysis operator in Brighton to provide the several sessions, over multiple days, that would be needed – all in the same week that I was at the Nuffield hospital. This was not a trivial matter to me and I was very concerned; the possible outcome of not removing the hair follicles could mean the neo vagina could be lined with skin that was capable of producing growing hair, something that was obviously gross and unacceptable to me and a recognised problem. I was getting really worried; you only get one chance at this surgery.

* * * * * * *

In February I received a letter from the Nuffield hospital. I was expecting this; it would be confirmation of my surgery date and consent form. Instead, it was the medical details of another patient, an 83 year old man who lived in Brighton who was due to be admitted for a completely different surgical procedure, two days prior to me. I was at first a bit annoyed, as they had obviously mixed up my medical information with someone else's. But then it occurred to me that If I'd been sent this man's information, including address and details of his condition, then he had probably been sent my personal information, too, including my intended surgical procedure, name and address!   I realised that the poor man would probably have no interest in 'outing' me as a transsexual woman and was probably as bewildered as I was with his letter from the Nuffield with another patient's details, but I was incensed by the slipshod way that they had made this mistake. I called them up to explain what I'd received in the post and to ask if, as I suspected, my details had been sent to this man in Brighton. The member of staff was less than helpful and didn't seem too bothered. She couldn't confirm if my information had been sent to the wrong address and anyway 'it was just a simple mistake'. They would send me the correct information in the next few days. She didn't even offer me an apology.

By this time I was getting really quite concerned about the casual way the NHS were treating me. I was always made to feel I should just be grateful they were willing to deal with a transsexual patient at all; after all, they were doing me a favour, and perhaps I should shut up.

Later on that week I was retelling Alice's mum Sue what had happened with the surgeon Mr Thomas, and the letter that the Nuffield had sent me, not forgetting the story of Anne that she was already aware of. Sue listened sympathetically; she knew I was becoming quite stressed at the prospect of visiting Brighton. Out of the blue she asked, "Would you prefer to go back to Dr Suporn?" Of course I would, I'd go in a heartbeat. But that would obviously cost money and would mean giving up free NHS surgery here in the UK.

Then Sue did the most wonderful thing. She asked me to contact the Suporn clinic and get a price for surgery over there. She would have a talk with Les, and they would fund me to go back to Thailand. I could repay them later. I could not believe their generosity; I was amazed. We were still repaying my facial surgery from the previous year! My own parents had completely disowned me and refused to even have any contact with me or my kids. And yet Sue and Les had proved to be so much more like family to me than anyone who was actually blood family. I gave Sue a hug. I was going back to Thailand!

Chapter 33 'Fix You'

Thailand 2

Right away I emailed Dr Kim. I needed to know when the Suporn clinic could offer me a date for surgery and how much it would cost. The answer was that I could come right away; as a member of the Suporn family they would fit me in and I could have surgery in March. Even better, as a returning client the cost would be almost a fifty per cent discount from the usual fee. I called the Nuffield and cancelled.

I booked my flights I'd arrive on the 9th March and have surgery soon after. This time I went with the Taiwanese carrier Eva Air, direct to Bangkok. It's true that Aeroflot had been fun the year before. But I definitely wanted comfort on this trip without a Moscow stopover, and no leaping around trying to catch a bag of salted peanuts!

As it turned out, two English girls I knew well, Jenny and Marie, were also going to be at the Suporn Clinic that month for sex change surgery, so I would have friends there with me. I called Sian, my friend who lived near Heathrow. I asked if I could park my car at her place again for a month. But she surprised me by saying she wanted to come along too. Like me she had been on the NHS waiting list for years, but on hearing my news decided to bypass them and come to Thailand if Dr Suporn could manage to fit her in the same month. I contacted Dr Kim to let her know Sian was a friend and it would be good if she came at the same time as me. Dr Kim agreed, and so now there would be four of us.

My second visit to the Suporn Clinic was like coming home. My first time I'd been so afraid and unsure what to expect, but now I knew. I was met by dear Wannee again at Bangkok airport, where we hugged and chatted like old friends. We both sang silly songs in the car all the way to Chonburi and Wannee filled me in on the latest clinic gossip. When we got to the Mercure hotel the staff were all very welcoming, too. It really was the best atmosphere to be having surgery, and literally a world away from the grim Sussex Nuffield.

The next morning I walked round to the clinic and met up with the girls again, Aey, Natta, Aoy, and Dr Kim. We all hugged and it felt good to be in a safe and happy environment. When it was time to see Dr Suporn, he politely welcomed me back. I felt like hugging him too, but you didn't hug Dr Suporn! It wasn't respectful. Instead he just smiled and said hello and welcome back. I responded "sawadee kha" and gave a small bow. He smiled, and we sat down and went over the surgical details, which didn't take very long because I was already well aware of his technique. I knew that I had no need to worry about electrolysis, as his method precluded any need for that. I did however have to produce my two referrals for sex change surgery and undergo another HIV blood test.

Once the medical side of things were completed I gave Dr Suporn a bottle of Scottish malt whisky I'd brought from the UK. He had given me a beautiful bronze angel figurine as a farewell present the last time I was here. He bowed slightly and thanked me. Then he told me my surgery date would be March 11th, which happened to be my birthday. "I picked a very suitable date for you," he smiled.

I soon met up with Sian, who had come with a different airline. My other friends, Jenny and Marie, were already in Aikchol Hospital, having arrived several days before. I'd meet up with them in a few days when we were all post op. At the Mercure hotel there were girls from all over the world - Canadian, American, Australian, several Thais and one absolutely stunning girl from Singapore. We all made friends quickly. There was a Swedish girl called Maja who was very young and very sweet. She was there with both her parents and we all felt very protective towards her. Many of us must have been thinking how much easier it would have been for us to have such supportive parents at that age. To be able to access treatment so young meant her sex change and subsequent life would be smooth in comparison with the trials most of the rest of us had endured.

* * * * * * *

It was time for me to book into the hospital. Wannee drove and Natta came along for the ride, chattering non stop to me in a mixture of Thai and English, giving me advice. Telling me I must eat after surgery, eat and sit up, don't sleep. Stay awake, go online, watch TV. Try to exercise my arms and move my legs in bed post op, then I will heal quickly. "I will visit," she promised.

At the Suporn floor I was given the same room as I'd had before. Everything seemed familiar as I looked out and took in the view again; the beach and the sea, a few fishing boats. Directly underneath my balcony eight floors below was the pretty house I remembered, with the red tile roof and the little dog running around the enclosed compound, yapping away. It was as if I'd not been away.

Then my door opened and 'hard face' Beam barged in, her face suiting her nickname at that moment. She looked at me and sneered. "Ah, you back." I wasn't sure if she was really pissed off with me or not. I put my hands together and said "Sawadee kha Beam'. I could see the corners of her mouth twitching as she scowled at me. Then her smile appeared, she came over and took my arm as she had done many times before and stroked it as she spoke. "no smokie, OK?" I agreed. No smoking. She smiled and pointed to her nose. "I know if you smokie, OK!" She gave me a quick hug and left.

I was left to my own thoughts that night. I recalled everything that had led me to this hospital bed some 6000 miles on the other side of the world from where I was born and grew up, the people who had stuck by me and those who had let me go. The violence, the heartache, the small victories that meant so much, such as when a stranger addressed me as 'her', or the spit on my face and threat of physical attack. The worst was probably the silent contempt. I thought of Maja, the sweet Swedish girl, who would be in a room along the corridor from me in a few days. She would not have to endure all that. She would lead a normal life untainted by testosterone poisoning and prejudice. I thought of poor Debbie Fox who never made it this far.

I had sometimes challenged others to accept me. My parents, for example, I had dared them to, and then was scathing of them when they didn't. But I realised now the only person I really needed acceptance from was myself. I was the child of my parents after all, regardless how progressive I imagined myself to be otherwise. Would I now, after this surgery, finally accept myself?

I'd never fitted the so- called stereotype of the typical male to female transsexual, or even the gay male. I liked sport. I was good at it. I didn't throw a ball or catch it 'like a girl'. I wasn't weak or scared to fight. I didn't burst into tears if someone upset me. This behaviour seemed at odds with what so many other trans women had told me about themselves or I'd read in books. It sometimes made me suspicious about my own trans credentials. I wasn't sexually attracted to men any more than I was to women; both were ok, but I could quite happily do without sex at all. I much preferred good friends who made me laugh. Would my sexual orientation or attraction change once I had a functioning vagina? With all those thoughts swirling around my mind I eventually drifted off to sleep that night. I hoped I was doing the right thing because there was no return from this surgery.

I awoke at six am. It was time to prepare. I had a shower and washed my hair using the medical soap and shampoo that had been left for me the night before. I thought it was probably too early to dress in the pink hospital gown, so I put on a clean long T- shirt and sat on the bed. I couldn't concentrate on anything, so I didn't bother going online or watching TV. I put the KD Lang CD 'Ingénue' on the player with the volume low and waited. I was feeling a mixture of occasional panic and peaceful blessing. I was here, where I was meant to be.

My serenity wasn't to last for long! At seven am Beam breezed into my room. "Happy Birthday," she smiled, "I have a gift for you." I'd forgotten today was my birthday. I looked at what Beam was holding; it was a couple of disposable razors. "Now you shave," she said, pointing to my pants area. Oh, yes, of course. I'd forgotten that was necessary. I took the razors. "You do all good, or I do it, ok?" She smiled again; I think she was enjoying this! I headed back into the shower room. Once the shaving was completed I came back into the room where Beam was waiting for me with a rubber tube and an enema bag. There is nothing glamorous about preparing for sex change surgery. "Now lie on side, OK?" Yes, I nodded. Beam was definitely all smiles this morning. I wasn't looking forward to this but it had to be done. I lay on my side and Beam began the procedure of introducing the liquid contents of the bag. When she was finished she took away the apparatus and sat down next to me. "Now we wait."

As I lay there I was desperately hoping for Beam's soft touch. And sure enough, she began to stroke my arm and neck. It felt so familiar to me that I instantly relaxed. After about 15 minutes, I was almost drifting off to sleep again, when I felt the sudden cramping in my tummy. I jumped up and ran for the loo. As I was slamming the door behind me I heard Beam shout, "One hour, be ready!". And she left.

An hour later I was dressed in the pink hospital gown, clean and prepared for surgery. The hospital porters arrived with the trolley bed. I didn't argue this time, I just climbed on and lay back. Beam held my hand the whole time as we travelled the corridors and descended in the lift, then once more I arrived in Dr Suporn's theatre and there was his gentle smiling face looking down at me. "Happy Birthday, Ally,'" he smiled." I will see you again very soon."

* * * * * * *

I woke up. I was back in my room. Was it over? I could hardly believe it. Just like before, it seemed as if I'd just seen Dr Suporn two minutes ago! But actually it had been six and a half hours. Aey appeared and came over to me. "Happy Birthday, Ally!" she chimed. I began to take in the room. There were streamers and balloons all over it, bouncing gently from the ceiling, On a table there was even a birthday cake surrounded by cards. "I'll be back!" Aey shouted, as she rushed out of the door. Two minutes later the hospital room was filled with nurses, porters and even cleaners. Aey directed them as they all burst into a rendition of Happy Birthday To You. I was still half asleep and wondering if this was a dream, it was so surreal. After the song everyone came by and blew me kisses or squeezed my arm. They all applauded as they left, chattering away happily in Thai. Aey brought the cards over to me; they had been received in the hospital from friends all over the world. The staff had kept them safe for this moment, so I would find them when I awoke. I was so touched, they all had messages -

to the 'birthday girl', to 'my sister', one from Sue and Les, to 'my daughter in law', and one from Alice, 'to my wife'. The cake was from Dr Suporn and Aey insisted I had a piece. She even took photographs of everything so I would remember. I managed a small piece of cake but then gave in, and drifted off to sleep again.

Dr Suporn came to see me that evening. The surgery had gone smoothly and he was very pleased with the result. I had depth of eight inches, which he demonstrated to me with rather graphic photographs of a measured off dilator, inserted in my neo vagina, taken immediately after surgery while I was still unconscious! He presented me with a beautiful padded box containing two dilators, one thicker than the other, both approximately ten inches long. These would be my constant companions for the next few years. 'Every day, for an hour, twice a day.' But for now I couldn't actually access the surgery site. I had a 'pack' in, which would remain for five days, and the whole area was bandaged up with a small rubber catheter tube exiting to a urine bag. As before, I had a saline drip in one arm, and a button controlled morphine drip in the other. Once everyone had left and I was on my own, I thought about the last time I was here, and I'd decided to have a cigarette immediately post op, and caused poor Beam so much hassle. But this time I didn't even feel the craving for nicotine. I was relaxed and had a radiant smile plastered across my face. The word that best described my mood that night was tranquil.

For the next five days I was confined to bed, as were my friends in other rooms along the corridor. We kept in touch by using the hospital internal phone switchboard. We would call each other up and chat, or to say watch channel 34, or just to talk about the food options. We all soon discovered you could phone for takeaway deliveries, McDonald's or Dominoes pizza. The days passed quickly enough and soon it was time for my 'pack' to be removed. Dr Suporn arrived one day with Beam and Wannee. I was told to lie back and relax. "It may be painful but only for a few seconds," I was warned. I pushed myself down into the bed, my head on the pillows and my hands gripping the guard rails on both side of the bed. I closed my eyes and let the three of them get on with it. "Let me know when it's done," I winced. "It's done!" Wannee shouted. I hadn't felt a thing! However, I still lay back and allowed them to clean up and gather up the dressing., At one point a camera came out and Dr Suporn took some photographs. I could tell, despite the conversation between them being in Thai, that they were all quite happy with the results. Eventually, Dr Suporn held up a mirror between my legs so I could see. "You look, is very good, yes?" he smiled. I looked, and I was amazed. I looked like a girl! It sounds silly- I mean what else was I expecting to see? But it really was just so wonderful. I felt clean. I felt a burden had been removed from me. I was finally me.

   In the next 24 hours Wannee taught me to pee, so hopefully I could leave hospital without a catheter. I had pain, but the bigger problem was reconfiguring my new physical reality to my brain. But Wannee insisted, over and over, sit. You must sit and feel it. Don't get up, sit and imagine it! This seemed to go on for hours. Eventually I heard a tinkle of liquid dripping into the toilet bowl. At first I feared it was blood and I jumped up and turned to look. It was urine. I'd done it! I was so pleased I shouted to Wannee, "Look, look! I peed!" I was like a little kid. She was smiling and clapping her hands. "I told you, it's OK now." From that moment on my brain understood how my new body worked, and I was able to leave hospital without a catheter.

I had good reason to want to leave without a catheter tube, and the urine container that was carried in a shopping bag, that some of my friends had had to put up with. Alice was flying in to Thailand from the UK, and I didn't want to be hampered with that inconvenience when we met up again, because we were going for a delayed honeymoon in Pattaya!

* * * * * * *

Dr Suporn, with his usual kindness, had arranged for a Suporn Clinic driver to go and collect Alice from Bangkok airport, and on the same evening that I was driven back to the Mercure hotel, I sat in the lobby on a lounge chair awaiting her arrival. When she came through the main doors I hobbled over and we embraced. Both of us were crying, she had stuck by me, and waited twelve years for me to finally have surgery. We both remembered so clearly the first time we'd met in Norwich all those years ago, and how I'd told her that one day I would have this surgery. She believed in me and now we could be physically together at last, as a lesbian couple. The truth is that we were so committed to each other through love that the surgery was by this time a side issue to our relationship. But it was very important to me, and good to have that all behind us now.

For me, finally achieving surgery and a female shaped body gave me much more self assurance and confidence. It's true that that no one knows what's inside your pants when you walk down the road. I've known many beautiful women over the years who lived and were accepted as female in almost every aspect of their lives, who didn't have surgery, whether through choice, lack of opportunity, or the funds to have sex change. But that would never have worked for me. I had always despised what had been between my legs to the extent that I could hardly bring myself to even mention it, even to doctors or surgeons. I avoided any possibility of seeing myself in a mirror, I would only undress in the dark, and kept myself 'tucked' in pants, even when sleeping. Now my underwear actually fitted me and I could happily look at my reflection without feeling sick. I have no wish or right to advocate about what other transsexual people do with their bodies, my views are always my own. But, just as my body accepted oestrogen like a cool oasis drink in the desert, my body accepted surgery as natural and corrective.

As usual, I was a fast healer. So when I heard there was a planned trip to Pattaya for the post op girls, who were a week ahead of me, I begged Dr Suporn for permission to go with Alice. I wanted to show her everything. It was unusual to leave the extensive aftercare of the clinic so soon after sex change surgery but he eventually gave me permission as long as I agreed to see the Suporn clinic nurse, who was resident in the resort, every morning. I also promised not to exert myself and just relax for a week. Alice and I needed some time to ourselves. We were driven down there as usual by Natta, and booked in once more at the Royal Palace hotel. It was fantastic to share this trip with Alice. She had heard so much about Pattaya from me, and now we were able to enjoy it together.

The first evening we had a gentle stroll along Walking Street and a nice meal in a beachside restaurant. As we walked hand in hand I'd never felt so much in love with Alice. After all we had been through, she was still there by my side.

The next morning we heard a knock on the door of our hotel room. I got up and answered, there was a Thai girl with a clip board. "Pen," she smiled at me. I assumed it was room service, because we had used that a lot for sandwiches and drinks. It was so easy to pick up the phone to call reception and order whatever we wanted. I assumed Alice had ordered something and I needed to sign for it. I invited the girl into the room and I began looking for something to sign with. But the girl kept following me and repeating 'pen' with a huge smile on her face. "I know, I'm looking, hang on, I'll find one,'" I replied. By this time Alice had come in from the balcony to see what was happening and I found myself asking her for a pen, so she began looking through her bag while I searched the bedside cabinet drawers. Meanwhile the Thai girl was at my elbow, following me and repeating 'pen'. She was becoming quite insistent! Eventually I found a Biro and turned to her. "ok, got one, where do I sign?" But she just looked at me in confusion. Then she began pointing her finger at herself and repeating 'pen'. I was getting exasperated by this time and passing the pen in front of her eyes to make sure she saw it. "Yes, a pen, here, take it." That's when Alice realised the Thai girl was referring to herself. And so I met 'Pen', who was actually Natta's sister and a nurse who also worked for the Suporn Clinic. What an idiot I was, it was hilarious! Anyway, I nodded to her, and told her I knew the routine. Lie back on the bed, pants off, knees up and legs open.

Pen smiled again and opened up her case with thermometer, stethoscope, swabs and cream. She visited every morning to check up on me and gave me a card with her phone number for emergencies. Happily there were no complications or infections, but it was great to know she was there if needed.

I promised Pen I would take things easy. Luckily she never found out we went elephant riding the next day!

After a wonderful week in Pattaya, Alice and I returned to Chonburi and the Suporn clinic. We spent the next couple of weeks sightseeing and went on occasional Bangkok shopping trips. My recovery went well and Dr Suporn was happy with the surgery. Finally it was time to leave. I was given a medical file written in English that detailed the surgery I'd had. This was for my GP records in the UK. It was also a lifetime guarantee that I could return to Dr Suporn at any time in the future if I had a problem.

It was time to leave, so with a few tears and a lot of hugs I went round all the staff at the clinic and the girls in the Mercure hotel and said my goodbyes. Alice had made friends with everyone too, so it took us a while, but eventually Wannee insisted we get in the car and she drove us to the airport. She was singing along, as usual, for the whole journey. We flew back to England and were collected by Les at Heathrow airport. It had literally been a life changing trip but I was glad to get home.

* * * * * * *

Weirdly, a few days after we got back I got a call from the local health authority regarding the Nuffield hospital, asking me why I hadn't turned up for my surgery. I told them that I'd informed the Nuffield by telephone seven weeks previously that I would be having surgery in Thailand. Predictably, this information was not passed on.

Back home, my recovery went well and I had no issues with post op infection. Which was just as well as the Norwich GIC discharged me with no after care provision. They seemed to be punishing me for going outside the system. I had to make check up appointments with my own GP, who had no experience of sex change surgery, and I could tell by his lack of enthusiasm to even examine me that he wasn't much interested. Likewise, when I presented the file of medical records from Dr Suporn, that I wished to be added to my NHS records, this was ignored. The NHS rationale regarding sex change surgery not done by their own surgeons seemed to be that it didn't happen. And in fact any surgery performed overseas was always suspect. This arrogance by the British medical profession prevailed for many years afterwards regarding my medical care.

I never expected having sex change surgery would be the answer to all my problems, and it was just as well I had that pragmatic assumption. But, attitudes were slowly changing; the work PFC and the Parliamentary Forum on Transsexualism had done behind the scenes was proving to be very effective.

* * * * * * *

The year I had my surgery, the Gender Recognition Act 2004 was voted through in parliament. That enabled transsexual people to apply to receive a Gender Recognition Certificate (GRC). This is the document that shows that a person has satisfied the criteria for legal recognition in the acquired gender. People whose birth was registered in the United Kingdom or abroad with the British authorities were then able to obtain a birth certificate showing their recognised legal sex. Sounds great, eh? But it was no use to me because to qualify I had to divorce Alice. That seemed very unfair to the woman who had stood by me all those years and who I was still very much in love with, not to mention our children. It was to be many years later that same sex marriage was legal and I could finally apply. But by then it hardly seemed to matter as the Gender Recognition Certificates had been devalued. I knew many people who had successfully obtained the who had never even taken hormones, far less had surgery, while people in my situation were often excluded.

But at least there was some progress in other areas The fear of AIDS as a 'gay plague' had diminished. The NHS had changed to accommodate LGBT people. The fact that a 'T' had been added to LGB was testament in itself to the great work carried out by Press For Change. Even the press stories now seemed slightly more sympathetic as this understanding chimed more with the public mood.

* * * * * * *

Around the end of 2004 I was offered a voluntary position with a private counselling agency, but this turned out to be a token gesture, a fact that was made obvious to me when the annual Christmas party was being discussed and I was told discretely that I would not be invited 'as there would be children present'. None taken!

I did however take up the offer of another voluntary job from my new GP when we moved house into a different practice area. Dr M seemed fascinated by my history and she asked if I would mind speaking with her medical students. I happily accepted, and I have found it to be very interesting and enjoyable over the years since to do a regular talk with a Q&A afterwards. I hopefully helped to enlighten some future GPs about transsexual people and their health requirements. My reward from the politically incorrect Dr M is always a very nice bottle of wine.

But none of that was paying the bills, so within 3 months of surgery I was back doing escort work. I still needed to finish hair removal treatment and we had to repay the money we'd borrowed for my surgery.

Now I needed a new angle. I could obviously no longer advertise as a pre op transsexual, and there was no demand for a post op transsexual girl. My options were limited. I certainly didn't want to have sex with clients, and anyway I knew I could never compete with the regular escort girls, who were much younger and prettier than I was. I needed to do something different that would allow me to stand out. So, after a bit of research, I advertised as a dominatrix. I'd dabbled with that kind of client previously and found it to be something I had the temperament for. I could still use the flat as before, and I had plenty of leather and metal restraint bondage gear left over from the old days of Metamorphose and the leather business. I also had a full wardrobe of female 'sissy' clothes to dress up and humiliate certain clients who enjoyed that kind of thing. But my main reason for taking this direction was that I also knew from reading the adverts online I would have very little local competition. So, it was settled, I became Dominatrix Suzanne.

* * * * * * *

The clients I attracted were far fewer in number, but they were also more loyal. I built up excellent relationships with several men who I saw on a regular basis, which meant that after a few months I rarely needed to advertise. I even did occasional 'out calls' for some of those men, visiting them at their own homes, because I knew they were trustworthy and I'd got to know them well. Over the next year I earned enough to repay my debts and give myself time to fully heal until I become completely accustomed to my new body configuration.

The time was approaching when I no longer needed to work as an escort. We were by no means well off, but we were in a stable financial position, and I needed only very occasional IPL sessions now to keep on top of my hair removal. Alice and I had always agreed that escorting was only a means to an end, and when the bills were under control, I'd stop. Now I understood why so many girls find it difficult to give up, but I'd promised myself that I would, and I also felt that if I carried on I'd become dependent on the money. Alice didn't put me under any pressure but I felt I needed to keep my word. However there was one last thing I needed to do while I had the opportunity.

What took place next was not really essential to my ability to pass completely as female. I had nothing to prove to anyone except to myself, but it had become a bit of an obsession. I needed to know what sex with a man felt like. And I knew I would not be content till I'd experienced it. Several of my post op friends had told me how wonderful it had been for them when they finally lost their neo virginity. It was time to test my new body. A one time only deal, it was time for a man.

March 2005

Norwich, England

I removed my black panties and began by smothering his penis with lubricant and invited him to do the same to my vagina. I kissed his shoulders and rubbed the back of his neck. I pushed my chain link covered breasts into his face and gyrated my hips. To be honest, I had no idea if it was a turn-on for him. I was just following what I'd watched my Thai bar girl friends do in Bangkok. I half expected him (or me) to burst out laughing. The situation was somewhat bizarre, and I just hoped Alice wasn't watching through the slightly-open door – she would definitely take the piss out of me later.

I straddled Clive and gradually lowered myself onto his upright penis, which by this time looked huge. Would that really fit inside me? I felt him enter me but I was still supporting myself with my legs and gently moving my hips slowly up and down. I intended to keep full control of this situation, and perhaps even bring him off by the gentle friction. But then he began to thrust violently upwards and was pulling me down on to him, his hands on my hips. His sudden strength was overwhelming, and pretty soon I'd lost control of the situation as he lifted me off my feet, thrusting deep inside.

I began to feel concerned! I wasn't used to the brute force of a man in the throes of sexual intercourse inside me like this. Would he damage me? I felt like a rag doll as he stood up, lifting me with him, and somehow manoeuvred me onto the bed and onto my back. I was helpless as he pounded into me, lifting my stockinged legs wide apart with every thrust. I tried to move my hips up and away as he pushed in, fearful of what damage this violent onslaught would cause to Dr Suporn's handiwork. This was not enjoyable in the slightest. In fact they were some of the scariest ten minutes of my life!

And then, thank god, it was over. Clive's face distorted as he arched his back for the final thrusts and I felt the shudder of his ejaculation inside me. Eventually he sighed and rolled over onto his side, panting and laughing – was he laughing at me? My paranoia was never far from the surface.

We both glistened with sweat. He smiled at me. "Did you come?"

"Yes," I lied.

Printed in Great Britain
by Amazon